INDIVIDUATION
PSYCHOLOGY
Essays in Honor of Murray Stein

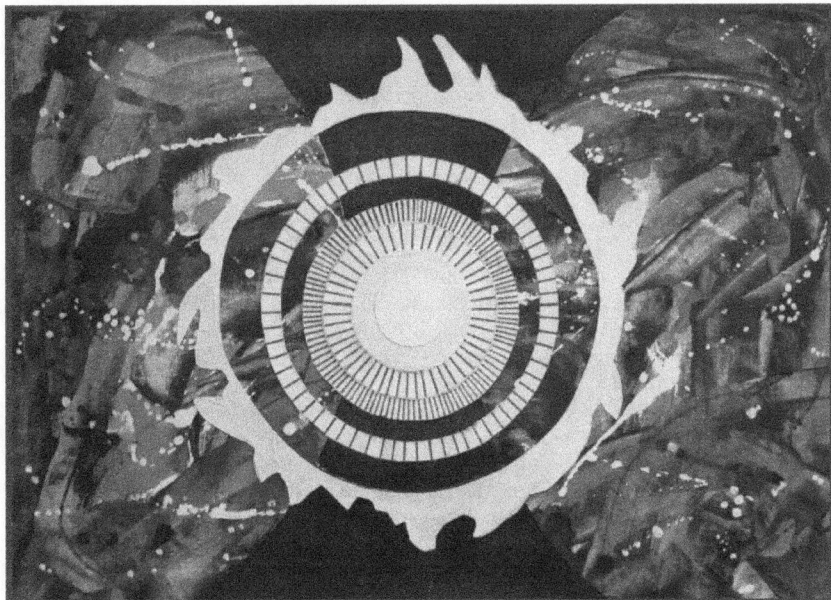

Festschrift in Honor of Murray Stein
on the Occasion of His 80th Birthday

Steven Buser & Len Cruz, Editors

CHIRON PUBLICATIONS • ASHEVILLE, NORTH CAROLINA

www.ChironPublications.com

Front cover painting by Diane Stanley
Interior and cover design by Danijela Mijailovic
Printed primarily in the United States of America.

ISBN 978-1-68503-183-1 paperback
ISBN 978-1-68503-184-8 hardcover
ISBN 978-1-68503-185-5 electronic
ISBN 978-1-68503-186-2 limited edition paperback

Library of Congress Cataloging-in-Publication Data

Names: Stein, Murray, 1943- honoree. | Buser, Steven, 1963- editor. | Cruz, Leonard, 1957- editor.
Title: Individuation psychology : essays in honor of Murray Stein : festschrift in honor of Murray Stein on the occasion of his 80th birthday / Steven Buser & Len Cruz, editors.
Description: Asheville, North Carolina : Chiron Publications, [2023] | Includes bibliographical references. | Summary: "This Festschrift celebrates Murray Stein, a man whose life and influence within Analytical Psychology has spanned several continents, wildly different cultures, several sweeping societal shifts, and now enters his ninth decade. He was forged in an American crucible, strengthened in Europe, and eventually matured into a world-wide phenomenon. These essays explore individuation in varied ways and reveal Dr. Stein's extensive impact on the world of Jungian psychoanalysis. An ambassador for post-Jungians, his own writings and the publication of others through his founding of Chiron Publications added valuable and novel insights about subjects as wide-ranging as Christianity, masculine psychology, and the practice of Jungian analysis. The diverse topics contained in these essays reflect the fertile, cross-cultural and interdisciplinary perspective that has characterized Dr. Stein's unique blend of scholarship, personal warmth, and far-reaching vision. From the times of the Delphic Oracle psychotherapists have illuminated the inner landscape where psyche dwells. Dr. Stein has witnessed countless developments and challenges in the decades after Jung's death. His gentle, wise stewardship reflects what Guinid says about individuation, it is "a testimony of the inner process". And Dr. Stein's lifework succeeds at re-enchanting a world stripped of mystery and meaning by modernity as Roderick Main and Len Cruz observe. After more than five decades of remarkable contributions, Murray Stein's lifework remains relevant and through his impact on the K-pop band BTS, he has appealed to a new generation of seekers after inner gold. This is a testament to a highly individuated man who fully demonstrates an ongoing individuation, and we are eager to see what his next decade will bring"-- Provided by publisher.
Identifiers: LCCN 2023037152 (print) | LCCN 2023037153 (ebook) | ISBN 9781685031831 (paperback) | ISBN 9781685031848 (hardcover) | ISBN 9781685031855 (ebook)
Subjects: LCSH: Individuation (Psychology) | Jungian psychology. | Stein, Murray, 1943-
Classification: LCC BF175.5.I53 I53 2023 (print) | LCC BF175.5.I53 (ebook) | DDC 150.19/54--dc23/eng/20230928
LC record available at https://lccn.loc.gov/2023037152
LC ebook record available at https://lccn.loc.gov/2023037153

Table of Contents

Crossing Borders

Introduction
Prima Materia: A Tale of Two Urinals
Steven Buser, Co-Editor

Like many of the authors in the chapters of this book, my journey with Murray Stein over the years has closely mirrored my own journey towards individuation. I first "met" Murray through his countless audiotapes at the *C.G. Jung Institute of Chicago*. I was a new psychiatrist at the time and engaged in a busy private practice in Asheville, North Carolina. Unlike many of my psychiatric colleagues, I deeply valued psychotherapy and devoted roughly half of my schedule to hour-long sessions. I had recently discovered C.G. Jung and Analytical Psychology and was devouring all I could find about them. When I came upon Murray's audio tapes in Chicago, I found the mother-load! There were nearly a hundred cassette tapes of Murray's lectures that could be rented for a dollar each! I feasted on a steady diet of Murray for the next 2 years.

A few years later, I enrolled in the 2-year training program at the C.G. Jung Institute of Chicago known then as the *Clinical Training Program* (CTP). I began flying up for a weekend of training once a month. Unfortunately, Murray had already left Chicago and was living in Zürich. While we had many wonderful analysts in Chicago, none of them were Murray.

Then, one month I heard that Murray was flying in to teach a weekend in Chicago. I flew up on a Friday and attended my first in-person lecture with Murray. As always, he spoke with profound elegance and grace. He was scheduled to teach the next day at the Institute as well; however, it was exclusively with the more in-depth *Analytical Training Program* (ATP) and not with the CTP. I was nonetheless hoping to speak with him, as I was itching to pitch an idea where we could set up online teaching seminars between Zürich and Asheville. This, however, was 2008, long before Zoom; online teaching was virtually unheard of and required the use expensive *Polycomm* systems that we could only access through universities. I waited for my chance to pitch my idea.

Urinal #1

As he was not teaching our class; my only chance was to catch him during a mutual break. I stalked their classroom throughout the day and eventually saw Murray leaving their room. Unfortunately, he went straight to the restroom. Fearing I would have no other chance, I followed him in. Standing side-by-side at the urinals, I pitched him my idea. Murray replied, "Sure. Let's give it a shot." Such was the humble beginnings of the *Asheville Jung Center*.

The Asheville Jung Center's first lecture was on individuation and was hosted on 8/8/2008 between Asheville and Zürich. It was the best explanation of individuation I had ever heard, and to this day remains my favorite lecture of his. His insights were profound. Listening to him talk felt like Jung himself had entered the room. Others seemed to agree and signed up to attend our online lectures by the hundreds. We were the only organization on the globe at that time to offer online Jungian education, and the number of attendees at our conferences quickly soared. We grew to have thousands of people taking part from over 50 nations. Over the next 10 years we hosted nearly a hundred seminars, most of which Murray led. Our little project blossomed beyond our wildest imaginings.

Urinal #2

It is said that mimicry is the highest form of flattery. Eventually, Skype, Go-to-Webinar, and Zoom made it easy to host such seminars and we were copied by dozens of groups leading to dwindling attendance. In 2018 I flew to Zürich and met with Murray to let him know that our numbers had dropped, we were losing money with every lecture, and we had to shut down the *Asheville Jung Center* seminars. We enjoyed our wine at dinner and reminisced over the years working together. Before we left to board our separate trains, we both headed to the restroom. I glanced over to the urinal next to me and suddenly laughed with him of how appropriate our ending was. It was the Alpha and the Omega.

In alchemy, it is the *prima materia* from which greatness is eventually made. That was the case for Murray and me. It was this base material from which something quite extraordinary grew. It was from our work together at the *Asheville Jung Center* that Murray asked me 10 years ago to take over *Chiron Publications*. He said he asked me to take it as he wanted to "keep it in the family." How could I say no to that? With tears of gratitude, I accepted. Stewarding Chiron for these many years has been an absolute delight. I have met incredible authors and read amazing works. As Murray turns 80, it is with great honor and joy that we publish this book as a testament to the deep transformative relationships he has made and the countless lives he has touched. I will be eternally grateful for Murray's presence in my life.

Steve Buser
Asheville, North Carolina
March, 2023

Introduction
From Adherent to Individualist to Sage:
Observations on C.G. Jung and Murray Stein

Len Cruz

Certain inflection points in life reveal themselves only retrospectively. Murray Stein's presence in the world is like a motif playing through the lives of the various contributors to this Festschrift. Murray draws out of others something essential capable of catalyzing psychic reactions that breathes life into the other authentic self. More than a dozen years ago, Murray invited me to write a review of a book by John Hill, *At Home in the World*. After decades of writing and editing in private, his prompting forced me to come out from the shadows. Since then, I have devoted myself to sustaining the legacy of Chiron Publications, a book publisher founded by Murray Stein and Nathan Schwartz-Salant.

Stein is that rare individual who courageously explores the deepest caverns of his inner life where he mines what Robert Johnson referred to as *inner gold* and then he re-enters the world to re-enchant it. Along the way, they animate the people they encounter. He has lived the life of a contemplative but not a hermit. I daresay that he has moved millions through his writings and continues to appeal to new generations of seekers as evidenced by his impact on the K-pop band *BTS* who titled an album after one of his books, *Map of the Soul*. He possesses an unusual blend of charisma, shrewd understanding of organizational life, deep spirituality, and mature psychological development that have equipped him to evolve throughout his 80 years.

This collection of essays is a testament to the impact that Murray Stein has had upon the continued development of analytical psychology. He was present for the founding and growth of training institutes and programs in North America, Europe, Eastern Europe, and Asia. Fifteen years ago, he pioneered online webinars that offered high-quality programming to anyone interested in analytical psychology who might be unable to attend an institute or Jungian study group. He has been at the vanguard of expanding training opportunities to people in Eastern Europe and the previous Soviet-bloc countries as well as Korea, China, Japan, and other regions of the world. To characterize Stein as an ambassador for analytical psychology would miss the fact that he has also advanced the field through his own study and writing. That Murray could be all these things to so many people from very different backgrounds is a testament to his warmth, sincerity, clear self-understanding, and the universality of what he offers.

I believe there is a striking similarity between C.G. Jung and Murray Stein. Early in their careers they seemed to be on a trajectory to becoming faithful adherents to conventional, even orthodox systems of belief. In time, they declared themselves as true individualists fashioning their own approaches to the times in which they found themselves. And in their later years, both these men did not retreat into a monastic or self-absorbed existence. Instead, they remained fully engaged with the world and went about re-enchanting it and animating the people they encountered. This passage from adherent to individualist to sage is open to anyone who commits to the process of individuation.

C.G, Jung began his training as a psychiatrist, a product of the latter part of the 19th century. This was a fertile period of scientific inquiry which produced Maxwell's equations on electromagnetism (1865), Darwin's insights into evolution (1859), Mendeleev's introduction of the periodic table of elements (1869), and Cantor's groundbreaking work establishing the foundations of set theory (1874). Jung's training as a psychiatrist was continued at the famous Burghölzi Hospital in Zürich where he was mentored by Eugene Bleuler, who introduced the diagnosis *schizophrenia* to replace the earlier designation of *dementia praecox*. His word-association studies undertaken with the help of Emma Jung, revealed an early interest in the unconscious, but it did not foretell the radical degree to which Jung would one day depart from convention to establish a radically new approach to psychology. He was traditionally trained, and soon after initiating his relationship with Sigmund Freud, appeared destined to be the heir apparent to the fledgling psychoanalytic movement. Though psychoanalysis was avant-garde, Jung initially appeared to be a faithful adherent. Within a matter of years of first writing to Freud, Jung was shouldering the responsibility for defending the field against its detractors. However, he had his own views and his own path to follow.

Jung recognized the importance of the whole experience of the individual, not just those aspects that cause illness or are repressed. Jung's emphasis on the spiritual dimensions of the individual put him at odds with the orthodoxy of his time and eventually led to his split with Freud in 1913. For Jung, analysis provided the means for a broad and deep inquiry into psychic life that encompassed all the best and worst of human nature. He envisioned a psychology that integrated not just repressed personal unconscious contents, but also collective unconscious elements whose roots extended deep and nourished things like myth, folklore, art, alchemy, religious symbolism, and more. His notion of the complex has in recent years born fruit when applied to the level of cultural complexes.

Jung's individualism was so forceful that he once denounced the tendency of his followers to enshrine his ideas as dogma by proclaiming, "Thank God I am Jung and not a Jungian" (Hannah, 1997, p. 78). This period of individual endeavor was enormously productive and provided others with a nearly inexhaustible fount of themes to be explored in the decades that followed.

By 1944, Jung had achieved considerable notoriety and fame. By any outward measure he was a success. In late February of 1944, following a fall in which Jung broke his ankle he suffered a heart attack most likely a result of a thromboembolism arising in his immobilized leg. Faced with similar circumstances he might have chosen to retire to a leisurely life in Küsnacht on the shores of Lake Zürich. He was accomplished in his outer life and had a keenly developed understanding of his inner life as would later be revealed with the publication of *The Red Book*.

Instead, Jung spent the next quarter century engaged in the world, inspiring people like Emma Jung, Marie von Franz, Erich Neumann, Mario Jacoby, Thomas Kirsch, James Hillman, Robert Johnson, Joseph Campbell and countless others to expand the boundaries of Analytical Psychology and to re-enchant the world around him.

Jung's father was a village pastor, but Carl Jung's understanding of the Christian faith and its symbols reflected a deeply personal, psychologically sophisticated perspective on God, the Christ, and faith in general. The spiritual dimensions of Jung's later adult years were richly textured and profoundly well integrated into his life. If *faith without works is dead,* then Jung's faith was vibrant and alive.

A similar trajectory can be surmised regarding Stein's evolution. His first two degrees were conferred at Yale where he received a BA in English literature and an MDiv in Theology. Stein's undergraduate years at Yale coincided with Robert Penn Warren's arrival to the English department. Penn Warren's *Understanding Poetry* first published in 1938, set the standard for *New Criticism,* an approach "that regarded the work at hand as autonomous, as an artifact whose structure and substance could be analyzed without respect to social, biographical and political details" (*The New York Times,* September 16, 1989, p. 1). New Criticism may have filled the air of Yale's English department, but Stein's curiosity that has often explored the liminal realms where certainty is sometimes forfeited in favor of breadth and depth. I have never asked him if he crossed paths with Professor Marie Borroff who translated the Gawain Poet.

Stein continued his studies at Yale in the Divinity School, the home of H. Richard Niebuhr, James Gustafson, and Henri Nouwen. One might have predicted from these early steps that Stein was destined for a traditional career in ministry; however, four years after completing his M.Div, he was finishing up his certificate training in Analytical Psychology in Zürich. More than a decade later in 1984, he earned a PhD in Religious and Psychological Studies at the University of Chicago. Like Jung, Stein has been a life-long learner

Stein has an unusual combination of political savvy, personal warmth, and an almost evangelical passion for spreading the message of analytical psychology. He would have undoubtedly been an effective minister, and his lifetime of service to the advancement of Analytical Psychology through his care of others, his writings, his teaching, and his organizational and leadership activities has made him an astoundingly influential force for this time. He was a founding member of the Inter-Regional Society for Jungian Analysts that helped extend training opportunities to people who did not live near a training institute. His work with the International Association for Analytical Psychology, helped extend training in analytical psychology to people living in places without registered training institutes. Fledgling Jungian groups in Russia, Eastern Europe, and Asia owe a great debt to Stein.

Chiron Publications recently re-published an early treatise Stein published on *Jung's Treatment of Christianity.* Nearly forty years ago, he posed the question "Why was a professional psychologist [Jung] so engaged in what is usually thought of as a theological task?" Who better to offer an answer to such an intriguing question than a man forged by early theological training at Yale. whose insights were seasoned in the crucible of the therapists consulting room, and fully ripened by doctoral education at the University of Chicago. Stein has returned to the topic of the problem of evil several times in the last four decades. If the backdrop for Jung's and Neumann's explorations of the problem of evil were dominated by World War I, we can surmise that Stein's examination was undertaken against the backdrop of Vietnam, the struggle for Civil Rights, the Women's Liberation Movement, the failure of Trickle-Down Economics, the rise of authoritarianism, and the commoditization of social interaction via social media. What Stein brought to his investigation of the problem of evil was a mature, deeply spiritual yet humanistic perspective.

One of the most remarkable things is that Stein remains relevant and timeless. Several years ago, the Korean-pop band *BTS* titled an album *Map of the Soul* after one of his books by the same title. Stein is a witness to sweeping societal changes that emerged in this period of post-modernism. What he continues to provide is more than the hard-won insights of years of unrelenting self-study and compassionate dealings with other seekers after personal and universal truths. Like Jung, Stein is in touch with the spirit of the times and the spirit of the depths. What I have observed of Stein, like what I have read about Jung, is that these are men who are thoroughly engaged in the moment in history in which they find themselves who bear witness without judgement. This may account for his ability to bring wisdom to bear without judgement in his dealings with others.

Since Max Weber declared that modernity was characterized by the "progressive disenchantment of the world" many have sought the means for re-enchanting the world. The deep interiority of people like Stein and Jung who remain engaged in outer life provides a roadmap for this endeavor. On those occasions when Murray has cast his benevolent gaze upon me, I have felt an affirmation of things that are deep and authentic. On a couple of occasions, the feeling was followed by profoundly meaningful insights. One example is that Murray has recognized a trickster quality in me and perhaps even named it, though I cannot really remember the occasion. This quality has sometimes been a sort of *daemon* whose tragic features have at times undone me, but when dedicated to nobler purposes has equipped me to be a consummate strategist and mover of the world. That this feature of my psyche has gradually been granted permission to step into the light and be unshackled from vestiges of shame and discomfort that arose in my youth is, in part, the result of my interactions with Murry Stein.

On the occasion of Murray's 80th year of life, I add my voice to the chorus of celebrants. Let this short essay attest to his profound influence on Analytical Psychology over the past 50 years. I also hope that by writing down my thoughts about how Jung and Stein traversed a path from adherent to sage that I might keep my feet upon a similar path for which I was destined. Furthermore, if another reader finds something about this notion illuminating for their own journey then I will have succeeded in honoring Murray in the most precious way I can imagine, by animating the soul of someone else and thereby re-enchanting the world.

I will close with the lines of the Spanish poet Antoni Machado who wrote:

> Caminante, son tus huellas el camino y nada más;
> Caminante, no hay camino, se hace camino al andar.
> Al andar se hace el camino, y al volver la vista atrás
> se ve la senda que nunca se ha de volver a pisar.
> Caminante, no hay camino sino estelas en la mar. (Machado, 1994)

> Traveller, it is your footprints that is the path, nothing else.
> Traveller, there is no road. You create your own path as you walk.
> As you go, you make your path.
> And when you look back, you will see the trail upon which you will never again step foot.
> Traveller, there is no road, only a wake on the seas. (My own translation.)

References

Hannah, Barbara. (1997). *Jung: His Life and Work*. Chiron Publications.

Machado,Antonio.(Dec.14,1994)."CaminanteNoHayCamino."EsPoesia, www.espoesia.com/poesia/antonio-machado/caminante-no-hay-camino-antonio-machado/. Accessed 18 Jul. 2023.

"Robert Penn Warren, Poet and Author, Dies." (September 16, 1989). *New York Times*, accessed July 17, 2023.

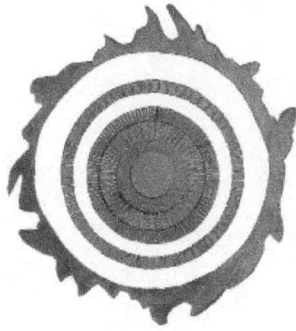

ON INDIVIDUATION

Individuation Psychology:
A Testament to "The Outer Reaches of Individuation"

Joseph Cambray, PhD., IAAP

Murray exemplifies the fullness of a well-lived Jungian life. His numerous writings, world-wide teaching, community building, administrative skills, and dedication, marked by numerous important developments he authored and championed over the past 50 years, have helped shape the Jungian approach for several generations.

"Who looks outside dreams; who looks inside awakes."
C.G. Jung to Fanny Bowditch 22 October 1916

A Tribute as Introduction

It is an honor and a pleasure to contribute to this festschrift for Murray Stein. Murray exemplifies the fullness of a well-lived Jungian life. His numerous writings, world-wide teaching, community building, administrative skills, and dedication, marked by numerous important developments he authored and championed over the past 50 years, have helped shape the Jungian approach for several generations. On a personal note, it was my great good fortune to serve as Murray's honor secretary during his presidency of the IAAP (2001-2004).

This was a time of opening and consolidation, starting with the "router" program, a term coined by Murray. Up until this time, those pursuing the individual membership route in the IAAP (in parts of the world without formal training possibilities), collected their hours of analysis and supervision, studied on their own and when they felt they were ready they attended the next IAAP triennial congress and sought to be examined. During Murray's administration we began to register those who were seeking the individual route, noting the broad geographic distribution and the unique problems that many faced. There were issues of availability of analysts in various regions of the world, of supervisors, of books in the mother tongues of those who wished to be trained, and access to instructors.

As stages of training at the international level were codified, pathways to progress were synthesized based on models from existing training institutes with their protocols for candidate advancement. By the end of Murray's presidency, we were surprised to find the numbers of people already invested and seeking to become analysts was well over 110. Subsequently, over the next decade the details of router training were further refined and codified. This in turn has been of enormous help in creating societies of analysts in locales outside the traditional centers (an effort that Murray had already been involved in within the US after he completed his analytic training). Stepwise advancement to training societies around the globe has emerged from these efforts. He has striven throughout his career to advance the individuation of the Jungian world as a whole and therefore this tribute to him is extraordinarily well-deserved.

Throughout the past several decades since completing his presidency, Murray has continued to serve in multiple roles assisting groups to become IAAP members. He is one of the most recognizable Jungians in the world; his acclaim was further enhanced a few years ago when the very popular South Korean band BTS selected the title of a two-album project from Murray's book *Maps of the Soul*. While turning 80 this year, Murray continues to be a vibrant, active force in the community. He edited in part with Thomas Artzt a five-volume series on *Jung's Red Book for our Times*. The final volume is composed of the papers given at an Eranos Symposium subtitled "Searching for Soul in the 21st Century" held at Monte Verità in the spring of 2022.

The rich body of Murray's writings has moved into a set of his own collected works. The first volume, published in 2020, is his book on *Individuation*. This is a fitting starting place for this festschrift in honor of Murray's depth of understanding and embodiment of individuation, in theory, practice, and life. The volume is a classic, a regal tour of the concept, explicating many of its arcane aspects. It introduces and deepens the readers engagement with this central concept to Jung's thought along a number of vertices. Not only individual development, but that of organizations and even the politics of nations are considered from an individuation perspective.

In the present essay I will explore the emergence of the concept of individuation during Jung's "confrontation with the unconscious," which is captured in *The Red Book* (2009). Within this context we will see that Jung needed to extend the notion of individuation beyond the realm of personal psychology, not only to include the transpersonal self, but also to expand our cosmology to include a synchronistic aspect to our vision of the universe. This will lead us to a "re-enchantment of the world" which is prefigured in the writings the 16th century alchemist Gerhard Dorn, discussed by Jung at the end of *Mysterium Coniuntionis*[4] and discussed in the last chapter of Murray's collected works volume 1.

Individuation Defined

A signature concept in Jung's thought, individuation is considered throughout his collected works, his letters, and his seminars. It is a broad, fulsome notion seeking to capture a great range of psychological phenomena about the adult human potential for maturation via vibrant engagement between our conscious and unconscious selves. It can never be fully realized within a single life but acts as if an instinctual force for self-realization is operating across our lifespans. The very idea of psychological development continuing throughout a person's life was a revolutionary idea at the time; Jung was a pioneer in the field of adult development. Later, London Jungian Michael Fordham (1996) extended this notion to childhood.

In reflecting back on the most intense period of his "confrontation with the unconscious" Jung commented:

> During those years, between 1918 and 1920, I began to understand that the goal of psychic development is the self. There is no linear evolution; there is only a circumambulation of the self. (1961, p. 196)

This captures the experiential encounter which forms the heart of the idea of individuation at a personal level. Indeed, Jung continued to record his dreams and experiences in pursuit of this goal throughout his lifetime, noting that it was:

> Some years later (in 1927) I obtained confirmation of my ideas about the center and the self by way of a dream. I represented its essence in a mandala which I called 'Window on Eternity.' (p. 197)

As we will see later this refers to his "Liverpool" dream, which we will explore to seek a possible reason as to why Jung continued his "confrontation" once he had this transformative dream. The "window on eternity" was an idea Jung would then paint and years later explicate in *Mysterium Coniunctionis* when discussing the three stages of alchemical unification found in the writings of Gerhard Dorn. There Jung attributes the concept to Leibniz (CW 14, para.670), one of the philosophers he identifies as postulating ideas that served as a forerunner to synchronicity with his notion of the pre-established harmony between psychic and physical events (CW 8, paras. 937-939).

For now, let us look at how Jung in 1921 first defined individuation in general terms as:

> ...the process by which individual beings are formed and differentiated; in particular, it is the development of the psychological individual as a being distinct from the general, collective psychology. Individuation, therefore, is a process of differentiation, having for its goal the development of the individual personality. (CW 6, para. 757)

There is a hint here that the formation of the individual is a part of a process, but this is left to others to develop. Jung's concern is the separation from mass psychology, in part due to having witnessed the horrors of the First World War. This concern will only grow over the years for him with the rise of Nazism and Stalinism. Thus, a socio-political aspect has entered into Jung's concept of the deeper goal of becoming as full and complete a personality as possible. He continues to stress the need for the person undergoing individuation to also stay reciprocally in relationship with the collective in which they live:

> ...only a society that can preserve its internal cohesion and collective values, while at the same time granting the individual the greatest possible freedom, has any prospect of enduring vitality....the process of individuation must lead to more intense and broader collective relationships and not to isolation. (para. 758)

The formal valuing of one's embeddedness in the world was not easy for Jung to live on a daily basis. After his break with Freud, he tended to shun most institutional involvement beyond teaching. This probably negatively impacted his role as a head of a movement (e.g., caustic remarks such as "Thank God I'm Jung, and not a Jungian" as reported by Hannah,1997/2018, p. 78) and was reflected in his leadership style as discussed by Eisold (2002, p. 501-524).

Jung saw individuation on an individual basis as proceeding via the active encounter between conscious and unconscious aspects of the personality:

> Individuation is closely connected with the transcendent function, since this function creates individual lines of development which could never be reached by keeping to the path prescribed by collective norms. (CW 6, para. 759)

Although he had not yet published his article on the transcendent function at this time, he had already written it but kept it under wraps until 1957 at the behest of students at the Jung Institute in Zurich. However, even in his 1921 definitions, he does mentions it, but refers the reader to the definition of symbol, where he clarifies that "this function facilitates a transition from one attitude to another" working through the combining of opposites in the "living symbol" (para.828).

He finishes his definition by focusing on the emergence of the personality from its source in the unconscious, but without clarity as to how this might best be achieved:

> Individuation is practically the same as the development of consciousness out of the original state of *identity*. It is thus an extension of the sphere of consciousness, an enriching of conscious life. (para.762)

From these basic notions, as he gains greater personal experience and knowledge, he will continue to refine his conceptions of the process. In terms of Jung writings as found in his Collective Works, brief summary documentation of the nuances of his views are captured by Samuels, et. al., in their *Critical Dictionary* entry on Individuation (1986, p. 76-79) as well in more detail in the book by Murray Stein on Individuation already mentioned above.

Moving Beyond the Personal

As previously noted, Jung continued his personal exploration of the unconscious beyond his personal realization of the Self in the Liverpool dream along with his representation of it in his painting of the window of eternity. The dream and associated artwork captured a profound personal experience but clearly did not bring a resolution of the dilemma Jung with which he had been struggling. From the inaugural waking visions of November 1913 of Europe filling up to the Alps with blood and debris, to the onset of WWI about 10 months later, Jung had been wrestling first with whether he was losing his grip on reality and then whether instead he had had prophetic visions portending the onset of war. Caught on the horns of this dilemma with neither choice palatable, Jung persisted in his personal exploration. However valuable the "Liverpool" dream, this did not provide a resolution. Hence a personal realization of the Self, a key element in the process of Individuation was insufficient an exit from his "confrontation with the unconscious."

As I have written about elsewhere, Jung's identified exit came through the experiences that led to his synchronicity hypothesis (Cambray, 2014, p. 36-53). Of particular importance was his receipt of a manuscript from his friend and colleague, Richard Wilhelm, of his translation of an ancient Chinese alchemical manuscript, known now as *The Secret of the Golden Flower*. The request was for Jung to consider writing a commentary. It had arrived as Jung was working on a mandala that puzzled him with its "Chinese" quality, which he had not been able to identify. He was captivated by the manuscript, with a close parallel to the vision of illuminated magnolia blossom of the Liverpool dream, and the cover page of the manuscript with the Vajra-mandala. As he later commented:

> ...the text gave me an undreamed-of confirmation of my ideas about the mandala and the circumambulation of the center. That was the first event which broke through my isolation.... In remembrance of this coincidence, this "synchronicity," I wrote underneath the picture which I had made so Chinese an impression upon me: "In 1928, when I was painting this picture showing the golden, well-fortified castle, Richard Wilhelm in Frankfurt sent me the thousand-year-old Chinese text on the yellow castle, the germ of the immortal body." (1961, p. 197)[1]

Receipt of the manuscript was the key event that led later that year to his first use of the notion of meaningfully linked, acausal but synchronous events, in a private seminar on dreams. He went on to develop this into the synchronicity hypothesis as discussed in my book on synchronicity (Cambray, 2009, p. 7-9). As Jung (2009) himself remarked, this allowed him to halt his work on the *Red Book*:

> My acquaintance with alchemy in 1930 took me away from it. The beginning of the end came in 1928, when Wilhelm sent me the text of the 'Golden flower,' an alchemical treatise. There the contents of this book found their way into actuality and I could no longer continue working on it. (p. 360)

The synchronistic receipt of the Taoist manuscript not only allowed Jung to close his "confrontation with the unconscious" as a chapter in his life, but also permitted his return to the world. I believe this was also the capstone to the individuation project. Synchronicity became the exit by allowing a transcendence of the dilemma of madness or prophecy—it indicated a new cosmology in which meaningful but acausal coincidences were fundamental to the nature of reality.

The more complete version of individuation would now include both a personal realization of the Self and the incorporation of a synchronistic

---

[1] This quote can also be found in German at the bottom of page 163 of the *Red Book*.

cosmology. In this way the Self could be simultaneously experienced as the mystery at the core of the personality and the world. The bifurcation of mind and matter characteristic of our disenchanted modernity might then be healed by this new vision. The *unio mystica* of Dorn, already mentioned several times, began to be a lived reality for Jung near the very end of his life, as found in last paragraph of *Memories, Dreams, Reflections* (1961):

> ...there is so much that fills me: plants, animals, clouds, day and night, and the eternal in man. The more uncertain I have felt about myself, the more there has grown up in me a feeling of kinship with all things. In fact it seems to me as if that alienation which so long separated me from the world has become transferred into my own inner world, and has revealed to me an unexpected unfamiliarity with myself. (p. 359)

The recognition of the intrinsic connection between the concepts of individuation and synchronicity in developing a project to re-spiritualize or re-enchant the world has also been explored from a parallel vertex by Roderick Main (2022) in his new book on *Breaking the Spell of Disenchantment*. In this Main makes important links between Jung and his contemporary Max Weber the sociologist who coined the idea of the disenchantment of the world. Main's study offers to build bridges between analytical psychology and sociology. In the final section of this paper, let us look at individuation and synchronicity from a collective perspective.

Individuation, Synchronicity, and Cultures

Already by 1928, Jung, with his Liverpool dream and several key synchronistic experiences[2], was seeking to expand his vision of individuation. In an important essay of that year, he wrote:

---

[2] In addition to the receipt of the "Golden Flower" manuscript, Jung had already had the clinical experience, with Maggy Reichstein in the mid-1920s which included the scarab beetle dream/synchronicity paradigmatic case. See Vincente de Moura, *Two Cases from Jung's Clinical Practice: The Story of Two Sisters and the Evolution of Jungian Analysis*, (London and New York: Routledge, 2019, 154-164

Every advance in culture is, psychologically, an extension of consciousness, a coming to consciousness that can take place only through discrimination. Therefore, an advance always begins with individuation, that is to say with the individual, conscious of his isolation, cutting a new path through hitherto untrodden territory. To do this he must first return to the fundamental facts of his own being, irrespective of all authority and tradition, and allow himself to become conscious of his distinctiveness. If he succeeds in giving collective validity to his widened consciousness, he creates a tension of opposites that provides the stimulation which culture needs for its further progress. (CW 8, paras. 937-939)

Jung is clearly writing about himself and his experiences. His model remains archetypally "heroic" but the relationship with the larger collective is gradually being considered. I believe he is on a trajectory which will continue to expand this, but he is suspicious of group activities, seeing them as vulnerable to descent to the lowest common denominator. In a few select statements later in his life he opens lines of inquiry about transformations in the collective. In one he states:

The activity of the collective unconscious manifests itself not only in compensatory effects in the lives of individuals, but also in the mutation of dominant ideas in the course of the centuries. This can be seen most clearly in religion, and, to a lesser extent in the various philosophical, social, and political ideologies. (CW 10, para.1161)

While the process of individuation itself is still not explicitly extended to groups or institutions, the deeper background in which they operate is at least seen as being impacted by similar forces. The possibility that archetypal patterns and dominants might change and put societies through collective transformations is an area that could be further explored, especially the possibility of the emergence of new archetypal patterns. This is an area I have begun to explore, as in the last chapter of my *Synchronicity* book on cultural synchronicities (p. 88-107). Individuation potentials in consequence of associated synchronicities are often complex and difficult to discern over the short term but deserve attention and reflection. There is wisdom to be had in group process, where the sum of knowledge can be greater than what is in the mind of any individual.

Might there be new archetypal patterns now emerging in our world that could draw upon such collective knowledge (conscious and unconscious)? I believe Jung did glimpse this at times, such as when he remarked:

> We are living in what the Greeks called the *kairos*—the right moment—for a 'metamorphosis of the gods,' of the fundamental principles and symbols. This peculiarity of our time, which is certainly not of our conscious choosing, is the expression of the unconscious man within us who is changing. (CW 18, para.585)

I believe this is even more true now than it was in Jung's day. How might Jung's own signature concepts be both part of the metamorphosis he speaks of, and undergoing their own metamorphosis in the process? This is an area I have begun to explore, reconsidering individuation in the 21st century (in press). From my perspective, this begins with attending to systemic aspect of the larger trends underway in our world, e.g., climate change, the associated rise of pandemics, the need to confront systemic racism as part of decolonialization and so on.

Conclusions

Murray Stein has been a living incarnation of Jungian principles and has helped the worldwide Jungian community to advance, both in terms of training and engagement with various other fields. Individuation has been a core value for him, not only in his writings but in his life. It is a privilege to contribute to this volume of essays, a commemorative publication in honor of his long, productive, and prosperous life as a Jungian.

In this short piece, I hope to have conveyed some of the inspiration I have experienced through my acquaintance with Murray. He has always been a collaborative supporter who I believe embodies the new pattern I am pointing to in this essay. Individuation as a task for the collective even more than for the individual. May his spirit inform the 21st century's view of analytical psychology as the tremendously valuable discipline that it is.

Joseph Cambray, Ph.D. is the Past-President-CEO of Pacifica Graduate Institute; he is Past-President of the International Association for Analytical Psychology; has served as the U.S. Editor for *The Journal of Analytical Psychology*. He was a faculty member at Harvard Medical School in the Department of Psychiatry at Massachusetts General Hospital, Center for Psychoanalytic Studies. Dr. Cambray is a Jungian analyst now living in the Santa Barbara area of California. His numerous publications include the book based on his Fay Lectures: *Synchronicity: Nature and Psyche in an Interconnected Universe.* He has published numerous paper in a range of international journals as well as book chapters and has edited three collections of research in analytical psychology.

References

Cambray, J. (2009). *Synchronicity: Nature & Psyche in an Interconnected Universe* (Fay Lecture Series). Texas A & M University Press.

Cambray, J. (2014). *"The Red Book*: Entrances and Exits," in *The Red Book: Reflections on C.G. Jung's Liber Novus*, (Ed. T. Kirsch and G. Hogenson). Routledge.

Cambray, J. (in press). "Reconsidering Individuation in the 21st Century: When Archetypal Patterns Shift."

Eisold, K. (2001). "Institutional Conflicts in Jungian Analysis," Journal of Analytical Psychology. 46(2): 335-353.

Eisold, K. (2002). "Jung, Jungians, and Psychoanalysis." Psychoanalytic Psychology. 19(3): 501-524.

Fordham, M. (1996). *Children as Individuals*-3rd Ed. Free Association Books.

Hannah, B. (1997/2018). *Jung: His Life and Work.* Chiron Publications.

Jung, C.G. (2009). *The Red Book: Liber Novus*. (Ed. S. Shamdasani, Trans. J. Peck, M. Kyburz, and S. Shamdasani). W.W. Norton.

Jung, C.G. (1969). On Psychic Energy (R. F. C. Hull, Trans.). In H. Read et al. (Eds.), *The Collected Works of C.G. Jung: Vol. 8. Structure and Dynamics of the Psyche* (2nd ed., pp. 3-66). Princeton University Press. (Original work published 1928) https://doi.org/10.1515/9781400850952.3

Jung, C.G. (1970). *The Collected Works of C.G. Jung: Vol. 14. Mysterium Coniunctionis* (R. F. C. Hull, Trans.) (H. Read et al., Eds.). Princeton University Press. (Original work published 1955-56) https://doi.org/10.1515/9781400850853

Jung, C.G. (1970). The Undiscovered Self (present and future) (R. F. C. Hull, Trans.). In H. Read et al. (Eds.), *The Collected Works of C.G. Jung: Vol. 10. Civilization in Transition* (2nd ed., pp. 247-305). Princeton University Press. (Original work published 1957) https://doi.org/10.1515/9781400850976.247

Jung, C.G. (1961). *Memories, Dreams, Reflections.* (Ed. Aniela Jaffe, trans. R. and C. Winston). Pantheon Books.

Jung, C.G. (1969). Synchronicity: An Acausal Connecting Principle (R. F. C. Hull, Trans.). In H. Read et al. (Eds.), *The Collected Works of C.G. Jung: Vol. 8. Structure and Dynamics of the Psyche* (2nd ed., pp. 417-519). Princeton University Press. (Original work published 1952) https://doi.org/10.1515/9781400850952.417

Jung, C.G. (1976). The Symbolic Life (R. F. C. Hull, Trans.). In H. Read et al. (Eds.), *The Collected Works of C.G. Jung: Vol. 18. The symbolic life* (pp. 267-290). Princeton University Press. (Original work published 1954) https://doi.org/10.1515/9781400851010.265

Jung, C.G. (1971). *The Collected Works of C.G. Jung: Vol. 6. Psychological Types* (R. F. C. Hull, Trans.) (H. Read et al., Eds.). Princeton University Press. (Original work published 1921) https://doi.org/10.1515/9781400850860

Main, R. (2022). *Breaking the Spell of Disenchantment: Mystery, Meaning, and Metaphysics in the Work of C.G. Jung.* Chiron Publications.

Samuels, A. (1986). *A Critical Dictionary of Jungian Analysis.* (Ed. B. Shorter and F. Plaut). Routledge.

Stein, M. (2022). *Jung's Red Book for Our Time: Searching for Soul in the 21ˢᵗ Century, An Eranos Symposium, Volume 5.* Chiron Publications.

Stein, M. (2020). *The Collected Writings of Murray Stein: Volume 1 – Individuation.* Chiron Publications.

Individuation As Testimony of Inner Process

Magi Guindi

Relentlessly following his keen guiding instinct and intuition, Murray has embarked with great care, courage, and dedication upon the construction of his own inner Bollingen Tower, so to speak, whose architectural design, still in the making, reflects his life's commitment to an ongoing individuation process, a pathway to wholeness. Stone by stone has been meticulously carved and laid in place with each of Murray's contributions; each of the many books he has written, each of the countless seminars and lectures he has given, each supervision, each analytic session, to name just a few, have been like brick, stone, mortar in the devoted and committed process of construction of his tower/lighthouse.

As I ventured to write this essay in honor of Murray Stein, whose bright mind, significant presence, gentleness of spirit, and gifted sensitivity have guided me along my own individuation path, the inspiring figures of Proust and Jung together with their valuable legacies rose to my mind. Each one of them, in their own individual way, embarked with great dedication and courage upon the search of their deeper being, a search which remains imprinted in their life work as a true testament for the generations to come.

The word testament, from the Latin *testamentum*, refers to a document, a "testamentary provision or requirement," that is the act by which someone places their possessions in order anticipating the end of

29

their life. This notion also comprises the meaning of the Hebrew word *Berith,* denoting an alliance, pact, covenant between God and humankind.

A "Covenant of God with Humankind..." introduces yet another dimension, which at an individual level alludes symbolically to the Self, the Godhead, the inner God image, intimating an alliance with the divine. This also resonates with the relationship between the ego and the Self, while highlighting the critical significance of maintaining a continuous link, an ongoing communication with the inner Other that seems to inspire and steer our lives towards the realization of a unique divine plan.

Yet, this "fragile and infinite variation of the soft inner music vibrating within each one of us," (Guillaume, 2020) often is, as Proust seems to suggest, rather difficult for us to hear. It is with this same soft inner music, i.e., this subtle inner voice, as Jung intimates, that the Self speaks to us.

It was using a very singular metaphoric symbolic language that Proust, while bringing his past to life, embellished his narrative, endowing his inner characters with more intensity and vitality. Similarly, Jung found a way to his soul by establishing an ongoing symbolic dialogue with the inner figures arising from the unconscious giving such powerful images a voice, a reality. Just as for Jung his life and work became indissociable, so for Proust his life experiences became a source of nourishment for his literary work. In this sense, their life stories became a solid foundation for their individuation process.

This individual adventure towards the realization of one's authentic being—adventure in the Latin sense of *ad-venire,* i.e., allowing the unforeseen or unknown that is to come to be revealed—this personal life path and destiny that unfolds of its own accord during a lifetime, presents each one of us with a different and unique challenging task.

This individuation pathway is itself an *opus contra naturam* that requires an almost religious attitude of devotion, dedication, and faithfulness to pay tribute to this valuable soul dimension. It is thus essential to honor one's existence, treasuring in all its plenitude the life one has been given, including its inevitable detours, contrasts and nuances, its ups and downs, its back-and-forth movements, its possibilities and limitations, its light and dark sides, its happiness, and sorrows.

This implies a commitment to the person that one is. This is not as a celebration of oneself as ego at the expense of or excluding our obscure sides, but rather as a dedication to discover the profound value that lies within each one of us, our deeper essence, which is not only beauty, but also shadow, limitation, adversity, and hardship. All this is part of individuation. It is engaging arduous labour for which a relationship to oneself must first be consolidated. This implies coming to terms with the totality of our being, including the not so pleasant aspects that are nonetheless an integral part of our uniqueness. It is like embracing our existence with its infinite hues and tonalities—including its somber and shadowy aspects—to remain loyal and truthful to who we are in our entirety.

In Proust, for instance, his individuation process ran parallel to his process of reminiscing. Through listening to memory and thus re-living his past, he gained access to his genuine emotions, to his authentic being. Jung, in turn, was led to the discovery of his own soul through his dedicated inner search that compelled him to take serious consideration of that which emerged from the depths of the unconscious. At the same time, throughout his individuation process he faced the difficult task of holding the inner tension of opposites pulling him in different directions.

It is along this individual life path that unfolds step-by-step into a particular destiny, that a testament reflecting our unique history—testament in the sense of covenant with the divine—is gradually interwoven with myriad-colored threads. It is along this very pathway that each one of us is called to live in genuine accordance with our essential inner reality while consciously engaging in a sincere process of individuation.

What a better testament as mortal human beings are there than to leave behind an eternal inner trace and turn our transitory passage on earth into immortal spiritual transcendent inner work?

By reminiscing the legendary stories of *One Thousand and One Nights* (Proust, 2003, p. 3049) resonating in the back of his mind, Proust was led to Scheherazade, to the anima. It is through the soft voice of the inner feminine that Proust was able to tell his story, a story of a narrator whose life also depends upon the prodigious use of his imagination. Threatened by profound uncertainty due to his pressing illness and unaware of how much more time he would be granted to live, night after night Proust sets out before a fierce and ferocious sultan, to write his narrative to remain alive. It is as if his need to remain alive, stirring him from within to tell his creative stories, would rely solely upon the nourishment from the unconscious. As long as he can maintain an ongoing connection to his anima through telling stories that emerge from his creative imagination, he can remain alive.

It is thus through his creative narrative that Proust rendered this world more luminous by enhancing life's most banal aspects with the boundless dimension of imagination. Such luminosity evokes the alchemical fire that, rather than destroying, transforms. This alludes to the anima's intervention, in the sense that by making use of his prodigious creative imagination, Proust was able to transform everything he had lived and experienced into symbolic psychic reality.

By narrating his own inner life within a perspective of memory and imagination, by bringing the past back to life and transferring it into the present through the vibrant use of metaphoric images, Proust created and gave birth to something that was able to survive and withstand the fleeting sense of time. There is a whole inner universe, a rich inner life that escapes the restricted limitations of time.

Proust's individual personal narrative, through a life in search of the seemingly lost time which paradoxically he had unexpectedly retrieved, inspires us to also set out in search of our own past. It is as if our life stories would also need to be told, expressed, written through the voice of the Self, as a living testimony, especially as we approach the end of our life. Perhaps the Proustian heritage is a memorial of his past set before the reader's eyes as an incentive to carry out the same significant yet challenging task of courageously embarking on our personal inner search.

For Proust, the years of our existence contain all those uninterrupted hours and moments that form our past, which can only be retrieved by stepping into the very depths of our being. By giving expression to our past, by giving it form through words and images emerging from our imagination, we not only transcend the limitations of time, at the level of imaginative expression, but we also endow the life we have lived with a dimension of dignity by transforming it into something more essential, more archetypal.

Both Proust and Jung had an intuitive awareness of the fathomless potentialities residing within the unconscious that needed to be brought to light and realized.

Jung, for instance, alluded to his inner experiences, including his dreams and visions, as a "fiery magma out of which the stone that had to be worked was crystalized" (1995, p. 18).

Proust, in turn, alludes to his imagination as a basin rich in minerals where "lay vast and valuable precious ores" (2003, p. 3042). He wondered, however, whether he would have the time to exploit them.

Proust rediscovered, retrieved a world that seemed to be hidden, buried so to speak within himself. We too are endowed with an immense reservoir of precious inner treasures we might not even suspect we possess. Perhaps by turning our gaze inward, like Proust and Jung, by being mindful of our dreams, visions, and life's mysterious synchronicities, we too can find an inner miner capable of descending into the very depths to extract such magnificent "minerals." When we can unlock the hidden meaning underlying the perplexing and symbolic language of dreams, we unearth invaluable treasures and riches.

By working on the *prima materia* of our life events and circumstances, while resorting to our memory and our imagination's transformative capacity, we too can extract the value contained within our inner experiences, endowing them with the quality of that which is lasting and essential.

Toward the end of his life, not knowing how much time would be allotted to him, Proust had this urge to pursue his inner search to write his book, which literally became his testament. Behind this inner urge, there appears to be an underlying need to create some kind of internal coherence. By giving an account of his existence, relying upon his creative imagination, he enhanced his life with depth and significance, i.e., with a quality of the individuation process, with a deeper dimension of creational timeless meaning.

As we approach the end of life, there seems to be an essential need to give expression to our individuation stories, enhancing them with a sense of duration and timelessness. It is as if we were compelled from within to leave a psychic testimony, a kind of testament that transcends time.

For Proust, everything fades, comes undone, due to the tragic degradation of all things. Life as it passes, as it slips by is nothing but lost time. Yet, paradoxically, when certain memories emerge during exceptional moments of inspiration in an unexpected and fortuitous way, when we witness through the experience of a particular sensation, the simultaneous presence of a memory coupled with such sensation, time is once again retrieved. It is then that those moments of the past, that are seemingly so far away, come closer to our memory. Yet, moments like those seem to be infinitely rare. And precisely because they are less intellectualized, they set our imagination into motion.

Therefore, by finding a past of which we were no longer aware, but that had nevertheless been dwelling within us all along, by the simultaneous presence of a sensation and a memory suddenly unfolding before our eyes, the time that appeared to be lost transforms into time regained. It is thus within this movement from lost time to lasting time that recovered memories are endowed with another reality.

Proust states: "But it is sometimes just at the moment when we think that everything is lost that an intimation comes to our rescue. We have knocked at all the doors that lead nowhere, and then we unexpectedly stumble on the only door through which we can enter—which we sought in vain for a hundred years—and it comes open" (p. 3042).

Involuntary memory seems to open a door towards eternity. There are moments in life in which we come to a dead-end and no door seems to open. This idea is reminiscent of the labyrinth motif in which—akin to experiencing an individuation process—an impasse-type experience must first be undergone before the centre can be reached. And although sometimes we may lose sight of the center, given the inevitable stumbling blocks encountered along the way, although the continuation of the path may not be visible, it is only by treading it that the way is thus revealed.

Alluding to the image of the labyrinth, Jung states: "One of the fundamental laws of natural development is that it moves in a spiral and the true law of nature is always reached after the labyrinth has been travelled" (1984, p. 100).

Antonio Machado, the Spanish poet, rightly says: "Traveller, there is no road. You create your own path as you walk. With each step, you pave your path. And when you look back, you see the pathway you will never tread again. Traveller, there is no road, only a ship's wake on the sea."

Psychic process is thus not linear, as we would consciously wish. Inner process cannot be predicted. Since life unfolds in a spiral movement, which includes difficulties, obstacles, moments of uncertainty, doubt, and disorientation, we cannot anticipate how such ever-shifting process will ultimately crystallize. All these stumbling blocks are inevitably encountered along the way. And it is only by taking the necessary risks and walking step-by-step that the path is gradually revealed.

Both Proust and Jung left a rich and fertile testimony that has survived the passage of time. What we write and pass on to future generations is indeed something that can survive. Throughout his writing process, Proust also awakens the reader's imagination:

> This idea of Time urged me, telling me that it was time for me to begin if I wanted to once again seize the feeling that had at times flashed ever so briefly throughout my life, intimating that life was well worth living. How much more worth living did it appear to me now, now that this life usually lived in darkness could be filled with light! Now that this life that we always distort, could be brought back to its original truth, could be realized within the confines of a book! How happy would the man who could write a book of such calibre, of such stature be! What an arduous task awaited him! To give some idea of this laborious undertaking, one would have to borrow comparisons from the loftiest and most varied arts; for this writer—who, moreover, would have to bring out the opposed facets of each of his characters in order to show its robust magnitude—would have to prepare his book with meticulous care, perpetually regrouping his forces like a general conducting an offensive, and he would have also to endure his book like a form of fatigue, to accept it like a discipline, build it up like a church, follow it like a medical regime, vanquish it like an obstacle, win it like a friendship, cosset it like a little child, create it like a new world without neglecting its mysteries whose explanation is to be found probably only in worlds other than our own... In this kind of grand books, there are parts that can only be sketched out and that may very well never be completed, precisely because of the breadth of the architect's blueprint. How many great cathedrals remain unfinished! The writer feeds his book, he fortifies the weak parts, he protects it, but, then, it is the book that grows, that designates our tomb, defending it against rumours and somewhat against oblivion. But coming back to myself, I thought more modestly of my book and it would be inaccurate even to say that I thought of those who would read it as 'my' readers. For it seemed to me that they would not be 'my' readers but the readers of their own selves, my book being merely a sort of magnifying glass like those which the optician at Combray used to offer his customers. (p. 3037-3038)

Alluding to this hard labour as the means to strengthen the soul, one is reminded of Paul Valery's words inscribed in golden letters on the pediment of Palais de Chaillot in Paris: "Every man creates, without knowing it, just as if he were breathing, but the artist feels himself creating, his act engages his whole being, his beloved sorrow strengthens him."[1]

This necessary and laborious task that Proust alludes to—which for the artist, according to Valery, is accompanied by an unavoidable sorrow that strengthens him—is contrary to what an ordinary person may experience who unaware of what they are doing, in an almost leisurely way, create just as if they were breathing. Instead, the artist, being emotionally conscious of his creative act that engages his whole being, must go beyond that. The artist must create amidst difficulties and despite his beloved sorrow, which he knows so well, and which deeply strengthens and inspires him.

In his relentless introspection to recover his seemingly lost childhood and despite his struggles with imminent death and time, his great enemy, Proust sets out courageously in search of a deeper knowledge of himself. It is through this quest to find the truth underlying that which he has experienced, by re-visiting and coming to terms with those painful feelings of disappointment, loss, and isolation, that he gains a deeper understanding of himself. This in a way reflects his individuation process. In the end, through such inner work, through such ongoing self-analysis, he is led towards a deeper introspection.

Individuation, therefore, also includes a connection to time and a certain timing, in the sense that we must be open to the fortuitous opportunities that life offers us at a given moment in time. Jung believed that if we do not take the specific opportunity that life has prepared for us, which could also present itself in the guise of difficulties or crises, if instead we try to avoid it because it seems deeply painful or too difficult to bear, we will inevitably regret it later.

Life's hardships are thus unavoidable, they form part of living. If we try to escape them, they just come back to knock on our door. Yet, if we courageously face such adversities, in whatever guise they may appear, if we consciously assume them, then we move forward in life and we further our individuation process. It is precisely during such critical

---

[1] "Tout homme creé sans le savoir, comme il respire, mais l'artiste se sent créer, son acte engage tout son être, sa peine bien aimée le fortifie."

moments that we are led to go in search of our deeper essence, which taps into the transcendent within, bringing us closer to the divine inner quality. Jung states:

> One way or another, suffering has been inevitable. However, I would rather suffer from the things that form part of my life. An important reason for this authentic way consists of knowing that if I do not fulfil my own life, then it will be passed on to my children as heritage. My unfully lived life will become a burden for them and will add to their own difficulties. (Jaffé, 2021, p. 22)[2]

As Jung illustrates, one cannot escape the inevitable suffering that is part of life. If one does not want to risk anything, if one just wants to live comfortably avoiding life's difficulties and insecurities, then such difficulties will be passed on, as a sort of psychological testament, as a kind of unpaid mortgage, to the subsequent generations. In other words, if we do not attempt to live our life in an honest and authentic way, and this also includes the difficulties of which it is made up, then we pass on this unlived part of our lives to our children, as inheritance, as an additional burden for them to carry.

Proust also believed that suffering could only be healed by experiencing it fully (p. 2089).[3] Therefore, by experiencing our individuation process fully, that is, by living in agreement with its natural unfolding, which includes its necessary challenges and difficulties, we not only create some kind of eternity, but we also spare subsequent generations from having to carry upon their shoulders this additional burden that does not actually belong to them. Interestingly, it is by virtue of the challenges and difficulties one is forced to face during life's critical moments that one is led into a self-searching process.

---

[2] The author's own translation into English of: "Leiden war so oder so unumgänglich. Aber ich will an *den* Dingen leiden, die wirklich zu mir gehören. Ein entscheidendes Motiv für diesen Weg war auch das Wissen: Wenn ich mein Leben nicht erfülle, dann wird es als Erbschaft auf meine Kinder übergehen und ihnen als Last meines ungelebten Lebens zusätzlich zu den eigenen Schwierigkeiten zufallen."

[3] On ne guerit d'une souffrance qu'a condition de l'eprouver pleinement." (Albertine Disparu)

According to Jung, the destinies of people who have avoided living or experiencing what life has intimated to them, who have eluded the possibilities and challenging opportunities that life has offered them, end up having terrible destinies. However, those who willingly live according to their vocation and with their best knowledge have no reason to regret. Jung claims that Voltaire was right when he stated that we must particularly repent of the opportunities we have missed.[4] In our old age, far from regretting what we did not see or experience, such as a trip we never took, we feel remorse for having eluded those opportunities that life put forth to us, whether good or bad, in the guise of a crisis or a difficulty, since it appeared to be too painful or challenging.[5]

Often it is this inner reality we call the Self, which for the purpose of our inner evolution arranges life's difficulties, struggles, sufferings, entanglements to awaken our consciousness. Behind such necessary crises lies a potential for change and transformation.

Proust feared that he was on the verge of dying. Incidentally, he must have suspected this since he wrote the word "end" upon completing his work. The word "end" came after the very last word in his narrative: "Time," which also happens to be the very first word of his work. The word testament, by the way, also alludes to the dimension of time.

Proust wrote the word "time," which paradoxically is the very beginning of his literary work. It is interesting to see how some thousands of pages separate the beginning from the end. Could this not also be a metaphor of our lives? An invitation to live our lives more fully?

It is as if a sort of enantiodromia would take place within this very fine delimitation between endings and beginnings, beginnings, and endings, pointing to the mysterious deeper significance underlying life paradoxes. Perhaps, the end of life in one form, the physical, may only be the beginning of another form of life, the spiritual, within which a mysterious process of transformation may unfold.

---

[4] The author's own translation of: "Die Schicksale, die ich gesehen habe, weil das eigene Leben nicht gelebt wurde, sind einfach schauerlich. Kein Mensch, der seine Bestimmung lebt und nach bestem Wissen und Können erfüllt, hat Grund zur Reue. In einem gewissen Sinne hatte Voltaire recht mit seiner Aussage: bereuen musse man "surtout ce que l'on n'as pas fait." Aniela Jaffe, *Streiflichter zu Leben und Denken CG Jung*, Erste Auflage, 2021, p. 22.

[5] The author's own translation of: "Im hohen Alter bereuen wir nicht die wunderbaren Dinge, die wir vielleicht nicht gesehen oder erlebt, sondern das, wo wir das Leben an uns vorbeizehen liesen." Aniela Jaffe, *Op cit.*

The process of individuation is made up of beginnings and endings, of right and wrong turnings. It entails many symbolic deaths which give rise at the same time to new births, to new beginnings, to new insights. All this forms part of the Self's movement.

Towards the last years of his life, when Proust realized the short time he had left, an intense urge sprang from within that drove him to write his book.

After his mother's and grandmother's death and until the time when his illness confined him in his flat, Proust never failed to visit his grandfather's tomb. In May of 1908, he wrote to a friend, Daniel Halevy, who had just lost his father: "There is no longer anybody, not even myself, since I cannot leave my bed, who will go along the Rue de Repos to visit the little Jewish cemetery, where my grandfather, following a custom that he had never understood, went for so many years to lay a stone on his parents' grave."[6]

The symbolic meaning behind this ritual in the Jewish liturgy is highly significant. The stone, contrary to a flower that withers and dies is something that endures. It marks the perennial characteristic of the imprint one leaves behind in this world. And although the deceased are no longer there, their memory remains as solid and stable as the stone that has been placed on their tomb. The word stone in Hebrew is *eben*, a combination of two words, *ab* and *ben*, meaning father and son. Therefore, to place a stone on a tomb literally alludes to the act of placing in such a space the mark of the connection between the generations. It also inscribes the person setting the stone on the grave as part of a direct line of descent with the one who has passed away.

This dimension of stone resonates with the symbolic meaning underlying the idea of testament, since it creates an ongoing link between the departed one and the one who remains alive. The stone lasts, prevails, survives the death of the individual... it endures, it continues to exist. Although here the image of the stone alludes to a temporal dimension of father and son, to a lateral dimension encompassing past, present, and future, in Jung, this same dimension of stone takes on a transcendental significance. Not only is the stone for him reminiscent of a process of transformation leading to a crystallization of the liquid fiery magma after

---

[6] *The Jewish Chronicle*, May 23, 1923.

the arduous labour has been carried out, but it also partakes of a dimension that goes beyond the realm of the ephemeral.

Compelled from within by a powerful need to embody the contents of the unconscious and place them "on a solid footing," Jung set out, with immense dedication and effort, to build his tower at Bollingen, which became for him a *temenos* of renewal and transformation (Jung, 1995).

The process of building such stone tower was akin to carving, capturing, expressing through such medium, his innermost thoughts and experiences with the intent of leaving an indelible imprint. This immortal dimension of stone, endowed with an eternal quality, survived Jung's death. Symbolically speaking, this might have been the very stone Jung had to work on.

Proust, in turn, after having struggled during arduous months of labour, finally birthed his completed work on his own. That is the precise moment in which Proust, the mortal flesh and blood writer dies, and the immortal pen and paper author comes to life. An alchemical transformation appears to have mysteriously taken place, bringing Proust's mortal time to an end, while lighting the everlasting flame of the immortal time of his work.

His literary masterpiece can be read as a living testament since it goes beyond this dimension of time and even further, expanding throughout the centuries. His childhood memories opened a door to the deeper archetypal layers of the unconscious. Having stepped into such a fathomless realm, he unexpectedly came across invaluable archetypal experiences. Such archetypal manifestations were indeed expressive of his own individuation process.

Proust's writings open a myriad of doors and windows through which we can also glance into the depths of our own being, inspiring us to go in search of our own childhood and give voice to the emerging memories.

Proust raises the question as to how to bridge the distance between the present and the faraway past. He speaks of an eternal time, a time that upon death does not withdraw from the body but is instead embodied; a time in which the human being occupies a far more important place than the restricted one reserved for him in space. This is the time of the imaginary, of imagination. So long as he occupies that place in time, he can journey to the deepest recesses of his being... "simultaneously touching widely separated years and the distant epochs that they have lived through" (p. 3054). It is within this idea of positioning the fleeting sense of time in the dimension of the eternal that we are able to occupy a place in Time, a time in which our imagination dwells.

Jung also refers to an eruption of the eternal onto the ephemeral, a process through which the ephemeral becomes eternal. In *Memories, Dreams, Reflections,* Jung states:

> Life has always seemed to me like a plant that lives on its rhizome. Its true life is invisible, hidden in the rhizome. The part that appears above ground lasts only a single summer. Then it withers away – an ephemeral apparition ... I have never lost a sense of something that lives and endures beneath the eternal flux. What we see is the blossom, which passes. The rhizome remains." (1995, p. 18)

In other words, there is something essential that lasts forever that exists at a root level. It is the foundation, that which lies at the very depths of our being, which is everlasting. It has an eternal dimension because it lies within. Thus, the significance of living in harmony and synchronicity with our essential inner reality entails an honest commitment to a process of individuation.

Proust goes in search of an essence that ultimately endures, allowing us to escape the limitations of time. Jung (1984) states: "Through individuation you create something timeless and eternal, which carries the quality of Immortality" (p. 284). He adds:

> The Process of Individuation has always been appreciated as the most valuable and important thing in life. It is the only thing that brings any lasting satisfaction to a man. Power, glory, wealth, mean nothing in comparison. These things are external and therefore futile. The really important things are within. Experience shows that there are certain psychological conditions in which man gets eternal results. They have something of the quality of eternity, of timelessness, they have the quality of reaching beyond man. They have a Divine quality and yield all that satisfaction which man-made things do not. (1984, p. 289)

Leaving a "testament behind," a sort of "psychic testimony," as evidence of our lived life and in reverence of our covenant with the divine is thus of crucial importance. A biography of an inner process . . . a psychic legacy in the form of an autobiography, of our own individuation experience.

One must remain open to the mysterious quality through which the individuation process unfolds. Proust unveiled such mystery by walking side by side with the narrator of his story, a narrator who embracing Proust's imagination sets out to search for his vocation as a writer, just as Parsifal, unknowingly, goes in search of his vocation as a knight of the Round Table.

After an arduous process through which the inert *prima materia* undergoes transformation, Proust finally discovered the alchemical gold. It was also throughout his individuation journey, through the spontaneous emergence of his childhood memories, that he was able to experience the numinous quality.

Perhaps, by partaking of Proust's individuation process, we too—as truthful readers of our selves—can set out in search of our very essence, our deeper being through the path of reminiscence, a pathway leading to our meaningful past. It is as if, paradoxically, we would need to retrace our steps to regain access to the dimension of soul which would, in turn, further our inner transformation process. While we continue to be endowed with life, we are unknowingly engaged in a ceaseless process of writing, editing, re-writing our own individuation narratives, the end of which we do not know.

Magi Guindi is a Jungian analyst in private practice in Los Angeles, California trained at ISAP, Zurich. Her main interest lies in the discovery and understanding of the mysterious language of the deeper psyche, as expressed through dreams, images, metaphors, and symbols. She has lectured at ISAP, at the Jung Institute, at the Centro Mexican C.G. Jung on a wide diversity of themes ranging from myths, dreams, and the archetype of the coniunctio, through depression and creativity to the individuation process, among other themes. She has lived in Mexico, Spain, France, Switzerland, and the United States. She speaks Spanish, French, Italian and English.

References

Gallienne, G. (2020). "Lectures de Marcel Proust," (podcast) February 1, 2020.

Jaffé, A. (2021). *Streiflichter*. Daimon.

Jung, C.G. (1995). *Memories, Dreams, Reflections: An Autobiography.* (ed. Aniela Jaffé). Fontana Press.

Jung, C.G. (1984). *Dream Analysis.* Princeton University Press.

Proust, M. (2003). "Time Regained," in *In Search of Lost Time*, Vol. VI, (Trans. A. Mayor & T. Kilmartin). The Modern Library.

Proust, M. (2023). "The Captive/The Fugitive," Vol. V. Yale University Press.

Individuation as Re-enchantment

Roderick Main

Just as Murray's publications are a go-to source for theoretical understanding of the full depth and range of individuation, so Murray himself, it seems to me, is a go-to person for experiencing what advanced individuation can look like in practice.

In this chapter, I consider Carl Gustav Jung's concept of individuation as a response to the cultural condition, process, or narrative called by Max Weber "the disenchantment of the world" (1919/1948, p. 155).[1] The narrative of disenchantment provided in Jung's day—and still provides today—one of the most powerful accounts of the nature of modernity. It implies, in ways I shall outline shortly, that the modern world has been stripped of genuine mystery, lacks inherent meaning, and is unrelated to any spiritual or divine reality. For many, such a condition is both a realistic and a positive development, for it is associated with a kind of rational and empirical outlook on the world that has proven conducive to the rapid development of science and technology, with all their economic, social, and cultural benefits (Gauchet, 1997; see also Main, 2022, pp. 8–9). Others, however, have highlighted that disenchantment also has profoundly negative aspects, in that the same dominant rationality and

---

[1] Most of the content of this chapter is extracted and adapted from my book *Breaking the Spell of Disenchantment: Mystery, Meaning, and Metaphysics in the Work of C.G. Jung* (Asheville, NC: Chiron Publications, 2022) and is reproduced in its present form with grateful acknowledgement.

empiricism can readily lead to stifling bureaucratic social structures, alienation from and attempted domination of both nature and other people, and a deep sense of meaninglessness, with proliferating mental health problems and general cultural confusion (Berman, 1981; see also Main, pp. 9–10). Weber himself (1919/1948) recognized both the positive and the negative consequences of disenchantment, but for him the condition was unavoidable, "the fate of our times," which needed to be endured "like a man" (p. 155).

Although Jung never used the term "disenchantment" (*Entzauberung*), he was acutely aware of the condition or process Weber had in mind and referred to it in alternative terms as "the historical process of world despiritualization" (1938/1940/1969d, para. 141) or as the world's being "desacralized" (McGuire & Hull, 1978, p. 230). Like Weber, Jung recognized both the positive and negative implications of disenchantment. But, unlike Weber, he did not believe that disenchantment needed to be acquiesced in as the default condition of modernity. In the following, I argue that Jung's psychological model, in particular its core process of individuation, can be understood as a forthright attempt to go beyond disenchantment and to reenchant the world. I suggest, however, that, importantly, individuation also acknowledges within its wider process both the perpetual need for disenchantment and the continuing presence of naïve enchantment. I first provide a sense of how Weber understood disenchantment by highlighting what he saw as its principal epistemological implications. I then briefly summarize the overall process of individuation as Jung classically presented it, before showing how the stages variously identified within individuation correspond to the conditions or processes of enchantment, disenchantment, and re-enchantment. I highlight that, for Jung, the most important, culturally most needed, and also most difficult stage is that associated with re-enchantment, and it is this stage that forms the focus of his psychological project. I conclude with some brief reflections on the value of viewing individuation in this light.

Disenchantment

"Disenchantment" is the usual English translation of the German term *Entzauberung*, which more literally means "de-magification" or "loss of magic"; it is sometimes also translated as "elimination of magic." In previous ages, Weber (1919/1948) relates, people used to believe in gods, spirits, and other mysterious forces that they could pray to and influence by "magical means" in order to acquire knowledge and achieve results in the world (p. 139). Over the course of the millennia, with "increasing intellectualization and rationalization" and eventually the development of science and technology, belief in these mysterious forces has become increasingly unnecessary and has waned. Although individual persons today might have no greater knowledge of the conditions in which they live than did those in earlier times, they have the belief, thanks to the empiricism and reason of science, that, if they wished to know or do something, it would be possible to know or do it by "technical means and calculations," without invoking any "mysterious incalculable forces" (p. 139). The disenchanted modern world for Weber is thus a world that has been stripped of genuine mystery.

However, there are for Weber important limits to what can be known by the empiricism and reason of science. Crucially, disenchanted modern science cannot obtain any knowledge of values or meaning. "Who," Weber asks rhetorically, "still believes that the findings of astronomy, biology, physics, or chemistry could teach us anything about the meaning of the world?" (p. 142) Indeed, he states, "these natural sciences . . . are apt to make the belief that there is such a thing as the 'meaning' of the universe die out at its very roots" (p. 142). The sciences have their presuppositions about the value of obtaining knowledge of the natural world, but these presuppositions cannot be proved correct (pp. 143–144); "still less," Weber reiterates, "can it be proved that the existence of the world which these sciences describe is worthwhile, that it has any 'meaning,' or that it makes sense to live in such a world" (p. 144). Any attempt to make such valuations would interfere with the proper activity of science, for "whenever the man of science introduces his personal value judgment, a full understanding of the facts ceases" (p. 146). The disenchanted modern world for Weber is thus a world that lacks inherent meaning.

Not only is it impossible to derive values from facts, but it is also, for Weber, impossible to obtain knowledge of any spiritual, divine, or "metaphysical" realities deemed to be beyond the empirical world. Whereas in the past, knowledge was pursued in order to access higher realities—providing "the way to true being," "the way to true art," "the way to true nature," "the way to true God," "the way to true happiness" (p. 143)—modern science no longer considers it possible to know these "former illusions" (p. 143) or indeed to access any reality beyond the empirical world; presuppositions about such things "lie beyond the limits of 'science'" and "do not represent knowledge in the usual sense" (p. 154). The disenchanted modern world for Weber is thus unrelated to any spiritual, divine, or other metaphysical realities.

This combination of features of the disenchanted modern world—it's being stripped of genuine mystery, lacking inherent meaning, and being unrelated to any spiritual or divine realities—has for Weber a further implication regarding how we are to understand the relationship between science and religion. Since the deliverances of science and reason provide no evidence for the putative transcendent realities and values of religion but can, alternatively, furnish credible naturalistic explanations of alleged religious phenomena (p. 147), one can, Weber argued, only make the step into religion by abandoning science and reason, making an "intellectual sacrifice" (p. 155). The disenchanted modern world for Weber is thus a world in which science and religion are irreconcilable.[2]

Individuation

Jung's concept of individuation can be seen as a response to the condition, process, or narrative outlined by Weber. Ultimately, in ways that will be made more explicit later, it attempts, contra disenchantment, to affirm genuine mystery, inherent meaning, sacred reality, and the reconcilability of science and religion. However, as we shall now see, it does so in a way that also continues to acknowledge the role of both disenchantment and naïve enchantment.

In brief, individuation is the developmental process of becoming a unique self through the ongoing synthesis of consciousness and the unconscious. Jung articulated the process in a variety of ways, of which the following is a summary (based mainly on Jung, 1928/1966b and 1951/1968a, paras. 1–67).

For Jung, psychological development begins in childhood and early adulthood by one's developing and strengthening an ego to deal with the

---

[2] The above account of the epistemological implications of disenchantment is based on the analysis by Egil Asprem in his book *The Problem of Disenchantment: Naturalism and Esoteric Discourse, 1900–1939* (Leiden, NL: Brill, 2014), pp. 32–40. A complementary analysis can be found in Jason Josephson–Storm, *The Myth of Disenchantment: Magic, Modernity, and the Birth of the Human Sciences* (Chicago, IL: Chicago University Press, 2017), p. 286.

forces that assail one from the psychic world within and the physical and social worlds without. Such an ego is inevitably one-sided, having been forced by the pressures of its inner and outer environments to develop and thereby make conscious some psychic potentialities at the expense of others, which remain unconscious.

In Jung's understanding, however, the unconscious has an innate drive toward expressing itself as a whole. An opposition is therefore set up between consciousness, centered on the ego, and the unconscious. From the unconscious, contents emerge spontaneously—for example, in the form of dreams, fantasies, symptoms, and acausal convergences of events—to compensate and regulate consciousness in the interests of greater overall realization of the unconscious.

This process of encounter between the ego and the unconscious, which can be facilitated by psychotherapy and the deployment of techniques such as dream interpretation, transference analysis, and active imagination, is marked by the appearance of certain typical themes or problems, which demand to be integrated and made conscious. Such typical themes, problems, or "archetypes" needing to be encountered and integrated with the ego include above all the disavowed, often dark, side of one's personality (the "shadow") and the contrasexual element of one's personality (the "anima" or "animus").

When a sufficient level of integration has been achieved between ego-consciousness and these archetypes, there can emerge a new center of the psyche, a center no longer only of consciousness, as was the ego, but of both consciousness and the unconscious. This new center is what Jung called the "self." The self is potentially there from the beginning as a kind of unconscious wholeness, but the aim of individuation is to realize it consciously. This is an extremely arduous, lifelong task, and it is full of pitfalls, not least the dangers of either the ego's becoming excessively assimilated by the self or the self's becoming excessively assimilated by the ego, both of which would result in pathological conditions, such as psychosis or inflation. "Conscious wholeness," Jung wrote more favorably, "consists in a successful union of ego and self, so that both preserve their intrinsic qualities" (1947/1954/1969b, para. 430, n.128).

Enchantment, Disenchantment, and Re-enchantment in the Process of Individuation

This overall process of individuation corresponds, I suggest, with the process of transformation from an enchanted state to a disenchanted state to a reenchanted state, with the reenchanted state being for Jung the overarching and decisive one. The correspondence can be shown by highlighting some aspects of the typical developmental stages within the process of individuation outlined above. For this purpose, I present two further, differently inflected summaries of individuation. The first is based on an account (Stein, 2006) aimed at tracking the typical stages in which the individuation process is encountered during psychotherapy. For convenience, I shall refer to this as the psychotherapeutic model. Whereas Jung generally emphasized two halves of life (1930–1931/1969e), this first additional summary subdivides the first "half" into two stages, producing a three-stage model. The second additional summary, presented in more detail, is based on Jung's last extensive discussion of individuation, in *Mysterium Coniunctionis* (1955–1956/1970), where he articulates the process in terms borrowed from alchemy. For convenience, I shall refer to this as the alchemical model. This model also recognizes three stages, though here the three stages all seem to be concerned with the second half of life. I shall return to these differences later.

Individuation Across the Lifespan: The Psychotherapeutic Model

Jung's model of individuation posits an initial undifferentiated and unconscious state, a preconscious fusion of subjectivity with the world. Drawing on the work of Erich Neumann (1954, 1955), Murray Stein (2006) describes this initial stage as the "maternal" or "containment/ nurturance" stage of individuation (pp. 199, 200–204). Jung considers this to be the state of mind of so-called "primitive" peoples and of children. This state, for which Jung also borrows Lucien Lévy-Bruhl's term *"participation mystique,"* broadly corresponds, I suggest, with the state of enchantment. It is a state characterized by identification, in which all aspects of the world seem animated and to behave according to the influence of magical forces.

With the development of ego-consciousness, there emerges increasing differentiation between self and world, subject and object. Greater critical capacities arise, including eventually the ability to notice and begin to withdraw projections. In Stein's terms, this is the "paternal" or "adapting/adjusting" stage of individuation (2006, pp. 199, 204–209). Jung considers this to be the state of mind of young adults who are coming to terms with life's realities and acquiring independence. It broadly corresponds, I suggest, with the state of disenchantment, experienced as freedom from former animistic delusions, in which the world is now seen as regulated impersonally by natural laws and hence as indifferent to human wishes.

The final, "individual" or "centering/integrating" stage of individuation (pp. 199, 209–212) is, according to Stein, "usually entered with a rather depressed and questioning attitude" (p. 210)—an attitude that can readily be seen to correspond with a state of disenchantment now experienced not as freedom from delusions but as de-animation. In this stage, once entered, writes Stein, "There is a shift in interest and emphasis towards reaching out to dimensions of living that have less to do with survival and more to do with meaning. Spiritual life becomes more crucially important and individualized" (p. 210). It is at this stage that the main work of integrating the opposites takes place (p. 212). A person comes to be centered less in the ego and more in the self, and as a result "feels less alienated from all of humanity and from the profound complexities of reality" (p. 212). The references here to dimensions of meaning, the importance of spiritual life, and the overcoming of alienation suggest that this stage corresponds with the state of re-enchantment.

Stein emphasizes the two major transitions between these stages— from the maternal to the paternal and from the paternal to the individual. These would be phases where in the first case disenchantment and in the second case re-enchantment appears not so much as states but as processes. But whether focusing on the three states of enchantment, disenchantment, and re-enchantment or on the two processes of transition from enchantment to disenchantment and from disenchantment to re-enchantment, the overall correspondence of the stages of individuation with these states or processes is compelling.

Late-Stage Individuation: The Alchemical Model

Jung believed that he had found a pre-modern parallel to the process of individuation in the symbolism of medieval alchemy, and he elaborated this parallel over the final three decades of his life in a series of studies of the relationship between psychological and alchemical phenomena and concepts. At the end of his final major study of alchemy, *Mysterium Coniunctionis* (1955–1956/1970), he encapsulated the process in terms provided by the sixteenth-century alchemist Gerhard Dorn (ca. 1530–1584). In summarizing the process below, I shall again note connections to the framing of individuation as a process of enchantment, disenchantment, and re-enchantment.

Dorn described the alchemical process as involving a series of three conjunctions. The first conjunction, which he called the *unio mentalis* ("mental union"), consists of a union of spirit and soul (Jung, 1955–1956/1970, paras. 664–676). Dorn considered that in the natural human state there was "an inextricable interweaving of the soul with the body, which together formed a dark unity (the *unio naturalis* [natural union])," variously referred to by the alchemists as "the *nigredo* [blackness], the chaos, the *massa confusa* [confused mass]" (para. 696). Jung describes it as "The original, half-animal state of unconsciousness" (para. 696). However, through the operation of spirit—that is, through the discriminating power of "conscious and rational insight"—it is possible to extract the soul from its "enchainment" to the body, to free it from "its fetters in the things of sense," and thus "to set up a rational, spiritual–psychic position over against the turbulence of the emotions," a position "immune to the influences of the body" (para. 696). In Jung's psychological and psychotherapeutic terms, this "overcoming of the body" involves "making conscious and dissolving the projections that falsify the patient's view of the world and impede his self-knowledge" (paras. 696, 673). Acquiring greater self-knowledge (paras. 674, 711) brings neurotic symptoms "under the control of consciousness" and fosters "inner certainty" and "self-reliance" (para. 756).

This first conjunction can be understood as depicting the transition from a state of enchantment to a state of disenchantment. The state of enchantment is the unconscious identity or fusion (*"participation mystique"*) between the psyche and the body and between the self and the world. The state of disenchantment is the differentiation, discrimination, or separation of the psyche from the body and of the self from the world with the aid of the spiritual intellect and its "conscious and rational insight." Becoming free of "the turbulence of the emotions," "the influences of the body," and "the projections that falsify [one's] view of the world and impede [one's] self-knowledge" and thereby bringing neurotic symptoms under the control of consciousness and fostering "inner certainty" and "self-reliance" are clearly major psychological and spiritual achievements. But these qualities and the discriminating, dualistic consciousness on which they are based come at a cost. Such "mental union [*unio mentalis*]" is, Jung notes, "purely intrapsychic" (para. 664); it is a state of "interior oneness" (para. 670). As such, it leaves the body and the material world unintegrated. Indeed, as Jung elaborates, it results in a deep split of the unified spirit and soul from matter and the body (para. 664). Jung does not for this reason denigrate the process, which he considers "indispensable for the differentiation of consciousness" (para. 672). However, since it was the soul that animated the body, a consequence of the soul's separation from the body by its union with spirit is that "the body and its world" appear "dead" (para. 742)—part of the very condition of disenchantment. The problem confronting the alchemists who reached this stage was how to reanimate the body by reuniting it with the soul in a way that was not simply a return to the confusion of the natural union (*unio naturalis*) (para. 742). This was the task of Dorn's second conjunction.

In Dorn's terms, the solution to the problem of how to reunite the *unio mentalis* with the body was the alchemical process resulting in production of the *caelum*, the "heaven," "the kingdom of heaven on earth," "a heavenly substance in the body," the "blue quintessence" (paras. 691–963, 703–706, 757–758, 764). Dorn described various alchemical procedures to produce this mysterious process and substance (paras. 681–685), but in Jung's interpretation such procedures are projected, symbolic expressions of the process of individuation and its facilitating method of active imagination (paras. 705–706). The *caelum* itself, the product of the process, is a symbol of the self. As such, the *caelum* was the *imago Dei*, the image of God, which could also be symbolized by the mandala (paras. 716–719, 757) and by the central alchemical figure of Mercurius, who, as both "matter and spirit," expressed for Jung that the self "embraces the bodily sphere as well as the psychic" (para. 717) and indeed represents not only a "spiritualization" of matter but also a "materialization of the spirit" (para. 764).

This second conjunction encapsulates the transition from a state of disenchantment to a state of re-enchantment. The dualistic state in which consciousness appears to be separate from the world, psyche from matter, self from other comes to be replaced by a more participative form of consciousness, in which this sense of separation begins to be dissolved. The world that seemed external, material, and other comes to be experienced as continuous with a wider sense of self. As a result, the world that had seemed to be inert and meaningless begins to show signs of animation, subjectivity, and participative relationship. Rather than being just material to be manipulated instrumentally for one's own ends, the world begins to make normative calls on one. From having been an "It," the world becomes a "Thou." The demands made by the world include that "the insights gained [in the second conjunction] should be made real," thereby "making a reality of the man who has acquired some knowledge of his paradoxical wholeness" (para. 679). The difficulty of effecting this transition from disenchanted to reenchanted consciousness cannot be overstated. It includes the work of integrating the anima/animus and of bringing about their union in the syzygy (cf. 1951/1968a, paras. 20–42; 1946/1966a). The greater sense of unity towards which this process leads is experience of the self.

Again, however, this is not the conclusion of the process. What the second conjunction achieved was "the representation of the self in actual and visible form"—through symbolic images—but this, for Dorn and for Jung (1955–1956/1970), was "a mere *rite d'entreé*, as it were a propaedeutic action and mere anticipation of [the self's] realization" (para. 759). The final realization, "a consummation of the *mysterium coniunctionis*," could be expected "only when the unity of spirit, soul, and body [i.e., the self or 'whole man' (para. 760)] [was] made one with the original *unus mundus* ['one world']" (para. 664). This was Dorn's "third and highest degree of conjunction" (para. 760).

The concept of the *unus mundus* refers to "the potential world of the first day of creation, when nothing was yet 'in actu,' i.e., divided into two and many, but was still one" (para. 760); it is the *mundus archetypus*, the "archetypal world" (para. 761). Jung was clear that the state of being united with the *unus mundus*, made one with the "one world," is not a case of "a fusion of the individual with his environment, or even his adaptation to it, but a *unio mystica* with the potential world" (para. 767). He emphasized that this potential world "is not the world of sense" (para. 767) but the "background of our empirical world," the "transcendental psychophysical background" in which the conditions of empirical physical and psychical phenomena inhere (para. 769), "the eternal Ground of all empirical being" (para. 760).

As we have seen, re-enchantment broadly corresponds with the stage of individuation that maps onto the second conjunction. What the third conjunction additionally does, theoretically at least, is to ground the process of re-enchantment in an experience of unity with the creative ground of reality. On the one hand, participative consciousness is thus consolidated and taken further through an experience of unitive consciousness. The "It" which became a "Thou" is now realized as an "I," as *the* "I." On the other hand, the unity of the self with the creative ground of reality means that creativity out of the *unio mystica* can create entirely new states of reality, which when they first emerge unprocessed would also be experienced as new states of enchantment. The creative emergence of these new enchanted states can thus recursively trigger further potential processes of disenchantment, re-enchantment, and mystical union.

Breaking the Spell of Disenchantment: The Countermagic of Individuation

In the psychotherapeutic model of individuation, the three stages with which enchantment, disenchantment, and re-enchantment have been correlated span the whole of biological life, from birth to late maturity. In the alchemical model of individuation, by contrast, the three conjunctions all seem to occur within late maturity and to be phases of consciously undertaken work of psychological and spiritual transformation, represented only by the third stage in the psychotherapeutic model. Moreover, disenchantment correlates with the first conjunction and re-enchantment with the second conjunction in the alchemical model, whereas these correlations are with the second and third (or at least the transitions to the second and third) stages in the psychotherapeutic model. Finally, the third conjunction in the alchemical model is not explicated in the psychotherapeutic model.[3]

These differences reflect Jung's predominant focus, especially in his alchemical work, on the second half of life and late-stage individuation. The alchemical model provides, as it were, a more focused look at the stage in which Jung is most interested, where individuation is taken up as a consciously abetted rather than just naturally unfolding process. Within this more focused perspective, the correlations with enchantment,

---

[3] The third conjunction is discussed in detail elsewhere in Stein's work (e.g., 2014, pp. 122–126; 2019).

disenchantment, and re-enchantment, despite the noted differences, remain apt. In both models, the process of transformation proceeds from an enchanted to a disenchanted to a reenchanted state, such that, crucially, disenchantment supersedes naïve enchantment but is not the culminating state. The culminating state is re-enchantment, and the alchemical model, as presented in *Mysterium Coniunctionis*, presents Jung's most advanced account of its reach.

Considering Jung's predominant interest in its late stage, the process of individuation is sometimes wholly identified with that stage (1939/1968b, para. 489), the earlier stages in the psychotherapeutic model being associated rather with processes of adaptation and integration (Samuels et al., 1986, p. 76). From the perspective of its goal, individuation can be said to be primarily concerned with re-enchantment. To clarify the sense in which individuation may indeed reenchant, we can now revisit the theoretical implications of disenchantment—that there is no genuine mystery, inherent meaning, or relationship to spiritual or divine reality, and that science and religion are irreconcilable—and show how, at a general level, individuation challenges them, breaking their spell with its own deeper magic, as it were.

First, disenchantment implies that there is no genuine mystery. Contrary to this, individuation, especially in its later stages involves acknowledging and relating to factors—the collective unconscious and its archetypes—that precisely are "mysterious incalculable forces" influencing human behavior as well as events beyond the sphere of human behavior (1928/1996b, paras. 266–406). Not only, for Jung, are intrapsychic archetypal events, such as dreams and visions, genuinely creative and hence irreducible to any set of psychological, social, or cultural determinants (1947/1954/1969b, para. 417; 1961/1977b, paras. 521–559). There can also be, for Jung, even more mysterious, externally occurring events of an archetypal nature that acausally coincide with psychic events—that is, synchronicities (1952/1969f, paras. 841, 843–846). Moreover, the process of individuation culminates in realization of a factor, the self, that as a paradoxical coincidence of opposites (1951/1968a, para. 423) is quintessentially mysterious, especially if one further realizes its union with the one world or *unus mundus* in the experience of mystical union (*unio mystica*) (1955–1956/1970, para. 771). Jung's affirmation of mystery is vividly expressed by his lifelong interest in mystical and paranormal experiences (Main, 2021; 2022, pp. 41–70).

Second, disenchantment implies that there is no inherent meaning in the world. Contrary to this, individuation for Jung presupposes a finality, purposiveness, and meaningfulness in the process of human development (1928/1996b, paras. 266–269, 405). He characterizes the archetypes that give structure to the process of individuation as each providing a "core of meaning" to a multiplicity of possible representations or experiences (1940/1968c, para. 266; 1947/1954/1969b, para. 417). He even describes the central archetype of the self, which guides individuation and is realized at its culmination, as "the archetype of orientation and meaning" (1963/1995, p. 224). In his essay "Synchronicity: An Acausal Connecting Principle" (1952/1969f), he makes clear that the kind of meaning he has in mind in discussing the archetypes that govern individuation is not just a subjective meaning projected onto external objects and events that in themselves are meaningless. He devotes a whole chapter, "Forerunners of the Idea of Synchronicity," to providing historical and cross-cultural support for the proposition that the archetypal meaning expressed by synchronicities is "objective" or "transcendental" (paras. 916–946). He even argues, with support from the physicist Wolfgang Pauli, that such archetypal meaning should be recognized as an intrinsic part of scientific understanding (Main, 2022, pp. 71–99).

Third, disenchantment implies that there can be no relationship to spiritual or divine reality. Contrary to this, individuation for Jung fosters relationship to numinous—spiritual—archetypes. More specifically, the process of individuation leads to realization of the archetype of the self, experience of which, Jung (1928/1996b) claims, is indistinguishable from experience of the God-image and as such represents "God within us" (para. 399). In Jung's understanding, individuation is precisely a religious process, whether he has in mind Western or Eastern forms of religion (1942/1954/1969g, paras. 414–448; 1939/1969a, paras. 906–907). As he asserted with emphasis, *"Individuation is the life in God"* (1956–1957/1977, para. 1624). Despite Jung's wariness of theology and philosophy, it is even possible to identify in his work an implicit panentheistic metaphysics, which supports an intimate and mutually transformative relationship between the world and the divine (Main, 2022, pp. 101–130).

Finally, disenchantment implies that science and religion are irreconcilable, that in order to possess religion it is necessary to make an "intellectual sacrifice." Contrary to this, individuation for Jung is a process that both is religious, in the ways just described, and yet is also scientific since, as he continually emphasized (1973, p. 529; 1976, pp. 294, 342), it is based on empirical observation of processes occurring in the psyche (see also Main, 2013).

Conclusion

The process of individuation, followed through to its later stages, thus fundamentally and precisely challenges the epistemological assumptions of disenchantment, with the aim, effectively, of reenchanting the world— that is, disclosing the world to be genuinely mysterious, inherently meaningful, and related to the sacred. In this way, individuation, which may seem to be primarily a psychological process, proves also to be psychosocial, loosening the grip of the dominant cultural condition, process, or narrative of disenchantment articulated by Weber. This psychosocial implication is entirely in keeping with Jung's claim that "Individuation does not shut one out from the world, but gathers the world to oneself" (1947/1954/1969b, para. 432), which highlights the reciprocity for Jung between individual and collective wellbeing.

Notably, we have also seen that, while individuation reenchants in the above way, it includes within its overall process continuing stage-specific roles for both disenchantment and naïve enchantment. This seems to be the case whether individuation is viewed as unfolding across the lifespan or, more specifically, as a task of late maturity. Such a perspective is helpful for at least the following two reasons: First, affirming re-enchantment does not entail outright rejection of disenchantment, including its positive benefits. The epistemological attitudes associated with disenchantment, including critical awareness, discrimination, and above all the ability to dissolve projections, are arguably essential to achieving the kind of participative and ultimately unitive consciousness associated with late-stage individuation and re-enchantment. Disenchantment becomes problematic, Jung's overall model suggests, mainly when it is identified with as the highest achievable state, when one is, as it were, under the spell of disenchantment.

Second, recognizing enchantment as a state or process distinct from re-enchantment, the former preceding and the latter succeeding disenchantment, is also helpful. In relation to naïve enchantment, disenchantment can be experienced as a liberatory and empowering state, and this experience may be one factor that encourages identification with disenchantment. If re-enchantment is then confused with naïve enchantment, re-enchantment may be criticized as a regressive retreat from the rigors and liberatory achievements of disenchantment. However, such criticism becomes inappropriate when re-enchantment is distinguished from naïve enchantment and envisaged not as a restored prior state but as an even more challenging and even more liberating state beyond disenchantment.

Roderick Main, PhD, works at the University of Essex, UK, where he is a professor in the Department of Psychosocial and Psychoanalytic Studies and Director of the Centre for Myth Studies. His books include *The Rupture of Time: Synchronicity and Jung's critique of Modern Western Culture* **(Brunner-Routledge, 2004),** *Revelations of Chance: Synchronicity as Spiritual Experience* **(SUNY, 2007), and most recently** *Breaking the Spell of Disenchantment: Mystery, Meaning, and Metaphysics in the Work of C.G. Jung* **(Chiron Publications, 2022).**

References

(In the following list, volumes of *The Collected Works of C.G. Jung* [H. Read et al., Eds.; London: Routledge & Kegan Paul/Princeton, NJ: Princeton University Press, 1953–1979] are abbreviated to CW plus volume number.)

Asprem, E. (2014). *The Problem of Disenchantment: Scientific Naturalism and Esoteric Discourse 1900–1939*. Leiden.

Berman, M. (1981). *The Re-enchantment of the World*. Cornell University Press.

Gauchet, M. (1997). *The Disenchantment of the World: A Political History of Religion*. Princeton University Press.

Josephson–Storm, J. (2017). *The Myth of Disenchantment: Magic, Modernity, and the Birth of the Human Sciences*. University of Chicago Press.

Jung, C.G. (1966a). *The Psychology of the Transference*. In CW16 (2nd ed., pp. 163–323). (Original work published 1946)

Jung, C.G. (1966b). *The Relations Between the Ego and the Unconscious*. In CW7 (2nd ed., pp. 121–241). (Original work published 1928)

Jung, C.G. (1968a). *Aion: Researches into the Phenomenology of the Self*. CW9ii (2nd ed.). (Original work published 1951)

Jung, C.G. (1968b). *Conscious, Unconscious, and Individuation*. In CW9i (2nd ed., pp. 275–289). (Original work published 1939)

Jung, C.G. (1968c). *The Psychology of the Child Archetype*. In CW9i (2nd ed., pp. 151–181). (Original work published 1940)

Jung, C.G. (1969a). Foreword to Suzuki's *Introduction to Zen Buddhism*. In CW11 (2nd ed., pp. 538–557). (Original work published 1939)

Jung, C.G. (1969b). *On the Nature of the Psyche*. In CW8 (2nd ed., pp. 159–234). (Original work published 1947, revised 1954)

Jung, C.G. (1969c). *A Psychological Approach to the Dogma of the Trinity*. In CW11 (2nd ed., pp. 107–200). (Original work published 1942, revised 1948)

Jung, C.G. (1969d). *Psychology and Religion*. In CW11 (2nd ed., pp. 3–105). (Original work published 1938, revised 1940)

Jung, C.G. (1969e). *The Stages of Life*. In CW8 (2nd ed., pp. 387–403). (Original work published 1930–1931)

Jung, C.G. (1969f). *Synchronicity: An Acausal Connecting Principle*. In CW8 (2nd ed., pp. 417–519). (Original work published 1952)

Jung, C.G. (1969g). *Transformation Symbolism in the Mass*. In CW11 (2nd ed., pp. 201–296). (Original work published 1942, revised 1954)

Jung, C.G. (1970). *Mysterium Coniunctionis: An Inquiry into the Separation and Synthesis of Psychic Opposites in Alchemy*. CW14 (2nd ed.). (Original work published 1955–1956)

Jung, C.G. (1973). *C.G. Jung Letters: Vol. 1. 1906–1950* (G. Adler, Ed.). Routledge.

Jung, C.G. (1976). *C.G. Jung Letters: Vol. 2. 1951–1961* (G. Adler, Ed.). Routledge.

Jung, C.G. (1977a). *Jung and Religious Belief*. In CW18 (pp. 702–744). Routledge & Kegan Paul. (Original work published 1956–1957)

Jung, C.G. (1977b). *Symbols and the Interpretation of Dreams*. In CW18 (pp. 183–264). Routledge & Kegan Paul. (Original work published 1961)

Jung, C.G. (1995). *Memories, Dreams, Reflections* (A. Jaffé, Ed.). Fontana. (Original work published 1963)

Main, R. (2013). "Secular *and* religious: The intrinsic doubleness of analytical psychology and the hegemony of naturalism in the social sciences." *Journal of Analytical Psychology, 58*, 366–386.

Main, R. (2021). Mystical experience and the scope of C.G. Jung's holism. In E. F. Kelly & P. Marshall (Eds.), *Consciousness Unbound: Liberating Mind from the Tyranny of Materialism* (pp. 139–174). Rowman & Littlefield.

Main, R. (2022). *Breaking the Spell of Disenchantment: Mystery, Meaning, and Metaphysics in the Work of C.G. Jung*. Chiron Publications.

McGuire, W., & Hull, R. F. C. (Eds.). (1978). *C.G. Jung Speaking: Interviews and Encounters*. Thames & Hudson.

Neumann, E. (1954). *The Origins and History of Consciousness*. Routledge & Kegan Paul.

Neumann, E. (1955). *The Great Mother: Analysis of an Archetype*. Routledge & Kegan Paul.

Samuels, A., Shorter, B., & Plaut, F. (1986). *A Critical Dictionary of Jungian Analysis*. Routledge.

Stein, M. (2006). Individuation. In R. Papadopoulos (ed.), *The Handbook of Jungian Psychology: Theory, Practice, and Applications* (pp. 196–214). Routledge.

Stein, M. (2014). Minding the self. In *Minding the Self: Jungian Meditations on Contemporary Spirituality* (pp. 111–126). Routledge.

Stein, M. (2019). "Psychological Individuation and Spiritual Enlightenment: Some comparisons and points of contact." *Journal of Analytical Psychology 64*, 6–22.

Weber, M. (1948). Science as a vocation. In H. Gerth & C. Wright Mills (Eds.), *From Max Weber: Essays in Sociology* (pp. 129–156). Oxford University Press. (Original work published 1919)

In the Still World of the Heart (*In des Herzens stille Welt*): Reflections on Goethe and Individuation Psychology

Paul Bishop

Murray has helped unlock the significance of Jung for making sense of (and responding to) the challenges of the twenty-first century. It is therefore an honour as well as a great pleasure to contribute to this Festschrift for Murray Stein, and to join with Chiron in celebrating his work as a Jungian who is a scholar—and a gentleman.

On several occasions I have suggested that C.G. Jung's legendary kinship with Johann Wolfgang von Goethe — said to have been regarded by Jung as annoying and amusing in equal measure (Jung, 1963, p. 52) — nevertheless points to an important truth, namely: the remarkable harmony between Jung's outlook and Goethe's. After all, the complex chiasmic parallelism of the remark in *Memories, Dreams, Reflections* about how Jung tried to "see the line which leads through my life into the world, and out of the world again" (Jung, 1963, p. 352) is strongly reminiscent, both rhetorically and conceptually, of Goethe's observation in "Significant Help Given by an Ingenious Turn of Phrase" (1823) that "the human being knows himself only insofar as he knows the world" and that "he perceives the world only in himself, and himself only in the world" (Goethe, 1988, p. 39). So here I intend to examine two shorter poems by Goethe (and, *en passant*, a couple of poems by Friedrich Nietzsche and one by Joseph von Eichendorff), whose themes intersect with the ideas — and the spirit — of Murray Stein's remarkable work over many years as an exponent and an exegete of analytical psychology (notably, the psychology of individuation) who is also a connoisseur of German literature and culture.

Nowadays the notion of medical humanities is still very much in vogue; yet, in a fundamental sense, to be engaged in the humanities has *always* been to be engaged in a therapeutic activity. As Karl Jaspers (1883-1969) once wrote:

> What health and illness mean in general are matters which concern the physician least of all. He deals scientifically with life processes and with particular illnesses. What is "ill" in general depends less on the judgment of the doctor than on the judgment of the patient and on the dominant views in any given cultural circle. (Jaspers, 1963, p. 652)

Recent work in medical humanities over the last couple of decades supports this view (Horowitz and Wakefield, 2007; Bolton, 2008 and 2010); and in *Studies in Hysteria* (1895) Freud himself once imagined telling his patients, "You will be able to convince yourself that much will be gained if we succeed in transforming your hysterical misery into common unhappiness" (Freud and Breuer, 1955, p. 305). Just two examples of the many possible approaches to mental health are furnished by the phenomenological analysis of moods (*Stimmungen*) developed by Otto Friedrich Bollnow (1903-1995) and subsequently of atmospheres by Gernot Böhme (1937-2022) (Bollnow, 1941; Böhme, 2013a; 2013b; 2017). Here, however, we shall use two short poems by Goethe, reflecting his classical temperament, to explore the fascinating intersection between the arts and humanities and psychoanalysis (and, in this case, between German literature and Jungian psychology).

"Calm at Sea" (*Meeresstille*)

In Schiller's *Musenalmanach* in 1796, Goethe published two poems, entitled *Meeresstille* and *Glückliche Fahrt*. Of these two texts, the first ("Calm at Sea") reads as follows:

> *Tiefe Stille herrscht im Wasser,*
> *Ohne Regung ruht das Meer,*

Und bekümmert sieht der Schiffer
Glatte Fläche rings umher.
Keine Luft von keiner Seite!
Todesstille fürchterlich!
In der ungeheuern Weite
Reget keine Welle sich.
    (Goethe, 1974, p. 242)

Silence deep rules o'er the waters,
Calmly slumbering lies the main,
While the sailor views with trouble
Nought but one vast level plain.
Not a zephyr is in motion!
Silence fearful as the grave!
In the mighty waste of ocean
Sunk to rest is every wave.
    (Goethe, 1882, p. 223)

Although it is a short poem, there is much that one could say about it, beginning with its meter: its consistent four-foot trochaic pattern (retained here by Edgar Alfred Bowring [1826-1911]) creates an almost oppressively sluggish feeling, compounded not only by the strictly regular *abab* structure, but also by syllable repetition ("Tiefe / Stille / herrscht im / Wasser"), word repetition ("**Keine** Luft von **keiner** Seite!"), and alliteration ("Ohne **R**egung **r**uht das Meer") (Lambert, 2004, p. 247).

When it was first published, Goethe's poem (like the following one) was accompanied by a musical setting by Johann Friedrich Reichardt (1752-1814), a friend of Goethe's and a member of the (Second) Berlin School of *Lied* composition, to which another of Goethe's acquaintances, Carl Friedrich Zelter (1758-1832) also belonged. As well as settings by Vaclav Tomášek (1774-1850) (and by several other composers), there exist well-known settings or interpretations of the poem by Franz Schubert (who wrote two versions, made on consecutive days), Ludwig van Beethoven, and Felix Mendelssohn. (The possibility of the use of music for therapeutic purposes opens a whole new set of questions.)

Among the manifold resonances contained within this text, one could point to the classical motif of "ships in danger," found in Homer, Alcaeus of Mytilene, and (in a political sense) in Horace (*Odes*, book 1, para. 14);

and, in particular, this metaphorical dimension of the voyage by ship is reflected in Cicero's political notion of the helmsman or pilot (*rector et gubernator rei publicae*), in a passage from opening of Virgil's *Aeneid* (book 1, ll. 148-55), and in Seneca's concept of the autonomous ego as *cursus per media tempestates* (Kuhn, 1996, p. 376, n. 19). (One notices that classical sources seem to be primarily concerned with weathering storms, not coping with becalment...!) At the same time, Goethe's poem could be based on his own experience, and there are two analogues, one natural, one cultural, for the situation described in his poem.

First, is there perhaps an echo of his experience during his first visit to Italy when, sailing back from Messina to Naples, the ship he was travelling on was becalmed off the coast of Capri (see Goethe's account in his *Italienische Reise* for 14 May 1787)? And second, the scenario depicted in the poem finds an important visual intertext in a painting by Caspar David Friedrich (1774-1840), his famous *The Monk by the Sea* (*Der Mönch am Meer*). As one critic has described this picture, "this is probably the most radical painting that Friedrich produced; the entire canvas consists simply of three layers: sand, sea, and sky, offset only by the diminutive figure of the monk who is dwarfed by his surroundings," and "the layers are essentially incompatible, for no one of them helps to define the scale of the other; the overwhelming sense of void is therefore created not so much by sheer physical scale as by its immeasirable quality" (Lambert, 2004, p. 243). According to another critic, in this painting "the sea is a symbol of the menacing vastness of the universe as well as the superiority of death over life" (Börsch-Suphan, 1974, p. 83). Among the admirers of Friedrich's painting was Heinrich von Kleist (1777-1811), who published a famous review of the work in 1810.[1] A few weeks before Kleist's review appeared, Goethe himself had been able to admire the painting, when he visited Friedrich's studio (in Dresden) on 18 September 1810.

Both before and after Caspar David Friedrich and Goethe, writers have understood the power of a flat, calm sea. In his epic ballad, *The Rime of the Ancient Mariner* (1798), for example, Samuel Taylor Coleridge (1772-1834) — an admirer and translator of Goethe, and a figure mediating German Idealism to English literature and thought — described the fate of sailors of a ship becalmed at sea (including the famous lines "Water,

---

[1] Did Kleist see the painting that we see today? For discussion of the changes made to the painting, see Lambert, 2004, pp. 244-245.

water, everywhere, / Nor any drop to drink"); and in the nineteenth
century, in *Moby-Dick* Herman Melville (1819-1891) described how the
young boy, Pip, is accidentally abandoned at sea.

Within Goethe's own corpus, too, there is a parallel of a different
sort: in the Dark Gallery scene in *Faust: Part Two*, in which Faust is told
about the existence of the mysterious Mothers, Mephistopheles describes
their abysmal abode beyond space and time, to which there leads, he
says, no road (2001, p. 177). Now, although Mephisto shifts the sense
of loss and abandonment into the metaphysical, the sense in which Jung
read the Mothers Scene, despite or because of its mystical overtones,
as a description of the psyche, invites us to consider the psychological
overtones to *Meeresstille*.

For Mephisto's warning to Faust, that "the danger is great," (2001,
p. 178) is echoed by Jung in *Transformations and Symbols of the Libido*
(1911-1912) and in its revised version, *Symbols of Transformation* (1952),
when he discusses the state of introversion. "These depths fascinate," he
says (1967, para. 449), because "they are the mother — and death" (1991,
para. 459). When the libido leaves "the bright upper world" — "whether
from the decision of the individual or from decreasing life force" (or, he
adds, in 1952, "from fate"), it "sinks back into its own depths, into the
source from which it has gushed forth" (1991, para. 459; 1967, para. 449).
The moment of introversion is a moment of crisis, which inaugurates
its own resolution: "Whenever some great work is to be accomplished,
before which a man recoils, doubtful of his strength, his libido streams
back to the fountainhead — and that is the dangerous moment when the
issue hangs between annihilation and new life" (1967, para. 449; cf. 1991,
para. 459).

"If the libido gets stuck in the wonderland of this inner world, then
for the upper world man is nothing but a shadow, he is already moribund
or at least seriously ill," Jung adds (1967, para. 449; cf. 1991, para. 459),
referring in a footnote to the Greek myth of Theseus and Peirithous
(1967, para. 449, n. 56; 1991, para. 459, n. 32). In introversion, according
to Jung, we return to "the world of memories," the "strongest" and
"most influential" of which are "the early infantile memory pictures"
(1991, para. 458; cf. 1967, para. 448). This is "the world of the child, the
paradisal state of early infancy," out from which we are driven by "a hard
law" (1991, para. 458) — namely, the "relentless law of time" (1967,
para. 448). We might compare this insight with Jung's later reference to

the German philosopher Karl Joël (1864-1934) and his description in his work, *Seele und Welt* (1912), of what he termed *das Urerlebnis* (or "primal experience") (1967, para. 500-para. 501; 1991, para. 513-para. 514; Joël, 1912, pp. 153-154).

In response to this passage from Joël, Jung comments that here, "in unmistakable symbolism," "the merging of subject and object" is depicted as "the reunion of mother and child" (1967, para. 501; 1991, para. 514). This "blessed state of sleep before birth and after death" is "rather like an old shadowy memory of that unsuspecting state of early childhood, when there is as yet no opposition to disturb the peaceful flow of slumbering life" (1967, para. 501) or "dawning life" (1991, para. 514). "Again and again an inner longing draws us back," but "the active life must free itself anew with struggle and death" (1991, para. 514), so that "it may not be doomed to destruction" (ibid., para. 514) or "fall into a state of sleep" (1967, para. 501).

Further on in this work (in its original and its revised versions), Jung returns to this theme. Here he writes that the individual "[does] not see his worst enemy in front of him, but bear[s] him within himself as a deadly longing for the depths within, for drowning in his own source, for becoming absorbed into the mother" (1991, para. 566) — or, as he puts it in more Faustian terms in his 1952 revision, a longing "to be sucked down to the realm of the Mothers" (1967, para. 553). This, then, is the death that threatens the individual in the introverted state: "A deep personal longing for quiet and for the profound peace [of all-knowing and] of non-existence, for a dreamless [or all-seeing] sleep in the ebb and flow of the sea of life [or in the ocean of coming-to-be and passing away]" (1991, para. 566; 1967, para. 553). For a second time, Jung turns to the mythological legend of Peirithous to make his point: "If, like Peirithoos, he tarries too long in this place of rest and peace, he is overcome by torpidity, and the poison of the serpent paralyzes him for all time" (1991, para. 566; cf. 1967, para. 553).

"The Prosperous Voyage" (*Glückliche Fahrt*)

Yet this sense of stasis is not the only dynamic that Goethe knows (and nor, for that matter, Jung). The second of the two poems published in 1796 is entitled *Glückliche Fahrt* (or "The Prosperous Voyage"):

> *Die Nebel zerreißen,*
> *Der Himmel ist helle,*
> *Und Äolus löset*
> *Das ängstliche Band.*
> *Es säuseln die Winde,*
> *Es rührt sich der Schiffer.*
> *Geschwinde! Geschwinde!*
> *Es teilt sich die Welle,*
> *Es naht sich der Ferne;*
> *Schon seh' ich das Land!*
> (Goethe, 1974, p. 242)

> The mist is fast clearing.
> And radiant is heaven,
> Whilst Æolus loosens
> Our anguish-fraught bond.
> The zephyrs are sighing,
> Alert is the sailor.
> Quick! nimbly be plying!
> The billows are riven,
> The distance approaches;
> I see land beyond!
> (Goethe, 1882, p. 223)

In his biography of Goethe, Nicholas Boyle suggests that *Meeresstille* and *Glückliche Fahrt*, published in Schiller's *Musenalmanach*, hark back to Goethe's visit to Sicily and his "eventful return voyage to Naples," but also "caught the atmosphere of the moment" — that is, his (and Schiller's) sudden emergence into a "new and productive phrase" (2000, p. 267). Goethe paused, then steamed ahead with work on his *Wilhelm Meister* novel. Both poems, however, speak to us above and beyond their compositional context.

Glückliche Fahrt is very much a poem about something that *happens*: in the original version as published in Schiller's *Musen-Almanach für das Jahr 1796*, the first line read "Suddenly it becomes" (*Auf einmal wirds*), placing an emphasis on the action of change and transition, rather than the sky, whether read literally or symbolically. As Gudrun Kuhn points out, "the departure and the fortunate voyage are contrasted by Goethe to the phrase of wearisome waiting in the first line through the different metre," i.e., two dactyls, introduced with an *Auftakt*; the second unstressed beat of the second dactyl merges with the *Auftakt* at the beginning of the following line. The lines are further connected by rhyme (ll. 2 and 8, 4 and 10, 5 and 7), as well as anaphoric parallelism of lines 5-6 and 8-9. And the four introductory form an introduction to the main part of the poem that remains: with their image, drawn from antiquity, of the release of the wind, they form a transition from the stillness to the breeze that fills the sails (Kuhn, 1996, pp. 375-376).

Amid these impersonal structures (*es säuseln, es teilt sich, es naht sich*) is, in fact, a person, even if introduced in a similarly impersonal way (*es rührt sich*); namely, the sailor or *der Schiffer*. Thus, Humankind and Nature form a unity, so that the imperative, *Geschwinde! Geschwinde!* of line 7, which separates the two pairs of anaphora's, can be equally applied to the activity of Nature or of Humankind alike (Kuhn, 1996, p. 375). The final line of the poem lends a new significance to the introduction of the poetic subject in the poem: the rhyme-pair *Band* (l. 4) and *Land* (l. 10) connects the two halves of the poem, its beginning to its end, while both monosyllabic substantives mark a caesura in the rhythmic movement. To line 9 there accrues a mediating position: in terms of form, its anaphora links it to the middle part of the poem, but in respect of its content, the approaching *Ferne* becomes concrete in the final line as *Land* (p. 376).

Thus, in Kuhn's words: "What a confusing interplay of divergent formal elements! The effect on the reader: hectic departure (*Aufbruch*) [2] *and* goal-oriented forward movement, chaotic wild confusion *and* orderly movement of the waves, all things are possible bar one: stasis" (Kuhn, 1996, p. 376). The final line of the poem is crucial for its comprehension: according to Hans Jürgen Geerdts, "the poetic 'I' foregrounds the great tension of its argumentative content in the curious interplay of the sailor and the lyrical ego, in the relation between object and subject" (1966, p. 56). (In general, one notes a preference among the commentators for a sociological or political, rather than a psychological, understanding of these poems.)

Geerdts identifies this "classical" outlook as an expression of the antinomy of being free and finding oneself at the mercy of the forces of nature — and as a "manifesto of hope" of overcoming this antinomy

---

[2] In German, the word *Aufbruch* has, unlike its most literal English translation ("break-up"), exclusively positive connotations, cf. *Aufbruchsstimmung*.

(1966, p. 66)! Whereas, in *Meeresstille*, the objective law — that the bourgeois individual of the age is at the mercy of forces that threaten his integrity — is expressed in laconic words that hint at tragic overtones; but then, in *Glückliche Fahrt*, the experience of Nature and History is viewed from the perspective of the individual who is conscious of his ability freely to choose. Whereas, in *Meerestille*, the question of fate is framed as a question about the relation of humankind to Nature; in *Glückliche Fahrt* the heroic answer is to be found in the sense of moral commitment on the part of the sailor (Geerdts, 1966, p. 66).[3]

Thus, the final line of *Glückliche Fahrt* stands in a superordinate position to both poems, emphasizing "the conscious overcoming of what brings danger through the activity of the creative individual" (Geerdts, 1966, p. 57), and thus forming an overarching bond between the two texts. For Gudrun Kuhn, the *Ich* of the final line does not stand in a complete contrast to either the sailor — the symbol of the human individual caught up in his (lack of) activity — or to nature: rather, as a *seeing* subject it stands in a relationship of analogy to the *Schiffer* in *Meeresstille*. Whereas, in *Meeresstille*, it was the sheer nothingness of the *glatte Gläche ringsumher*, or the pure void that drew the gaze of the sailor into the distance, in *Glückliche Fahrt* the reverse is the case — the horizon approaches the speaker, *Es naht sich die Ferne*. And whereas, in *Meeresstille*, Nature was placed in opposition to Humankind, in *Glückliche Fahrt* it is Nature who approaches *him* (Kuhn, 1996, p. 376).

In other words, a good deal of their significance accrues to the *relation* between these two poems. For Lawrence Kramer, this relation can be expressed with reference to the Goethean concept of *Steigerung*, i.e., ascent or increase, or enhancement, or evolutionary process (1992, p. 69). (In an essay of 1828, Goethe described the principle of *Steigerung*, or "intensification," as a property of matter "insofar as we think of it as spiritual," as "a state of ever-striving ascent" [1988, p. 6].)[4] On Kramer's account, *Meeresstille* and *Glückliche Fahrt* do not only "presuppose this principle as a cause," but they also "celebrate" it: "the semi-allegorical movement from the stasis of the first poem to the eager motion of the second" suggests "an ascent from paralytic self-consciousness to the

---

[3] Or to put it another way, the relation between these poems reveals the transformation of fate (understood as exterior constraint) into destiny (understood as interior liberty) — a project at the heart of the thought of Epictetus (Vergely, 2007, p. 17).

[4] For further discussion, see Wilkinson and Willoughby, 1962, p. 189.

liberatory energy of *Steigerung*," a reading which is "concretized most strikingly in phonetic terms." Thus the "tight rhyme scheme" of *Meeresstille* (i.e., abab cdcd) presents itself as "the embodiment of an involuted and mechanical energy," while *Glückliche Fahrt* "limbers this energy up, throwing off rhymes in an intricate, irregular pattern" (i.e., (abcd ef ebgd), that seems "both vital and spontaneous" (Kramer, 1992, pp. 69-70).

On the difference between the two poems, Geerdts has observed that, if *Meeresstille* tends toward "a laconic expression of motionlessness," offering "a static, silent and gloomy picture," then by contrast *Glückliche Fahrt* is "an expression of movement" — "a dynamic threading-together of individual image motifs, which order themselves in relation to each other in order to illustrate the flow of the action" (1966, p. 54). Indeed, as the German musicologist Fred Büttner has pointed out, *Glückliche Fahrt* depicts an action that develops out of the motionless *Meeresstille* (1999, p. 11); so that, taken together, Goethe's two poems "enact," as Joe Haney has put it, "an exhilarating journey from the depths of existential doubt to a state of overwhelming affirmation" (2004, p. 113).

Such a dynamic is, of course, eminently Jungian. In *Transformations and Symbols of the Libido* (and in its revised version, *Symbols of Transformation*), Jung writes that, "if the libido manages to tear itself loose and force its way up again, something like a miracle happens: the journey to the underworld was a plunge into the fountain of youth, and the libido, apparently dead, wakes to renewed fruitfulness" (Jung, 1967, para. 449; cf. Jung, 1991, para. 459). As he explains in his revised version of 1952, "the great psychotherapeutic systems which we know as religions" serve to oppose this "regressive tendency," and they do so through the construction of an "autonomous consciousness," achieved by "weaning humankind away from the sleep of childhood" (Jung, 1967, para. 553). Drawing on the work of the third-century alchemist and Gnostic, Zosimos of Panopolis, Jung highlights the image of the μεσουράνισμα ἡλίου (or the position of the sun at midday as a symbol of the initiate's illumination):[5] when "the sun breaks from the mists of the horizon and climbs to undimmed brightness at the meridian" (Jung, 1967, para. 553).

---

[5] See *The Treatise of Zosimos the Divine concerning the Art*, III.v (cited in Berthelot, 1888, p. 126), which involves a figure referred to as the Meridian of the Sun. For further discussion, see Jung on "The Visions of Zosimos" (1938; 1954) in Jung, 1970, para. 86 and para. 95.

For Jung, Friedrich Hölderlin's poem "Patmos" reveals that "wisdom dwells in the depths, the wisdom of the mother: being one with it, insight is obtained into the meaning of deeper things, into all the deposits of primitive times, the strata of which have been preserved in the soul" (1991, para. 661), constituting "a vision of deeper things, of the primordial images and primitive forces which underlie all life and are its nourishing, sustaining, creative matrix" (1967, para. 640). Thus *Glückliche Fahrt* marks a moment Jung might describe as *a miracle* — "an unconscious irrational happening, shaping itself without the assistance of reason and conscious purpose," as he writes in *Psychological Types* (1921): "It happens of itself, it just grows, like a phenomenon of creative Nature, and not from any clever trick of human wit; it is the fruit of yearning expectation, of faith and hope" (1974, para. 233). The poem enacts a moment of "unfolding," "a streaming outwards and upwards," or "a diastole, as Goethe called it," or "a motion embracing the whole world," as described in Friedrich Schiller's famous ode *To Joy* (*An die Freude*) (Jung, 1974, para. 234). It could even be called, following Nietzsche, "Dionysian expansion" — "a flood of overpowering universal feeling which bursts forth irresistibly, intoxicating the senses like the strongest wine"; indeed, it *is* "intoxication in the highest sense of the word" (Jung, 1974, para. 234).

This dynamic is introduced by the motion Jung credits to Heraclitus, *enantiodromia*: "the play of opposites in the course of events," or "the view that everything that exists turns into its opposite" (Jung, 1974, para. 708). In the specific psychological context, Jung understands the phrase to mean "the emergence of the unconscious opposite in the course of time" (para. 709). If the process is called enantiodromia, the mechanism it uses is — the symbol: "With the birth of the symbol, the regression of libido into the unconscious ceases. Regression is converted into progression, the blockage starts to flow again, and the lure of the maternal abyss is broken" (para. 445). Thus "the redeeming symbol," Jung writes (with reference to a passage from the biblical Book of Isaiah, cited at the beginning of the *Red Book* in "The Way of What Is to Come"),[6] "is a highway, a way upon which life can move forward without torment and compulsion" (para. 445). Another word for the symbol is the "primordial image," one example of which is "the whole mythological complex of the

---

[6] Isaiah 35:5-8; cf. Jung, 2012, pp. 118-119.

dying and resurgent god," which expresses "a transformation of attitude by means of which a new potential, a new manifestation of life, a new fruitfulness, is created" (para. 325).

On Jung's account, "the great problems of life […] are always related to the primordial images of the collective unconscious," and these images are "balancing or compensating factors that correspond to the problems with which life confronts us in reality" (1974, para. 373). Yet another word for the symbol is borrowed by Jung from Schiller — "living form" (*lebende Gestalt*) (para. 184). Engaging with Schiller's idea on the type problem in his treatise *On the Aesthetic Education of Humankind* (1795), Jung writes that devotion (in German, *Andacht*) is "a regressive movement of libido towards the primordial, a diving down into the source of the first beginnings," out of which then rises, "as an image of the incipient progressive movement, the symbol," or "a condensation of all the operative unconscious factors" (para. 202). And if the mechanism is the symbol, its *function* is transcendence, in the sense that Jung uses this word when he speaks of the "transcendent function" (para. 205; cf. para. 828): "The natural flow of libido," Jung writes, "means complete obedience to the fundamental laws of human nature, and there can positively be no higher moral principle than harmony with natural laws that guide the libido in the direction of life's optimum" (para. 356).

Earlier, in *Transformation and Symbols of the Libido* Jung had suggested that the second discourse of Yahweh in the biblical Book of Job (40:6-41) shows us how "the unconditional and inexorable, the unjust and the superhuman, are truly and rigidly attributes of libido" — and are, moreover, aspects of the "primitive power" which, in the words of another poem by Goethe, "leads us into life" and "lets the poor [man] be guilty."[7] Against this backdrop Jung remarked that "nothing remains for humankind but to work in harmony with this will," adding that Nietzsche's *Zarathustra* "teaches us this impressively" (Jung, 1991, para. 111). This optimum can, Jung now adds in *Psychological Types*, be reached "only through obedience to the tidal laws of the libido, by which systole alternates with diastole — laws which bring pleasure and the necessary limitations of pleasure, and also set us those individual life tasks without whose accomplishment the vital optimum can never be attained" (Jung, 1974, para. 356).

---

[7] See Goethe's poem, *Wer nie sein Brot mit Tränen aß*, in *Wilhelm Meisters Lehrjahre*, book 2, chapter 13 (in Goethe, 1959, p. 136).

As well as in *Thus Spoke Zarathustra*, we find this dynamic in Nietzsche's poem "Toward New Seas" (*Nach neuen Meeren*) in the "Songs of Prince Vogelfrei" appended to the second edition (1887) of *The Gay Science* (1882):

> *Dorthin — will ich: und ich traue*
> *Mir fortan und meinem Griff.*
> *Offen liegt das Meer, ins Blaue*
> *Treibt mein Genueser Schiff.*
>
> *Alles glänzt mir neu und neuer,*
> *Mittag schläft auf Raum und Zeit—:*
> *Nur dein Auge — ungeheuer*
> *Blickt mich's an, Unendlichkeit!*

> That way is my *will*; I trust
> In my mind and in my grip.
> Without plan, into the vast
> Open sea I head my ship.
>
> All is shining, new and newer,
> Upon space and time sleeps noon;
> Only *your* eye — monstrously,
> Stares at me, infinity!
> (Nietzsche, 1974, p. 370)

For a representation of those psychological states in which the "vital feelings and energies flow with greater freedom and joy," however, Jung turns in *Psychological Types* to a different poem by Nietzsche, one which serves as a proemium to Part Four of *The Gay Science*, entitled *Sanctus Januarius*:

> *Der du mit dem Flammenspeere*
> *Meiner Seele Eis zerteilt,*
> *Daß sie brausend nun zum Meere*
> *Ihrer höchsten Hoffnung eilt:*
> *Heller stets und stets gesunder,*
> *Frei im liebevollsten Muß: –*
> *Also preist sie deine Wunder,*
> *Schönster Januarius!*

With a flaming spear you crushed
All its ice until my soul
Roaring toward the ocean rushed
Of its highest hope and goal.
Ever healthier it swells,
Lovingly compelled but free:
Thus it lauds your miracles,
Fairest month of January!
(Nietzsche, 1974, p. 221)

In *Psychological Types* Jung compares this text with the *Rig Veda* and its notion of *Rta* (glossed as "established order, regulation, destiny, sacred custom, statute, divine law, right, truth" [1974, para. 348]), citing the following invocation — "May the divine gates open, the increasers of *Rta* […] that now the sacrifice may proceed. I invoke here at this sacrifice Night and Dawn […]. […] The three comfort-giving goddesses, they who not fail, shall sit down on the sacrificial grass" —[8] as offering an "analogy with the sunrise" which is "unmistakable" and as illustrating how *Rta* "appears as the sun, since it is from night and dawn that the young sun is born" (para. 354).

In turn, Jung associates this idea with a concept found in Stoic philosophy, *heimarmene*: "For the Stoics *heimarmene* had the significance of creative, primal heat, and at the same time it was a predetermined, regular process (hence its other meaning: 'compulsion of the stars')" (para. 355). In *Symbols of Transformation*, Jung translates this "compulsion of evil stars" into the "*compulsion of libido*" (pointing to Schiller's words in the *Piccolomini*, "The stars of thine own fate lie in thy breast" [II.6]) (Jung, 1967, para. 102; cf. para. 644), and in *Psychological Types* he concludes that "the path is *Rta*, the right way, the flow of vital energy or libido, the predetermined course along which a constantly self-renewing current is directed," and that "this path is also fate [*das Schicksal*], insofar as fate depends on our psychology" and is "the path of our destiny [*Bestimmung*] and the law of our being [*Gesetz*]" (1974, para. 355). In the words of the first stanza of Goethe's *Primal Words. Orphic* (*Urworte. Orphisch*; written 1817, pub. 1820), this "law" is "the law by which you started" or "the law presiding at your birth" ([*das*] *Gesetz, wonach du angetreten*),

---

[8] *Vedic Hymns* (Mandala I, Hymn 13) (Oldenberg, 1964, p. 8). This translation of the *Rig-Veda* belongs to the series *Sacred Books of the East*, edited by Max Müller — one of the philological, cross-cultural influences on the *Red Book*.

for — in words echoed by Jung in the *Red Book* — "Thus must you be, from self there's no remission" or "None but yourself, from self you cannot flee" (*So mußt du sein, dir kannst du nicht entfliehen*).[9]

Eichendorff and the "Still World of the Heart"

The "exemplary connection" of stasis and movement in Goethe's poems can also be found in a short story, *Eine Meerfahrt*, written in 1835 by the Romantic poet and novelist Joseph von Eichendorff (1788-1857) and published posthumously in 1864. The subject of the story is the crew of a Spanish ship, which becomes becalmed during its voyage to the New World in 1540. At one point in the story, Antonio, a young student, gazes out across the still sea and sings a song entitled *Meeresstille* (Eichendorff, 2007, pp. 263-264). Despite the obvious differences between this text and Goethe's poem, there are significant similarities: above all, the uncanny situation of a complete lack of wind, described by Eichendorff as *eine entsetzliche Zeit*. Moreover, just as Goethe's poem echoes his experience during his sea-journey between Messina and Naples, so there is analogy between Eichendorff's text and his account in his diary of a journey to the Baltic Sea in 1805.

In Eichendorff's story, no sooner has Antonio sung his song, than the wind suddenly picks up, and the boat begins to sail again — towards, as it turns out, a group of islands and a series of exciting adventures. At the end of the story, Antonio's uncle, Don Diego, waves off the crew — wishing them a "fortunate journey" (*eine glückliche Fahrt*). In fact, Eichendorff also wrote a poem with the title "Glückliche Fahrt" — published in 1816:

> *Wünsche sich mit Wünschen schlagen,*
> *Und die Gier wird nie gestillt.*
> *Wer ist in dem wüsten Jagen*
> *Da der Jäger, wer das Wild?*
> *Selig, wer es fromm mag wagen,*
> *Durch das Treiben dumpf und wild*
> *In der festen Brust zu tragen*
> *Heil'ger Schönheit hohes Bild!*

---

[9] See Goethe, 1998, p. 123; and Goethe, 1983, p. 231. Cf. Jung, *Liber primus*, "Soul and God": "But you cannot flee from yourself" (*Du kannst dir aber nicht entfliehen*) (in Jung, 2012, p. 134).

Sieh', da brechen tausend Quellen
Durch die felsenharte Welt,
Und zum Strome wird ihr Schwellen,
Der melodisch steigt und fällt.
Ringsum sich die Fernen hellen,
Gottes Hauch die Segel schwellt —
Rettend spülen dich die Wellen
In des Herzens stille Welt.

Wishes battle other wishes,
Desire is never satisfied.
In this hunt amid the desert
Who's the hunter, who's the prey?
Truly blessed whoever dares
Through the hustle vague and wild
Firmly in the breast to carry
Sacred beauty's image high!

Look! a thousand water sources
Burst the world's too solid cliffs,
And their stream becomes a torrent
Whose rise and fall sounds musical.
All around the distances grow brighter,
God's breath makes the sails swell full —
Redeemingly the waves propel you
To the still world of the heart.
(Eichendorff, 2007, pp. 217-218)

Aside from the date of the poem, its content demonstrates that it does not stand in an immediately significant relationship to the later poem called *Meeresstille*, nor to Goethe's own poem of the same name.

Yet the idea that, within the individual, salvific forces may be found is entirely compatible with the essential spirit of Goethe's second poem, following *Meeresstille*, with the title *Glückliche Fahrt*. Indeed, Eichendorff's very phrase *In des Herzens stille Welt* ("in the still world of the heart") interiorizes those divine powers symbolized in Goethe's poem in the figure of Aeolus, and both Eichendorff's and Goethe's poems allude to the most profound part of the individual which, come what may, can never be harmed. The Stoics called it the "interior citadel";[10] Jung would have called it the Self; but more broadly and recognisably within the Western tradition it is known as *the heart*. To explore one's interiority without losing contact with the world; and, after setting sail, to make it safely home to harbour — in psychoanalytic terms, to *individuate* — remains the existential goal for Goethe, Eichendorff, and Jung alike.

Paul Bishop is William Jacks Chair of Modern Languages at the University of Glasgow, UK. After studying at Oxford and (for a year) at Harvard, Paul has lived and worked in Glasgow for nearly three decades. He is interested in all aspects of German culture and thought, in tracing the progression of ideas through time, and in uncovering links between German culture and the concepts of psychoanalysis, with particular emphasis on analytical psychology. Although he is currently researching the philosophy of Ludwig Klages, the publication of the Red Book (and subsequently the Black Books) means he keeps returning to Jung's remarkably rich and fertile thought. He is the author of *Reading Goethe at Midlife: Ancient wisdom, German classicism, and Jung* (2011; republished in 2020 by Chiron); and other studies on aspects of Jung's thought in an intellectual-historical perspective (published by Routledge).

---

[10] Compare with the title of Hadot, 1998; and see Marcus Aurelius, *Meditations*, book 4, para. 3; book 8, para. 48; and Epictetus, *Discourses*, book 4, para. 1.

References

Berthelot, M. (1888). *Collection des anciens alchimistes grecs: Traduction*. Steinheil.

Böhme, G. (2013a). *Atmosphäre: Essays zur neuen* Ästhetik [1995]. Suhrkamp.

Böhme, G. (2013b). *Architektur und Atmosphäre*. Fink.

Böhme, G. (2017). *Atmospheric Architectures: The Aesthetics of Felt Spaces*, ed. and trans. A.-Chr. Engels-Schwarzpaul. Bloomsbury.

Bollnow, O.F. (1995). *Das Wesen der Stimmungen* [1941]. Klostermann.

Bolton, D. (2008). *What is Mental Disorder? An Essay in Philosophy, Science and Values*. Oxford University Press.

Bolton, D. (2010). Conceptualisation of mental disorder and its personal meanings. *Journal of Mental Health*, vol. 19, no. 4 (August), 328-336.

Börsch-Suphan, H. (1974). *Caspar David Friedrich*. Braziller.

Boyle, N. (2000). *Goethe; The Poet and the* Age, vol. 2, *Revolution and Renaissance (1790-1803)*. Clarendon Press.

Büttner, F. (1999). Meeres Stille und glückliche Fahrt: Theodor Göllner zum 70. Geburtstag. *Musik in Bayern*, *58*, 5-42.

Eichendorff, J. von (2997). *Sämtliche Gedichte und Versepen*, ed. H. Schulz. Insel.

Freud, S. (1955). The Psychotherapy of Hysteria. In J. Breuer and S. Freud, *Studies in Hysteria* [*Standard Edition of the Complete Psychological Works*, vol. 2], ed. J. Strachey. London: Hogarth Press; Institute of Psycho-Analysis. 253-305.

Geerdts, H.J. (1966). Zu Goethes Gedichten "Meeresstille" und "Glückliche Fahrt." In H. Holtzhauer (ed.), *Natur und Idee: Andreas Bruno Wachsmuth zugeeignet*. Weimar: Böhlau. 53-66.

Goethe, J.W. (1882). *The Poems of Goethe, translated in the original metres*. Cassino.

Goethe, J.W. (1959). *Romane und Novellen*, vol. 3, ed. E. Trunz. Hamburg: Wegner.

Goethe, J.W. (1974). *Gedichte*, ed. E. Trunz. Beck.

Goethe, J.W. (1983). *Selected Poems* [Goethe Edition, vol. 1], ed. C. Middleton. Suhrkamp/Insel.

Goethe, J.W. (1988). *Scientific Studies*, ed. and trans. Douglas Miller [Goethe Edition, vol. 12]. Suhrkamp.

Goethe, J.W. (1998). *Selected Poems*, trans. J. Whaley. Dent.

Goethe, J.W. (2001). *Faust: A Tragedy*, trans. Walter Arndt, ed. Cyrus Hamlin, 2nd edn. Norton.

Hadot, P. (1998). *The Inner Citadel: The "Meditations" of Marcus Aurelius* [1992], trans. M. Chase. Harvard University Press.

Haney, J. (2004). Navigating Sonata Space in Mendelssohn's *Meerestille und glückliche Fahrt. 19th-Century Music, 28*, no. 2 (Autumn), 108-132.

Horowitz, A.V., and Wakefield, J.C. (2007). *The Loss of Sadness: How Psychiatry Transformed Normal Sorrow into Depressive Disorder.* Oxford University Press.

Jaspers, K. (1963). *General Psychopathology* [1913; 3rd edn, 1923], trans. J. Hoenig and M.W. Hamilton. Chicago University Press.

Joël, K. (1912). *Seele und Welt: Versuch einer organischen Fassung.* Jena: Diederichs.

Jung, C.G. (1963). *Memories, Dreams, Reflections*, ed. A. Jaffé, trans. R. and C. Winston. Collins; Routledge & Kegan Paul.

Jung, C.G. (1967). *Symbols of Transformation: An Analysis of the Prelude to a Case of Schizophrenia, The Collected Works of C.G. Jung: Vol. 5.* trans. R.F.C. Hull, 2nd edn. Princeton University Press.

Jung, C.G. (1970). *Alchemical Studies, The Collected Works of C.G. Jung: Vol. 13.* trans. R.F.C. Hull. Princeton University Press.

Jung, C.G. (1974). *Psychological Types, The Collected Works of C.G. Jung: Vol. 6.* trans. H.G. Baynes and revised R.F.C. Hull. Routledge & Kegan Paul.

Jung, C.G. (1991). *Psychology of the Unconscious: A Study of the Transformations and Symbolisms of the Libido*, trans. Beatrice M. Hinkle. Routledge.

Jung, C.G. (2012). *The Red Book: Liber novus* [Reader's Edition], ed. S. Shamdasani, trans. M. Kyburz, J. Peck, and S. Shamdasani. Norton.

Kramer, L. (1992). *Felix culpa*: Goethe and the image of Mendelssohn. In R.L. Todd (ed.), *Mendelssohn Studies*. Cambridge University Press. 64-79.

Kuhn, G. (1996). "Schon seh' ich das Land!" Über Stille und Ankunft in Mendelssohns Konzertouvertüre opus 27 *Meeerstille und Glücklicher Fahrt* nach Goethe. In H. Helbig, B. Knauer, G. Och (eds), *Hermenautik – Hermeneutik: Literarische und geisteswissenschaftliche Beiträge zu Ehren von Peter Horst Neumann*. Würzburg: Könighausen & Neumann. 371-379.

Lambert, S. (2004). Schubert and the Sea of Eternity. *The Journal of Musicology*, 21, no. 2 (Spring), 241-266.

Nietzsche, F. (1974). *The Gay* Science, trans. W. Kaufmann. Vintage.

Oldenberg, H. (1964). Vedic Hymns. Vol. 2, *Hymns to Agni (Mandalas I-V)* [1897]. Motilal Banarsidass.

Vergely, B. (2007). *Pascal ou l'expérience de l'infini*. Milan.

Wilkinson, E.M. (1962). "Tasso – ein Gesteigerter Werther" in the Light of Goethe's Principle of "Steigerung." In E.M. Wilkinson and L.A. Willoughby, Goethe: Poet and *Thinker*. Arnold. 185-213.

Active Imagination and Testament:
A Window on the Other Side of Life

Chiara Tozzi

During Murray Stein's presentation, I couldn't help but notice the true "state of grace" I was in. But there was more: I was surprised to realize that being there during his lecture seemed related to synchronicity! What had appeared to me as a thoughtless and irrational bet applying for a conference overseas that required me to invest a great amount of money and energy—seemed to have suddenly transformed into a meaningful, reasonable and providential choice, a true "act of creation in time."

The word testament comes from the Latin *testamentum*, which comes from *testari*, "to bear witness." Moving beyond its legal meaning, I want to refer to the so-called *spiritual testament*, defined by the Italian Treccani Encyclopedia as *the set of dispositions... that represent the spiritual legacy of the testator, who gives others . . . the task of continuing the work he/she undertook in life, or recommends carrying on the worship of his/her own ideals. Figuratively speaking, the expression also refers to written texts and works—sometimes acts, attitudes, life examples; although that was not their conscious objective, they truly represent the spiritual legacy of a person who was important for survivors and posterity.*

In the last years of his life, Jung said: "The years when I was pursuing my inner images were the most important in my life — in them everything essential was decided. It all began then; the later details are only supplements and clarifications of the material that burst forth from the unconscious, and at first swamped me. It was the prima materia for a lifetime's work." (Jung, 1961, p.137). These words are found at the end of the fundamental chapter "Confrontation with the Unconscious" in *Memories, Dreams, Reflections*, one of the last writings by Jung in which, through Aniella Jaffé, he passed on to us the meaning of his life and his idea of analytical psychology. In *The Red Book* (2009), he extensively described what happened during what he had referred to as the most important years of his life, telling us how, exactly through them, for the first time he had the courage to experiment on himself a confrontation with the unconscious, which he defined as active imagination. We can therefore conclude that active imagination is Jung's spiritual testament, his spiritual legacy, very important to us Jungian analysts as his *survivors and posterity*. Given the nature of its content, I will try to explore this precious testament mainly through images.

Testament, Symbol, and Active Imagination

When I think of the meaning of the word testament, the first image that comes to my mind is that of a bridge that creates a meaningful and enriching connection between two parties, in spite of time and space. A testament is a way of leaving a legacy that has a special value for the bequeather. The term *symbol* (σύμβολον) also refers to the bridge that connects. It derives its etymology from ancient Greek and means "identification card" or "hospitalitatis (hospitality) card" (Curi, 1997), based on the tradition whereby two individuals, two families or even two cities, would break a card or a ring. Each party would keep one of the two parts as a testimony to an agreement or alliance to be maintained and passed on. Being able to find the perfect match after some time proved the true existence of the agreement, and therefore of a relationship between two parties, which is exactly what I want to focus on.

We might say a symbol can nullify time, significantly reducing it along the load-bearing axis of the relationship and not along that of linear time, conceived by logic. Throughout decades or millennia, symbols continue to reunite and bring back to the origin of the union: two parties reunite although they may be completely unknown when this happens.

Testaments, just like symbols, create a meaningful bridge between a before and an after, and at the same time, in playing this role, a possible eternization, a spreading, an amplified and renewed expansion that gives new meaning and presence to that and those who have passed on "to the other side," even if that side can no longer be physically and sensorially perceived.

Active imagination, in turn, is a bridge that connects the part that lies over there – the unconscious, darkness, and the unknown, the night, the Shadow – and the part that lies over here – the Ego consciousness, what is known, bright and clear, the day, reason, logic. It is a bridge built through an affective personal experience; a brave practice passed on to us by Jung precisely in *The Red Book*. Active imagination allows us to give life to a different way of being in the world, a way that can be reached by the possible passing from one side to the other, defined by Jung himself as the activation of the *transcendent function*, "a movement out of the suspension between two opposites, a living birth that leads to a new level of being, a new situation." (Jung 1916/58, para.189). In this regard, going back to the similarity between testament and symbol, Jung emphasized that the images emerging from the unconscious and encountered through active imagination should not be interpreted semiotically and reduced to signs through a predominantly logical interpretation; rather, they should be interpreted "symbolically," respecting their complex appearance which has not yet clearly been grasped by consciousness.

Based on the above considerations, I find it necessary to focus on the symbolic meaning of the "legacy" left by Jung through his statement on what he considered most precious and important about his life and work. Jung does not *reductively and literally* tell us that what he wants to pass on and deliver is a pattern, a technique or a method; rather, he leaves a testimony (testament) on *how* he symbolically lived the years when he practiced active imagination. His reluctance to present a "technical" pattern and outline the practice of active imagination shows us how important it is to leave more space for the *individuative and transformative meaning and outcome of active imagination*, as seen in *Memories, Dreams, Reflections* and in *The Red Book*.

Different Ways of Approaching Active Imagination

When I was in training to become an analyst, I already perceived a twofold approach to the possibility of learning and teaching active imagination within the Jungian community:

1. As a mainly mentalized repetition of a technique.
2. As a personalized integration of a different way of being in the world, of a capacity for equal comparison with the unconscious, related to synchronicity and fundamental in the process of *individuation.*

To become more familiar with active imagination following the first method, in addition to learning theoretical notion and clinical suggestions for applying the method, it could seem enough to be aware of the four phases in which active imagination can unfold, mentioned by Jung and further described by M.L. von Franz (1980a) as follows:

Phase 1

The first phase of active imagination can be defined as *letting things happen.* A deliberate emptying of one's mind which Jung defined as *doing-by-not-doing,* a receptive abandonment, an inclination to opening up to images characterized by unselfconsciousness, and devoid of conscious controls, corrections and denials.

Phase 2

The second phase of active imagination occurs when *you can also accept the irrational and incomprehensible,* because they both represent the process of becoming. An acceptance capable of allowing the unconscious images to surface to the consciousness. The image is not dissociated; it is examined and therefore becomes "pregnant." Jung believed something new can originate from this quality of being "pregnant," since the image is alive, it changes and reproduces itself.

Phase 3

The third phase of active imagination is that of *recording of images transforming themselves.* The progressive change of the contents of imagination is carefully followed and described, either writing down the images or expressing them through other means, such as painting, sculpture, music, dance, etc. Regardless of the form, Jung recommends avoiding both the aesthetic satisfaction and the uncontrolled drift towards rational interpretations and explanations of the image itself.

Phase 4

In the fourth phase, when active imagination comes to life, *an actual dialogue with the unconscious takes place, through an "ethical comparison"* with anything that was previously created. It is the individual stance, fundamental to really come to terms with one's inner images and Shadow. Jung turns the metaphor of theater around, speaking of "making the scene." From an accepting audience, we now become co-protagonists and interlocutors of the generated image. We enter into the field of the imaginary, we ask ourselves questions, we try to understand, to feel and to find answers. For Jung, this particular encounter with the unconscious, that is also the final goal of active imagination, means being able to simultaneously face the points of view of the unconscious and the Ego, as occurs in a dialogue between two people with equal rights (Jung, 1916/1957). Considering it as the main stage of active imagination, Jung highlighted that often in psychiatry one only reaches the third phase but not the fourth. He also highlighted the importance of moral responsibility toward images, which we must know, but we must also take such knowledge in a confrontation that has a moral duty, because "It is equally a grave mistake to think that it is enough to gain some understanding of the images and that knowledge can here make a halt. Insight into them must be converted into an ethical obligation. Not to do so is to fall prey to the power principle, and this produces dangerous effects which are destructive not only to others but even to the knower." (Jung, 1961, p.237).

Last but not least, as rightly pointed out by Joan Chodorow, "later on," to these four phases, "she (von Franz) adds: Apply it to ordinary life." (Chodorow, 1997, p.11). This recommendation cannot be compared to a technique since it suggests making active imagination natural and connatural to our way of being in the world. And this is directly related to what I am about to discuss.

An Attitude of Active Imagination

Since I first started studying, analyzing and holding seminars on active imagination, it became clear to me that, both in Italy and abroad, active imagination was mainly approached as a notional technique to be applied repetitively, with no personalization, especially through the thinking function and therefore with the predominant guidance of the Ego consciousness.

As far as I am concerned, I certainly find it necessary to know and implement the four phases described above. But if the images and contents resulting from reducing the practice of active imagination to a mere technique may seem apparently satisfactory to the person who only encounters/produces them this way, they instead resonate as artifacts and not as the result of a real exercise of active imagination to those who authentically experienced those images and contents. If we reduce active imagination to a mere technique, what von Franz said—i.e., to make active imagination part of one's way of life—seems to be completely missing. Gerhard Adler very efficiently clarified this, arguing that one cannot speak of a "technique" of active imagination, "just as one can hardly speak of a 'technique of dreaming' (...) By 'active imagination' we understand a *definite attitude* towards the contents of the unconscious (...) The right attitude may perhaps be best described as one of 'active passivity' (...) It is not unlike watching a film or listening to music (...) Only the difference is that in active imagination the 'film' is being unrolled inside." (Adler, 1948, pp. 56-57).

But how can we best explain the difference between an *attitude* of active imagination that becomes part of our way of living, and a mere *technique* of active imagination? Jung believed creative people have the advantage of having a more permeable diaphragm between consciousness and the unconscious (Jung, 1916/58) and therefore find it easier to have a confrontation with the unconscious, as occurs in an experience of active imagination. I have extensively described the surprising similarity between the process that leads a screenwriter to imagine and write a film, and the experience of active imagination (Tozzi, 2015a). Both my patients and trainees in active imagination seminars have often heard me share a metaphor I came up with after dancing professionally for many years, following the Martha Graham technique: the experience of body balance centered on the swinging of two opposite movements (*contraction and release)*, as well as the experience of, equal and opposite, physical tension exerted toward the Earth and the sky (downward/upward) and the resulting balance; and again, the possibility of "falling" without necessarily tumbling to the ground. Actually, in almost all falls in the Graham technique, the dancer exerts a strong upward force to counteract the force of gravity, creating an art effect by suspending the body in space. I believe the following definition of "falling" in the Graham technique effectively represents what is attempted through active imagination:

"falling," letting go, giving in to the unconscious without getting trapped by it while falling. "Falling is not a literal representation of reality, but instead an embodiment of inner experience; not a reductive language, but a poetic language that derives its meaning from the layering of the physical and psychic." (Graff, 2004).

Since the very beginning, I always based my research, practice and teaching of active imagination on the second approach—taking from the attitude described by Adler. I wanted to make sure my approach did not become a "thought" exercise of the evocative examples presented by Jung in *Memories, Dreams, Reflections* and in *The Red Book*. I did not want my approach to only occur by imitation (mainly unconscious). However, I very often noticed my patients and students seemed skeptical and unsure when I told them to try to find the courage to face an experience of active imagination in a way that was truly individual and detached from the examples provided by their analyst and by Jung himself; and to renounce the predominant Ego (and the thinking function) with regard to the contents emerged from the unconscious. There is a widespread tendency within the Jungian community to underestimate the importance of active imagination and to actually warn against its danger and the danger of exposing patients to "the risk of being overwhelmed by the unconscious." Of course, we first need to assess the psychic state of the patient, but I think these concerns actually show an even greater lack of knowledge and practice of active imagination. They show a dark and shared fear of this special and distinctive therapeutic practice bequeathed by Jung, and a tendency to be anchored especially to the thinking function in therapy. Sadly, meeting the unconscious images and contents without immediately trying to interpret and classify them still seems dangerous (Tozzi, 2020). Describing, reading and thinking about what emerges from the unconscious from a superiority standpoint—that of the Ego consciousness—seems mostly right and acceptable. Therefore, the feeling, intuition, and sensation functions, so present in active imagination, tend to be subordinate and decreased in favor of the thinking function. As a result, active imagination still remains on the sidelines within the Jungian community compared to other therapeutic approaches.

Perceiving this clear differentiation between the experience of the actual "meaning" of a "confrontation with the unconscious" and the premature interpretation of the images and contents emerging from the unconscious guided especially by the Ego consciousness, when I first started holding seminars on active imagination (about 10 years ago) I was constantly looking for a way to better explain to colleagues and trainees what is meant by *attitude of active imagination*, and the big difference between using logical and rational thinking in therapy, and that way of thinking defined by Jung as "symbolic thinking" (von Franz, 1980b), with regard to which Marie Louise von Franz believed: "This is something hard to learn, and the more you learn to think in the traditional way, the more difficult it is to get used to this kind of symbolic thinking [...]. I would encourage you to try to do so, however, because in this way you can extract otherwise unintelligible new light and gain new understanding."

While I was struggling in that complex search, I was helped, in a way that I can now say was providential for my future work, by the inspiration provided by a lecture by Murray Stein, and the following professional and personal friendship that followed.

Time, Synchronicity, and the Piano Lesson

In the summer of 2015, at Yale University[1], I attended Murray Stein's incredible conference, *"Synchronizing Time and Eternity"* (Stein, 2017). On that same occasion, I presented *"The Experience of grace: The possibility of transformation in Vladimir Nabokov and Carl Gustav Jung"* (Tozzi, 2015b). During Murray Stein's presentation I couldn't help but notice the true "state of grace" I was in. But there was more: I was surprised to realize that being there during his lecture seemed related to synchronicity! What had appeared to me as a thoughtless and irrational bet—applying for a conference overseas that required me to invest a great amount of money and energy—seemed to have suddenly transformed into a meaningful, reasonable and providential choice, a true "act of creation in time" (Jung, 1952/1969a, para. 965), just like Jung defined synchronistic events. Stein's presentation was unfolding all my doubts and dilemmas related to my choice to teach, practice and experience active imagination as an *attitude* and not as a *technique*. In his lecture, he addressed the apparent oxymoron of "time/eternity" through the representation of Pauli's World Clock, which Jung interpreted "as a symbol for the intersection of time and eternity, or 'real time' and 'imaginary time,' to

---

[1] As part of the Fourth Joint Conference IAAP and IAJS: "Psyche, Spirit and Science: Negotiating Contemporary Social And Cultural Concerns," Yale University, New Haven, USA, July 2015.

use a more modern terminology." (Stein, op. cit., p.44). Following this symbolic representation, Stein presented an active imagination done by Pauli in 1953, defined by Pauli himself as "The piano lesson." See below some parts of the full text of Stein's lecture:

> In the autumn of 1953 (…) Pauli wrote 'Die Klavierstunde – Eine aktive Phantasie *über* das Unbewusste' (The piano lesson – An active fantasy about the unconscious), 'dedicated to Dr. Marie-Louise von Franz in friendship.' (…) It begins like this: 'It was a foggy day, and for a long time now I had had a serious problem (a Kummer). Namely, there were two schools: in the older of the two one understood words but not meaning, while in the newer one understood meaning but not my words. I could not bring the two schools together.' (Atmanspacher, Primus, 1995, pp. 317-330) At one level, this is a reference to the schools of nuclear physics and analytical psychology; at another level, it refers to the explanations that science offers and the meanings that derive from a depth psychological and spiritual orientation. Here Pauli was stuck. (Stein, p. 50)

At this point in active imagination, Pauli found himself in a room with a classy woman who gave him a piano lesson. Pauli opened up to her, told her about his hard relationship with the Captain and with the Master (representing the Self, a guide). He then mentioned a charlatan and said:

> Once there was a charlatan (a theologian, a Captain from Keopenick), (…) who taught that the black keys on the piano are nothing but holes where white keys are missing, and that all teachers are therefore either all white or totally black. The Lady laughs out loud and tells him that one can equally well play pieces in a minor key on white keys and in a major key on black ones. This depends only on how one plays the piano. (…). He replies that the white keys seem to him to be the 'words' and the black ones the 'meaning.' Sometimes the words are sad and the meaning is joyful, sometimes it's the opposite. (…) Here, by her, Pauli concludes, it is not the same as in that place where there are two schools, where he had such a worrisome

problem; here there is only one piano. (He is finding a way to bring the schools together, to link Ego-consciousness to the unconscious.) (Stein, p. 55).

After sharing Pauli's touching and meaningful active imagination, Stein added:

It has seemed until now impossible to have a dialogue, a meeting of minds, between modern positivistic science and the giver of meaning (the Master, the self), or make a link in consciousness between the world of the Ego and the realm of the unconscious, between time and eternity, so estranged are they from each other. This is the same division that Jung sought to bridge in his alchemical work, especially in Mysterium coniunctionis. Pauli faces this issue head-on in this 'active fantasy.' The piano symbolizes a possible point of meeting. It represents the transcendent function, a synthetic mind. Of course, the question is: Can he play the piano? Well, he is learning. (…) At any rate, Pauli has given us in the image of the piano a useful metaphor for the transcendent function, which may assist our efforts to create a sustained and sustaining link between time and eternity for ourselves and with our patients. (Stein, pp.55-56)

Following this inspiring lecture, after I was back in Rome I decided to write to Murray Stein, although I did not know him personally. I wanted to tell him I appreciated his lecture at Yale and share with him the synchronistic reason that had pushed me all the way to Connecticut. I wanted to describe to him the state of grace I had experienced. I told him that by presenting Pauli's active imagination on "The piano lesson," he had given a symbolic answer to my consideration on the two ways of experiencing and passing on active imagination. After all, my question on how to explain an attitude of active imagination had already been answered in the title of his lecture: it is… "A matter of practice!"

Murray sent me the text of his presentation and asked me to send him mine. Following that exchange, I suggested to the AIPA Executive Committee to invite Stein to the AIPA Rome headquarters to hold that same conference. The full text of the conference was then published in the AIPA Journal *Studi Junghiani* (Stein, 2015), for which I was the editor at the time. Murray accepted the invitation and asked me to spend some friendly time with him and his wife Jan before and after the conference.

Acts of Creation in Time

Murray Stein came to Rome in April 2016 and his lecture was greatly appreciated by AIPA colleagues. I truly started to know Murray and his lovely wife Jan right then, in those spring days in Rome. The weather was nice and mild, and the city streets and squares gleamed at day and night. I learned how lively, funny and kind Murray and Jan were. When I think of an effective attitude of active imagination, I immediately think of the natural, fluent, original, divergent, intense and joyful attitude that first characterized and still characterizes my relationship with Murray and Jan. Bonding over meaningful connections linked to analytical psychology, especially active imagination (my lecture at Yale also referred to active imagination and the "state of grace" resulting from learning a new way of being in the world), inevitably allowed us to refer to those "acts of creation in time" which, for Jung, defined synchronicity. So, time and acts of creation in time became the protagonists of our thoughts and stories.

One evening we were driving through the city center. Roman ruins kept looming in the streets and squares, when Jan said: "In Rome, you live in archetypes!" That striking, true and meaningful image allowed us to think together and ask ourselves about the possible coexistence of past and present, and therefore of the possibility of "*Synchronizing Time and Eternity.*" The past that lives in the present, the layering of what existed in time and continues to exist in the present—archetypically, but also truly, partly buried in darkness, partly in sunlight—was all incredibly symbolized by the historical complexity of Rome.

We told each other and shared our life stories and experiences we considered relevant as they had to do with synchronicity and an attitude of active imagination related to the process of individuation.

When Murray and Jan went back to Zurich, we carried on our conversation through an exchange of letters that continues to this day. In one of those letters, Murray asked me to send him and his wife "A memory for the future," a meaningful memory of mine that had truly impressed them. In turn, I asked Murray to send me the episode that happened to him and Jan which he had told me about during our conversations in Rome and that had truly impressed me. With Murray Stein's permission, see below the two stories taken from a correspondence between Murray and me.

Dear Murray, here is my memory for the future.

It was a Spring morning in 1969, in Florence. I was 15, and I was on my way to school. I walked at a fast pace, thinking about the day ahead of me: a morning with schoolmates, my friends from the Liceo Classico Michelangiolo high school, studying all those new subjects, full of contents. It was not notional and dull like in middle school: Art History, Italian, History, Ancient Greek, French, Physics, Chemistry... My new professors were good and openminded, and they connected each topic to the others. In the afternoon, there were the meetings of the Student Movement: new things to discover, to learn. Politics, Economics. We read newspapers and magazines that explained to my school friends and me for the first time what the world was like, what was happening in other countries, what worked and what did not. Justice and rights to defend, along with old and new friends, with some of our teachers and new classmates and schoolmates. In the afternoons and evenings we went to the theater, we saw concerts, we watched movies. On Sunday mornings, we went to the film club. We discovered Eisenstein, Tarkovskij, Dreyer, Bunuel, Fellini, Antonioni, Godard, Truffaut, Wilder, Kubrick... And then there were the volleyball workouts and matches. The parties with the vinyl records, the thrill of dancing at the sound of the Beatles and the Rolling Stones, wearing grown-up clothes.

I was finally a grown up. And I was free. Free and ready to jump forward: life welcomed me like the salty air and the sea water while I looked around waiting to dive off a cliff.

As I kept walking, and thinking about all of this, I found myself in front of a wall of blooming wisteria. The intense and sweet scent filled me and mixed with the full growing feeling procured from the concatenation of my thoughts... And, suddenly, I was totally flooded and overwhelmed by an uncontrollable happiness. I was almost out of breath. I wanted to cry; the joy was so intense, it seemed I could not keep it in. So I stopped. I looked around. I was grateful for everything around and inside me, and so I thought: "I must do something with this happiness, otherwise I'll burst. It's too much for me, now!" Then, I told myself: "Remember this moment. You are here, on the corner of Via Masaccio and Via Botticelli, it is an April morning, and you are totally, irresistibly happy. Remember this in ten days or ten, twenty, forty years, if things do not go well."

I sent myself this message, my memory for the future, in the same way you can write something on a piece of paper, put it into a bottle, throw it into the sea, trusting it can arrive somewhere and it will not be lost.

Today I can say: I received that message. It is still here, with me. Again, the light of that morning continues to brighten my soul.

Warmly,

Chiara

Dear Chiara,

Here is the story I told:

Helmut and Ellynor, a couple who we knew well and were very fond of, died within a short time of one another, perhaps a year or two between the husband's death and the wife's. We had attended both funerals, and on this day we were driving home from the funeral ceremony of the wife. As we were making our way up the road that leads to our home in the hills above Lake Thun and talking about our memories of our dear friends, a strange thing happened that we have never forgotten. It is a small two-lane road, and as we were proceeding as usual we suddenly saw that a car had stopped on the other side of the road up ahead of us, and the driver was standing in the road and holding up his hands to warn us also to stop. We wondered what was happening. We had never been stopped like this on the road. Soon enough we understood. A pair of beautiful mallard ducks was slowly crossing the road, and the other driver had stopped his car and was warning us to do the same so we would not run over them. Slowly and with dignity the pair of colorful ducks made their way across the road, walking from the left side of us to the right and then disappearing into the trees beyond. This type of bird is not common in this area. In fact, we have never seen them here before or since that day. As we finally were able to drive on, I said to my wife: "Isn't that just like Helmut and Ellynor?" They had been a couple since they were high school students, and we never saw one without the other. They were always together. Mallard ducks are famous for mating for life. We read this manifestation as a "signal of transcendence": The spirits of our friends were greeting us that day and were assuring us that they are still together as a couple.

Warmly,

Murray

A Window on the Other Side of Life

The stories Murray, Jan, and I exchanged during their stay in Rome reminded me of the final part of an autobiography book which is very important to me, *Il cerchio che si chiude* (Balducci, 1986), by Ernesto Balducci, a well-known and knowledgeable Italian theologian who was also a dear friend of mine and my family. I sent that final part to Murray, who was touched.

I wish to conclude with this text that poetically summarizes what I presented so far: being able to collect and pass on, from one side of existence to the other, the symbolic understanding of an attitude of active imagination and the acts of creation in time.

When I was a young boy, my room had a window overlooking a cliff (the house is still there, perched over medieval walls). Beyond the cliff was a glimpse of small hills. On the side of the cliff, the long outline of an old Clarisse convent. On several occasions, at night time, a bell called the monks with "matins to her Spouse." Every now and then, when I heard the bells, I would get out of bed to look at those tiny windows of the cells turn on and off, one after the other, in darkness. I now understand my fascination for that night-time show, which I watched by myself, almost surreptitiously. It was as if I were looking at the other side of life, where time follows different rhythms, where time is a useless time; it is the time of Being, time that turns on itself like a dance step, and doesn't care about our time, the time of existing. I could say I never moved away from that window. (Balducci, p.154)

Chiara Tozzi is a psychologist and psychotherapist. She is a Training Analyst and Supervisor of Associazione Italiana di Psicologia Analitica (AIPA) and of the International Association for Analytical Psychology (IAAP). She is also a writer, screenwriter, and screenwriting professor. She lectures internationally and is visiting professor to different IAAP Developing Groups. She is the author of a research on active imagination supported by the IAAP which will be published by Routledge. She is artistic director of the international "Mercurius Prize for Films of particular Psychological Significance and Sensitivity to Human Rights," based in Zurich. She is former editor of "Studi Junghiani," the Journal for AIPA. Email: chiarat652@gmail.com

References

Adler, G. (1999). *Studies in Analytical Psychology*. Routledge.

Atmanspacher, H., Primus, H, and Wertenschlag-Birkhauser, E.(eds.). (1995) *"Der Jung-Pauli Dialog und seine Bedeutung fur die moderne Wissenschaft,"* Springer.

Balducci, E. (1986). *"Il cerchio che si chiude,"* Marietti, Genova.

Bannerman, H. (1999) "An Overview of the Development of Martha Graham's Movement System (1926–1991)." *Dance Research: The Journal of the Society for Dance Research.* 17 (2): 9–46. JSTOR 1290837).

Chodorow, J. (1997) "Jung on Active Imagination," Routledge.

Curi, U. (1997). La cognizione dell'amore: eros e filosofia, Milano: Feltrinelli Editore.

Franz, M. L. von (1980a), "On Active Imagination," in *Inward Journey: Art as a Therapy (La Salle and London: Open Court, 1983*, 125-33.

Franz, M. L. von (1980b). *The Psychological Meaning of Redemption in Fairytales*, Inner City Books, Toronto.

Graff, E. (2004) "When your heart falls: The drama of descent in Martha Graham's technique and theater." *Women & Performance: A Journal of Feminist Theory.* 14 (1): 107–115. doi:10.1080/07407700408571443. S2CID 191443452.).

Jung, C.G. (1929/1976) "Commentary on *The Secret of the Golden Flower," The Collected Works of C.G. Jung: Vol. 13.* Bollati Boringhieri. Princeton University Press.

Jung, C.G. (1916/58) "The transcendent function," *The Structure and Dynamics of the Psyche, The Collected Works of C.G. Jung: Vol. 8.* Princeton University Press.

Jung, C.G. (1952/1969) "Synchronicity: An Acausal connecting principle," in H. Read, M. Fordham, G. Adler (eds) *The Structure and Dynamics of the Psyche, The Collected Works of C.G. Jung: Vol. 8.* Princeton University Press.

Jung, C.G. (1995) *C.G. Jung, Memories, Dreams, Reflections.* Fontana Press

Stein, M. (2015) *Sincronizzare tempo ed eternità. Una questione di pratica,* in Studi Junghiani, vol.21, N.2, Milano: Franco Angeli Ed.

Stein, M. (2017) "Synchronizing Time and Eternity: A Matter of Practice" in *Outside, Inside and All Around,* Chiron Publications.

Tozzi, C. (2015a) "En Route: from Active Imagination to Film Language," in "Copenhagen 2013: 100 years on: origins, innovations and controversies" Proceedings of the 19th Congress of the International Congress of Analytical Psychology.

Tozzi, C. (2015b) *"Jung e Nabokov,"* in Succedeoggi.it

Tozzi, C. (2020) "From horror to ethical responsibility: Carl Gustav Jung and Stephen King encounter the dark half within us, between us and in the world," Journal of Analytical Psychology N.65(1).

Seeking the Divine:
Reflections on Steinbeck's "To a God Unknown"

Robert M. Mercurio

Even more than the quality of his lectures, what we have all appreciated in Murray so much over the years is his very presence, a presence characterized by gentleness, humility, discretion, wisdom, honesty, and authenticity. Being around Murray Stein provides one with a living example of what Jung meant by the process individuation, and his way of being in the world is a beautiful lesson on how to continue living and working in that spirit.

The commemorative volume published in honour of the late great Edward Edinger (2009) bears the title "An American Jungian" and indeed, from his birth in Iowa, through his professional training at Yale, and his psychiatric work at Rockland State Hospital, Edinger's roots were firmly planted in American soil. The frequent references to thinkers such as Henry David Thoreau, Ralph Waldo Emerson, and Herman Melville attest to the ingenious way in which Edinger dug deep into our American heritage and found wisdom and guidance there. His analytical practice on both coasts of the United States almost seemed to be a symbolic representation of the way in which he managed to keep the opposites and contrasts of American life and culture in relation to one another while reading and interpreting the tension those opposites tend to generate. Edinger was a keen observer of all that transpired in the cultural unconscious of the

American continent, and he commented on this so eloquently in many of his works.

Our friend, colleague, and mentor, Murray Stein, is likewise an alumnus of the prestigious Yale University and Yale Divinity School where he studied before earning his doctorate at the equally prestigious University of Chicago, so his roots are also deeply American and yet somehow the appellative "American Jungian" does not seem to fit him, indeed it might even be reductive for a man who spent and continues to spend so much of his life abroad. Murray's analytical training was in Zürich where many of the people who had worked directly with Jung were still actively teaching and supervising. His own analytical work was done with analysts of the calibre of Hilde Binswanger and Richard Pope. His interests do not seem to lie so much in observing and interpreting the American cultural unconscious as in tracing movements in the unconscious of the world at large. It is difficult (though not impossible) to find in his numerous books and articles anything specifically American. His interests lie in areas of research and an inward search related to questions of spirituality and the interface between religious sentiment and depth psychology, and indeed his contributions in this area have been precious. Stein's 2014 *Minding the Self* is, to my mind, a magnificent testimony to the analysis and reflection he has always brought to bear on questions connected with transcendence, interiority, and the way the life of the spirit enriches and completes our humanity.

I have recently dedicated a great deal of attention to a small novel by John Steinbeck which I read years ago but which continues to resonate and offer food for reflection. Steinbeck is undoubtedly as American as they come and yet he too is much, much more. The book I am referring to, *To a God Unknown* (1933/1976) is small only in terms of the number of pages which comprise it, but it is immense in the topics it deals with and the probing questions it raises. In a 1932 journal entry, the author writes "The story has grown since I started it. From a novel about people, it has become a novel about the world...The new eye is being opened here in the west...the new seeing" (p. vii). And Steinbeck was using that "new eye" to bring into focus a serious religious crisis and the need to find a stronger, more genuine connection with the beyond. Steinbeck originally published *To a God Unknown* in 1933 and it obviously antedates his major works such as *Grapes of Wrath* and *East of Eden.* Throughout the book he seems to be experimenting with style and the result is a sort of lyrical and highly expressive language which gives an almost mystical tone to the whole tale.

From this book, Steinbeck emerges as an *ante litteram* ecologist and feminist and the ingenious story he spins says as much about the changes going on in American society as it does about fundamental questions of how our relation to nature moulds and reflects the rapport we have with transcendence. Steinbeck too then is thoroughly American but again, it would be reductive to stop there.

Towering archetypal figures such as the *Cosmic Man* and the *Anthropos* emerge in the text almost unexpectedly in a way which is at once surprising and yet convincing. It is a book about projection and *participation mystique*. The title of the book, with its reference to the unknown god of the Vedic hymn that Steinbeck himself quotes, cannot but remind us of St. Paul's second missionary journey to Athens where he attempts to instruct the Athenians as to the real identity of the unknown god to whom they had reserved an altar on the areopagus, or of the *deus absconditus* the alchemists were convinced to have discovered hidden in the mystery of matter.

The whole text resoundingly seeks to answer the age-old question of how and where we can find a fresh and vibrant contact with the divinity when the old ways of doing so are no longer viable or credible. In the *Red Book,* in the section of the *Liber primus* entitled *"The conception of God,"* Jung (2009) writes "He who plays is a child: his god is old and dies. He who lives is awakened: his god is young and goes on...so leave the play to the players. Let fall what wants to fall; if you stop it, it will sweep you away" (p. 170). Everything Steinbeck describes in this tale is part of what Jung (1989) calls in his Zarathustra seminars, "the continuous revelation of religious thought" (p. 206) while being at the same time a chronicle of collective social movements in the United States.

The Plot

Young Joseph Wayne, heir apparent to the wealth and wisdom of his patriarchal father, despite his age and secondary place in the line of family succession, takes his leave from the family farm on the east coast of the United States and sets out to stake his claim to land in California. Collectively speaking, he seems to have heard and heeded the call "Go west, young man" to a place where the rising sun of the east coast could shine in all its force and brilliance and offer not only intuitions of a new life, but the real concrete conditions needed to realize it.

Joseph's departure from the traditionally Christian atmosphere of his family and of the Atlantic coast is also a departure from the world of institutions, banks, and conventionality. (Steinbeck will take up this theme in his later works in which he harshly criticizes financial institutions for depriving farmers of their homesteads when drought and misfortune leave them practically destitute.). While Joseph's father is carefully described, no mention is made of the mother figure, showing just how deeply patriarchal the situation he is about to leave really is.

Joseph finds the land he wants near a forest aptly dedicated to and called by the name of "Our Lady." With the help of local *latino* peasants, he constructs his house and successfully begins farming the land. His three brothers soon join him in the wake of the death of their father, a loss that strikes Joseph to the heart and leads him to recognize the presence of his father's spirit in a mighty oak tree not unlike the oracular oak of Zeus at Dodona or the oak in the Grimm fairy tale *The spirit of the bottle*. Joseph marries Elizabeth and fathers a son whom, in honour of his father, he names John.

Working with his brothers, the farm flourishes until a fearful drought strikes as indeed, he feared it sooner or later would. Joseph's youngest brother, Benjy, a hopeless rake, is killed by an irate father as he, Benjy, is trying to seduce a young girl; his brother Burton abandons the farm in disaccord with the way Joseph connects with the land in a mysteriously religious way, going so far as to accuse him of blasphemy; while Thomas, the brother who communicates best with animals, takes what is left of the starving and dwindling livestock in search of richer pastures. Joseph himself dies of a self-inflicted wound convinced that the blood which flows from the cuts on his wrists will correspond in some way to the rain which the land so desperately needs. And indeed, as his blood trickles down onto the ground, the first drops of rain begin to fall. "The rain swept through the valley…the earth turned black and drank the water until it could hold no more" (p.185).

The Characters

Steinbeck had read the few works of Jung that were available in English in the early 1930's and his close friendship with Joseph Campbell as well as his widespread reading of the Latin and Greek classics had given him a remarkable mythological sensitivity. His characters are *types* and even though he did not apply Jungian typology the way W.H. Auden (1948) admittedly had in his "Age of Anxiety" where each of the four characters corresponds to a precise "superior function," it is not difficult to find expressions from our Jungian vocabulary to describe them. Steinbeck foresaw difficulties in selling the book principally because the characters were not "home folks." The patriarchal figure of John, father of the Wayne clan, is indeed a "wise old man" and as Jung (1934-9) tells us, in speaking of such a figure "the older he is the more he is worshipped or feared" (p. 112).

Joseph and his brother Thomas will also encounter another mysterious wise old man who lives, as he himself says, "500 feet above the beach." He incarnates the fact that the wise old man, who inevitably appears when the predominate God image is dead or dying, is "a system of beautiful ideas. He consists of a tissue of the most marvellous ideas that have ever been visualized, but nowhere is it said how to do it" (p. 112). Joseph's youngest brother, Benjy, is witty and entertaining with little desire to do any sort of hard work. He is a dreamer but also a heavy drinker who seems more at home in a drunken world of fantasy than in the world of repetitive farm chores. He is highly seductive and is killed while attempting to seduce the young daughter of Juanito, a workman well-known and respected by Joseph. He is in short, a self-destructive *puer type* who lives in what von Franz (1970) called "a continual sleepy haze" (p. 2). When he dies, Joseph comments that his end had been dictated by fate long before the stabbing; they knew it would happen but were helpless in the face of destiny.

Burton Wayne is the oldest of the brothers and is a stiff and rigid traditionalist who can only slavishly apply the Christian principles he has learnt by heart, to every situation. He epitomizes an intolerant *senex* who, by damaging the tree Joseph considers sacred, brings the entire operation of the flourishing farm tumbling down. There is no room for imagination or originality in him, he is dogmatic and unforgiving, a perfect example of that "ice of the absolute idea" (2009, p.166) that Jung refers to in the *Red Book*.

Thomas is the brother who is in continual, direct communication with the farm animals and emerges in the story as a prefect representation of the *homo naturalis*. He has few if any human contacts but prefers the company of horses, sheep and cattle, and his wife, Rama, is equally at home in the unspoken mysterious ways of nature. The local friar, Father Angelo epitomizes more than any other character the constant tension which the locals feel and express between their ancient pagan heritage and the rites and sacraments of the Catholic Church. At times he gives way to the needs and spontaneous pagan ways of the people in his care, while at other times he stiffly defends the "Christian way." He seems to know that at least a part of the unknown god we are always seeking is embedded in the deep and distant heritage of his people, but he cannot bring himself to really admit it. Like Paul in Athens, he preaches that the God we are all seeking is the Lord Jesus who was crucified and raised from the dead. He is, in a way, a modern-day crucified Christ figure himself, suspended between the new and the old, unable to leave room for the necessary mediation between the two.

And Joseph, the key and central character of the entire book is as mysterious as he is fascinating, and even tragic. The depths of his personality and knowledge instil fear in those who would like to know him but who feel totally inadequate to the task. After his marriage to Elizabeth, his brother's wife, Rama, explains to the new bride that she has married a man she will never really know or understand. Despite his sincere efforts to be close to his new wife, it is evident that Joseph cannot belong to any one person; he has been burdened with a challenging prophetic task that goes well beyond family: he must recognize and embrace a new god image, an image so closely linked to the land and the manifestations of nature as to emerge as a genuine nature divinity in all of its archaic force.

The Crux

The crux of the entire story centers on and circles around the challenge of honestly searching for the unknown god capable of restoring in human hearts a truly religious sentiment. Paul's attempts on the areopagus to convince the Athenians that the revelation he so desperately needed to proclaim would solve the problem of the "unknown god" has always struck me as being pathetically inadequate and beside the point The masterful and detailed way in which ancient Greek theology had described and circumscribed the various gods and goddesses shows how keen their attention to the movements of the unconscious really was. Their divinities were a clever and convincing combination of immanence and transcendence who at times participated and interfered in human events but who then retired to their Olympian heights where they remained distant and ethereal. It seems to me that their recognition of an "unknown god" indicates how, despite all of efforts made by the Greeks, they realized that there was and always would be something in the divine that escapes us, something so deeply mysterious and ungraspable that we cannot describe or even imagine.

In a poem from his youth entitled "To the unknown God," Nietzsche at 24 writes

I want to know you, Unknown One
You who are reaching deep into my soul
And ravaging my life, a savage gale
You Inconceivable and yet Related One
I want to know you – even serve (Kaufman, 1950, p. 371)

Joseph Wayne's departure from his patriarchal home is the gesture of an *everyman* in search of a meaningful contact with the divine. He epitomizes the religious search that the soul of humanity must confront repeatedly. Though Joseph never explicitly says so, it is evident that the entire synthesis of his life is at stake. He abandons the comforts of his east coast existence in Vermont with this unusual blessing imparted to him by his aging, blind father, "May the blessing of God and my blessing rest on this child. May he live in the light of the Face. May he love his life" (p. 3).

The forest of "Our Lady," which strikes him so powerfully because of the "curious femaleness of the interlacing boughs" leaves him "half-drugged and overwhelmed" (p. 6). He quickly intuits that his father has died and that now, his father and this new land are one and the same thing. The land for Joseph is as much mother as father, a bisexual divinity not unlike the Etruscan Voltumna, also a numinous figure of the land. His contact with the land and with nature is intimate and erotic to the point of being, in the end, a total identification. "I should have known" he says as he lies dying, "I am the rain" …"I am the land, I am the rain. The grass will grow out of me in a little while." (p. 184). And like Osiris himself or the sprouting white grain that grows out of the dark "sepulchres" that Italian Catholic churches still set up for the Holy Thursday liturgy, Joseph himself is the sprouting new life, absorbed and totally integrated into nature. In the words of the Vedic hymn that gave the novel its name, "He is the giver of breath and strength is his gift, the High Gods revere his commandments. His shadow is life, his shadow is death; who is he to whom we shall offer our sacrifice?....May He not hurt us, He who made earth, who made the sky and the shining sea. Who is the God to whom we shall offer sacrifice?" (p. xxxv). Joseph Wayne offers the ultimate sacrifice, the sacrifice of his very life to the mysterious divine movements of the earth and of nature, and he does it so that nature might live anew and the divine be recognizable again.

It appears that Joseph the "subject" and nature as "object" have merged into a state of archaic identity or of *participation mystique,* but in a conscious and knowing way. As the primordial cosmic man, Joseph assumes onto himself all worldly reality in order to then, through his death, re-create a world. His could equally be seen as an outdated personality structure that dies so that imagination (rainwater) can revive life itself. As von Franz comments, "...the quaternary structure of the primordial man would mean then that the image of the Anthropos contains the possibility of a progressive development of human consciousness, an inner dynamic" (p. 141). Joseph is also the alchemical *filius macrocosmi* compensating the one-sidedness of the *filius microcosmi* who limits his redemptive work to the soul of men and women while leaving out the body with its instincts and nature at large.

Sacred Symbols

Two objects in the story are consecrated by Joseph as sacred representations of *mana.* The first is the huge oak tree we have already mentioned. It is a sacrament to him in every sense of the word, an image and an act that opens a channel of grace and activates energy. Each time Joseph needs to make a difficult decision, each time he is weighed down by a problem or by one of the dilemmas connected with the organization and management of his life and the life of his family members, he sits beneath the tree and is inspired by its wisdom, or better by the wisdom of nature that the tree channels. When his son John is born, Joseph and his wife Elizabeth baptize the boy by placing him in the limbs of the tree. From his initial sensation that the tree contained the spirit of his deceased father, Joseph gradually experiences the tree as a universal source of counsel.

Jung reminds us in his essay on the Philosophical Tree (1967/1954, CW13) that "if a Mandala may be described as a symbol of the Self seen in cross section, then the tree would represent a profile view of it: the Self depicted as a process of growth" (para. 304). It can, as Jung further states, "be interpreted as the Anthropos, or the Self" (para. 458). It is evident in the story that there beneath the tree, to which he goes so far as to offer sacrifices of food, Joseph is in intimate contact with the Self and the way contact of this sort unites and reconciles that which is most personal and private with the universal concerns of mankind and of the gods. Naturally, it is his *axis mundi,* linking the mysterious movements below in the bowls of existence itself with all that is sublime and spiritual. The god image, as Joseph lives and transmits it, is in a process of transformation here. The old dogmatic images are long gone and the reader who is familiar with the spiritual evolutionary view of Teilhard de Chardin (2002) cannot help but be struck by the way Joseph's unitary way of seeing earth, humanity and divinity seem to be leading us through the *noosphere* towards the ultimate *omega point.* Again, Jung sums it up for us so well, "In so far as the tree signifies the opus and the transformation process 'tam ethice quam physice' (both morally and physically), it also signifies the life process in general. Its identity with Mercurius, the *spiritus vegetativus,* confirms this view" (CW13, para 459).

But the old, traditional dogmatic view of the divine and of the separation between divinity, humanity, and nature cannot bear what looks like such a blatant form of blasphemy. It does not know how these three elements could possibly be united in a synthesis, indeed it seems outrageous to even imagine it or to try bringing it about. When Burton accuses Joseph of relating to the tree in a sinful way, Joseph answers that if Burton were to do what he does, it would indeed be a sin but for him, for Joseph, it is simply the fulfilment of what he feels and sees, it is the realization of his synthetic role. Like an ancient crusader, Burton must intervene and during the night prior to his departure, he severs the roots of the tree which quickly starts shedding its leave and gradually dies. What ensues is the tragic drought that marks the end of the rich experience the family had lived on this, their promised land. The land seems lifeless, the lymph which kept everything alive and in connection all but dried up completely leaving behind a veritable Wasteland of starving livestock and parched arid earth. This is what happens, Jung and von Franz would have said, when the imagination dries up and dogma has the last word.

There was a mystical rock in the forest of "Our Lady" that was truly numinous. It filled Joseph and both his friend Juan and his wife Elizabeth with awe and with fear. It was covered with slippery moss and the water which flowed from the opening on its side fed a stream which in turn formed a pool. Even when water became scarce and the rivers and streams were about to dry up, the rock continued to be a source of moisture. Joseph often went there as if on a pilgrimage, he rested and prayed in the shadow of the rock. He felt it was somehow alive. Like the rock in the desert that opens for the gushing waters when Moses taps on it with his rod, this rock continued to be a source of comfort and of counsel whenever Joseph was in need.

Elizabeth, after seeing the rock and being frightened by it, had dreamt of it, again in a frightening way. When she later goes back to the place with Joseph, she wants to show him and herself that it is after all, only a rock and there is nothing to be afraid of. In a gesture of pure *hubris,* she climbs up on it to show that she is its mistress, that rational consciousness is mightier than the mystical nature of this sacrament. In one of the most tragic sequences of the story, Elizabeth loses her footing, slips on the rock's moss, falls, and breaks her neck, victim of a "nothing but" attitude which sought to tame and control something far greater than what human consciousness can handle. As the drought continues, even the rock dries up, its slippery moss becomes a dry brown blanket. Joseph seems to know that the only thing that can heal this disturbed situation is first, the recognition of his role as Cosmic Man like the Chinese P'an Ku or the Persian Gayomart or the Germanic Ymir, and secondly, to offer the ultimate sacrifice of himself. Joseph's affirmation that "This land is mine" turns into a declaration of identity "I am the land."

"According to numerous creation myths" writes Marie-Louise von Franz, "the universe arose from the scattered parts of a gigantic human figure" (pp. 136-7). He descends into that "ungraspable inchoate unity" making it possible for new life and a new form of consciousness to gradually emerge. The rock of Moses becomes the rock of the sacrifice, as if Abraham were once again about to slay his son Isaac, but here there is no *deus ex machina* to stop the process and the renewal of the land passes through the blood of Joseph. And that same stone seems to be akin to the mysterious Philosopher's stone whose soul, according to Dorn, is in its blood (Jung, CW 13, para. 390). As Joseph bleeds, the rock too bleeds and that bleeding, like the bleeding that returns to the Fisher King's sterile wound when Parsifal finally asks the right question, renews the land and all of life. The flowing of red blood points to the ultimate victory of Eros over the *hubris* displayed by Elizabeth and over the dogmatic rigidity and arrogant certainty of Burton.

The Process of Renewal

Steinbeck's story is a saga of renewal, renewal of the land, of the human spirit and of the rapport between earth and nature on the one hand, and earth, our humanity and the divine on the other. It is then a tale of Eros, of relationship. Joseph incarnates that mysterious symbolic dimension where things *are* and *are not* what they seem. He is a man of course, but he is much more than an ordinary man and everyone who has contact with him seems to realize this. He incarnates the symbolic dimension of *esse in anima* where reality is the imaginal dimension that bridges the gap between subject and object but can never be reduced to just one of these. Through his death, Joseph sloughs off what remains of his ego identity and truly emerges as the cosmic, universal Anthropos who is the collective soul of humanity.

Murray Stein (2018) sums up all the rest better than I ever could:

> This is the Way, the door, the bridge between conscious and unconscious, between time and eternity, between ego and Self. To find this psychic factor within as a living spiritual presence gives the individual access to the eternal realms of the archetypes as well as comfort in the perspective that the ego's limitations in time and knowledge are not the ultimate definitions of human life. (p. 207)

There is more, there is always more, in the mysterious beyond.

Robert Michael Mercurio completed his undergraduate studies in philosophy and then moved to Rome for graduate studies in theology at the Gregorian University. He later completed a Master's degree in Management with a thesis project on the application of Jung's typology to teaching methods adopted in language schools. He subsequently enrolled in the C.G. Jung-Institut in Küsnacht, where he took his diploma in Analytical Psychology. Previously a member of the Centro Italiano di Psicologia Analitica (CIPA), he is presently a member, training analyst, and President of the Associazione per la Ricerca in Psicologia Analitica (ARPA). His interests include the practice of active imagination, the interface between spirituality and psychology and myth and fairy tale interpretation.

References

Auden, W.H. (1948). *The Age of Anxiety: A Baroque Ecologue.* Faber & Faber.

Chardin, T. (2002). *The Heart of Matter.* Harper One.

Elder, G. & Cordie, D. (Ed.) (2009). *An American Jungian: In Honor of Edward Edinger.* Inner City Books.

Jung, C.G. (1967). The philosophical tree (R. F. C. Hull, Trans.). In H. Read et al. (Eds.), *The Collected Works of C.G. Jung: Vol. 13. Alchemical Studies* (pp. 251-349). Princeton University Press. (Original work published 1954) https://doi.org/10.1515/9781400850990.251

Jung, C.G. (1989). *Nietzsche's Zarathustra: Notes on the Seminar Given in 1934-1939.* J. Jarrett (Ed.). Routledge.

Jung, C.G. (2009). *The Red Book: A Reader's Edition.* S. Shamdasani (ed.) Norton & Company.

Kaufmann, W.A. (1950). *Nietzsche: Philosopher, Psychologist, Antichrist.* Princeton University Press.

Steinbeck, J. (1933/1976). *To a God Unknown.* Penguin Books.

Stein, M. (2014). *Minding the Self: Jungian Meditations on Contemporary Spirituality.* Routledge.

Stein, M. (2018). *The Bible as Dream: A Jungian Interpretation.* Chiron Publications.

von Franz, M.-L. (1970). *Puer Aeternus.* Sigo Press.

von Franz, M.-L. (1999). "The Cosmic Man" in *Archetypal Dimensions of the Psyche.* Shambhala.

An Interview with Murray Stein
in Celebration of His 80th Birthday

Jan Wiener

Murray's knowledge and loyalty to Jung the man and his ideas and Murray's own belief in the power of deep unconscious forces, including dreams to generate hope and tolerate dark times have sustained my own faith in what it means to be an analyst in clinical practice and helped me to discover greater resources to manage challenging times in my own life. He has generously passed on some of his great wisdom.

JW: Murray, it is always a real pleasure to meet up with you and talk in depth together. I am pleased and honoured that you have asked me to interview you on the occasion of your 80th birthday as part of your Festschrift. The first interview, held in person in Zurich was around 4 years ago and is published in the JAP in 2019. It was filmed and I know it has had more viewings online than any other JAP listing. Four years is actually quite a long time, and much may have happened during that time. I wanted to begin by asking you how you feel about 80 approaching in a few months' time?

MS: Presently, I feel well (knock on wood!), and I don't feel "old." One has a picture in one's mind of how an 80-year-old person should look and feel based on our experience perhaps with our grandparents and earlier generations, but I don't feel like that. I'm relatively healthy and looking forward to the next decade.

JW: That sounds an excellent way forward, I hope so too. I was re-reading my first interview with you in Zurich, published in the JAP, and I wonder what for you has changed both personally and professionally since that time, including any significant events and experiences?

MS: There have been quite a number of changes, some of them externally driven and some more internally motivated. And of course some are more significant than others, but they do add up. Externally, it was of course the Corona pandemic, covering the world with a very somber shadow in 2020, an *Umbra mundi* as I called it. As a result, a lot of things had to be postponed. For instance, I was planning to co-host a conference at Eranos with my friend and colleague, Thomas Arzt. We had created a series of books by Jungian analysts and scholars on *Jung's Red Book for Our Time,* a total of 4 volumes by 70 different authors. We were then going to top this project off with a grand finale symposium at Eranos in Ascona, Switzerland, and this was scheduled for April 2020. In March, Corona hit Europe and everything more or less was shut down for a spell. But then on Easter Sunday 2020, Thomas died, suddenly and very surprisingly. I was in shock. This had a big impact on me personally, of course. The symposium took place two years later and was dedicated to the memory of Thomas.

Also, when the Corona pandemic set in, I began working exclusively with clients and supervisees online from home, and I have continued doing so ever since. Also my teaching and lecturing online have picked up significantly during this time. Online work seems to be the wave of the future, at least for me. I didn't travel much during those two years, and paradoxically other doors and windows opened and this expanded the horizon because online you can meet with people anywhere in the world without leaving home.

The other thing that has changed, probably more due to the aging factor, is that I've been feeling myself pull back, especially from organizational activities, which previously had been a big part of my professional life and which I found very meaningful and interesting. As a result of this combination of Covid restrictions and personal pulling back, my daily life has changed a great deal. I haven't been on an airplane for 3 years. I used to travel a lot, but I must say I don't miss it, the hotels and airports, although I do miss the human contact.

JW: I always think of you as somebody with huge internal resources which probably helped a lot during the time of Corona but I wanted to ask you what the losses have been? It's something I've been thinking and writing about too.

MS: I had a few sessions in my office recently, and I really do feel quite a difference. Sitting together in a room you get a much fuller experience of the relationship and the other personality. There's a depth to it that I don't find in the online work. It's certainly a trade-off. There's always a hair in the soup, as Jung was fond of saying. Or as we say in America, there's no free lunch.

JW: So you only realize what you haven't had when you have it again. Thinking about the Ascona conference, how have you found hybrid events? How do they work from your point of view when you've got some people in the room with you and some people online?

MS: When I'm with a group of people in a room, I see whom I'm addressing, and I get their response immediately and directly. Online and with the hybrid model, I don't get this. I don't see the people who are attending online, and then when it comes to Q & A and discussion, I'm discussing mostly with the people in the room. The hybrid is ok as far as getting the content out, but for discussion and interaction it doesn't work very well. It's impossible to have a discussion online of the type I would have in the same room with the audience.

JW: I suppose what you're saying about Covid is that in some ways, it has expanded possibilities and in other ways there are restrictions. It sounds as though you do not miss travel around the world.

MS: That's right. I travelled a great deal for the IAAP. You and I were together in Russia many times. and I really enjoyed that. It was nothing to jump on a plane and go there, and I didn't think twice about it, but I wouldn't do it now and it's not about Covid. It's about age and diminished physical stamina. My last big trip was to a conference in China, and on the return I had to spend six hours at night in the Beijing airport. I realized as I sat there alone in the empty and dark great hall of the airport, I'm too old for this!

JW: But it hasn't changed your active mind.

MS: No. My mind is active as ever. But my memory, oh dear, it does lag behind my thoughts. I have to wait patiently on Mnemosyne these days. She's quite slow on the uptake sometimes, especially for names.

JW: What are your main interests and preoccupations at present would you say?

MS: I have several projects going, and they really consume all the time I have to spare. One is putting together my *Collected Writings*. So far, six volumes have been published, and there will be three or four more. I find it engaging to go back to papers and books that I have written over the past fifty years. I revise them a bit but don't change the substance. I've also got a continuing project going with our mutual friend, Henry Abramovitch. We wrote a play a couple of years ago, *The Analyst and the Rabbi*, which is based on a conversation between Carl Jung and Rabbi Leo Beck that took place in 1946 in Zurich. Now we've written a follow-up play. It's titled *Eranos* and is a five-person conversation that takes place a year later at the Eranos Conference. Rabbi Beck was one of the Conference speakers that year, and Eric Neumann attended Eranos that year for the first time. The other characters are C.G. Jung, of course, Aniela Jaffé, and Olga Fröoe-Kapetyn. And we've also recently written a third playlet, which is a conversation between Henry and myself while on a train trip from Zurich to Eranos. The conversation is about my work with Thomas Arzt and is titled "My Lunch with Thomas."

JW: What's it like co-working with Henry. How does it work between you in terms of writing something?

MS: We've become brothers in this process of creating these plays together over the past seven years. It's very much a back-and-forth between us as the plays develop. We accept each other's differences and are both committed to focusing on the work and not insisting on our personal preferences. We both went to Yale, which we discovered while visiting Masada in Israel together. This was the beginning of our collaboration. He's a younger brother, and I insist on priority! Not so easy with Henry. We were both born in Canada, and we share so much in common in our interests. It really has worked out well. Henry's is a beautiful soul.

JW: I really enjoyed the play in Avignon. Do you think sometimes when you get caught up in differences, there's a sort of parallel process that gets into your joint writing which actually comes from some of the interactions with the characters in the play?

MS: That's absolutely true. We really try to capture the characters as we've come to know them in our reading and studies, and we put the words in their mouths that we feel they would say. But of course these are also our words. In the first play, we were both working out our feelings about Jung's relation to Germany in the Nazi period. Henry is Jewish and I'm Christian, and this difference often comes into our working out positions and dialogues among the characters we're creating because they share the same difference. This gets into the debates and conversations amongst the characters. Henry is very direct and I like that. He doesn't mince words; he says what he thinks. It's a very dynamic co-creative process we're engaged in. Never a dull moment.

I've also been doing some other writing. I sent you *The Mystery of Transformation,* which I began writing in 2019 when I was invited to give a lecture on Dante's *Divine Comedy* from a Jungian psychological perspective. The conference took place in 2021 in Ravenna on the 700th anniversary of Dante's death. I hadn't paid too much attention to Dante in the past. Of course, everybody knows *of* Dante and has read a few lines of *The Divine Comedy*, but Claudio Widman, who invited me to the conference in Ravenna, has spent his whole adult life reading Dante and collecting many editions of Dante's works. His love and dedication stimulated me to really study the *Commedia* seriously, and the further I went into this extraordinary masterpiece of world literature, the more I was smitten with a similar enthusiasm. I fell in love with Dante's breathtaking creation. After reading several translations, I found I could best get a psychological handle on the poem by reading it through the lens Jung offers in the last chapter of *Mysterium Coniunctionis,* which he published when he had just turned 80, by the way! There he uses Gerhard Dorn's three stages of transformation to speak about the individuation process, and this offered me the intellectual guidance I needed for understanding Dante's journey through the three realms of the afterlife, Hell, Purgatory and Paradise. This intense engagement also took me into a closer study of Jung's late work and especially into his thinking about individuation as culminating in a state of consciousness in which the individual unites with *unus mundus* and becomes one with the world on a spiritual level. As I see it now, this work was a pivotal point in my own self-understanding. After working on this, synchronicity has led to several meaningful meetings and conversations with people who are familiar with mystical experience and non-duality. This has really absorbed my interest in the last couple of years. It seems fitting to be thinking about these things as I approach the end of my eighth decade. Dante died in his sixth decade, by the way, shortly after completing the 100ᵗʰ Canto of the *Commedia*.

JW: I want to come back to that in a second, but just to ask you about your friend Thomas Arzt who died. Are these volumes on *The Red Book* going to be published, even though he died in the middle of the publishing process. I feel sure they will be so interesting.

MS: Four volumes were published before he died in 2020, and the fifth, which consists of the essays that were given at the Eranos Symposium at Ascona on 2022, has now also been published. This completes the Series that Thomas and I began in 2017. It's a miracle, and I want to express my gratitude to Chiron Publications for making this dream a reality. Steve Buser, Len Cruz, and Jennifer Fitzgerald have been marvellous facilitators in this project.

JW: It is my impression that you are working really hard in different ways, even if your practice is less extensive these days.

JW: I wanted to talk to you about your book, *The Mystery of Transformation* that you kindly sent me to read in advance of this interview. I was particularly interested in the first and last chapters. In the first chapter you write about a numinous dream of somebody and in that dream you talk about a 5th dimension from the image in the dream where the dreamer dreams of a house with a 5th floor and a room with a self-sustaining fire.

MS: I borrowed the term "fifth dimension" from John Hick, a philosopher of religion, who wrote a book with that title. He refers basically to mystical experiences in which one has the very strong impression that another world exists that is not available to our senses but is to the mind under certain conditions. We occasionally catch glimpses of that dimension in visions and dreams. The young Jakob Boehme (1575-1624), for instance, came into his shoemaker's workshop one day and was struck by a ray of light hitting one of his tools at a certain angle. Suddenly, he has a vision: he sees an invisible world revealed behind the visible one, and when he steps outside, he can see it for the first time in his life. It's numinous! That's the fifth dimension beyond the three dimensions of the material world plus time (the four dimensions we have ready access to with our senses and normal state of mind). Boehme can now see it and experience it visually, not only intuitively. It's a brilliantly vivid experience, and he spends the rest of his life philosophizing about it. His writings became very influential in European culture through the works of people like the poet William Blake and the philosopher Hegel. Jung had such experiences too and more often than he writes about, I'm quite sure. He does talk about them a bit in *The Red Book* and *Memories, Dreams, Reflections (MDR)*.

In *MDR*, he says of the visions he had while in hospital in 1944 that they were not imagination but absolutely real. These experiences open our consciousness to a level of the psychic world that is normally closed off. We live in the temporal world where we have to organize our lives by the clock, but every now and then we get a glimpse of eternity. In the first chapter of *The Mystery of Transformation,* I report a dream in which the dreamer discovers the fifth dimension in her house. She goes into this room on the fifth floor, and she sees a fire burning brightly in the middle of it and realizes that it is not consuming anything. It is a self-sustaining fire that will never go out, an eternal flame that is self-nourishing and self-sustaining. It is the fifth dimension and located within the four walls and above the four floors of her temporal house. This experience is part of her individuation process and needs to receive central importance in her conscious life. I feel we should make people who are training to become analysts aware of this dimension so they keep an eye out for it, in their own lives and when they work with clients. This type of experience is a key element in the individuation process.

JW: Is it something you can teach or is it something you have to discover?

MS: That's a good question. We can point a person in this direction and refer them to literature and say this is a part of the individuation process, but can we effectively teach about this dimension unless the student has already experienced it? Maybe we can find methods for fostering the experience. For Jungians, this would involve active imagination. We need to spend more time with this method in our teaching. Another question is: what do we do with such an experience? Jung once said he was shocked at how little people make of their numinous experiences. The analyst can help by giving such an experience meaningful emphasis. It's not something to overlook and forget. It belongs in the household of ego-consciousness as a point of orientation. Religious people put a Crucifix or a Star of David somewhere in their homes, and this is to remind them daily of their spiritual guidance system. Jung built his tower at Bollingen and wrote calligraphically in his famous Red Book to give such experiences concrete reality. We could encourage students to practice active imagination and do something with the images that appear to them. I think this would go some way toward educating them about the fifth dimension.

JW: I went from your first to your last chapter which is about the role of faith for the analyst. In that chapter, you really develop so beautifully I thought an understanding of what faith is and what it is not.

MS: As an analyst, one frequently finds oneself with clients in periods of time that seem to be dead ends, to be going nowhere. To stay with the process requires faith. It's faith that psyche will continue to move and will find a way in its own time. This is faith that 'it' knows – "the big *it*" – it knows better than we do. The unconscious will lead the way. I think that's very much a part of the Jungian approach, that the unconscious knows things that we don't know. The self has a way and an intention of its own beyond what the ego does or can know. We aren't conscious of it, and we have to make our choices and decisions as best we can and live with them. But there is a guiding hand in the background.

JW: That was the phrase that I liked particularly "a hand far above my reach." I liked that so much because the hand is human and embodied.

JW: I was thinking too that although I am a few years younger than you, I am also aging of course. Do you think these topics of the 5th dimension and faith are a more serious domain of interest as we get older?

MS: I think that is the normal tendency as people get older. For most people, the first half of life is occupied with getting their feet on the ground and adapting to society, getting an education and developing a profession, beginning important love relationships and partnerships, and generally getting established in this four-dimensional world of time and space. In the second half of life, the question of finding deeper meaning becomes more urgent as they begin to recognize their finitude more realistically: I too will die. People then begin the search for spiritual meaning in their lives, and some return to the religious tradition they had left in earlier years. I remember Judith Hubback telling me that she was having meaningful conversations with a clergyman in her church. She had not been a church-goer for many years. Religious traditions have tremendous resources because they offer what Jung called "living symbols" that connect us to the eternal.

JW: Judith of course was my analyst. She was a wise woman and she helped to pass on something to me about a profound belief in the unconscious and in numinous experiences if we remain open to receive them.

JW: Going back to that first chapter on the dream, are you still interested in your dreams, and do you feel the themes of your dreams have changed as you approach 80?

MS: I do pay attention to dreams, of course. This is a longstanding habit, and I consider it to be an important part of living in relationship with the unconscious. And every now and then there's a big symbolic dream that brings me new insight. I had one of those just recently in which it was shown to me how temporal objects—all objects, not only human beings but also animals, plants, stones, everything that exists—are related to the eternal spirit: They are woven tightly together like two threads in a string. This has given me food for thought and feeling. I've also dreamed quite a lot in these past several years of being in meetings and conferences with colleagues, which is quite contrary to my daytime life. I think of these as compensatory to my present stay-at-home life. I also quite often dream of friends who have passed away, people like Tom Kirsch, for example, with whom I had so many meaningful experiences. I take these as welcome visitations and opportunities to spend some time again with them. I take dreams with me on my daily walks and in a way, I take them on. I get some of my best creative ideas while walking through the hills around my home with their views of the snow-covered mountains in the distance.

JW: I find that so interesting thing because I can see that for some people movement generates ideas whereas for other people, sitting absolutely still fosters the development of creative ideas. I am with you on that one and for me too, ideas come through movement. Presumably, in your lovely woods, you've got so much that is evocative about nature around you too.

JW: I think the world is in a really bad place at the moment with climate change destroying our own environment, the war in Russia and Ukraine; poverty in the world, the big post-Brexit mess here in the UK and so on. I was wondering whether you think a lot about these social and political issues and what your thoughts are about how best to reflect on these dark places. Is there much in Jungian psychology that we might draw on?

MS: It's very distressing to be aware of all the suffering in the world today—due to war and politics, climate change, racism and all the rest of the illnesses that beset humankind. It seems that humanity is in the midst of a massive change, and it may be that we are in the turbulent phase of a major worldwide transition from one paradigm to another. It's disruptive when old patterns of thinking and perceiving meaning are challenged and new ones aren't established yet.

What's generally called globalization is far from over. The world is shrinking as fast as the glaciers are melting, and the differences and divisions among cultures are becoming more apparent. With communication media so rapid and ubiquitous now, it's clear that all the far-flung enclaves of humanity are coming ever closer together. On the other hand, people and groups want to be unique and not all just mixed together into a *potpourri*. We have a lot of disruption because there are obvious differences among peoples and cultures, and those differences are going to be fought over—religious differences, cultural and linguistic differences, political differences. Before there is a possibility of transcending those differences and overcoming them for something higher that creates a sense of unity, there is going to be a lot of conflict. We are in the midst of a gigantic transition toward a new type of world culture, but we don't know what that will be. I'm hopeful, though. What we can draw on from Jungian psychology is faith in the "hand far above our reach." The healing symbol will appear in time and gather us all into a common human community with unity in diversity and diversity in unity.

JW: I wish I felt as hopeful of that as you do Murray. In a way, what you say here echoes the last chapter of *The Mystery of Transformation* again. It's about your definition of faith, which is a belief in greater processes and dynamics and also having the faith to live through dark times whether it's with a patient in analysis or in the world.

MS: There's not a lot one can do as an individual in these times to make things better on the collective level. The individual can't solve the problem of war in Ukraine. We can make some contributions, of course. Also about climate change, we can each do our small part. But we can also work on the inner level. As Jungian analysts, we have the methods and tools for working with dreams, imagination, reflection. This contributes to consciousness on a personal level, and each contribution will have an effect on the larger world in the long run. They add up.

JW: When you were talking earlier about re-publishing the papers that you've written in the past and bringing them together. I was thinking that these would be part of the legacy you will leave when you are no longer with us.

JW: This leads me to ask you whether death and dying feature in your dreams and whether you think about death on a day-to-day basis?

MS: I wouldn't say I think obsessively about death, but I do find myself reflecting on it quite often and quite spontaneously. I also work in analysis with people in their later years. I have some clients now who have been with me for 20 or 30 years, and they're roughly my age. Speaking regularly with them also makes me very aware of the body's limitations and ailments as we approach end of life. I also have thoughts about the afterlife. These are based on dreams and also on experiences I've had around death, synchronistic events that vividly appeared as communications from the person who has died. Many other people have told me stories of a similar kind. Of course, from a rational scientific point of view it sounds strange to the modern ear, but for me this isn't a matter of faith but of fact. It calls for observing dreams and visions and synchronistic experiences as they come to one. Such manifestations of the mysterious and inexplicable have given me a degree of confidence that the psyche continues in another form, let's say in the fifth dimension.

JW: Before you go to the other world, what do you feel personally and professionally are on your bucket list?

MS: I want to do some more writing. This gives me a great deal of pleasure and satisfaction. More travel on the other hand is not on my bucket list. There isn't some place in the world that I haven't visited and really long to see before I die. But there are books on my bucket list that I'd like to read, and I'm eager to continue studying the classics more deeply than I have had time for in the past. Delving into Dante's *Divine Comedy* was thrilling. I'd like to do more of that.

JW: Are there any fun things on this bucket list?

MS: For me, that's all fun. But good meals, yes, that too, with friends. Zurich has some very fine restaurants. Visits from our children and grandchildren are also fun. We had a grand get-together last summer in Sils Maria, the village in the mountains of Switzerland where Nietzsche wrote *Thus Spoke Zarathustra*. Things like that are really fun, and I look forward to more of them.

JW: Do you feel Jungian analysis has a future in the world and can it evolve in different cultures and in different times?

MS: Yes, definitely. I had a dream a few years ago when I was ruminating anxiously about precisely this question. In the dream, Jung came to me and told me not to worry. "Analytical psychology has a long future," he said. I was comforted. Jung has not appeared in many of my dreams, and so this was quite special. I take it as a message from the other side and from a perspective that has vision into the future that I cannot see. I think Jung's psychology is perfectly suited for a world culture because it transcends cultural differences with the theory of the collective unconscious and the archetypes. At that level, all human beings belong naturally and instinctively to one world culture. If we can lift this awareness into the consciousness of people, there will be a chance for unity within all the wonderful diversity among the peoples of the world. I certainly see a strong future for Jung's psychology. I think Jung will be read for a long, long time. His legacy is so rich and interesting.

Last year, I was invited to join a committee that Misser Berg, the President of the IAAP, has set up called the Fundamental Values Committee. This is an attempt to address the question: What does analytical psychology represent to the world? What is our message? This must be carefully considered. Jungian psychology is on the line now and must take a position on major issues facing humanity. Simply saying we are for more consciousness is not enough. This has to be spelled out socially, clinically, politically and culturally.

We must also face up to the fact that our practice of performing analysis is going through some major changes. This is going to make some analysts very uneasy. The fifty-minute hour conducted two or three times a week in an analyst's office has already begun to change significantly because of the online sessions that were necessary during the Covid pandemic. I think that will continue to evolve because in some cultures the traditional form doesn't work. Time commitments don't fit the program, and many people aren't accustomed to those kinds of patterns and rhythms. We have to remember that this form was originally developed in the major city centers of the West. I think there will always be some of that type of practice, but what I see is other forms emerging. For instance, I talked recently to a Jungian psychotherapist in Asia and asked: "How often do you see your clients?" "I see most of them once a month" they said. "Do you really get a process going in that very infrequent rate?" I asked. I was told: "That's what they're used to, that's as much as they can afford, and that's as often as they are willing to attend sessions. Sometimes, I can see them every other week, but weekly sessions are not part of our culture; they just won't do it." We have to become more flexible and adapt to changing times and climes.

JW: That's very interesting, because I had a very thought-provoking conversation with a Danish colleague who was talking about a candidate who was in their own therapy once a fortnight, sometimes once a month. I asked why not weekly? Her point was that the work goes on between the sessions......I said what happens if nothing goes on between the sessions? It was a cultural difference....

MS: You had a lot of exposure to that when you worked in Russia. You were right on the front lines there in a very different culture from the one you had worked in previously in London.

JW: Yes, absolutely, and I learned so much from that. Murray, you clearly have so much more to contribute to the Jungian world. I hope very much that you will invite me back to do this interview again for your 90th birthday celebrations!!

MS: I look forward to it, Jan!

Jan Wiener is a Training Analyst and Supervisor at the Society of Analytical Psychology in London. She recently completed a second term of office as Director of Training. She was Vice President of the IAAP from 2010-2013 and co-chair of the IAAP Education Committee. She has taught and supervised extensively in the UK and abroad, especially in Eastern Europe. She is author of many papers and four books, the most recent of which, *Jungian Analysts Working Across Cultures: From Tradition to Innovation*, was edited with Catherine Crowther and published by Routledge in 2021.

References

Hick, J. (2013). *The Fifth Dimension. An Exploration of the Spiritual Realm*. OneWorld Publications.

Stein, M. (2020-). *The Collected Writings*. Steven Buser and Lenard Cruz, General Editors. Chiron Publications.

Stein, M. (2022*) The Mystery of Transformation*. Chiron Publications.

Stein, M. (ed.) (2022). *Jung's Red Book for Our Time: Searching for Soul in the 21ˢᵗ Century. An Eranos Symposium*. Chiron Publications.

Stein, M. & H. Abramovitch (2019). *The Analyst and the Rabbi*. Chiron Publications.

Stein, M. & T. Arzt (eds.). (2017-2020). *Jung's Red Book for Our Time: Searching for Soul Under Postmodern Conditions*, Volumes 1-4. Chiron Publications.

Wiener, J. (2019). "Interview with Murray Stein." *Journal of Analytical Psychology*, Volume 64, No. 3, 406- 421.

Jung's Dream of the Arab Prince

John Beebe

By the time Murray's popular textbook, Jung's Map of the Soul came out, he had a large international audience ready to join him on his voyage of discovery. There's a bit of Marco Polo to Murray, and at 80 he's still letting us know what he's just managed to see.

In the spring of 2018, during a meeting in Guangzhou with Jungian psychotherapists on the eve of the 8th International Conference of Analytical Psychology and Chinese Culture in Xian which Murray Stein had helped Professor Heyong Shen to organize on the theme of "Enlightenment and Individuation: East and West," I was asked to comment on the dream that Jung shares in Chapter IX, part I, of *Memories, Dreams, Reflections*. It occurred on the last night of his visit to North Africa in the spring of 1920, when he would be sailing from Tunis the next morning back to Marseilles as his point of return to his home continent. This is the well-known dream of Jung's encounter with an Arab prince.

We had been talking about the eight functions of consciousness and how not just the ego but also the shadow has a psychological type. The shadow expresses itself through the same four functions as the ego-identified part of the personality, but for each of those functions it prefers the opposite attitude with respect to extraversion or introversion from what is preferred by the ego-syntonic personality (Beebe, 2017). Someone thought of the dream because, within it, Jung encounters a shadow figure, the Arab prince, with whom Jung had to wrestle before they found themselves able to come together in an eight-sided room.

Having passed through one of the entrance gates of a four-gated city, Jung immediately found himself attacked by an Arab Prince and at first had to quell the latter's combativeness, but then was able to sit more peacefully with the Prince after they had gone into a beautiful and large vaulted octagonal room. Jung's move from the four gates to an eight-sided chamber had apparently made enough inner room for the shadow to tolerate the kind of *auseinanderzetsung* Jung (by now seven years into recording similar imaginal dialogues in his Red Book) would have had in mind. I could not help thinking, however, that the move from four to eight function types within his typology was why the octagonal room seemed such a capacious holding environment for such a conversation in this dream. It was, after all, dreamed by Jung in Tunis in the spring of 1920, and that trip most likely took place just after he had delivered the manuscript of *Psychological Types* to his Swiss publisher, who was then able to publish it that fall. With these details in mind, I decided to include as part of my presentation the dream encounter with the Arab prince as Jung recounts it in *M.D.R.*:

> I dreamt that I was in an Arab city, and as in most such cities there was a citadel, a casbah. The city was situated in the broad plain, and had a wall all round it. The shape of the wall was square, and there were four gates.
>
> The casbah in the interior of the city was surrounded by a wide moat (which is not the way it really is in Arab countries). I stood before a wooden bridge leading over the water to a dark horseshoe-shaped portal, which was open. Eager to see the citadel from the inside also, I stepped out on the bridge. When I was about half-way across it, a handsome, dark Arab of aristocratic, almost royal bearing came towards me from the gate. I knew that this youth in the white burnous was the resident prince of the citadel. When he came up to me, he attacked me and tried to knock me down. We wrestled. In the struggle we crashed against the railing; it gave way and both of us fell into the moat, where he tried to push my head under water to drown me. No, I thought, this is going too far. And in my turn I pushed his head under water. I did so although I felt

great admiration for him; but I did not want to let myself be killed. I had no intention of killing him; I wanted only to make him unconscious and incapable of fighting.

Then the scene of the dream changed, and he was with me in a large vaulted octagonal room in the centre of the citadel. The room was all white, very plain and beautiful. Along the light-colored marble walls stood low divans, and before me on the floor lay an open book with black letters written in magnificent calligraphy on milky-white parchment. It was not Arabic script; rather, it looked to me like the Uigurian script of West Turkestan, which was familiar to me from the Manicheaean fragments from Turfan [吐魯番 Turpan in Xinjiang]. I did not know the contents, but nevertheless I had the feeling that this was "*my* book," that I had written it. The young prince with whom I had just been wrestling sat to the right of me on the floor. I explained to him that now that I had overcome him he must read the book. But he resisted. I placed my arm around his shoulders and forced him, with a sort of paternal kindness and patience, to read the book. I knew that this was absolutely essential, and at last he yielded. (1963, pp. 266-275)

In his analysis of the dream, Jung asserts that the "dark Arab" is a shadow figure, an appealing face of the unconscious who might attract and overwhelm him. The detail however that really engaged me when I was discussing Jung's dream with the Guangzhou group, almost a hundred years after he dreamed it, was the colorful detail of the book written in Uigurian script, the book that Jung associated with Manicheaan fragments from Turfan that he feels is a book that he himself has written. What significance, I wondered, did a Manichean manuscript have for Jung?

That question eventually led me to a letter that Jung handwrote in April 1929 to a 19-year-old Swiss writer Walter Robert Corti who would one day be famous. At that time, however, Corti's father had urged his son, not yet 20, to consult Jung. He was concerned about the young man's emotional intensity. Jung explained to the young man why he had told his father that young Corti was suffering from "hypertrophy of intellectual intuition." Jung said he would have made the same diagnosis of Nietzsche and Schopenhauer and that he himself was one-sided in this respect. Apparently, Corti had written to Jung in dismay that Jung would so diagnose him to his human father after Corti had told Jung that he lived for God.

"That you 'live for God' is perhaps the healthiest thing about you," Jung wrote back. And then Jung said, in what may be the most explicit and completely Jungian "religious" advice he ever gave to a young man bent on living for spirit is that one who does this needs to make himself "an earthly tabernacle" because "God needs man in order to become conscious, just as he needs limitation in time and space." For this reason, Jung explained, the suggestion he would always want to give to those like Corti and himself whose introverted intuition is too strong would be: "Let us therefore be for him limitation in time and space, an earthly tabernacle" (1973, p. 65-6).

The biblical "tabernacle" is "a portable sanctuary consisting of a rectangular wooden framework covered with curtains and carried by the Israelites during their wanderings in the Exodus as a holy dwelling place for their God and as a place for worship," thus called also a "tent for meeting" (meaning, I think, meeting God) and whose second meaning is "the human body when it becomes a temporary dwelling for God" (Posner, 2023).

Further on in his letter, Jung provides the 19-year-old with examples of people from history whom he felt actually understood how to use an embodied existence to house the holy spirit: "Jesus—Mani—Buddha—Lao-tse are for me," he told Corti, "the four pillars of the temple of the spirit. I could give none preference over the other" (1973, p. 66).

To me, the inclusion of Mani in this list of the four personalities who have formed the central pillars of Jung's embodied religious attitude, is amazing. I think Jung respected Mani in part because he was able to grasp the autonomy of evil. Jung knew that any temporary victory over evil would not produce lasting peace of mind until the core problem of the shadow had been faced.

He may have been influenced in this vision by Richard Wilhelm, who wrote in his commentary to the top line of the Yijing's 11th *gua* [hexagram] 'T'ai', Peace, in which defenses against evil collapse:

The Wall falls back into the moat. Use no army now. Make your commands known within your own town. Perseverance brings humiliation. Wilhelm adds: "Should we persevere in trying to resist the evil in the usual way, our collapse would only be more complete, and humiliation would be the result." (1967, p. 52)

Jung offers Corti an aesthetic amplification of the power that for him inheres in the figure of Mani, who had created the first Gnostic world religion on the basis of a dualism that not only included man alongside God, but asserted evil as well as good as being essential to the transformation of God into something that can actually become a human-enough shelter. Jung felt he had seen this in the beautiful art of the Manicheans, and so he writes to the young man, "Sometime I will show you some Manichean Turfan frescoes," (Idem.) meaning 7th century AD images from the days of this first Gnostic world religion, founded by Mani in the 3d century AD, which survived more or less intact in Turkestan until the 13th century. The frescoes Jung saw had recently been unearthed by German archeologists between 1902 and 1914 in Xinjiang, at a site along the Silk Road of the Turfan Oasis in what is now known as the Uygur Autonomous Region of China.

Jung's next three letters in this volume of his selected *Letters* (1973) are to Richard Wilhelm and then we find on September 12th, 1929 Jung writing to Walter Corti again, mentioning that he was at work on "a thousand-year-old Chinese text which the China Institute sent me for a commentary." It was *The Secret of the Golden Flower*. This, as we know, is a book that understands how to use the body in meditation as a way to return light from the darkness of an embodied self to the ego in such a way as to illuminate the latter as well. Manichean art depicts such illuminated figures, which manage in their colorful dark outlined radiance to concretize what Jung puts more drily in the oft-quoted passage from his later alchemical essay, "The Philosophic Tree" in which he rails against a religious conception that does not give the dark its human due when the light of the spirit is encountered:

Filling the conscious mind with ideal conceptions is a characteristic feature of Western theosophy, but not the confrontation with the shadow and the world of darkness. One does not become enlightened by imagining figures of light, but by making the darkness conscious. The latter procedure, however, is disagreeable and therefore not popular. (1967b, p. 265-66)

The necessity and difficulty of confronting and transforming our own evil as imaged in Jung's dream of meeting the Arab prince can also be seen in cultural images of every time. To convey this in Xian, I shared a key passage, thirteen minutes long, from one of Alfred Hitchcock's most neglected masterpieces, *The Wrong Man,* a movie I had first seen in 1956—the year it came out. This film was based on an actual case of mistaken identity that very nearly sent a man to prison for a robbery he did not commit, simply because he looked like the man who actually performed the robbery.[1] It was because that case had attracted a great deal of attention in New York papers that Warner Brothers wanted Hitchcock to make it the subject of a film that though semi-documentary could also be done in noir style, with the shadow so prominent in both the development and the denouement of the drama involved, which touched on the psychological conflict between guilt and innocence that ensues from a mistaken projection. Adhering to the story, Hitchcock's screenwriters kept the actual name of the man who had been wrongly accused and had to find a way to dissolve the projection that has been laid upon him. Given how Manichean this forced brush with evil was for an essential good man, it should not entirely surprise us that the man's name, though not exactly Mani, was close enough: Manny! In Hitchcock's film, as in real life, Christopher Emmanuel "Manny" Balestrero, the son of Italian immigrants, is a bass player at the most famously patronized of New York City elegant nightclubs, The Stork Club. As played by Henry Fonda, he is a mild and preternaturally innocent man who thinks of himself as so harmless that he is astonished when he is wrongly accused of robbing an insurance office. He is assumed to have returned to rob again when he shows up in the office looking to the woman at the desk a lot like the man who did rob the office some weeks before.

The scenes that I showed in Xian[2] begin with Manny in court, being tried for the robbery. Several of the women from the insurance office he is charged with robbing are now the state's witnesses, and they are certain that Manny is the man who robbed their office. Of course, they are wrong, so this whole proceeding is a study in irony. Here's what ensues in the

---

[1] See Isralowitz, 2023 for a full account of the story, which shows that Hitchcock's scenario for *The Wrong Man,* written by Maxwell Anderson and Angus MacPhail, largely matches the actual facts of this grim coincidence

[2] On the Blu-ray disk of *The Wrong Man* they are located within the running time of the film from 1.28.54 -1.40.43.

dozen minutes I chose to show my audience in China. Keep in mind, if you think these scenes would bore you, that they are perhaps the best cinematic example of what Hannah Arendt (1963) seven years after *The Wrong Man* was released, called "the banality of evil":

1) In a courtroom, we see the reading of the charges against Manny in the presence of the jurors who have not yet been sworn in. Manny is required to stand as the charges are read.

2) Then we cut to the opening statement of the prosecutor, giving an overview of how he expects to prove Manny's guilt to the satisfaction of the jurors. Manny is seated, holding a rosary in his hand.

3) The defense counsel makes his opening statement, telling the jurors that the evidence presented will readily convince them that Manny did not commit the crimes he is charged with, but that he has, instead, been mistakenly identified as the man who committed the robbery.

4) We see testimony of a witness for the prosecution, Mrs. James, a woman who was working in the insurance office on the day it was robbed. She identifies Manny as the robber, actually touching his shoulder as she is instructed by the prosecutor. At this point in the film, an uncanny effect is pulled off by Hitchcock, as D.A. Miller has revealed in his extraordinary book, *Hidden Hitchcock*. While the prosecutor is importuning the witness, saying, "Mrs. James, will you look around the courtroom and tell us if you see the man who was in your office on July 9 in this courtroom," and Mrs. James says, "I do," poor Mrs. James, who is still terrified, is made to come down from the witness stand and put her hand on Manny's left shoulder. Miller, a Professor of English at Berkeley who has made what he calls "too-close viewing" of Hitchcock films one of his specialties, which he can do in this age that has made starting and stopping DVDs and BluRays on a computer easy, testifies, as if still answering the prosecutor's question too, "I did see; and unlike Mrs. James, I didn't just see Manny; I also saw, peeping behind Manny's right shoulder like a wary rabbit from its hole, the face of Alfred Hitchcock" (figure 3.26; 1:29:29–30). Professor Miller also tells us that the head of Hitchcock disappears and then reappears a few frames later. I have followed Miller's time indications on the BluRay player on my own computer, and I have indeed seen Hitchcock appear and disappear twice in the back of the courtroom in the midst of Manny's ordeal. Given Hitchcock's supreme role in the cinematic universe he creates, this really is the face of God, in a Manichean universe where even he cannot stop the evil of unfounded accusation from doing its damage,

but can let us know he sees it, and witness what we do with the awful opportunity this evil has provided us to do something about it. This feels to me in close accord with Jung's view. Murray Stein has written:

> As opposed to a theorist who would root the reality of good and evil in metaphysical nature itself and then rely upon inspiration, intuition, or revelation to decide upon what is actually good and what is evil, Jung puts forward a theory that places the burden for making this judgment squarely upon ego-consciousness itself (p.10).

At this point in *The Wrong Man,* Manny is being wrongly (and projectively) identified by Ann James. Hitchcock demonstrates what Jason Isralowitz calls the "casual indifference" with which the prosecutors of Manny exercise their power to nail Manny in this way. Even as Manny's lawyer, Mr. O'Connor is able through cross examination to reveal "that Ann James' husband was in Manny's lineup" Hitchcock, showing Manny's point of view, "cuts to a close-up of the prosecutor laughing" (Isralowitz, p.191). In fact, we see the prosecutor's face wrinkle in a mean crude laugh that almost certainly connotes that he has just been told a very dirty joke. Everyone else in the courtroom looks distracted or bored. Obviously, no one believes the trial is more than a formality because Manny is obviously guilty, and they feel they don't need to weigh the evidence further. Watching this sequence as filmed with Hitchcock's command of telling minor characters acting out something like the cardinal sin *accidia* of the Medieval Catholic Church has much the same effect as surveying a Hieronymus Bosch painting: we know we are in hell.

    5) A second woman who was at work in the insurance office when it was robbed testifies.

    6) Miss Willis, another employee of the insurance office who witnessed the robbery, testifies.

    7) Miss Willis is cross-examined by the defense attorney, who questions her about the police lineup in which she identified Manny as the robber. He asks her various detailed questions about the lineup in an effort to show the jurors that she is actually not a very observant person, doesn't remember clearly what she has seen, and therefore cannot be trusted to have correctly identified the robber.

8) A male juror interrupts the cross examination to ask the judge if the jury really has to sit and listen to this line of questioning. The implication is that the juror has already decided that Manny is guilty and therefore does not have an open mind to hear the defense's case when it will be made.

9) The defense attorney asks for counsel to approach the bench.

10) The judge declares a mistrial.

11) The defense attorney, Mr. O'Connor, explains to Manny that it was necessary to ask for a declaration of mistrial and that it means now that the entire trial process including scheduling dates and selecting new jurors must start all over. We see that although Manny feels he must steel himself to go through the whole thing again, he is not sure he has the heart for it.

12) Cut to a scene of Manny talking with his mother as she does some sewing. He complains about having to endure the restarting of the court case, blaming himself for everything that has gone wrong in his life. His mother, Mama Balestrero (played very badly by Esther Minicotti) asks if he has prayed. He says he has prayed for help; she says he must pray for strength. Her ethnicity seems to be in the shadow of her highly gentrified, cultured Italian American son played by the always understated Henry Fonda, and the functions of consciousness she exhibits, introverted intuition and extraverted thinking, are shadow functions from the standpoint of his extraverted feeling and introverted sensation. Though Manny himself has been wearing a crucifix to court, the picture of Jesus that is on his mother's wall, a savior with his sacred heart displayed, would have looked rather kitsch to Manny's wife, who as played by Vera Miles, looks like a Lutheran of Northern European ancestry, one of Hitchcock's cool blondes trained to remain austere and unemotional, and in this movie conscience-stricken that her need for money to pay for dentistry had led to this crisis. Manny at first rejects his mother's call to ask God for Fortitude, as if she had floated a cardinal virtue from an old Tarot deck for him to try to live by. He dismisses that as superstition and says that what he really needs is luck—for the real robber to be found and charged.

13) Manny dresses to go to work. And then, he does show that his mother's advice has somehow reached him from the shadow in which he and Hitchcock had placed it, folk religious superstition. Seeing the picture of Jesus on the wall, he prays.

14) As he prays, we see behind his face the face of another man, a man in a dark trench coat who is about Manny's size but whose features are sharper and more feral. The man is walking down a commercial street at nightfall. He has a lean, hungry look. The man's face merges with Manny's and takes its place so that Manny's image fades away leaving only the lean man.

15) The lean man goes into a delicatessen and asks the proprietress for a pound of ham. No one else is in the store. The man comes around the edge of the counter and holding what he says is a gun in his coat pocket tells her to give him the money from the cash drawer. The woman is holding a knife that she would use to cut the ham. She stamps her foot twice on the floor, which the robber takes to be merely an expression of her anger.

16) Her husband, signaled by her stamping on the floor, comes quietly into the store and, unseen by the robber, grabs him from behind and overpowers him. The woman calls the police.

17) A police car with the robber inside pulls up at the police station. The officers take the man inside to book him.

18) In the police station hallway, they pass the police lieutenant who was in charge of the insurance robbery case. The lieutenant has his overcoat on and seems to be leaving work for the day.

19) The lieutenant comes out onto the darkened street but hesitates, presumably realizing the physical similarity to Manny of the man he has just seen the officers bring in. He turns around and goes back into the station. Those, like me, who notice the types of consciousness when they are accurately dramatized in films, will not fail to recognize this example of verification, the hallmark of the function Jung called "introverted sensation." It also happens to be the type I feel characterizes Hitchcock the director, whose close attention to specific detail throughout the film enables him to record the many examples of bad introverted sensation that have led the justice system to ignore before now the evidence that Manny was probably not the robber of the insurance office. In these ways Hitchcock has inserted himself into the near documentary that can seem so boring to so many viewers that this film has not been recognized as the cinematic masterpiece it is. But now that the "right" man to be tried for the robbery of the insurance office has finally been recognized, Hitchcock helps us to remember how often the film has documented pseudo-evidence. We see once more two women who testified wrongly against

Manny come out from a second line-up, not yet fully ready to give up their trust in their ability to see. Their shadow extraverted sensation is still linked to pride, and they are ashamed to find Manny watching them exit the police station (and the film). If God is in the details, so is the Devil, and thus perception of reality itself requires that distortions be dissolved in accurate perception if any kind of healing truth is to be achieved.

This Manichean truth is lost on Manny, however, who has little sympathy for what the right man will now be put through by the very same justice system. All Manny knows, in Hitchcock's film as in Christopher Emmanuel Balestrero's account, is that he has prayed, and his prayers were answered. When he visits her later in a psychiatric hospital, Manny's wife, still suffering from a post-traumatic major depression can only say to him, "That's fine for you."

So, all I would claim for the section I showed from of this complex film, we see a man's first important step in encountering the shadow as something he has to deal with on his own. Hitchcock's cinematic rendering of the psychological process involved suggests that the shadow that up to now has merely been projected onto him, making him the wrong man to carry it, is finally allowed entry into Manny's religious conception of himself, where its evil can be held and transformed. Notice, though, that Manny does not triumph by heroically vanquishing evil, but by praying for the strength to endure it. Only then is he strong enough to bring the evil close enough into himself to transform the situation for him that it has created. In his "Commentary on *The Secret of the Golden Flower*," Jung (again famously) wrote:

> Now and then it happened in my practice that a patient grew beyond himself because of unknown potentialities, and this became an experience of prime importance to me. In the meantime, I had learned that all the greatest and most important problems of life are fundamentally insoluble. They must be so, for they express the necessary polarity inherent in every self-regulating system. They can never be solved, but only outgrown. (1967a, p. 15)

In Hitchcock's film, however, there is a solution of sorts—a slow dissolve of Manny's image as the man wrongfully carrying a shadow projection into the face of the man who is the actual criminal, and this is a sort of solution, rather like the prophet Mani's idea that evil needs to be diluted. Murray Stein has written in his introduction to his edited collection aptly titled *Jung on Evil* that from the Jungian standpoint, "At bottom, good and evil must be united, both derivative from a single source and ultimately reconciled in and by that source." To be able to do this requires the virtue Manny's mother begs him to pray for, strength. It is growth through endurance, and a healthy respect for the shadow is what we see enacted both in Jung's dream, when he fights the shadow figure, not to kill it but only to subdue it, and when he later puts his arm around the recalcitrant prince and forces him, with "paternal kindness and patience" to read the book that Jung has written, and when Manny imitates the Passion of Christ in having to live with the projection he cannot for a time get off him, until his strength unties him enough with his lookalike through prayer and the synchronicity that attends upon the integrity of that prayer dissolves his guilt in the realization by everyone that another man who looks like him has committed the crimes. The dissolving of the projection upon Manny that Hitchcock achieves cinematically as the real perpetrator of the series of robberies comes into view for us, replacing Manny's lost face with his own, is very like a Manichean dilution of evil by good when the latter is allowed to get close enough to it. This idea is echoed by Jung's idea of integrating the repressed shadow into the ego, in the recognition that both are powers that pertain to what it is to be ethically human. This co-sovereignty of these powers in the shaping of an ethical sense, which can do what God alone cannot, would seem to be the message of Manichean scripture, to the degree we can still make out its intended meaning (Baker-Brian, 2011). But for Jung it also is the meaning of our consciousness, and thus also of our types of consciousness, which as four ego-syntonic functions are inevitably shadowed by a twin quartet, because any function we use with the attitude we prefer, that is, in an extraverted or an introverted way, will be shadowed by the same function used with the opposite attitude.

Since we have four functions each of which can be used with either an extraverted or an introverted attitude, that means we have eight function-attitudes of consciousness. There is considerable evidence that the four function attitudes Jung preferred were superior introverted intuition, auxiliary extraverted thinking, tertiary introverted feeling, and inferior extraverted sensation (Beebe, 2017, pp. 167-180 & 165-167). This means Jung's ego would have an antagonistic relationship to the Arab prince, who most probably used each of the functions with an opposite attitude from Jung with respect to introversion and extraversion. The same could be said for Manny and the man who actually committed the crimes. Oppositions like these were coin of the realm for the Manicheans, and they were sure that God has left it to us to deal with this way ego and shadow are doomed to coincide and collide. For just that reason, Jung might have said, for he certainly implies it in *Psychological Types,* we have been given eight functions of consciousness and not just four, so that we can learn from the battle of ego and shadow. As we have seen with the uncanny positioning of Hitchcock in the courtroom as the God who both watches the banality and as Jesus responds to the prayer to endure the coincidence of shadow and ego that can bedevil our lives, he is also the one who rewards Manny's integrity in allowing himself to pray for strength with the synchronicity that will bring ego and shadow close enough together that the latter can be dissolved in the former.

When Stein heard me discuss this dream in Xian, he thought it likely the book that Jung shared with the Arab Prince was the Red Book, in which of course there was calligraphic script. But as I said then, and I say now with the permission a Festschrift gives to honor a respected colleague who is also one of his longest-time professional friends by restating his own opinion on a matter in which they have previously disagreed, I think the book represents Jung's in some ways Manichean effort to include the shadow in his account of how consciousness is constructed. That was surely one of the aims of *Psychological Types*, and thus in his 1920 dream to speak cordially to a shadow figure in the well-lit octagonal room is to suggest the power of an eight function-attitude model of consciousness to establish a container for the type problem we all hold within (Jung, 1971).

From this perspective, shadow consciousness, when viewed with neighborliness inside, can become a twin, a needed compensation to our typically four-square mindsets, which we may have mistaken for wholeness. That means, we not only have the chance to make peace with darkness, we can get over being the wrong men and women we are apt to become when we do not know how to have the dialogue with our shadow. The latter is not just an encounter that serves the completion of consciousness. The integrity that results will allow synchronicities to emerge, and it is those that will make at least some deliverance from evil possible. What else we can do with that deliverance is more human work, which we do not see in the Hitchcock film, but still needs to be achieved before we can believe that the story of Manny has truly a happy ending.

John Beebe, past president of the C.G. Jung Institute of San Francisco, is the author of *Energies and Patterns in Psychological Type: The reservoir of consciousness* and also of *Integrity in Depth.* He is co-author, with Virginia Apperson, of *The Presence of the Feminine in Film,* and co-editor, with Ernst Falzeder, of *The Question of Psychological Types: The Correspondence of C.G. Jung and Hans Schmid-Guisan.* He founded the quarterly publication that is now called Jung Journal: Culture & Psyche and was the first American co-editor of the Journal of Analytical Psychology. John has spearheaded a Jungian typological approach to the analysis of film. In his over 200 publications, he has often used type and archetype to explore developments in the cultural and political unconscious. His eight-function, eight-archetype model, which Murray Stein was the first editor to encourage John to present to an audience of Jungian analysts and candidates, is now widely studied and applied.

References

Arendt, H. (1963). *Eichmann in Jerusalem: A Report on the Banality of Evil*. Viking.

Baker-Brian, N. J. (2011). *Manicheism: An Ancient Faith Rediscovered*. T&T Clark International.

Beebe, J. (2017). *Energies and Patterns in Psychological Type: The Reservoir of Consciousness*. Routledge.

Hitchcock, A. (1956). *The Wrong Man*. Warners Home Video (Blu-Ray).

Isralowitz, J. (2023). *Nothing to Fear: Alfred Hitchcock and the Wrong Men*. Fayetteville Mafia Press.

Jung, C.G. (1967a). Commentary on "The Secret of the Golden Flower." In *Alchemical Studies,* R.F.C. Hull (trans). *The Collected Works of C.G. Jung: Vol. 13.* pp. 1-56.

Jung, C.G. (1967b). The Philosophical Tree. In *Alchemical Studies,* R.F.C. Hull (trans), *The Collected Works of C.G. Jung: Vol 13.* Princeton University Press, pp. 251-350.

Jung, C.G. (1971). A Psychological Theory of Types (1931). In *Psychological Types*, R.F.C. Hull & H.G. Baynes, vol. 8, Princeton University Press, pp. 524-541.

Jung, C.G. (1973). *Letters*, vol. 1. Selected and Edited by Gerhard Adler in collaboration with Aniela Jaffe, R. F. C. Hull (trans.) Princeton University Press.

Jung, C.G. (1995). *Memories, Dreams, Reflections,* recorded and edited by Aniela Jaffe, Richard and Clara Winston (trans.) Fontana Press (paper).

Miller, D. A. (2016). *Hidden Hitchcock.* University of Chicago Press.

Posner, M. (2023). What Was the Mishkan (Tabernacle)? A Brief Overview of the Tabernacle of Moses. www.chabad.org/parshah/article_cdo/ aid/2133493/jewish/What-Was-the-Mishkan-Tabernacle.htm (consulted online 3.1.23).

Stein, M. (1995). Editors Introduction to *Jung on Evil*. Princeton University Press, pp. 1-24.

Wilhelm, R. (1967). *The I Ching or Book of Changes.* German Translation rendered into English by Cary. F. Baynes. Princeton University Press.

"Love…can unite opposites and reverse the paradox": The Individuation Process of the Medieval Mystic Hadewijch

Maria Grazia Calzà

Dr. Stein was one of my favorite lecturers, my trusted supervisor and cartographer of the soul, and, eventually, my encouraging thesis advisor, my Doktorvater, as the Germans say. In short: an educator, who thanks to his broad psychological knowledge, brilliant mind, depth of soul and, last but not least, his heart-full generosity was able to "draw out" (Lat. ex-ducere) of me what was within, and at the same time to support it over my years of training and beyond. For these gifts and more, I will forever carry a deep and enduring gratitude to him.

As soon as a more honest and more complete consciousness beyond the collective level has been established, man is no more an end in himself, but becomes an instrument of God, and this is *really* so.
—C.G. Jung, *Letter to Father V. White* (1955)

Vivere è un continuo cammino di trasformazione, è questo il segno dell'uomo.
—S. Tamaro, *Ogni angelo è tremendo*

In the chapter "Roads of Life" in *Out of Africa*, Karen Blixen tells us that as a child, she was often told a story about a man who lived near a pond.

As the storyteller spoke, he illustrated the story by drawing a sequence of lines. The story—always told in the same way, always with the same words—runs like this: One night a man who lives in a round house with a round window and a little triangular garden, is awakened by a terrible noise coming from the pond filled with fish. So, he leaves the house and rushes down the road to the pond in order to find the cause. It is dark. The man first walks to the south. Here, he stumbles over a big stone, falls down into a ditch, gets up, and stumbles again on another stone and falls again into another ditch and gets up again. Then, realizing that he has been mistaken, he decides to walk back to the north and then, hearing the same noise coming from another direction, again back to the south. There, he trips again over a stone, falls again into a ditch, and so on. At the end, when he finally realizes that the noise is coming from a big leak in the dam, he succeeds in repairing the hole and then goes back to bed. In the morning, when the man looks out of his little round window, he recognizes in the set of footprints he left on the soil the previous night, the outline of a stork.

The protagonist of this story encounters all the obstacles on his way with great determination, with "faith." Blixen remarks:

> [The man of the story] must have wondered what was the idea of all his trials: he could not know that it was a stork. But through them all he kept his purpose in view: nothing made him turn round and go home; he finished his course, he kept his faith. That man had his reward. In the morning he saw a stork. He must have laughed out loud then (1954, p. 215)

And then, the author concludes her musing wondering about herself:

> The tight place, the dark pit in which I am now lying, of what bird is it the talon? When the design of my life is completed, shall I, shall other people see a stork? (p. 215)

The significance of this beautiful and mysterious story lies in the end result, in the *stork* that appeared only at sunrise. Does the course of a life, as Blixen wonders, reveal itself as meaningful design? Will we—or others on our behalf—eventually see a bird drawn with the markings of our singular journey? "The figural unity of the design, the unifying meaning of the story," suggests philosopher Cavarero, "can only be posed, by the one who lives it, in the form of a question. Or perhaps in the form of a desire" (2000, p. 1). Perhaps only questions and desires are available to us as we stumble along in pursuit of a mysterious call.

It is no accident that the Danish author chose a stork as the figural pattern of her story. The stork is an ancient symbol of new birth and life and has other symbolic connections with the development of the human individual. As a wading bird, it has an intimate relationship with those fertile, womb-like wetland habitats (swamps, marshes, bogs, ponds, and rivers) where, according to ancient belief, not-yet-born children float within their dark waters, waiting to be born. Moreover, the stork's uncanny ability to navigate its precise route during its long annual migrations has given rise to the idea that it has a sort of divine orientation to which it holds true. This is why since ancient times the stork was held to be the *pia avis* (devout bird) or the *pietatis cultrix* (devout worshiper), as Roman writer Petronius († 66 B.C.) called it. Since the stork obeys its own laws without ego judgement, it can therefore be understood as a symbol of functioning in accordance with a deep inner guidance that is beyond the conscious mind and control (von Franz, 1995, pp. 53-54; Jung, CW 13, para. 417; Caspari, 2003, 259).

While the stork was an allegory of piety in ancient Rome, in the Christian tradition this "religious" bird was associated with Christ himself because it hunts and eats snakes, often a symbol of evil. C.G. Jung writes as follows: "Just as the snake or dragon is the chthonic numen of the tree, so the stork is its spiritual principle and thus a symbol of the Anthropos." (CW 13, para. 417). Yet, there is another reason why this migratory bird was associated with the figure of Christ: in Europe, its punctual return from its migration made it a genuine herald of new life after the long, dark winter, and, consequently, an apt symbol of Christ's birth as divine child and re-birth as resurrected savior.

The stork points to a person's singularity, *who* and not *what* a person truly is, to her or his unique life story that can be neither presaged nor planned. A story that is temporal and fragile. The image of the stork, with its unerring migratory capacity, that appeared after that night of work, was not only unintentional but also ephemeral. "It is the fleeting mark of a unity that is only glimpsed" (Cavarero, p. 3)—the meaningful or, better, meaning-creating or meaning-giving (the Ger. *sinngebend*) gift, Blixen's reward, of a moment. Only at the end of our lives we, or others for us, might clearly distinguish to which winged animal its contours belong and, after the completion of our existence's course, eventually see the *pia avis*.

The story Blixen tells us is the literary illustration of what C.G. Jung would have described as an *individuation process*; a mysterious path, a personal process involving a lifelong development of personality. And although it is unique to each person, the sequence of this individual developmental process has common features, including obstacles, back-tracking, delays, and dangers. Each of us, in her or his own way, experiences what the man in the story experienced; that is, to be carried along by an inexplicable and powerful current without a notion of where it might lead: "[T]he goal of psychic development *is* the Self," says Jung (1995) in his *Memories, Dreams, Reflections*; and continues, "[t]here is no linear evolution; there is only a circumambulation of the Self" (p. 222).

Often, during this *circum-ambulating process*, we wonder what is the point of all these twists and turns or "struggles," "why we undertake this wearing and often fearsome journey…why we strain and strive and seek," as analyst June Singer (1972) in her *Boundaries of the Soul* beautifully affirms, "to know more, when knowing more is only to open the gates to deeper mysteries" (p. 281). Nevertheless, those of us who are called are compelled to persevere. And if we are fortunate, we keep our faith like the puzzled man in the story or the stork in its mysteriously guided navigation. So, "robbed by our fancied freedom of will," as Jung would say, we continue on our way moved by something that keeps its "intentionality"— our so-called "self-realization" or, better: the *realization of the Self.*

In his *Psychological Approach to the Trinity*, C.G. Jung argues that:

> Individuation is a heroic and often tragic task, the most difficult of all, it involves suffering a passion of the ego: the ordinary empirical man we once were, is burdened with the fate of losing himself in a greater dimension and being robbed of his fancied freedom of will. He suffers, so to speak, from the violence done to him by the Self. (CW 11, para. 233)

Ultimately, our life "ends with the defeat of the ego despite the many so-called victories it may have won during its time." Regardless of "how long or short our personal life may be, that 'identity' so bravely achieved by the ego" is replaced by "the anonymity and greater dimension of the unconscious" (Singer, p. 281). It is the mysterious "non-ego" or, what Esther Harding called the "not-I," the Self, that wins the final battle. Theologically speaking, we could say with *Matthew* 16:24-26:

> Anyone who wishes to follow me must deny himself, take up his cross, and follow me. For whoever wishes to save his life will lose it, but whoever loses his life for my sake will find it. What will it profit a man if he gains the whole world and forfeits his very life?

We might like to reassure Blixen that yes, we are able to see the shape of a winged bird formed by the gradual unfolding of her life; that she did take up her own "cross" and, in so doing, came to accept and consciously realize her own particular pattern of wholeness. However, the main subject of my essay is not the destiny of this imaginative writer and the "figural unity" of her life. It focuses on another writer from the North whose life also formed a *pia avis*: Hadewijch of Antwerp, a mystic woman who lived in the 13th century Low Countries.

In contrast to Blixen, the life of whom is very well documented through both autobiographical writings and several biographies, Hadewijch remains a mystery—not only for the "paradoxes and perplexity of her writings," as medievalist McGinn points out, but also, and especially, for her life story. The historical figure is veiled in mystery that medievalists still are unable to lift despite their best historiographical endeavors. It is worth emphasizing that the fact that we know so little about her not only makes our attempt to delineate Hadewijch's process of individuation complicated, but also may more easily trigger our projections and fantasies—projections and fantasies that modern people carry when we turn toward the past in the light of much post-cartesian thought, especially if this past is a "Dark Age," as several modern historians still call the Middle Ages.

But let us start with what we do know about this fascinating medieval mystic. Hadewijch lived in the first half of the 13th century, probably in the vicinity of Antwerp, Belgium. We do not know where and when she was born or died (approximately 1240) nor about her family or social origin. We do not even know about her education, nor do we have clear documentation of it. Yet, her many allusions to the "School of Love" (p. 164, 171, 345) in her poems lead us to suppose that she likely attended school. Her education, wherever she acquired it, is reflected in her writings: the familiarity with Latin, with the liberal arts (rhetoric, dialectic, astronomy, music, etc.), with the rules of letter writing, the so-called *ars dictaminis*, and of versification. She knew the works of great theologians—like St. Augustine, Isidor of Seville, the Victorines, to mention only a few. And that she was familiar with French chivalry and courtly love and showed a certain refinement of character has brought scholars to the conclusion that she must have belonged to the higher class.

Hadewijch was a Beguine and probably founded the *beguinage* of Antwerp or functioned as its head and as spiritual guide in her community. In the course of time, it seems that she was criticized for her views, perhaps forced out of her community, and separated from those women with whom she lived and for whom she cared. Did she then experience a life wandering through the countryside in punishment? Or was she imprisoned after having been denounced to the Inquisition? These questions remain unanswered. It seems, however, that some of her sister Beguines secretly engaged in undermining her position—perhaps her ascendancy, mystical gifts and knowledge (based on personal inner experiences) aroused envy, jealousy and fear in them.

In his essay, *Adaptation, Individuation, Collectivity*, Jung stresses how few people are really capable of individuating since this difficult and painful process requests the sacrifice of personal conformity to the collective. In his view, individuation and a life submitted or adapted to the collective values and demands are two divergent destinies and are related to one another by guilt—a "tragic guilt," he explains. In order to expiate one's absence from the collective, this "desertion" or guilt, the individual is called to create something of worth, new values, for the benefit of society. "[O]nly so long as substitute values are produced," Jung emphasizes, *is* individuation possible. Clearly, the withdrawal from society causes the individual an intense solitude and isolation "in which one experiences the contempt of the collective" (CW 18, para. 1095). Paradoxically, this alone will allow for the creation of a new set of values that possesses a collective validity.

In my opinion, Jung's understanding captures perfectly the modern psychological description of what Hadewijch experienced and achieved: "What happens to me," she emphasizes in a letter to a young Beguine, "whether I am wandering in the country or put in prison—however it turns out, it is the work of Love [*read*: the Self]" (Letter 29, p. 114).

In solitude and isolation and despite the contempt of her community, the deep need to continue to teach, encourage and share with her Beguines the "creation of a new set of values" seems to have led to her writings. They include: 31 letters *(Brieven)*, 14 descriptions of visions *(Visioenen)*, 45 poems in stanzaic form *(Strofische Gedichten)*, and 16 to 29 poems in mixed form *(Mengeldichten)*.

In the context of the variety of genres through which she expressed her deep spiritual message, it is worth mentioning that like all the mystic women of the Late Middle Ages, Hadewijch wrote in her *mother* tongue (in her case, the Medieval Dutch), the language considered to be opposed to Latin, the language of the Church, of authority, the *father* tongue. And why? First, because the nearly inexplicable is best described in one's mother tongue rather than in a formally or later learned language. But also because the direct, sensory, visceral experience of the divine as incarnated Love (Christ himself) that Hadewijch and other medieval mystic women lived out, may have required the immediacy and potency of a language that is directly learned from the mother. A language from the so-called "first relationship," from the mother and her life-giving and nourishing body with its familiar scent, touch, expression, and gesture; a tongue that hovers within the need to suck, to babble, coo, and cry, and evolves into the need and capacity to speak. In sharp contrast to Latin, referred to as *grammar* because of its reliance on rules and structure, to logic *(Logos)*, the "new" language was able to express the symbolic and daily life, the poetic *(Eros)*, and thus able to challenge—and probably this was also the intention of these women—the dominant way of thinking and speaking of the Church. Through the use of the vernacular, Hadewijch and her like-minded women writers foreshadowed, decades in advance, Dante's decision to choose his own mother tongue *(lingua naturalis)* over Latin *(lingua articifialis)* when writing the *Divine Comedy* (1304-1321). In his linguistic essay *De vulgari eloquentia* (Lib. I, Cap. I, 1-3), he explains that speaking about matters of the heart and God requires the language which the infant acquires by imitating her or his mother or wet nurse; the language learned through suckling, maternal embraces, caring love—the language, according to Dante, of "sì" (*"sic,"* i.e. "thus it is," or "yes").[1]

---

[1] The famous pianist Hélène Grimaud affirmed during an interview: "My first memory of music is my mother's voice. That was the first incarnation of music in my environment—my mother's voice."

As I mentioned before, Hadewijch was a Beguine. Who were these Beguines and what does it mean to have belonged to that spiritual Christo-centric women movement that began to unfurl in the Low Countries around the end of the 12th century?

In the age of chivalry, women were not only able to reach new positions by personifying the *Anima*-ideal of a knight or the hidden dream of a troubadour but were also able to discover new ways of giving form to their unique, feminine spirituality and of defining *ex novo* a precise role within the Church. Having been fundamentally misunderstood by the ecclesiastical world, women began leaving their families and their convents to live lives of poverty, to become recluses in their own homes, hermits in the woods or mystics in the world. The Beguines who slowly appeared against the backdrop of the Flemish landscape were just one expression—though, in my opinion, the most creative—of this emerging religious life adopted by medieval women in northern Europe. This was a phenomenon of great significance, considered by scholars to be the earliest movement ever created by women for women and in which women alone took leadership.

In this context, I want to stress that during the Middle Ages the concept of a person as an object of experience formed an unbreakable bond with the realm of the sacred. This was particularly true for women, since within the religious dimension, the devotion to Christ represented the only possible path through which they could savor a certain freedom and autonomy, and the opportunity to pursue both self-awareness and spiritual maturity. In modern terms: a path upon which one's individuation process might unfold.

The primary characteristic of the Beguines is what anthropologists call "liminality" (V. Turner) or historians of spirituality term "semi-religiosity" (H. Grundmann). The Beguines represented a paradox: an anomalous half-lay, half-religious vocation that positively demanded a crossover or "relation-*between*" mentality. They were, in fact, not nuns. They were neither within the strict medieval socio-religious hierarchy nor outside of it. They were neither celibate nor sexually active, neither married to an earthly man nor to Christ. Yet, at the same time, they were exactly all that.

The Beguines lived and worked in a twilight just as their settlements, the *Beguinages*, miniature heart-shaped courts or, as scholar Rosenwein (2006) proposes, "emotional communities," (p. 2) reflected geographically a "betwixt and between" (V. Turner). These settlements were enclosed by a wall, yet had a bridge that linked the urban, secular world to the religious one. And because they were "suspect hybrids," as historian Le Goff describes, they were often persecuted by the official male Church. As stated before, we do not know exactly what happened to Hadewijch; but we do know the tragic fate of Marguerite Porete (†1310), a French Beguine: she and her treatise, *The Mirrors of Simple Souls*, were both burnt at the stake.

Behind historical facts, events or changes, as Jung affirms in his essay, *The Psychological Foundations of Belief in Spirits,* living contents of the collective unconscious are at work, and such a change always means a change or modification of the psychological attitude. Jung asserts that "external circumstances often serve merely as occasions for a new attitude to life and the world, long prepared in the unconscious, to manifest." Such a change, thus, does not have its origins only in a collective conscious mind, a conscious attitude of a social group or a nation, but can be attributed also to those inner psychic contents which are activated by social, political and religious conditions,

> in the sense that all those factors which are suppressed by the prevailing view or attitude in the life of a society gradually accumulate in the collective unconscious and activate its contents (CW 8, para. 594)

In seeking to comprehend the emergence of the Beguines, their message, and their incarnational theology during this period, there are certain, special individuals, according to Jung, gifted with a deep intuition who are able to perceive that newness that has been long gestated in the unconscious, and to bring it into the world in a physical form—a "newness" that can spread rapidly, since a parallel new attitude lies in wait within the unconscious of many others, ready to be sparked by the proper catalyst. However, as Jung explains—for some of these people both long past and present—the spreading of the new and still unknown idea is met not only with a certain receptivity, but also with violent resistance. "New ideas," concludes Jung, "are not just the enemies of the old; they also appear as a rule in an extremely unacceptable form" (para. 594).

Often, the Beguines were lacking in advanced theological training (unlike Hadewijch), but the religious feeling that inspired them was such that they sought only to imitate Christ and, to use a Patristic ascetic formula, to "nudely follow the nude Christ" (*nud[ae] nudum Christum sequi*). In fact, the religious fervor of these women was so dominated by the incarnated Son of God as the Love-made-Flesh, that they gave up their worldly goods and wealth and sacrificed themselves in order to be united with Him.

And this is in fact what Hadewijch calls the "new commandment" that Christ gave to her, his beloved friend:

> If you wish to be like me in my Humanity…you shall desire to be poor, miserable, and despised by all men…If you wish to follow Love…it will become so alien to you to live among persons, and you will be so despised and so unhappy, that you will not know where to lodge for a single night, and all persons will fall away from you and forsake you, and no one will be willing to wander about with you in your distress and your weakness, whatever the state in which you find yourself. (Vision 1, p. 268)

Is it not true that an awareness of radical separateness is a prerequisite for individuation, as described before? Meaning, to embrace and so incarnate one's own particular "pattern of wholeness?" It is not easy at all "to live a life that is modelled on Christ's, but it is unspeakably harder," as Jung further asserts "to live one's own life, as truly as Christ lived his" (CW 11, para. 522).

This was the landscape within which Hadewijch moved, created, taught, and suffered: the soil, so to say, where she laid down her own footprints while "taking up her own cross," and, following Jesus' example, to accept and consciously realize her own particular pattern of wholeness.

Today, Jungian psychoanalysts recognize in this harrowing psychological and biological process of self-unfolding we call *individuation*, three main stages which mark an entire lifetime: the *first* stage, the containing/nurturance stage, refers to childhood, the *second*, the adapting/adjusting stage, to early and middle adulthood, and the *third*, the centering/integrating stage, to middle and late adulthood and old age. Although this three stage-model of the individual development is a useful tool for psychotherapy when applied with a certain caution, these three stages of growth cannot be understood as three clearly delineated phases that we leave behind when we enter the next one, but rather as stages that, as Stein (2020) writes, "shade gradually from one into the next, and features of each continue, but less in a predominant way, as a person makes the passage through a whole life" (p. 7).

Now, can we actually apply our concept of individuation process with its characteristic three-stage-movement to a medieval person? And, if not, what might an individuation process look like to a person living in medieval times?

Some historians assert that the High Middle Ages—the time period between 1000 and 1250, in which "our" Hadewijch lived—was a time in which the "discovery of the individual" (C. Morris) occurred. However, I want to emphasize that this period did not actually include modern concepts of the "individual" or the "personality." What medieval people believed they were *dis*-covering when they turned within to reflect was what they called "soul" (*anima*), or "self" (*seipsum*) or, even, the "inner man" (*homo interior*). Yet, this "soul" or "inner man" was not what we define as "individual." As medievalist Caroline Bynum (1982) clarifies:

> When we speak of "the individual," we mean not only an inner core, a self; we also mean a particular self, a self that is unique and unlike other selves. When we speak of "the development of the individual," we mean something open-ended. In contrast... the [High Middle Ages] regarded the discovery of *homo interior*, or *seipsum*, as the discovery within oneself of human nature made in the image of God—an *imago Dei* that is the same for all human beings. (p. 87)

In other words: when medieval writers or thinkers explored themselves, they did it with a precise purpose; namely, the development of the self toward God. Again in Bynum's words:

> One might say...that to the ancients the goal of development is the adult human being, for which one finds a model in the great works of the past; to the [High Middle Ages] the goal of development is likeness to God, built on the image of God found in "the inner man"; to [a person of this time period] the goal is the process itself. (p. 87)

In the light of this, we might say that the process of individuation of that medieval period could be considered a long process of returning to love of and likeness to God, a love and likeness in which the person did not dissolve into God but rather became God's special friend and partner, as Hadewijch concretely demonstrated. Moreover, unlike what occurs in our rather "narcissistic" modern time, this new concern with the "inner man" went hand in hand with a devotion to the process of belonging to groups and filling roles—to the "outer man."

A concrete example of this relates to our mystic woman: Hadewijch's psychological change or development unfolded in the open-closed frame of a *beguinage* and with an awareness of a deep commitment to belong to this religious women's group even after she was forced to leave it. We might even say that if she was concerned with her own inner landscape, it was also because of her concern for the "emotional community" of young Beguines, her own "School of Love," to which she belonged and within which she filled the role of spiritual guide. Moreover, this community with which she shared her spiritual intention—what Edward Edinger calls a "living mythology"—provided Hadewijch (and other mystic women as well) with a secure container or holding within which her utterly distinct, powerful, immediate encounter with the Divine (always understood as incarnated Love) could be experienced and integrated while managing the threat of overwhelming new contents emerging from the unconscious.

Now, there is another aspect that we have to consider before we move to Hadewijch's soul's journey. In the Middle Ages, our modern tripartite division of biological development in infancy, puberty, and adulthood did not exist. The individual went from childhood directly into adulthood—since puberty is an invention of modern times. A person was considered to be an adult at roughly 11 years old. Soon after her first menses, a woman, for instance, was ready to be given in marriage and to be the mother of numerous children, often dying during one of her many deliveries. In a time where death was constantly present through birth, miscarriage, famine, illness and plague, crusades and never-ending war, the average life expectancy was approximately 35 years. In the light of this, the inner development of an individual or, better, the "long process of returning to love of and likeness to God" of a "soul," as Hadewijch and her sisters testify in their writings and deeds, was unfolding within a very brief and "compressed" life.

We might briefly describe, as Singer does, the individuation process as that *movement* that leads an *individual* through the "confrontation with the opposites until a gradual integration of the personality comes about, a oneness with oneself, with one's world, and with the divine presence as it makes itself known to us" (p. 388). If we translate this definition into Hadewijch's words, it would sound like this: "to become what [God himself] wills you to be: that is your peace in the totality of your nature" (Letter 6, p. 60).

In a letter to a young Beguine, Hadewijch writes as follows:

> Since I was ten years old I have been so overwhelmed by intense love that I should have died, during the first two years when I began this, if God had not given me other forms of strength than people ordinarily receive, and if he had not renewed my nature with his own Being. For in this way he soon gave me reason, which was enlightened to some extent by many a beautiful disclosure; and I had from him many beautiful gifts, through which he let me feel his presence and revealed himself. And through all these tokens with which I met in the intimate exchange of love between him and me—for as it is the custom of friends between themselves to hide little and reveal much, what is most experienced is the close feeling of one another, when they relish, devour, drink, and swallow up each other—by these tokens that God, my Love, imparted to me in so many ways at the beginning of my life, he gave me such confidence in him that ever since that time it has usually been in my mind that no one loved him so intensely as I. (Letter 11, p. 69)

"So overwhelmed by intense love" at ten years old! In this letter, we can perceive the presence of an intentionality that was already at work in her as a child. This purposive force—the "goal-directedness of the psychic energy"—is referred by Hadewijch as *Love* (*Minne*). What was this intense Love and what did it request from Hadewijch while she was "individuating," or in her words, becoming what the divine Love wanted/ planned her to be?

The passing of time always leaves behind its traces. On a fresco, for instance, these many traces can be called aesthetic and structural deterioration, discoloration, signs of cracking or disintegration;

periodically, time swallows up even entire painted areas. In the restoration process, although all the marks and alterations from which the fresco suffered can be repaired, the loss of the painted parts, on the contrary, is allowed to remain, to be visible. It is the eye of the observer then that fills in the lost area by "re-creating"—in a sort of optical illusion—the whole fresco.

And this is exactly what happens when we observe the "fresco" of Hadewijch's life. Although the ravages of history have discolored, deteriorated and cracked her outer profile and have worn away the precise lines of her soul's journey, our intuition as inner eye can indeed recreate her specific features while we consider and contemplate her writings. And, in that moment, the entire woman is miraculously there. What she intended affirms itself forever in the fragments of her design; that is of becoming what God/Christ/incarnated Love himself wanted her to be in the totality of her own nature.

Given the frame of my essay, it would be impossible to share all the "fragments" that mark Hadewijch's path toward the realization of the Self/God, so I will focus on those I consider most eloquent and profound. I do so with the fervent hope that eventually these few glimpses might re-*veal* Hadewijch's union with herself, her world, and the Divinity as it made itself known to her; in short: her "wholeness."

On one Easter Sunday, Hadewijch received a vision. After having embraced her in her interior senses and taken her away in spirit, Christ, the Love-made-Flesh, told her as follows:

"Behold, ancient one, you have called and sought me, what and who I, Love, am, myriads of years before the birth of man... With regard to all things, know what I, Love, am in them! And when you fully bring me yourself, as pure humanity in myself, through all the ways of perfect Love, you shall have fruition of me as the Love who I am. Until that day, you should love what I, Love, am. And then you will be love, as I am Love. And you shall not live less than what I, Love, am...In my unity, you have received me and I have received you. Go forth, and live what I am; and return bringing me full divinity, and have fruition of me as who I am." Then I returned to myself and I understood all I have just said. (Vision 3, p. 272)

Jung (1989) too emphasized how vital it is, after an encounter with the divine, to return to the reality of the ordinary world, when in his seminar on *Nietzsche's Zarathustra* he argues as follows:

> It is...a dangerous thing to devote one's soul entirely to God, since we are living in the world. Do it and see where you land. You get out of the world and might as well be an eternal ghost—you don't live any longer and are not in time; you cannot devote yourself to the nowhere because you are here. So it is impossible for the human being to devote himself entirely to God. The mystics knew that the remoteness from God was an intrinsic part of the union with God. (Vol 2., part 1, p. 595)

Jung's "remoteness from God as part of the union with Him" represents the play of love, the *ludus amoris*, the coming and going of erotic mysticism. According to Hadewijch, what she called "the pure Divinity and the entire Nature of Love" resembles a "pouring out and keeping back." (Letter 17, p. 82). A diastolic and systolic movement in which mysteriously God remains,

> always untouched, and so deep to touch that he must be moved with compassion because so few men seek or long, with eagerness or by force of ardent works, to touch him even slightly in his mystery: who he is, and how he works with love. (Letter 3, p. 52)

In *this* ordinary world, in service and in love, Hadewijch did "break her body like bread" (Etty, 2002, p. 549) to share and disburse among humanity. To the dismay of her family, she distributed her riches among the poor and ill as living icons of the suffering Christ; in short: she did not live less than what Love itself is, namely, incarnated Love, as Love itself required from her. —Then, wrote Hadewijch,

> ...the naked
> circle can grow wide,
> enlarging,
> embracing all (ed. J. Hirschfield, 1994, p. 206)

What did Hadewijch actually intend to convey?

In deepening the meaning of this "naked circle," a transformative, all-embracing circular process, Hadewijch repeats the word *Love* (*Minne*) so often that when reading or hearing it our senses reel:

I greet what I love
With my heart's blood.
My senses wither
In the madness of Love...
O Love, were I but love,
And could I but love you, Love, with love!
O Love, for love's sake, grant that I,
Having become love, may know Love wholly as Love! (p. 350)

The endless spiraling, whirling, centripetal process that the experience of *Love* triggered, transformed Hadewijch into *love* itself—so that woman and "Lady Love" became one thing through each other, yet at the same time remained two different selves, as Hadewijch so often stressed in her writings. Hers is a process that might remind us of Gertrude Stein's poetic, "cubistic," and dizzying attempt to reach and so become the essence of the rose as symbol of love *par excellence*, of love's pain (the thorns) and joy (the perfumed petals), by repeating the noun "rose" over and over again: "Rose is a rose is a rose is a rose" (Ed. L. Bond, et al., 2011, p. 173).

In the same way, it seems that after Hadewijch's rapture has receded, a spiral of the same words curled inside themselves, creating a vortex and at the same time a path toward the infinite, divine Being. In his commentary to *The Secret of the Golden Flower*, Jung explains that this kind of *circumambulatio* or "circular course" represents not only a movement around a circle, but it marks off a *temenos* and, at the same moment, facilitates a focused concentration. When the *Love*-wheel begins to turn, so to say, *Love* itself is activated and begins to take over fully. In this manner, action is transmuted into non-action and all that is peripheral is drawn into the center. Movement, as Jung (Wilhelm, 1947) summarizes, means mastery. From a psychological point of view, according to Jung,

this circular course, would be the "turning in a circle about oneself," by means of which, apparently, all sides of the

personality become implicated [...] Thus the circular movement
has also the moral significance of activating all the light and dark
forces of the human nature, and with them, all the psychological
opposites of whatever kind they may be. That means nothing
else than self-knowledge by means of self-incubation. (p. 101)

Hadewijch's own process of self-incubation is reflected during one vision
within the "space of the perfect virtue." On a day after the Eucharist,
Hadewijch was guided by an angel through a wondrous garden where
various trees stood. The angel then accompanied her from tree to tree
and revealed to her their names and the quality that each name unveiled:
self-knowledge, humility, the gift of discernment, the knowledge of God,
Love—that *Love* that has to be felt, carried and incessantly transformed
into deeds, to be incarnated. Then, at the very end of this unusual
"itinerary" her beloved Friend, Christ himself, was waiting for her.

After He had spoken with her about the commandment and the
significance of Love and had fully recognized her in her nature and
longing, in her sacred calling and charitable works, in her value and in
her heart and soul's desire, since exactly all that was He himself, Christ
said to her:

you must go back quietly [now] and do what I have commanded
you. If you wish, take from this tree a leaf to symbolize the
knowledge of my will. And if you are saddened, take a rose
from its summit and one petal from the rose to symbolize Love.
And if you cannot bear it, take from the rose what is within it.
This signifies that I will grant you myself in fruition. You shall
always have knowledge of my will, and experience Love; and
at the expedient time you shall feel me in fruition. So my Father
did for me although I was his Son; he left me in affliction but
never abandoned me; I felt him in fruition, and I served those to
whom he had sent me. The heart that is found so full in the rose
symbolizes the fruition of Love through feeling. My beloved,
help all persons in their affliction impartially...Love will make
you capable of it. (Vision 1, p. 270)

It is characteristic of Hadewijch and women mystics in general to pick
the heart of the rose, the true and incorruptible Being, with the same

immediacy of feeling, without concepts or complex logical acts or associations.

As Hadewijch reminds us, as symbol of love, the rose has been preeminently associated with the Great Goddess and her sensuality, fertility, and unlimited compassion. It was sacred to Aphrodite (and therefore to Love, *Minne*, or, as she called it, Lady Love), its petals enveloped the Phrygian Cybele, its scent was the expression of the Virgin Mary's and other women's sanctity and their incorruptible bodies. Like the Lotus flower or Golden Flower in the Orient, the "mandalic" rose also symbolized the heart and the womb, the opening and closing vessel where transformation occurs. If for the (male) alchemists (Jung, CW 12, para. 388), the whole process of psychic transformation took place projecting onto the *prima materia* and *sub rosa* (under the rose), for Hadewijch as *prima materia* herself, the *opus* unfolded—soon after having passed through its petalled and perfumed folds and plunged into—not *sub rosa*, but rather *in rosa*, within the inner rose as the birthplace of herself and her *Self.*

In a letter to Pastor Bernet (1955), C.G Jung not only asserts that the course of individuation is a dialectical one, but also points out that the so-called "end" of this course is represented by the confrontation of the ego with what he calls "the emptiness of the centre." At this point the ego reaches its "limit of possible experience" and dissolves as reference-point of cognition. This dissolution, however, does not mean that the ego coincides with the center, but it comes only so close—it is at best "an endless approximation," as he writes—that it is able to keep its sensibility and to avoid falling into inflation. Jung (2020) further remarks then:

> The ego can merely affirm that something vitally important is happening to it. It may conjecture that it has come up against something greater, that it feels powerless against this greater power; that it can cognize nothing further; that in the course of the integration process it has become convinced of its finiteness, just as before it was compelled to take practical account of the existence of an ineluctable archetype. The ego has to acknowledge many gods before it attains the centre where no god helps it any longer against another god. (p. 259)

Thus, after having "approximately" reached this all-inclusive divine center, and so having been transformed into Love, Hadewijch's countenance and body became transparent: in her we can recognize a true capacity to realize, hold, and affect the miraculous, the invisible, the sacred in the ordinary—her likeness to God. In her, immanence and transcendence seemed to have been overcome: The Divine proved to be an Absolute that "occurred" in the world or coincided with it (Muraro, 2001, p. 151)— "Love...can unite opposites," says Hadewijch, "and reverse the paradox" (Stanzas 28, p. 206). Or, in Jung's words:

> As a result of the integration of conscious and unconscious, [man's] ego enters the "divine" realm, where it participates in "God's suffering" [*that is*: Hadewijch's "uniting the opposites"]. The cause of the suffering is in both cases the same, namely "incarnation," which on the human level appears as "individuation" [*that is*: her "reversing the paradox"] (CW 11, para. 233)

It is the circularity as wholeness, the enlarged "naked circle," that is celebrated by Hadewijch. Like an enclosure, a *temenos*, it marks the many points of convergence at which the soul and body, heaven and earth, beginning and end, and all the opposites meet and unite; a *temenos* that represents the place where paradox is reversed and the mystery of a union occurs, whether with a human or a divine "other."

The importance of the "other" is not only expressed by Hadewijch, but also by Jung while affirming that the Self cannot exist *per se* but only inasmuch as it is mirrored in the reflections created/produced by "others": "Only when the Self mirrors itself in so many mirrors, does it really exist," Jung writes. And he continues:

> You can never come [in fact] to your Self by building a meditation hut on top of Mount Everest; you will only be visited by your own ghosts and that is not individuation....The Self only exists inasmuch as you appear. Not that you are, but that you do the Self. The Self appears in your deeds and deeds always mean relationship. (1989, p. 795)

The understanding that Hadewijch (and with her other mystic women of that time) had of her individual self, mirrored the highest ideal of the Western spiritual culture in which she was reared, that is, Christ himself as incarnated God and as Love—yes, she was not Christ, but she "did" Christ. From this incarnated Love came the conviction and strength that as an individual she was carrying a responsibility not only for herself (the personal) but also for others and beyond that for the world known to her (the collective). In short: she *experienced* that wholeness or totality of Self, her "naked circle," which can only occur through a consciousness that enlarges to that of a greater consciousness. Or, again with Jung's words:

> When a summit of life is reached, when the bud unfolds and from the lesser the greater emerges, then, as Nietzsche says, "One becomes Two," and the greater figure, which one always was but which remained invisible, appears to the lesser personality with the force of a revelation. (CW 9ii, para. 217)

I want to conclude my essay with those encouraging words that Hadewijch wrote with the very ink of her being in a letter to her spiritual friends and, as I like to imagine, to us, women and men, who, through obstacles, back-tracking and delays, dangers and losses of faith and direction, are designing our own individual path in the hope to eventually see *"piae aves,"* religious birds:

> If you wish to follow your being in which God created you, you must in noble-mindedness fear no difficulty; and so in all hardihood and pride you must neglect nothing, but you should valiantly lay hold on the best part—I mean, the great totality of God—as your own good. (Letter 6, p. 60)

Yes, when Hadewijch reached the summit of her life, the great totality of God appeared with the force of a revelation. And now, as reflected in her words above, she inspires and challenges each of us to pursue the same, to be "hunters of epiphanies" (Tamaro, 2013, p. 236).

Maria Grazia Calzà grew up among the olive trees along Lake Garda, Italy. After a diploma in Art Restoration in Venice, she continued her studies at the Albert-Ludwigs-University of Freiburg, Germany receiving a MA and later a PhD in Medieval History, Theology, and Psychology. She has written a book on the role of the body in the mysticism of the first Beguine, Marie d'Oignies, published various articles (e.g. "The Thinking Heart: The individuation process in late medieval mystic women," in: Jung Journal. Culture & Psyche, 10:3, 3-14, 2016) and lectured internationally. In 2017 she graduated from the International School of Analytical Psychology (ISAP) in Zurich, Switzerland. Dr. Calzà works in Riva del Garda as a Philosophical Counselor and Jungian Psychoanalyst. She is a co-founder of the Embodied Jung Conference held in 2022 and is currently completing a book, entitled *The Feminine Taste of God: The Individuation Process of Medieval Women Mystics*.

References

Blixen, K. (1954). *Out of Africa*. Penguin Books.

Bond, L., et al. (ed.) (2011). *Literary Cubism–Geography and Plays. Selected Works of Gertrude Stein*. Traveling Press, 173ff.

Bynum, C. W. (1982). *Jesus as Mother. Studies in the Spirituality of the High Middle Ages*. University of California Press.

Caspari, E. (2003). *Animal Life, Myth and Dream*. Chiron Publications.

Cavarero, A. (2000). *Relating Narratives. Storytelling and Selfhood*. Routledge.

Etty, H. (2002). *The Letters and Diaries of Etty Hillesum. 1941-1943*. Complete and Unabridged. (Ed. By K.A. D. Smelik). W.B. Eerdmans Publishing Company.

Hadewijch. (1980). *The Complete Works*. Trans. by Mother Columba Hart, O.S.B. Malwah, Paulist.

Hirschfield, J. (1994). *Women in Praise of the Sacred. 43 Centuries of Spiritual Poetry by Women*. HarperCollins Press.

Jung, C. G. (1967). Commentary on "The secret of the golden flower" (R. F. C. Hull, Trans.). In H. Read et al. (Eds.), *The Collected Works of C. G. Jung: Vol. 13. Alchemical Studies* (pp. 1-56). Princeton University Press. (Original work published 1929) https://doi.org/10.1515/9781400850990.1

Jung, C.G. (1989). *Nietzsche's Zarathustra*. (Ed. by J.L. Jarrett). Routledge. 1989.

Jung, C.G. (1995). *Memories, Dreams, Reflections*. Fontana Press.

Jung, C.G. (2020). *Letters, Vol. 2*. (Ed. by G. Adler). Princeton University Press.

von Franz, M.-L. (1995). *Shadow and Evil in Fairy Tales*. Shambhala.

Muraro, L. (2001). *Le Amiche di Dio. Scritti di mistica femminile*. D'Auria.

Rosenwein, B. H. (2006). *Emotional Communities in the Early Middle Ages*. Cornell University Press.

Singer, J. (1972). *Boundaries of the Self. The Practice of Jung's Psychology*. Doubleday.

Stein, M. (2020). *Individuation. The Collected Writings, Vol. 1*. Chiron Publications.

Tamaro, S. (2013). *Ogni angelo è tremendo*. Bompiani.

Wilhelm, R. (1947). *The Secret of the Golden Flower*. Kegan Paul.

Schopenhauer: The Grand Disabuser

Ann Casement

Analyst, author, academic, administrator – Murray excels in every arena in which his positive attributes are abundantly on display. Above all, he exudes innate authority - a rare quality in the psychoanalytic profession - where he is an able spokesman for that international field.

Putting together this composition has been something of an alchemical process in distilling 6,000 words from the mass of material produced by the three extraordinarily creative men who are its central focus; in this instance, there is no question of transmuting lead into gold, nor, it is to be hoped, the opposite. This essay has been compiled as a tribute to my distinguished friend and colleague, Murray Stein, whose considerable talents have augmented *analytical psychology* over many decades. I recall a formal dinner we attended together in Yokohama, one of the world's beautiful cities, at which Murray and I compared our typologies in accordance with Jung's theory on that topic. If memory serves me right, we concluded that our strengths lay along the vertical axis of Jung's *typological* model; whereas our deficits were most definitely situated along the horizontal axis. A summary of this would be the following: our typological make-up shares in common what Jung calls *thinking* as our primary function with *feeling* as the secondary. Murray skilfully deployed this *duo* to help make him a great President of the International Association for Analytical Psychology (IAAP), giving a masterclass each-time he presided over one of the many meetings I attended as a member of the

IAAP's Executive Committee under his Chairmanship. That is where his *feeling* function proved to be an asset in enabling him to pick up the *feel* as well as the conceptual input of a meeting, which was then processed through his primary *thinking function* into *feedback*— the latter being a central pillar of *Information Theory* now in common usage—regarding what was under discussion to all the Committee members present at that meeting. An understanding of how to receive and give *feedback* is an essential component of a leadership role.

Preamble

Several of the themes that are explored in this essay have, over the years, provoked stimulating exchanges between Murray and myself as we are dedicated *Wagnerites* as well as *Jungian psychoanalysts*, albeit from somewhat different orientations of that worldwide mental health field. The focus of this piece is on the *chef-d'oeuvre* of the greatest of all composers, Richard Wagner's *The Ring of the Nibelung,* itself a panorama of good and evil; attempting to combine it with Jungian psychology. With regard to *The Ring*, I have had to take for granted in this essay that the reader has some working knowledge of the four operas which make up that *music drama* as there is no space to even attempt a summary of the whole of that magnificent work in this short piece.

The Ring itself is populated with what in Jungian psychology would be thought of as *archetypal* characters such as *Wotan*, embodying *the law of the father* in the earlier operas – *Rheingold* and *Valkurie* - who returns as the sadder, wiser *Wanderer* in the third opera, *Siegfried.* The latter figure represents the *archetypal hero* who eventually brings himself down as *heroes* are wont to do – *Jason* of the *Argonauts* being another prime example of that fate. The *music drama* depicts *Brünnhilde* as a supreme exemplar of what Jung calls the *puella*, or eternal youth, who evolves in the course of *The Ring* from being a "daddy's girl" to her father, *Wotan*, into becoming grounded as a mortal woman before her self-immolation in *Götterdämmerung*. This evolution and dramatic end come about as the result of her suffering at the hands of both her father, *Wotan,* and her lover, *Siegfried.* The heartbreakingly sublime aspect of *Brünnhilde* is her resigned acceptance of the *law of the father* condemning her to lose her divine status and to become mortal, and of the mutual betrayal by *Siegfried* of her and of him by her before both of their deaths. Just preceding that fateful climax, *Siegfried* redeems himself – *redemption* being one of the motifs that will run through this chapter. The notion of redemption is possibly the most important message taken by Wagner from Schopenhauer, who, in his turn, discovered it in the ancient religious philosophical texts of the Hindu *Vedas* and of *Buddhism*.

As Schopenhauer was one of the first Europeans to discover these *Eastern* religious/philosophical texts, and, as they came to be of the highest importance for his philosophy, it is necessary, at this point, to touch on his own writings on those texts. Schopenhauer's interest was particularly drawn to *Hinduism* and *Buddhism* as both have compassion for everything doomed to carry the burden of existence, and for their awareness of the deeply suffering nature of the world. Another vital notion he takes from these religious philosophical works is that the outer world is illusory or *maya* as it is expressed in the *Vedas*. Furthermore, this worldview incorporates the idea that each person is connected to everything that exists so that to harm anything or anyone is also self-harming. From his readings of the ancient *Buddhist* texts, Schopenhauer comes to the realization that dying is the moment of liberation from the one-sidedness of being an individual person as, according to him, that does not constitute the innermost core of our essence. To die willingly, to die gladly, to die joyfully, is the prerogative of one who is resigned, of one who surrenders and denies the *Will for Life*.

Schopenhauer's *Will* is, of course, derived from Kant's notion of the *numenon* and incorporates the *Will for Life* - Nature's blind thrust for reproduction somewhat akin to Darwin's notion of *fitness*.

For only he wishes *actually* and not merely *seemingly* to die, consequently he needs and demands no survival of his person. He willingly surrenders that existence with which we are familiar: what he gains in its stead is in our view *nothing*; for our existence, in relation to that is *nothing*. The Buddhist faith calls that existence *Nirvana* i.e. extinction. (Schopenhauer, 2011, para. 581)

Wagner felt that in espousing Schopenhauer's *"pessimism,"* which the latter yet again derives from Hinduism and Buddhism, he, Wagner, had emerged ten times stronger and the characters in his last great *music dramas* also espouse death willingly, *viz.,* Wotan, Brünnhilde, Siegfried, and, of course, *Tristan* from *Tristan and Isolde,* another great operatic work of Wagner's late *music dramas.*

Introduction

Some of life's most profound insights are to be found in the work of these three creative individuals of the 19th and 20th-centuries, who are at the very heart and mind of this piece. Each of them was only too aware of the *shadow* side of this world and each went on to explore it in depth through his work. The all-important link between Schopenhauer, Wagner, and Jung (not forgetting Freud) is their focus on what is going on *inside* people – not on their activities in the *phenomenal* world of outer reality. For his part, Schopenhauer derived this, as has already been alluded to, from his own immersion in the Eastern religious philosophies of the Hindu *Vedas* and those of Buddhism.

Furthermore, there are telling links between Wagner and Jung, which I tried to demonstrate in a presentation I gave at the Vienna IAAP Congress in August 2019, a revised version of which was reproduced in a book that was published in 2021 titled *Jung: An Introduction.* In that piece, I conjectured that Jung's significant dream recounted early in *The Red Book* was a vital milestone in his own psychological shift from identifying with Siegfried. The latter may be thought of as Jung's youthful heroic side as one sees him journeying on the quest for his *soul* through his reflections recorded in *The Red Book.* This writer's contention is that that is not dissimilar to the way *Wotan* develops in Wagner's portrayal of him in *The Ring.* It is generally agreed there are elements of Wagner in *Wotan*, which, presumably, is the reason why the emphasis in the evolving production of *The Ring* shifts from Siegfried as the central character to Wotan.

To return to Jung, the following is a recital of the significant dream of his mentioned above:

I was with a youth in the high mountains. It was before day-break, the Eastern sky was already light. Then Siegfried's horn resounded over the mountains with a jubilant sound.

We knew that our mortal enemy was coming. We were armed and lurked beside a narrow rocky path to murder him. Then we saw him coming high across the mountains on a chariot made of the bones of the dead. He drove boldly and magnificently over the steep rocks and arrived at the narrow path where we waited in hiding. As he came around the turn ahead of us, we fired at the same time and he fell slain. Thereupon I turned to flee, and a terrible rain swept down. But after this I went through a torment unto death and I felt certain that I must kill myself, if I could not solve the riddle of the murder of the hero. (1963, p.173)

The central figure in the dream, that of *Siegfried,* represented the following for Jung: "...the blond and blue-eyed German hero" who "had everything in himself that I treasured as the greater and more beautiful; he was my power, my boldness, my pride" (Shamdasani, 2009, p.163). Siegfried, who exemplified everything personified by the Germanic heroic ideal, who has also at times been compared to a storm trooper, now lies dead as the *self-ideal* for Jung. As already stated, Wagner, similarly, started *The Ring* with *Siegfried* as its central figure but that centrality gradually transferred to *Wotan*, the latter increasingly a portrait of Wagner himself. Nietzsche's insightful explanation for this shift in Wagner may be summarized as Wagner's shift to *pessimisms*—an evolution from *optimism* to *pessimism* applied equally to Jung as I shall set out to explore in both in what follows.

Another important *archetypal* figure in Jung's metapsychology is that of the *archetypal Earth Mother.* She bears an obvious resemblance to *Erda,* the personification of earthly wisdom in *The Ring,* who gave birth to the nine *Valkurie*, including Brünnhilde, and the three *Norns,* the weavers of fate. Jung's contribution to the importance of the mother in psychoanalysis represented a major transformation in that discipline from the overriding import of the *Oedipal* father in Freud's metapsychology. One sees this shift in, for example, Freud's ascribing "two mothers" to Leonardo da Vinci as the key factor in the artist's development in that eponymous paper. Jung's response to it was as follows: "*Leonardo* is wonderful...the transition to mythology grows out of this essay from inner necessity...it is the first essay of yours with whose inner development I felt perfectly in tune" (Maguire, ed., 1974). His response is unsurprising as this was Jung's own sphere of interest.

Schopenhauer has significant things to say about mother/son relations in his work – mostly positive which is surprising as his personal relationship to his mother was negative and always remained so. She was, however, an accomplished, intellectual woman through whom he met scholars who introduced him to Eastern philosophy and religion that became such a vital part of his *weltanschauugen*. In paragraphs 590-

602 of his masterpiece, he puts forth his hypothesis that sons inherit their intellects from their mothers and cites Goethe, Hume, and Kant as examples of this claim. Wagner, too, was greatly attached to his own mother which we see brought to life in the form of *Erda*, the Earth Mother in *The Ring*.

Jung also inherited his mother's intellectual curiosity as she was the one who told him: "You must read *Faust* one of these days" (Jung, 1963, p. 68). This turned out to be all-important in the development of the reality of *evil*, one of his most vital contributions to the world. "Here at last, I thought, is someone who takes the devil seriously and even concludes a blood pact with him – with the adversary who has the power to frustrate God's plan to make a perfect world" (p. 68). This all-important notion for both Schopenhauer and Jung will be elaborated further in this text.

Schopenhauer

The main thrust of this essay is an attempt to demonstrate how much the last of the great Kantian Idealist philosophers, Schopenhauer, was the *homme inspirateur* for both Wagner and Jung in what one may think of as their personal quests for the Grail. As an important aside, Schopenhauer was also the most formative influence on Freud's development of *psychoanalysis,* in particular his emphasis on the vital role sexual pleasure plays in life later to be taken up Freud in his first *topological theory*; and the *Nirvana Principle* (from the Buddhist *Nirvana* meaning *nothingness)* central to the all-important shift in Freud's thinking in his later *structural theory.* The Contemporary Freudian, Mark Solms, went so far as to acknowledge a contribution I was making at a conference on Freud's usage of the term *Nirvana* attributing it to Schopenhauer, when he added that one could say the whole of Freud's *oeuvre* was prefigured by Schopenhauer. To mention another vital link between them, they are both thought of as "pessimistic" thinkers. My view of that epithet is that it is put about by the unthinking generality who seek always to deny truth where it is glaringly obvious.

Another noteworthy resemblance between those two great thinkers is that they are among the most articulate writers and, in that way alone, an absolute delight to read. It is to be regretted that the same cannot be said about Wagner or Jung, and the reader is advised to focus on the *music dramas* of the former and the psychological insights of the latter instead of the style in which they write. If either had had to make his living through clarity of expression or elegance in writing, they would not have become the world-renowned figures they did.

Schopenhauer as religious thinker

Putting forward the idea that Schopenhauer's philosophy is one of the most important influences on the work of both Wagner and Jung is hardly an original thought but the fact that his influence was around the religious is perhaps a little more surprising— albeit religion without a god as he was a self-proclaimed atheist. There are as many references to Schopenhauer in Jung's *Collected Works* as there are to Kant although Jung is quoted as saying: "Kant is my philosopher" (Shamdasani, 2012, p.22). For Schopenhauer, as for Jung, Kant was the greatest thinker above all other modern philosophers leading them to dismiss Hegel as "bombastic"—even though the latter's dialectical thinking is unmistakably present in Jung's most important contribution—*psychological alchemy.* The ideas of one major philosopher per essay is quite enough for this short piece of work to carry but a brief word here about Hegel's dialectic, which is itself an ongoing *process* of *negation* not dissimilar to Jung's ongoing *alchemical* process of *distillation,* may suffice to show there is a *family resemblance* (Schopenhauer, 2008, Vol. I, para: 184) between the two.

I doubt anyone would argue the fact that Hegel's writing is about the most indigestible in the whole of philosophy, but his ideas on the *spirit* and its historical progress through a dialectical *process* to *absolute knowledge* are amongst the greatest contributions to *Western* thinking. When, as often happens, the well-known tripartite of *thesis/antithesis/ synthesis* is wrongly attributed to Hegel's dialectic - anyone hearing this is advised to run for their life according to the philosopher, Johannes Niederhauser. Hegel, himself, was dismissive of this tripartite model, which was in fact the creation of Fichte, also a well-known *Idealist* philosopher, who was another of Schopenhauer and Jung's pet hates whom they dismissed as a "repulsive charlatan" (Schopenhauer, Vol. II, 2011, para. 75). Jung also expresses his heartfelt dislike of Hegel in similar fashion through his intense reading of Schopenhauer—the latter at his most acerbic when referring to Hegel's philosophy. This is in part due to his corresponding adulation of Kant—feelings that were shared by Jung himself.

This well-known tripartite of *thesis/antithesis/synthesis* was dismissed by Hegel himself and attributed by him to Fichte in *The Phenomenology of Spirit*. I had a set-to with psychiatrist Ian McGilchrist when he was misattributing the above tripartite to Hegel, who became defensive when I took him up on this. As a result, anyone reading *The Master and His Emissary*, should be on their guard in relation to the philosophical and scientific overreach in that book; the literary sections are good not least because his tutor at Oxford was John Bailey, the eminent English scholar and literary critic.

To return to *the* topic in the heading of this section, Schopenhauer has this to say: "…to demand that even a great mind—a Shakespeare, a Goethe—should adopt the dogmas of some religion is like demanding that a giant put on the shoes of a dwarf" (Schopenhauer, 2011, Vol. II, para. 186). It is of interest to note though that he does not dismiss all religions as worthless; for instance, *Hinduism, Buddhism,* and *Catholicism,* are ranked well above all the others - the latter for its "pessimism" in acknowledging "…that our condition is both exceedingly miserable and also sinful" (para, 188) with a consequent need for *redemption*. The last word is put in italics as it is key to both Schopenhauer's as well as Wagner's thinking, who took it from the philosopher and, as has already been said, made it the central motif of his *music dramas*.

The *Will*

Schopenhauer's most significant contribution to philosophy and, forty years after his death, to psychoanalysis is his notion of the *Will*. It is italicized and capitalized in this chapter to differentiate it from the ordinary usage of the term. For Freud, this laid the foundation for his theory of *primary process*; equally for Jung, in that it underlay his creation of the notion of the *collective unconscious*.

As already stated, Schopenhauer was one of the first Europeans to interest himself in the religious philosophy of the *East*, namely, the Vedas and Buddhism. Jung borrowed freely from Schopenhauer's writings on these great religious philosophies, including his usage of terms like *Maya,* and the *Atman,* the former denoting the illusory quality of everyday life; the latter equivalent to Jung's development of his notion of the *self* which he defines as a quantity of the *collective unconscious* that is supraordinate to *ego* (Jung, 1966, p.177). Jung's disillusionment with Christian dogma resulted in his turning to these *Eastern* philosophies, which he discovered from his reading of Schopenhauer.

To turn now to the definition of the *Will* which is central to Schopenhauer's masterpiece *The World as Will and Representation* is that it is the *thing in itself*, the awe-inspiring contribution by Kant for what underlies the *phenomena* of ordinary mundanity. Schopenhauer's own philosophy relies heavily on this phrase which he borrowed from Kant's differentiation of the *noumenon* (*thing in itself*) from the *phenomenon*, the latter denoting what could be experienced through the senses. Jung notions of the *collective unconscious* and *archetypes*, seminal concepts of his psychology were inspired by Kant's *noumenon*. Jung was reading Schopenhauer avidly during his student years and, by his own admission in *Memories Dreams Reflections*, discovered Kantian philosophy from that source. There are several other concepts to be found in Jung that also owe their existence to his early reading of Schopenhauer that will be explored further in this chapter.

Intellectualizing emotion

At this point, the focus will turn to Schopenhauer's immense influence on Wagner's composition which was inspired to reach even greater heights by the former's view that music was the supreme art form. "Because music does not, like all the other arts, depict the *Ideas,* or levels of the objectification of will, but immediately *will itself,* it is thereby explicable why it is immediately effectual with respect to the *will,* i.e., the feelings, passions, and emotions of the listener, so that it quickly elevates them, or even retunes them" (Schopenhauer, Vol. II, 2011, para. 510). And again: "...music, which indeed often spiritually exalts us to such an extent that we might believe that it speaks of other and better worlds than our own" (para. 521). These ideas from the philosopher had a profound influence on Wagner's own thinking about music as well as on the many in-depth characterizations that make up the *dramatis personae* in the late *music dramas.* A final quote from the philosopher on music says it all: "Thus music is in no way like the other arts....For the latter speak only of shadows; it, rather, speaks of the essence of things" (Schopenhauer, Vol. I, 2008: para. 304).

Redemption

The theme of *redemption* runs through Wagner's *Ring* as the leitmotif of the whole *music drama*. Likewise, in the other two great music dramas *Tristan and Isolde* and *Parsifal*. This is the supreme notion he takes from Schopenhauer which is well illustrated in the following quotations from the latter:

> Christianity is the doctrine of the profound guilt of the human race through its very existence and of the heart's pressing for redemption from it...Optimism in religions as well as in philosophy is a fundamental error that obstructs the path to all truth...Catholicism seems to me to be shamefully abused...and to have suffered the fate to which all that is noble, sublime and great falls prey as soon as it is meant to exist among humanity. (Schopenhauer, Vol.II 2011, paras. 716 -717)

For Wagner, reading and re-reading Schopenhauer changed him completely from a politically committed revolutionary idealogue harbouring wish-fulfilling fantasies of a *Utopian* future for humankind once the oppressive shackles of the state were overthrown, to a far more reflective philosophical thinker.
Wagner himself puts it as follows:

> Everything depends on facing the truth, even if it is unpleasant. What about myself in relation to Schopenhauer's philosophy— when I was completely Greek, an optimist? But I made the difficult admission, and from this act of resignation emerged ten times stronger. (1978, Vol. 1, p. 291)

This change, which he attributed solely to his reading of Schopenhauer, elevated his late *music dramas* i.e., *Tristan and Isolde, The Ring Cycle,* and *Parsifal* to the greatest heights achieved in music. In this essay, I shall be dealing only with brief extracts taken from *The Ring* as even that is beyond the scope of this short piece in which to do justice. The theme of *redemption* is the leitmotif that runs through these great works which Wagner gets from Schopenhauer as exemplified in the following, one among many quotations by the latter on *redemption:* "...the *will for life* requires greater consideration than simply packaging the world with the label 'God' attached to it…Hence there is no need for redemption; consequently there is none" (Schopenhauer, Vol.II, 2011, para. 406).

Archetypal incest

Archetypal incest is amongst the many ideas Wagner and Jung share; it is, for example, a feature of *The Ring* in the incestuous love between the twins Siegmund/Sieglinde and also between Brünnhilde/Siegfried. The four characters mentioned from *The Ring* are cognates of Wotan, all of whom find *redemption* through love and death, themes which sound only too familiar to ears attuned to psychoanalytic speech.

Schopenhauer, who held to a strong moral standard based on Kant's *moral order within,* was horrified at the incest depicted in *The Ring* and told Wagner to rid his *music drama* of it. This was the scanty response the latter received from Schopenhauer to his libretto for *The Ring* along with the assertion that Schopenhauer, himself, preferred the works of Mozart and Rossini to Wagner's operatic *oeuvre.* He would, most probably, have been equally horrified by the *archetypal incest* to be found in Jung's *psychological alchemy.* It needs to be said here that Schopenhauer had completely misinterpreted Wagner as all the "incestuous" figures in *The Ring* previously mentioned in this essay are cognates of Wotan, and, therefore, semi-divine - incest being an acceptable practice amongst gods. In this, Wagner and Jung are closely allied as mythological incest leads to the birth of the symbolic *Divine Child*—for Wagner, this was Siegfried; for Jung it was what he termed *individuation.*

Schopenhauer would most likely also have been horrified by Freud's adaptation of his *Will* converting it, as Freud did, into his major early theory of *primary process* that itself was governed by instinctual drives, sexual libido above all. As is apparent from this, Schopenhauer had a strong moral sense, one of the reasons he is drawn to Kant's lofty "moral order within" – one of the well-known aphorisms from that philosopher.

Some of these figures also feature in Jung's all-important contribution to psychology namely, *psychological alchemy.* The end goal of the latter process was for Jung what has already been cited *viz., individuation;* this is the achievement of *wholeness* (by which he means self-knowledge (1963, p.305) whereby everyone is capable of a union with everything. The term *individuation* is identical with another Schopenhauerian concept, *viz., The Principle of Individuation,* which he derives from the *Vedas* and *Buddhism*. Schopenhauer's theory proposes that any one individual actually existing in time and space is only one of the species of humans or *Ideas* as Plato puts it: "…the eternity if the Idea (species)…is expressed in the individual…it is true that we always have before us a different being in the individual…But in another sense it is not true, namely in the sense in which reality belongs solely to the persistent forms pertaining to things, the *Ideas,* which was so clearly evident to Plato that it became his fundamental thought, the centre of his philosophy" (Schopenhauer, Vol.II, para. 550). These *Platonic Ideas*, along with Kant's *noumen* or thing in itself, are themselves the founding structures of Jung's *archetypal* theory. In this way, I am attempting to show that Jung's concept of *individuation,* inspired through his reading of Schopenhauer, bridges *Eastern* and *Western* thinking *viz.,* the *Vedas* and *Buddhism* with Platonic and Kantian conceptualization. This process of continuous change within *Oneness* is yet another of Schopenhauer's concepts derived from the Eastern sacred texts that were such an influence on Jung's seminal thinking about *archetypal theory.*

Schopenhauer's thinking, like every great philosopher, is preoccupied with death and, as usual, he turns to the East for inspiration. "Brahmanism and Buddhism, entirely consistently with survival after death, have an existence before birth, for which this life exists to atone for its guilt" (para 557). And, from a source that was also an important inspiration for Jung, Hermes Trismegistus: "For what is must be eternally" (para. 559).

Another frequently alluded to symbol of *wholeness* by Jung is the circle which again we see prefigured in Schopenhauer as follows: "…the true symbol of nature is the circle, because it is the schematic representation of recurrence. It is in fact that most general form in nature, which it implements in everything, from the course of the stars to the death and originating of organic beings" (para. 543).

Meister Eckhart

Another figure frequently referenced by Schopenhauer is Meister Eckhart, the 14th-century Catholic theologian, whose teaching is comparable to the *Vedas* and to *Buddhism* teachings in relation to *Being* in not seeing God as akin to human projection as male or female, nor he or she but as *Being* itself. Jung was inordinately predisposed to Eckhart's teachings and there are innumerable references to the latter in the *Collected Works*. In his own *working through* of the *alchemical process*, the *archetypal* incest that is portrayed therein is symbolic *not* literal. It is pointing to fundamental union in wholeness i.e., with everything that exists, that Jung calls *individuation.*

Schopenhauer links Meister Eckhart with the Buddha's prescription to his followers to cast away everything and become beggars. This later became the founding ethos of the mendicant order of St. Francis, founder of the Catholic Franciscan monks. "I therefore say that the spirit of Christian morality is identical with that of Brahmanism and Buddhism. In accordance with the whole of the view set forth here, Meister Eckhart also says: 'The fastest animal to carry you to perfection is suffering'" (Schopenhauer, para.550). Schopenhauer advocates compassion for our fellow sufferers in this world. Thus, compassion linked to redemption repeatedly make their appearance in Wagner's *Ring,* as well as in his other *music dramas* inspired by Schopenhauer.

Jung echoes Schopenhauer's emphasis on compassion in the following: "…the love of one's neighbour in the Christian sense as well as in the Buddhist sense of compassion, and the love of mankind as expressed in social service" (1970, para. 200).

Evil

Jung's life-long investigation into the reality of *evil* started with his questioning of his father's passive acceptance of Christian dogma which categorically states that God is only good. This was something Jung questioned from an early age—though the knowledge that this way of thinking made him an outsider from the Christian Church "filled me with a sadness which was to overshadow all the years until I entered the university" (1963, p. 65). One can readily imagine his joy reading Schopenhauer on the reality of evil once he, Jung, was at university. To quote Schopenhauer:

> I know of no greater absurdity than that propounded by most systems of philosophy in declaring evil to be negative in its character. Evil is just what is positive; it makes its own existence felt. Leibnitz is particularly concerned to defend this absurdity. (Schopenhauer, 2017, p. 5)

The critical reference to Leibnitz was in reaction to the latter's proclaiming that this is the best of all possible worlds, which led Voltaire to parody him as Dr Pangloss tutor to the eponymous hero of *Candide,* who wanders in a world littered with rape, murder, pestilence, enslavement, and natural catastrophe—all of which has an uncanny resonance with today. Jung would have readily concurred with the criticisms of Leibnitz on this score as he thought much of Christian dogma is at one with that philosopher's worldview and led to Jung's life-long critique of that side of Christianity.

Jung's difficulties with his father over Christianity's dismissal of evil in Christianity's conception of God resurfaced in his relationship with the English Dominican priest, Father Victor White. This was centred on Father White's defence of the Christian doctrine of the *privatio boni* i.e., that evil exists only as the privation of goodness. As already stated, Jung, like Schopenhauer, saw evil as a force and set out his argument in *Answer to Job* about the reality of evil and his critique of Yahweh/Jehovah, which criticism also first appeared in Schopenhauer's writings. One major difference between the two thinkers on religious matters is that Jung accepts the existence of "God" whereas Schopenhauer was a self-declared atheist. His interest in religion was quite apart from any belief in "*God.*"

In drawing this section on *evil* to a close, I shall yet again as I have in a book I wrote in 2001 titled *Carl Gustav Jung,* reference the following wonderful quotation taken from the black dog that appears in Goethe's *Faust,* which is the devil in disguise: "Part of that power, not understood. Which always wills the bad and always creates the good." This paradox is at the heart of Jung's approach, and he often quotes it to support his contention that without evil nothing can be created (Casement, 2021, p.80).

Shadow

As already alluded to in this essay, Schopenhauer and Freud are always referred to as "pessimists" although from even a quick glance at Jung's work no one is likely to think of it as "optimistic." The following extract will serve to illustrate the point:

> Only an infantile person can pretend that evil is not at work everywhere and the more unconscious he is, the more the devil drives him. It is just because of this inner connection with the black side of things that it is so incredibly easy for the *mass*

man to commit the most appalling crimes without thinking (Jung, 1966, p.166).

Compare this with Schopenhauer's own thinking:

> ...it is with evil, ills and death that qualify and intensify philosophical amazement not merely that the world exists, but still further that it is such a sorrowful one, is the point of difficulty of metaphysics, the problem that sets humanity into a disquiet that neither skepticism nor criticism can assuage (Schopenhauer, Vol. II, para.190).

Jung's childhood dream about the unacknowledged dark side of Christianity developed into what became one of his most vital contributions to psychology which he called *shadow*. What follows is the best possible depiction of this all-important concept by Jung himself:

> The shadow personifies everything that the subject refuses to acknowledge about himself and yet is always thrusting itself upon him directly or indirectly, for instance, inferior traits of character and other incompatible behaviour. (1959, p. 284)

Jung focused so much of his thinking on this concept that one may conceive of it as representing the whole of his notion of the *unconscious*— both *personal, collective*, and *archetypal*. I have followed suit by writing and lecturing on *shadow* for much of my professional career so shall, for now, leave this short contribution on that topic as it stands.

Persona

The comparisons between Schopenhauer and Jung will end with exploring another important concept, that of the *persona*. In so doing, we shall witness a considerable overlap in the contributions from Schopenhauer and Jung to this important psychological topic as follows.

The real meaning of *persona* is a mask, such as actors were accustomed to wear on the ancient stage, and it is quite true that no one shows himself as he is, but wears his mask and plays his part. Indeed, the whole of our social arrangements may be likened to a perpetual comedy;

and this is why a man who is worth anything finds society so insipid, while a blockhead is quite at home in it. (Schopenhauer, 2017, p. 27).

In a similar vein Jung writes the following:

> This arbitrary segment of the collective psyche – often fashioned with considerable pains— I have called the *persona*. The term *persona* is really a very appropriate expression for this, for originally it meant the mask worn by actors to indicate the role they played….It is only because the *persona* represents a more or less arbitrary and fortuitous segment of the collective psyche that we can make the mistake of regarding it *in toto* as something original. It is, as it name implies, only a mask of the collective psyche, a mask that *feigns individuality,* making others and oneself believe that one is individual, whereas one is simply acting a role through which the collective psyche speaks (1966, p.157).

Conclusion

Pessimism, in other words, telling truths about life is the thread that connects Schopenhauer, Wagner, and Jung (not to forget Freud). All these in-depth thinkers focus on the need for redemption of humankind: for Schopenhauer it is redemption from the suffering in the world he found confirmed in Buddhist and Hindu texts; for Wagner redemption is through self-sacrifice; for Jung redemption is through self-knowledge; for Freud redemption is from neurotic misery.

Wagner came to the realization that it was only through music that he could be in touch with the intensity of feelings expressed in the *music dramas* that sound as if they have been dredged up from the depths of the *collective unconscious.* It is salutary to remember that both Wagner and Jung in their thirties suffered from what the erudite psychiatrist/historian, Henri Ellenberger, called a *creative illness.*

Professor Ann Casement LP, is a London-based licensed Jungian psychoanalyst, a member of professional bodies including the National Association for the Advancement of Psychoanalysis (NYC), The British Psychoanalytical Council, The British Psychological Society, and founder member of the International Neuropsychoanalysis

Society. She served on the International Association for Analytical Psychology's Executive Committee as well as its Ethics Committee, the latter two terms as its Chair. She is a Fellow of The Royal Society of Medicine and the Royal Anthropological Institute, has worked in various parts of the world including the USA, Europe, Russia, Latin America, Israel, South Africa, China, and Japan. She served in the House of Lords on a Private Member's Bill for the statutory regulation of psychotherapists/psychoanalysts. She contributes to The Economist and professional journals around the world, has authored articles, reviews, book chapters, eight books, the last titled: *Integrating Shadow: Authentic Being in the World* (in press).

References

Casement, A. (2001). *Carl Gustav Jung.* Sage Publications.

Jung, C.G. (1959). *The Archetypes and the Collective Unconscious.* Routledge & Kegan Paul.

Jung, C.G. (1963). *Memories, Dreams, Reflections.* Random House.

Jung, C.G. (1966). *Two Essays on Analytical Psychology.* Princeton University Press.

Jung, C.G. (1970). *Civilization in Transition,* Vol. 10. Routledge & Kegan Paul.

Maguire, W. (Ed.) *The Freud/Jung Letters.* The Hogarth Press/Routledge & Kegan Paul.

Schopenhauer, A. (2008). *The World as Will and Representation, Volume I.* Pearson Education, Inc.

Schopenhauer, A. (2011). *The World as Will and Representation, Volume II.* Pearson Education, Inc.

Schopenhauer, A. (2017). *Studies in Pessimism.* Diderot Classics published in Great Britain by Amazon.

Shamdasani, S. (2009). *The Red Book: A Reader's Edition.* W.W. Norton.

Shamdasani, S. (2012). *C.G. Jung: A Biography in Books.* W.W. Norton & Co.

Wagner, C. (1978). *Cosima Wagner's Diaries.* Harcourt.

Individuation, Soul Making, and Cultural Complexes

Thomas Singer, MD

This chapter is dedicated to Murray Stein, whose life long work on individuation has inspired me.

The psychology of individuation is a topic filled with promise and uncertainty. The promise of a life lived with purpose and the full development of the personality is a deeply appealing, prospective attitude toward the psyche. At the same time, the uncertainty of what it means to individuate is daunting. If threading one's way through the notion of individuation in the individual is hard to define, much less live, transposing that notion to the life of the group is exponentially more difficult. What does it mean for a group, such as a nation-state, to individuate? Does it even make sense to try to apply that notion to the life of groups? Is there anything in the life of groups, including nation-states, analogous to the individuation process of a single person becoming whole, not perfect?

This chapter will explore the development of my thoughts about individuation and the life of groups. I will start this exploration by telling the story of one of my first experiences of the Jungian community. In 1968, as a young medical student interested in Jung, I was invited to attend Esther Harding's eightieth birthday party celebration in Bailey Island, Maine. Harding was one of the first Jungian analysts trained by Jung to return to the United States and open an analytic practice in New York. She was most well known for her book *Women's Mysteries,* which was very influential in the small but lively group of Jungians. I stayed with Joe and Helena Henderson who had rented a house for the occasion. I drove with Joe to and from the conference center over the course of the weekend conference. Joe, blind in one eye from early childhood, drove a bit like the cartoon character Mr. Magoo. He was a very quiet and introverted man—in some ways more strangely quiet than anyone I had ever encountered before. If we exchanged more than ten words during that entire weekend, I would be surprised. But Joe gave a lecture at Bailey Island that remains a fundamental building block of my understanding of how we encounter complexes over time and a glimpse of how we might conceive of the individuation process both in the individual and larger groups of people.

Henderson's Notion of the Minoan Spiral Image and Complexes

In his lecture, Henderson explored the symbolic image of the spiral as it appears in Minoan wall paintings. He elaborated a most interesting visual interpretation of how our relationship to complexes evolves over time, and in that notion, how the individuation process might unfold in a lifetime. In Henderson's interpretation of the Minoan image, the fate of our complexes and the trajectory of our individuation path are inextricably bound together in the development of the individual. Here is a rendering of the spiral that I drew in my little black diary:

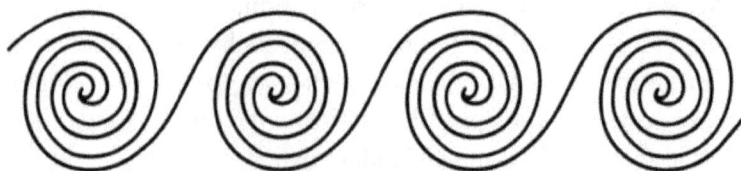

The Minoan Spiral

The first thing to notice is that the movement is not linear. It goes in and out, up and down, backward and forward. And yet there is a progression from left to right over time. Henderson postulated that the psyche develops by alternating between movement forward in progression and movement backward in regression and then progression and regression, again and again.

In a more detailed image of a single spiral, Henderson elaborated that the center of the spiral, (**b**), is when the psyche has spiraled back in on itself in a "regression" (not centered) and then unfolds again outward and forward in what he termed a "peak of progression" (**a**).

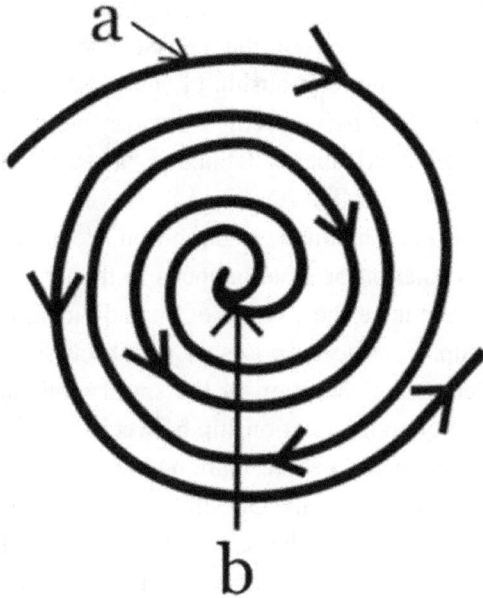

A spiral showing **a** the peak of progression and **b** the center of regression.

Michael Fordham evoked a similar image in describing infant development in terms of integration and de-integration, or breathing in and out. Henderson noted that this can also be seen as a movement from order to chaos to order to chaos. I like the spiral image in its nonlinear movement that also shows both progression and regression.

Another notable feature of the spiral is that when one is in a regression, or caught in an old complex, **b**, it seems as if they are in the same spot they have always been in and nothing has changed—the same old feelings, the same old attitudes, the same old thoughts, the same old crummy mood. But the fact is that there has also been movement in time, and although the psyche experiences it in the same old way, there may have been some development or real progress. And when one comes out of the complex, or moves into a phase of progression (**a**), there can be a sense of forward movement, of opening to new worlds. I remember Elizabeth Osterman, a San Francisco Jungian, remarking that some of her complexes had gone on uninterrupted for years, but as she grew older, the same old complexes would sometimes last only five minutes when triggered.

Henderson's notion of the spiral can also be seen as complementary to Edward Edinger's notion of the ego-Self axis in which Edinger elaborated on an evolving relationship of ego to Self over a lifetime. He labeled this the *ego-Self axis*, a term I always found a bit too rigid or linear in the idea of an axis that is defined as "a straight line about which a body rotates." (Merriam-Webster).

The fact is that no one image or definition adequately captures what is meant by individuation or what happens in the psyche as it develops over time—whether it be the psyche of an individual or the collective psyche of a group. For the purposes of my discussion, I am going to stay with Henderson's elaboration of the spiral motif in the context of how I imagine the evolving relationship between cultural complexes and individuation in groups of people, nation-states, or even larger entities such as the European continent. One thing is certain, whether it be an individual or a group, when the same old complex takes hold of the individual and collective psyche, it can seem as if you have always been in this same place, and nothing has changed and certainly nothing has progressed.

An Evolving Perspective on Individuation in Groups

But, before continuing, I need to regress or go backward to the rudimentary beginnings of my thinking about groups, complexes, and individuation because my own notion of what groups do with their complexes and whether or not groups individuate has gone through its own spiral development over time. Many of us in the United States who came of age during the Vietnam War abroad and the intense racial conflict at home in the mid- and late 1960s began to think we were witnessing a decisive moment and movement toward greater maturity as a country— that the Vietnam War was the manifestation of a late stage of adolescent development of the country out of which we needed to grow in our understanding of the limits of our power and authority in the world. We were young enough to believe that we were witnessing and creating the birth of a new American identity in which we were outgrowing our identification with heroic military victory against the forces of darkness that marked the World War II (WWII) generation.

The Vietnam War was a dangerous "regression" to our older view of war as heroic conquest (**b** in the spiral), especially in the divided world of Democracy versus Communism, which was also beginning to feel outdated. Protests against the war in the name of peace was a "peak of progression" (**a**) in the sense of disidentifying from our identity of military heroes or conquerors and the dominant authority in the world. We saw ourselves as part of a generation that would lead to a more mature, more individuated stage of development of America at home and abroad. So you might say that I and many of my generation bought into a notion of emerging American individuation around issues of war and race and our role in the world. (It seems odd to think that now many of us are embracing the notion of coming to the aid of Ukraine against the Russians—once again assuming the role of defenders of democracy in the world.)

If we imagined that America was an adolescent on the verge of growing up, it turns out that our dream of that process was perhaps much more a reflection of our own adolescent idealism than a grounded vision rooted in the reality of the American collective psyche and in the unfolding of American history. In short, we were, at best, overly optimistic in our assessment of America's emerging individuation. I have become more skeptical of the notion of individuation in large groups of people, but not without hope of a kind of soul-making process that can take place in large groups of people.

In my spiraling view of the topic of individuation of groups of people, I now want to jump forward in time to another encounter with the notion of individuation in large groups of people. With my German colleague, Joerg Rasche, I coedited a book in 2016 about European cultural complexes entitled *Europe's Many Souls*. We followed Joerg's lead in framing much of the book based on his experience of Europe, which grew out of the nightmare of WWII, the post-war divisions of Europe symbolized by the Berlin Wall, and the attempts at healing between Germany and its neighbors after WWII. It is worth noting that Joerg was personally honored for his work on reconciliation between the Polish and German people by the Polish president who presented him with the Polish Golden Cross of Merit. Out of all the regression of WWII, with its massive, chaotic destruction and then the truly miraculous rebuilding of post-WWII Europe, deep hopes for further renewal emerged after the fall of the Soviet Union.

As we were working on the book, Joerg was informed by a spirit of hopefulness (Henderson's "crest of progression," or **a**, on the spiral image) in which the European continent itself was undergoing a positive individuating experience. Our book was modeled on the notion that the individuation of Europe was happening in front of our eyes with individual nations more fully affirming their own unique identities while at the same time joining in a new collaborative European Union. In the work of the contributors to *Europe's Many Souls,* who were from many different European nations, we felt as though were getting glimpses of the individuation processes in Europe, or at least soul-making encounters with cultural complexes of multiple countries. Each author labored at understanding their individual country's cultural complexes while simultaneously contributing to the overall individuation of Europe as a whole: many individuating nation-states contributing to one individuating European whole. It seemed like we were recording the dream of European individuation coming into reality. The dedication of our book celebrated this idea of the many and the one coming together, with an emphasis on diversity as essential to unity:

> Cultural diversity is a precious heritage that we should treasure and protect. The soul loves variety and the human psyche needs the freedom to imagine, to play, and to create. When globalization and homogenization join forces with militaristic thinking and its unceasing expansionist politics, the soul in all its variations is endangered. This book is dedicated to *Europe's Many Souls*. (2016, p. vii)

At the time of our putting together *Europe's Many* Souls in 2016 we were witnessing Europe at a "crest of progression," and we rode that spirit in the belief of its coming into being. Within a few short years, however, with Brexit and the Russian invasion of Ukraine, this shattered into chaos and has given way to the most serious "regression" since WWII. In personal terms, this was especially hard on Joerg who had given all of his energies to the development of an individuating European world in which countries maintained their individual identities while belonging to a large whole that was truly integrated.

If individuation signals something about an individual or group psyche that has both differentiated out its different parts while cultivating a relatedness and wholeness among its different parts, that dream of individuation has failed us again—as it did in the hopefulness of the Vietnam era in which we imagined a world at peace with the end of racism at home and war abroad. Clearly that version or definition of individuation seems to elude us. Individuation or soul making in groups does not occur in a straight-line progression and is not marked by the "crests of progression" alone but is characterized by the movement of progression and regression, in and out, up and down—and surely it doesn't exclusively follow the beautiful organic form of a spiral. To talk meaningfully and accurately about what actually happens with our cultural complexes and with our group individuation processes in the context of historical process, it still may be helpful to incorporate a notion of cyclical or spiral processes. At the archetypal level, there is no question that individuation or soul making at the individual and group level does not occur without multiple serious encounters with the shadow as well as, perhaps, an occasional burst from the Self as with Martin Luther King's "I have a dream" visionary speech. In fact, we might argue that soul making, or individuation, at the individual and group level may occur only because of multiple serious encounters with the shadow over time.

Complexes, Soul Making, and Individuation

This brings me to a discussion of my current thinking about the use of the term *individuation* in the discussion of group life. For me, individuation implies the movement toward a state of wholeness as the goal of the process. I am sure many use the term *individuation* by dissociating it from some final goal and focus on the process. Perhaps because it focuses primarily on process, I have personally gravitated more to the phrase *soul making,* which I prefer as a way of talking about what others might think of as individuation in groups. As I see it, soul making doesn't necessarily imply some sort of state of wholeness, which I think is implicit in the notion of individuation. And, at the heart of the matter in the context of groups, I think of soul making occurring specifically in the context of what a group does with its cultural complexes. By linking individuation, soul making, and cultural complexes, I can give some specificity to what I am talking about. Here is what Jung said about personal complexes: "We all have complexes; it is a highly banal and uninteresting fact ... It is only interesting to know what people do with their complexes; that is the practical question which matters" (1968, p. 94).

If I extend Jung's insights about personal complexes to cultural complexes, what is most important is not that individuals or societies have cultural complexes. This is just a basic psychological fact of being human and living in human societies. Jung even calls it "banal and uninteresting" to indicate that the recognition that complexes exist at all is "so lacking in originality as to be obvious and boring."

Complexes are simply part of being human. What is not banal, however, and what does matter enormously is what we do with our personal and cultural complexes. Do our cultural complexes remain unchanged for decades, centuries, even millennia—whether they be about race, ethnicity, gender, religion, or any other primal human concern? Or are cultural complexes transformed over time? Stated another way, *what a group does with its cultural complexes determines its relative position of progression and regression in the spiraling cycle of its soul making or individuation.*

To be clear about what a cultural complex is, I offer the following characteristics as a working definition:

1. A cultural complex expresses itself in powerful moods and repetitive behaviors—both in a group as a whole and in its individual members. Highly charged emotional or affective reactivity is the calling card of a cultural complex.

2. A cultural complex resists our most heroic efforts at consciousness and remains, for the most part, unconscious.

3. A cultural complex accumulates experiences that validate its point of view and creates a store house of self-affirming, ancestral memories.

4. Cultural complexes function in an involuntary, autonomous fashion and tend to affirm a simplistic point of view that replaces more everyday ambiguity and uncertainty with fixed, often self-righteous attitudes to the world. Especially prominent in today's world are the cultural complexes that emphasize victimhood and perpetrator.

5. Cultural complexes have archetypal cores; that is, they express typically human attitudes and are rooted in primordial ideas about

what is meaningful, making them very hard to resist, reflect upon, and discriminate.

6. And finally, not all cultural complexes are "pathological." There are cultural complexes that are ego syntonic with the identity of the group—that is, they can strengthen and affirm a sense of identity in a positive as well as negative way.

Racism: An example of the relationship between cultural complexes, soul making, and individuation

A meaningful way, then, to begin thinking about individuation in terms of groups would be to think of recurring encounters over time with cultural complexes. I first started getting glimpses of this notion in an article that I wrote for *Spring Journal* in 2007. [1] There, I defined a series of seven cultural complexes that have dominated the American collective and political psyche over much of our history (p. xxvii–xxix).

1. Our relationship to money, commerce, consumer goods
2. Our relationship to the natural environment
3. Our relationship to the human community, including family life, social life, and the life cycle from conception to death
4. Our relationship to the spiritual realm
5. Our relationship to race, ethnicity, gender—all the "others"
6. Our relationship to speed, height, youth, progress, celebrity
7. Our relationship to the world beyond our borders

I do not take the number seven as being fixed and magical, nor do I take the concept of soul making or individuation in groups too literally. As I wrote in the *Spring* article in 2007:

> My thesis, then, is that the American soul is embedded in our various cultural complexes. Furthermore, our cultural complexes are what give political life its dynamism and its content. Both the energy and the issues of political debate spring from the autonomous, highly charged emotional material of our core cultural complexes. Political life is the natural social arena in which cultural complexes play themselves out. We forge the

---

[1] This article later became much more elaborated in *Cultural Complexes and the Soul of America* (Thomas Singer, ed. *Cultural Complexes and the Soul of American* [London: Routledge, 2020]).

American soul in our struggle with our cultural complexes. In the political arena, cultural complexes seem mostly to generate heat, division, hatred; they are inflammatory and polarizing; they usually end in a stalemate without any resolution, only to recur in the next election or the next generation; sometimes they are ignored or kept unconscious for decades; occasionally they can be worked out slowly in engagement, compromise, reconciliation, and healing after generations of recurring battle. In short, they behave like complexes. (p. 137)

The soul of America then and, by extension, our individuation as a nation depend on what we do over time—sometimes hundreds of years or more—with our cultural complexes. This is nowhere truer than with the cultural complex of racism in America. And also it is nowhere truer that the progress with racism in the United States over time has been anything but a straight line. It is marked by progression and regression over and over again, sometimes with both progression and regression occurring at the same time. No one symbolic image of that process, such as the spiral, can do justice to the unpredictable vicissitudes of the course that racism has taken in America through the centuries. But Henderson's image of the spiral as being apt for the course that personal and cultural complexes can take is not a bad place to begin as it sees the natural course of such processes as one of progression and regression.

We get a glimpse of this spiral unfolding over time in the recent March 2023 fifty-eighth anniversary of Bloody Sunday in Selma, Alabama. President Biden presided over the event, which honored the occasion on March 7, 1965, when black Americans began a planned march from Selma to Montgomery, the state capital. As they tried to cross the Edmund Pettus Bridge, which was named after a former Confederate brigadier general, US senator, and "Grand Dragon" leader of the Alabama Ku Klux Klan, (Whack, 2015) the marchers were stopped by white law enforcement officers in a bloody confrontation in which the police used tear gas and billy clubs. Fifty-eight years later the same battle for voter rights in the face of voter suppression is going on, in spite of the tremendous progress achieved by the civil rights movements of the 1960s. This spiral movement of progress and regression in the soul-making journey of dealing with our racial cultural complex led President Biden to state on that day: "On this bridge, blood was given to help 'redeem the soul of America'" (Richardson, 2023).

To get a visceral feel for why it is right for Biden to speak of redeeming the soul of America in our battle with the racial complex, I believe readers get the best sense of the damage done to both white and black souls through our long history of racism in Toni Morrison's description in *Beloved* of a house haunted by the spirits of black ancestors. She speaks through the experience of her character, Stamp Paid:

> he believed the undecipherable language clamoring around the house was the mumbling of the black and angry dead. Very few had died in bed ... and none that he knew of ... had lived a livable life. Even the educated colored: the long-school people, the doctors, the teachers, the paper-writers and businessmen had a hard row to hoe. In addition to having to use their heads to get ahead, they had the weight of the whole race sitting there. You needed two heads for that. Whitepeople believed that whatever the manners, under every dark skin was a jungle. Swift unnavigable waters, swinging screaming baboons, sleeping snakes, red gums ready for their sweet white blood. In a way, he thought, they were right. The more coloredpeople spent their strength trying to convince them how gentle they were, how clever and loving, how human, the more they used themselves up to persuade whites of something Negroes believed could not be questioned, the deeper and more tangled the jungle grew inside.
> But it wasn't the jungle blacks brought with them to this place from the other (livable) place. It was the jungle whitefolks planted in them. And it grew. It spread. In, through and after life, it spread, until it invaded the whites who had made it. Touched them every one. Changed and altered them. Made them bloody, silly, worse than even they wanted to be, so scared were they of the jungle they had made. The screaming baboon lived under their own white skin; the red gums were their own. (1987, p. 234)

The souls of both white and Black people have been infected for centuries with the psychic virus of racism and its virulent spread of the toxic archetypal image of the jungle and its black natives as being like "swinging screaming baboons, sleeping snakes, red gums ready for their sweet white blood."

I now offer a very rough sketch of the spiral progression and regression over time of the virulence of the racial complex in the United States.

The Spiral:
Imagining a Spiral Process of Soul Making/Individuation
in the American Experience of the Racial Cultural
Complex

Abolitionists 1830–1870
Civil War 1861–1865
Emancipation Proclamation–1863

Civil Rights Movement 1955–1968
Voting Rights Act 1965
Martin Luther King

Black Lives Matter
2013–present

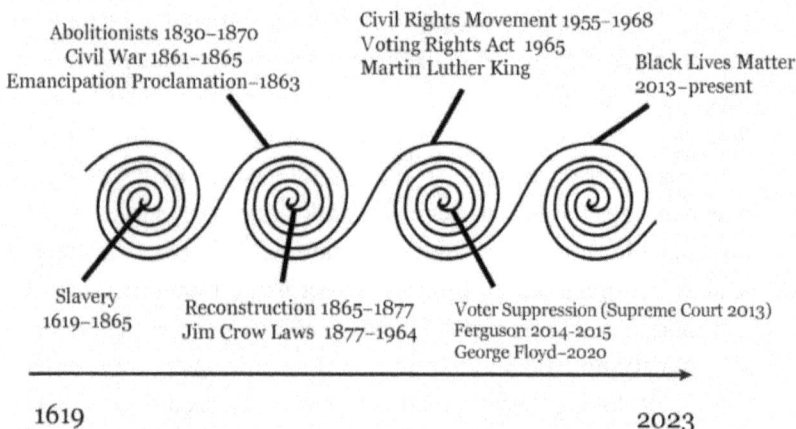

Slavery
1619–1865

Reconstruction 1865–1877
Jim Crow Laws 1877–1964

Voter Suppression (Supreme Court 2013)
Ferguson 2014–2015
George Floyd–2020

1619

2023

I will not go through a detailed history of each phase as others have done it much better and more thoroughly than I ever could. But by teasing out in some broad strokes the movement of progression and regression, I hope to suggest one way to imagine the relationships between a cultural complex, soul making, and perhaps individuation at the level of the collective psyche. These nodal points on the spiral are the tip of the iceberg or landmark moments when the complex breaks through to collective consciousness by expressing itself in a significant event that symbolizes a turning point or peak of progression or regression. It is important to note that in bipolar cultural complexes, what one group defines as progression may be seen by its polar opposite group as regression.

For more progressive Americans, a soul-making and individuating engagement with the deeply entrenched American racial complex has expressed itself positively in the following landmark moments of our history: Abolitionists (1830–1870), the Emancipation Proclamation (1863), the civil rights movement (1955–1968) and Voting Rights Act (1965), Black Lives Matter (2013–) and other contemporary protest movements against racism. The negative nodal points of regression for progressives in the history of the racial complex are most prominent in slavery itself (1619–1865), Reconstruction (1865–1877), and Jim Crow laws (1877–1964), and now renewed voter suppression (2013–present) and increased police brutality against blacks, as seen in the deaths of Michael Brown in 2014 in Ferguson, Missouri; Breonna Taylor in Louisville, Kentucky, and George Floyd in Minneapolis, Minnesota, in 2020, among many, many others.

I simply reverse this perspective for racists who tend to see the peak positive moments in the racial complex in slavery itself, Reconstruction, and Jim Crow laws, renewed voter suppression and increased police brutality against blacks. And racists will tend to see the peak "regressive" moments of the racial complex in the abolitionists and the Emancipation Proclamation, the civil rights movement and the Voting Rights Act, and the emergence of Black Lives Matter and other contemporary anti-racists movements.

In looking at this spiral representation of the evolution of the racial complex in America, I am forced to ask whether or not there has been any progress. There is certainly movement over time, but it would be easy enough to say that the moments of regression are simply a recapitulation of the original sin of slavery. It is in the very nature of a complex to see the same old issues recycling with self-selecting memories that reinforce one's point of view, with the same potent emotions that simply accumulate more and more power over time, and the same old convictions that express themselves in black-and-white simplistic ideas that are autonomous, repetitive, and self-perpetuating. Nevertheless, that prompts the question of "is there any real change?" On the one hand, there is the critique of the progressive myth of history that says, "History does not have sides. It does not take sides. The progressive view of history is a myth. History is perfectly capable of slamming into reverse and backing up at 50 miles per hour" (Deresiewicz, 2023).

On the other hand, Eric Ward, a civil rights leader for more than thirty years, gives a clear sense of the underlying progress in the movement over time with the nation's encounter with the racial cultural complex.[2]

I know 2020 is fundamentally better in this country than 1920. And I absolutely know 2020 is better than 1820 in this country. And that doesn't mean that I think everything is marvelous. It doesn't mean that I'm ignoring the inequality and the injustice that exists in our society. What I'm noting is that we're in a better place. Now, why are we in that better place? As a person on the left and as a progressive, are we in a better place because capitalism made this a better place? I'm skeptical, though capitalism has had its own role to play, and I'll acknowledge that. Are we in a better place because folks who were bigoted decided "It's time to be in a better place?" No. We are in a better place because folks like me and folks like you and folks like those listening really struggled for generations, for hundreds of years, to get us to this point. And one of the things that the impact of authoritarian thinking does to our movement in its insistence on purity and a unilateral narrative is, when we look back, to disregard the work that people did for us to get us to this point. They died for it. They were beaten for it. They were ostracized for it. They were persecuted for it in ways that I can't even imagine.

If we are building a society that cannot acknowledge the work that got us to this point, how do we acknowledge the work that it's going to take to get us to 2120? And what type of democracy do we want or what type of society are we saying we want in 2120? And so I feel like that long-arc thinking is really important. I also think this is critically important—life has been unfair for the majority of Americans, for the majority

---

[2] Eric K. Ward is a nationally recognized expert on the relationship between authoritarian movements, hate violence, and preserving inclusive democracy. In a civil rights career spanning more than thirty years, he has worked with community groups, government and business leaders, human rights activists, and philanthropists. Eric is executive director of the Western States Center. He's also a senior fellow with the Southern Poverty Law Center and Race Forward, and he's co-chair for the Proteus Fund.

of people of color and other marginalized communities in this country, and for the majority of the world. Life is unfair. It is harsh in ways that are unnecessary. It is costing in ways that are unnecessary. This has benefited a smaller grouping of folks in our society who have benefited from that privilege—whether they are male, whether they are straight, whether they are white—in lots of different ways. But the truth is that we're not seeking revenge here. That shouldn't be our goal, ever. (2020)

Eric Ward knows deep in his bones the evolution over time of the racial complex in America. He has inherited the sensibility of Stamp Paid's deep suffering from Toni Morrison's *Beloved*. Ward knows there has been progression and regression. Ward also knows that there has been real progress. And, Ward knows that struggling with our racial cultural complex is a most arduous soul-crushing as well as soul-making process, perhaps even an individuating process for the American people and the American psyche.

Thomas Singer, MD, is psychiatrist and Jungian analyst who trained at Yale Medical School, Dartmouth Medical School, and the C.G. Jung Institute of San Francisco. He is the author of many books and articles that include a series of books on cultural complexes that have focused on Australia, Latin America, Europe, the United States and Far East Asian countries, in addition to another series of books featuring Ancient Greece, Modern Psyche. He serves on the board of ARAS (The Archives for Research in Archetypal Symbolism) and has edited ARAS Connections for many years.

References

Deresiewicz, W. (2023). "There Is No Right Side of History," *The Free Press,* January 2, 2023, https://www.thefp.com/p/there-is-no-right-side-of history?utm_source=substack&utm_medium=email.

Jung, C.G. (1968). *Analytical Psychology: Its Theory and Practice (The Tavistock Lectures)* Vintage Books.

Merriam-Webster Dictionary, s.v. "Axis," accessed March 21, 2023, https://www.merriam-webster.com/dictionary/axis.

Morrison,T. (1987). *Beloved.* Alfred A. Knopf.

Rasche, J. & Singer, T. (2016). *Europe's Many Souls.* Spring Journal Books.

Richardson, H. C. (2023). *Letters from an American.* Substack. https://heathercoxrichardson.substack.com/p/march-5-2023-sunday.

Singer, T. (2007). "A Personal Meditation on Politics and the American Soul," *Spring Journal* 78:121–147.

Singer, T. (2020). *Cultural Complexes and the Soul of America.* Routledge.

Ward, E. (2020). "Justice, Rage, and Peace," *Mind of State* podcast, December 9, 2020, https://mindofstate.com/justice-rage-and-peace/.

Whack, E. (2015). "Who Was Edmund Pettus? The March to Freedom Started on a Bridge that Honors a Man Bent on Preserving Slavery and Segregation," *Smithsonian Magazine,* https://www.smithsonianmag.com/history/who-was-edmund-pettus-180954501/.

Balancing: Weight, Wings, and Wind

Linda Carter, MSN, CS, IAAP

Murray Stein's capacity to carry joy and pleasure on one shoulder while carrying the sorrows that life brings on the other— simultaneously— is a lifetime achievement. A well-known leader for many years, he has consistently held and maintained perspective and an overview of the worldwide Jungian community in remarkable ways. Perhaps Odin's ravens Huginn and Muninn fly across the world at sunrise and return in the evening, perching on his shoulders, to whisper news of evolving life from far and wide. Murray's wise listening abilities and consultation with thoughtful companions have been fundamental in his functioning as a kind of axis mundi centering our complex community; the result has been a gathering together of creative energies into a collaborative whole— benefitting the ongoing emergence of our field.

Introduction

As Murray Stein approaches 80, I myself approach 70. With substantial life lived and feet squarely on the ground, I imagine that Murray, as I have come to know for myself, is capable of carrying grief and sorrow on one shoulder while simultaneously carrying joy and pleasure on the other. Having traveled the snake-like path of the *Via Longissima* and faced terror as well as creative surprise along the way, the capacity to hold ambivalence as a life-long achievement has taken hold. Of course, there are shifts and sways that ebb and flow as do energies in the multiple worlds surrounding us; we are always and forever surrounded by concentric fields of influence. However, such balance requires honest confrontation with the inevitability of death as a goal of life and full-on engagement with experiences of lamentation as part of the process. Anxious defenses against grief and mourning lead to physical, psychological, emotional illnesses and sickness of the soul that prevent a fullness of being that comes with integration and ultimately, individuation. The truth of sadness and the flow of tears open to a deep solace and communion with both the living and the dead and to the capacity to bravely carry suffering that, paradoxically, can open to creativity within individuals and within collective groups. The almost unimaginable disruptions over these past few years including the pandemic, environmental disasters, unprovoked wars, political strife, and societal fragmentation have stripped away the denial of death that had previously been the norm (Becker, 1997).

This paper will address the importance of facing lamentation as essential for the achievement of balance through a clinical case amplified by a painting by Fra Angelico. To do so, I look to Complex Adaptive Systems (CAS) and theories of emergence as they resonate with Jungian ideas. Reflections on worldwide upheavals leading to grief and mourning during Jung's time and our own will be considered along with the human tendency, when confronted with invisible, incomprehensible forces to seek cohesion, coherency and meaning through mythical systems. Doing so helps to stabilize individuals and groups so that creative life can proceed. Of note is that various systems often share remarkably similar fundamental structures as exemplified by the tree as an *axis mundi* that is both symbolic and practical for grounding and survival.

Carrying

During the past few years, I have been wondering how we carry and balance burdens that, at times, have felt to be overwhelming. Mary Oliver (2007): wisely addresses this struggle in her poem "Heavy":

> It is not the weight you carry
> but how you carry it—
> books, bricks, grief—
> it's all in the way

you embrace it, balance it, carry it
when you cannot, and would not,
put it down.[1]

From the beginning of time, myths, stories, religious rituals, music and poetry have *carried* forward memories from the past and the past influences each present moment even when no future seems possible. Repeated from generation to generation, such reminders have offered structural containment and opened portals within communities for the *essential* expression of lamentation that needs to flow when unbearable loss is encountered. Through enlivened and embodied storytelling, continuity with the ancestors can be felt in the here and now and be perpetuated so that threads of memory are grasped and a sense of belonging restored over time. At the personal level, acute and shattering moments of profound sorrow may be eased by the presence of loving friends and family and by contact with inner helpers who hold us up when consumed with states of near collapse. Artwork may sometimes convey an empathic presence in remarkable ways.

An Emergent Pattern Amplified

Such was the case when an anguished mother facing the loss of her child was softened within a substantial empathic analytic relationship that opened to a resonant amplification. A Fra Angelico painting created a portal for collaborative imagination and an accurate pattern match between her current emotional state and the configurations inherent in both the story content and the affective expressions visible in the characters depicted. In particular, we entered a central scene showing Mary, the suffering mother of Christ within a larger fresco called the "Crucifixion" (1441) by Fra Angelico in Florence. The actual painting is almost life size and is located in the monastery's Chapter Room across from the entrance, a place where outer and inner meet.

---

[1] "Heavy" by Mary Oliver

Fra Angelico, *Crucifixion and Saints* 1441, Fresco and fresco painting, 18 ft. by 10.3 yds
Convento di San Marco, Florence[2]

I call your attention to the particular section (enlarged below) where Mary, at the foot of the cross, seems to be fainting into her own crucifixion. Notice her arms outstretched and eyes downcast. One would assume that her son has just died, and she is gripped by sorrow and lamentation. But she does not apparently fall to the ground; instead, she is held up and surrounded by caring and intimate companions who have walked by her side and witnessed the agonies of torture and death.

Firmly kneeling in front of her, offering physical support as if rooted to the ground, is Mary Magdalene; on one side is her tearful sister-in-law Mary Cleophas (possibly the wife of Cleophas, brother of Joseph) and on the other, a rueful looking John the Evangelist. Given that some art historians see St. John here and in other Medieval and Renaissance artwork as androgenous, the sense of a feminine surround is emphasized.[3]

---

[2] https://commons.wikimedia.org/wiki/File:Crucifixion_with_Saints_%28Angelico%29_1.jpg

[3] St. John is often shown in androgenous or feminized forms with the assumption that he would be more relatable to women. It is argued that portraits of an androgenous John could "function as an 'image of a third or mixed gender' and 'a crucial figure with whom to identify' for male believers who sought to cultivate an attitude of affective piety, a highly emotional style of devotion that, in late-medieval culture, was thought to be poorly compatible with masculinity" (McNamer 2010, p. 145 in Christianity 2022).

Mother Mary, Mary Magdalene, Mary Cleopas, John
the Evangelist
Detail, Fra Angelico 1441, *Crucifixion and Saints*

The fresco, in which this scene is held, is layered with symbolic meaning within Catholicism, bringing together various aspects of a rich tradition and history. The archetypal pattern related to the anguish of a mother who has lost her child is one that has been continuous across cultures and time. This painting emerged as a specific visual amplification within the emotional analytic field constellated as a present moment of both the recent and primeval past. From art history, we understand that each figure has a detailed story within Catholicism but what binds all of the elements together is that of resonant deep feelings creating an atmosphere of embodied grief and lamentation, a field that the analysand and I could enter together.

Some Brief Art Historical Reflections

When considering those whose likenesses populate the fresco, you will find, either standing or kneeling, various saints revered by the Dominicans whose grieving faces are, for the most part, turned toward Mary, not the cross. On the left are saints venerated by the Medici family who wielded significant political and financial power and who were deeply connected to San Marco during the period when this fresco was commissioned.

In the diamonds, linked by the upper overarching lunette, are faces of the Old Testament prophets, whose writings foretold of the death and resurrection of Christ. In the central diamond is the image of a pelican feeding young hatchlings with her own flesh and blood, as the self-sacrificial mother. The pivotal position of this bird whose body and wings create a crucifix form when diving for fish, emphasizes the deeper archetypal roots of the generative, nurturant mother who gives birth, suffers pain, even in the feeding, and who will suffer deep loss. She connects us to the animal world of which we are members and as a winged creature, to the spirit world above. This cameo scene of maternal care is at the pinnacle of a vertical line flowing through the cross, to a skull and then to an encircled portrait of Saint Dominic. At community meetings, the living prior sat directly beneath Domenic, thus representing the founder and, simultaneously, the savior embodied in the current leader (Hood, 1995, p. 62). Moving from the verticality of linear chronological time, we find at the bottom, a horizontal movement depicted by a vine or root linking the Dominican genealogy, composed of seventeen portraits of the most illustrious members of their society (popes, cardinals, bishops, saints and blesseds) up to that date (Menarini, 2021).

Mary and her immediate caregivers are contextualized within what we might see as nested systems including the living and the dead, surrounded by the ineffability of the Divine. Those who have gone before are represented along with tendrils of new growth naturally bringing together words of the gospel with hope of an unfolding future. Reminiscent of a family tree or an *axis mundi*, this complete image consolidates an overall gestalt of a belief system with ongoing meaning as evident in the case of my analysand.

The Value of Tears

Although long dead himself, the artist Fra Angelico shows us the ancestors of import to his community and his church so that we, as engaged viewers, share sentiments with others whose spirits and emotions touch us now, in this moment, in this time. A very small but essential element, easily missed if not carefully scrutinized, is the tear of Mary Cleophas (see enlarged image below). In harmony with this detail, it has been said of Fra Angelico that:

Whenever he painted a Crucifixion, the tears would stream down his face; and it is no wonder that the faces and attitudes of his figures express the depth and sincerity of his Christian piety [and likely, resonant emotional empathy.] (Mormando, 2005)

Tears of a Compassionate Companion

Fra Angelico conveyed the lives of his characters with deft painterly skills saturated with authentic feeling. He revealed what Hegel called 'the investigation of inner coordination, the indwelling meaning of facial expressions' (Delistraty, 2019). Further, Fra Angelico's "art is the kind of art that might make us weep or yell or find within ourselves beliefs and thoughts and depths that we did not otherwise know we had" (ibid.). This artist reaches through time and continues to be successful in transmitting "…emotions from the mind of the artist to the mind of the viewer" (ibid.). Or, we might say that emotions have been channeled through the artist and the painting to us as current day receivers, within an emergent constellation of similar human tribulations.

We experience Fra Angelico's compassion and, in some ways, the compassion of the painting itself as it seems to have developed a life of its own. Jung was very clear that a painting cannot be reduced to the psychology of the artist. The interactions between the painting and the viewer and the viewer and the painting create an atmosphere, an environment, a field full of psychoid aliveness. The paint, color, texture, shapes, images, religious history, cultural backdrop of the Italian Renaissance come together and meet us and our perceiving presence to co-create conjunctive moments within the liminal territory between ourselves and the artwork that carries over to conjunctions within ourselves and with outer others.

The tears of Fra Angelico and our tears as co-participants in the shared field are amplified by those of Mary Cleophas; engagement with this painting affected my patient deeply, shifting internal agony to an outer expression of hot wet streams of sorrow that had been waiting to find release. This turning point moment heralded the transition from a dry, arid wasteland to a natural flow of emotion critical for the replenishment of her own life. Visual art, music, dance, religious rituals and other embodied forms of lamentation "can elicit tears as 'material signs of the liquefaction' of grief" (Seremetakis, 1991, p. 115 in Cools, 2021, p. 48). Cools citing Danforth comments:

> Tears can mediate between the apparent opposites of life and death. For the mourner, they are bitter, representing the poison of grief leaving the body, while for the deceased, they bring relief: 'Tears are associated with death in this world but with life in the underworld.' (2021, p. 48)

I agree with these writers that tears represent a liquifying flow through the body, breaking out of constricting blockages on the path toward restoration of health and vitality.[4]

Jung on Life and Death

Jung notes paradoxical responses: "Death is indeed a fearful piece of brutality" while on the other, it "appears as a joyful event. In the light of eternity, it is a wedding, a *mysterium coniunctionis*. The soul attains…its

---

[4] I offer my thanks to Barbara Miller and the candidates from Netherlands Association for Analytical Psychology (NAAP) who participated in a seminar that I taught on February 10, 2023. Their reflections and comments on the theme of lamentation influenced and shifted my ideas about the composition of this paper. I especially thank Rob Polmann who recommended the excellent book cited here by Guy Cools called *Performing Mourning Laments in Contemporary Art* (2021).

missing half, it achieves wholeness" (1965, p. 314). However, coming into such a balanced perspective is complicated; the process of grief can be a roller coaster that takes time before the acuteness abates and loss can fall into the background where it becomes an essential aspect of one's truth and a source of self-compassion and compassion for others. Grief never disappears even if the loved one has physically disappeared. However, a solace can be found in the ongoing relationship between the one who has died and the one left behind as a cocreated emergent and transcendent third; it continues as an internalized interaction pattern instantiated in mind, body, emotion and soul. Through implicit knowing usually outside conscious awareness, presence of the other lives on and can be accessed.

Transgenerational Patterns

We now know from neuroscience that we internalize interaction patterns as neural pathways from ongoing repeated experiences. From trauma research, we know that intergenerational trauma is perpetuated when a young, vulnerable child is persistently terrorized by an overpowering adult and then grows up behaving abusively toward his own child and often does so without conscious, explicit awareness.

Hirsch notes two forms of identification with the aggressor: Ferenczi first described it[5] as an introjection of the parent's guilt and the terror in such a way that the adult child tends to identify himself as "…victim throughout his life by repetition compulsion" (Ferenczi, 1932 in Hirsch, 1996, p. 198). Secondly, Anna Freud, in her studies of the ego and mechanisms of defense, used the term to describe children with more ego strength "…who are able to defend aggressively a feared attack by identification with it" (Freud, 1936 in Hirsch p. 198). Ferenczi early on attempted to address the maltreatment of children by their parents at a major psychoanalytic conference in 1933, while Anna Freud elaborated her theoretical ideas about this concept that emerged from empirical observations of young children. From immersion in work with patients, Ferenczi mapped out behaviors and symptoms including dissociation,

---

[5] Ferenczi's ideas about "identification with the aggressor" were first presented in his "Confusion of Tongues" paper at the Twelfth Psychoanalytic Congress at Weisbaden at 9 A.M. on September 4, 1932. It was published in German a year later but was withdrawn from circulation by Ernest Jones and was not published in English until 16 years afterward (Hazen 1993, p. 333).

fragmentation and trance states that we currently see with adult patients suffering intergenerational trauma.[6]

Neuroscience and trauma research have shown that someone previously abused is then inclined to live out patterns that have been seared into his brain over time and that these patterns are automatically triggered from the nonconscious, implicit system. Hebb's Law affirms that "neurons that fire together, wire together" so that instantiated networks are present and at the ready. The goal of psychotherapy is to help patients create new neural networks by internalizing healthier relational interaction patterns emergent in intersubjective therapeutic exchanges thereby creating alternatives to problematic older childhood ones. As new options gain strength through repetition, the previously dominant networks are de-potentiated over time. However, under stress the old patterns can once again become activated, affecting emotion regulation leading to enactment of unwanted past behaviors. (Jungians might see this as possession by a powerful complex or due to a weak ego.)

Practicing new ways of relating can make a huge difference in lifestyle in the present moment and for future generations. Further, from epigenetic studies, we have learned that trauma can be intergenerationally transmitted, as noted; in other words, the demons from previous eras persist, as in identification with the aggressor. Such inherited behaviors can be enacted and seem like disembodied, possessing spirits that are not within the bounds of actual lived memory but are invisibly passed on. Just as such problematic behaviors can be intergenerationally inherited, I believe that positive traits can pass from generation to generation, as well. Through the implicit domain, we internalize the facial expressions, voice

---

[6] We can imagine Ferenczi's bravery in presenting his ideas at the 1932 conference with Freud in attendance given that Freud had abandoned the seduction theory in 1904 by stating that he did not believe that actual abuse reported by his patients led to their symptoms of hysteria; rather from his view, their suffering was attributed to fantasies and or memories of fantasies. Consider this disavowal in light of the struggles in the 1990s that erupted around "false memory syndrome" and the conflicts around the Freud archive, the views of Jeffrey Mason reported by Janet Malcom related to traditional theorists who tended toward intrapsychic ideas rather than sufficiently considering the actuality of outer physical abuse that Ferenczi early on was addressing. In addition, feminists took strong issue with those who adhered to orthodox Freudian perspectives and practices. The emergent field of neuro-psychoanalyis has been moving toward a synthesis of analytic perspectives with findings from neuroscience, trauma research and infant studies and the value of Complex Adaptive Systems, a conceptual framework that brings together mind, body and brain as one system embedded within ever widening systems of influence.

tones, body movements and rhythms from those surrounding us during early childhood that persist throughout the lifespan. (See Carter 2008 on bidirectional influence and how a colleague recognized my analyst in me through implicit non-verbal relational knowing.) My mother often noted that she sounded "...just like Nanna Mick..." and I now say, "I sound just like my mother AND Nanna Mick." This idea has the potential to offer comfort for those grieving by knowing that, despite the death of a loved one, we have truly embodied them at the level of neural circuitry as well as at the level of soul and they are, therefore, alive in us (and likely, alive in members of previous generations). Even now, when I say certain words in certain ways, I can viscerally feel the love and presence of my psychoanalyst (now dead for many years), a great and ongoing comfort that brings tears of gratitude to my eyes. In this way, a progressive chain of embodied memory can offer a sense of cohesion and well-being in positive ways; alternatively, the chain of embodied memory can continue in negative ways, through fragmentating and destructive patterns. Such is the case exemplified above, as a defense against vulnerability and feelings of worthlessness that can manifest as rage, operating to hold back anxieties about annihilation that, at root, stem from profound sadness and grief unexpressed or understood.

Facing Titanic Forces: Life and Death

During these past few years, we have been profoundly affected by the emergence of miniscule, invisible viral molecules that continue to mutate and collaborate to stay alive while infecting and killing the human population with Titanic power; they operate as an emergent system, fatal and dangerous for humans but creative in their ability to hold onto life through the trickster's shape-shifting and morphing through mutation; they will manage to perpetuate ongoing generations unless and until halted by vaccines and herd immunity. We can see an analogy of the battle between our species and this powerful virus as similar to the epic wars between the Olympians and the Titans, for example.

Our recent massive catastrophes have forced us to confront death in unimaginable ways. Entering such dark places may be more palatable if done in metaphoric, derivative form in a context of myth and story that offers containment and companionship but *does not* diminish the truth of the emotions that surge forward. Moves into amplification can help protect against re-traumatization if pattern match is accurate and empathic emotional resonance is present. Of course, a certain amount of healthy ego functioning is important when crossing the threshold into lamentation and often needs to be done incrementally within a holding context whether that is through psychotherapy, friendship, family or religious ritual. Companionship reminds us that we are still here, and that death is necessary even though there are strong pulls to avoid accepting that there is an endpoint to life. Here are some reflections from Jung (2009) on life and death from the *Red Book*:

> We need the coldness of death to see clearly. Life wants to live and die, to begin and end. You are not forced to live eternally, but you can also die, since there is a will in you for both [See footnote #74, p. 266]. Life and death must strike a balance in your existence....For the completion of life, a balance with death is fitting. If I accept death, then my tree greens, since the dying increases life. If I plunge into the death encompassing the world, then my buds break open. How much our life needs death. (p. 266-267)

However, this lovely, philosophical perspective is hard-won as evident in earlier passages within this same section on death. See the lines below:

> I looked around me and I saw that the solitude expanded into the immeasurable, and pierced me with the horrible coldness. The sun still glowed in me, but I could feel myself stepping into the great shadow. I follow the stream that makes its way into the depths, slowly and unperturbed, into the depths of what is to come.
> And thus I went out in the night (it was the second night of the year 1914), and anxious expectation filled me. I went out to embrace the future. The path was wide and what was to come was awful. It was enormous dying, a sea of blood. From it the new sun arose, awful and a reversal of that which we call day. We have seized the darkness and its sun will shine above us bloody and burning like a great downfall.
> When I comprehended my darkness, a truly magnificent night came over me and my dream plunged me into the depths of the millennia, and from it my phoenix ascended.

But what happened to my day? Torches were kindled, bloody anger and disputes erupted. As darkness seized the world, the terrible war arose and the darkness destroyed the light of the world, since it was incomprehensible to the darkness and good for nothing anymore. And so we had to taste Hell. (p. 265)

We can easily imagine that Jung's words, here, could have been spoken during March of 2020 predicting experiences *now* well-known to us. For example, he speaks of an expanding and immeasurable solitude that we certainly felt surrounding us as we stepped into the coldness of the great shadow of pandemic lockdowns. Jung seems to be referring to the sea of blood vision that he had in 1913 that he ultimately saw as a precognition of WWI. However, until war was actually declared, he worried that this remarkable vision indicated that he was fragmenting and "doing a schizophrenia." Phrases such as "bloody anger and disputes erupting" and that "war arose" certainly resonate with the horrific invasion of Ukraine, the insurrection attempts on January 6th and with the ongoing threats of violence in word and deed that have manifested with school shootings, aggressive behaviors targeting minorities, conflagrations fired by political adversities globally and by the menacing potential of nuclear decimation. There is no doubt that we all have "had to taste Hell."

Response to Catastrophe: Pandemics and Wars

During this time of worldwide upheaval, true scenes of lamentation and grief have been remarkably lacking in our culture and there has not been a sense of shared national mourning as we experienced with 9/11 or President Kennedy's assassination. Prior to the distribution of vaccines, we faced horrifying scenes of bodies waiting to be buried, often far from home. The dead along with loved ones were deprived of the "dignity of death" as Caterina Vezzoli, so very well puts it, when individuals die within the context of family and the atmosphere is one surrounded by love, appreciation and even beauty. During the height of the pandemic, funerals, memorials and gatherings of any kind were suspended or, if attended, the risk of contamination persisted, and the chain of infection and premature death were real possibilities.

Commerce with the Dead

Turning toward the spirit world has been an important means of coping with loss throughout history. Commerce with the dead was a source of fascination and terror during the mid-19th and early 20th centuries in the West. Jung grew up within this time frame when spiritualism was enacted with seances and consultations with ancestors via clairvoyants were prevalent. Many link the collective interest in spiritualism to the loss of young family members due to the Civil War, the 1918 Flu Pandemic and World War I. The Civil War (1861-1865) was the bloodiest in the nation's history to that date with 750,000 fatalities (Kommel 2019).

World War I (1914-1918) claimed the lives of 8,500,000 soldiers as a result of wounds or disease along with as many as 13,000,000 civilians (2023 *Encyclopedia Britannica*). The 1918 Flu Pandemic death toll was at least 50 million, killing about a third of the world's population (Klein 2020). To put these historical numbers in perspective, the World Health Organization reports as of June 13, 2023, there have been 767,984,989 confirmed cases of Covid-19, including 6,943,390 deaths. A total of 13,397,334,282 vaccine doses have been administered[7]

Along with these cataclysmic blasts and overwhelming numbers killed, *millions more were devastated by the loss of loved ones.* During the time of the Civil War, young men left home vital and alive when last encountered, and then they were *gone*, never to be seen again. Bodies not returned from battlefields during wartime or buried in collective graves following the global pandemic disallowed a needed facing of reality; families were not given the opportunity to view the beloved body and see, for themselves that the soul had departed. We might imagine that they struggled with gaps, emptiness and confusion; how do we cope with "the disappeared"?

My grandmother was a student nurse during the 1918 Spanish Flu Pandemic and worked night and day in a hospital in Camden, NJ. It was not until recently that I really grasped that a family joke about Nanna was not a joke at all: she was nearly expelled from nursing school because she had tagged a body incorrectly---meaning that the corpse in the casket was not the family member expected by those grieving. In fact, in hard-hit cities like Philadelphia, a short ride over a bridge from Camden, funerals were suspended to avoid contamination and due to the complete

---

[7] Accessed June 19, 2023, WHO, https://covid19.who.int/

overwhelm with dead bodies heaping up, funeral homes, grave spaces, casket makers and gravediggers were in drastically short supply. Some believe that burial rituals in the US were, consequently, forever altered, shifting communal grief held by rituals to more private experiences for individuals and nuclear families (Klein, 2020).

> In many communities, processing the loss of loved ones entails a series of rituals and rites and laying a person to rest in a respectful way. In many cities, the restrictions on public events meant that families and communities had those rites interrupted, so grieving didn't take place in public but became an individual process, which had long-term consequences. Without an opportunity to share it with them, that grief was carried around for decades. (Bristow, 2017 in Klein, 2020)

During 2020, we, too, witnessed morgues filled to capacity with lines of tractor trailer freezers parked outside hospitals in New York that held corpses as if they were a commodity reduced to contaminated pieces of meat of no use and requiring expeditious disposal. Caterina Vezzoli, in Milan, reported that she was unable to sit on her outdoor balcony for some fresh air during the early lockdowns as she could not bear the constant sound of ambulances rushing critically ill people to local hospitals, on otherwise empty highways. In her hometown of Bergamo, the graveyard had become full, and bodies were being transported across Italy to places very far from home and family, to be buried without ceremony and the care that offers respect to the dead. Consequently, the sense of being cut down and cut-off was, and continues to be, prevalent leaving those of us remaining with a cloud of existential angst and adrift from the experience of "belonging" that comes with shared community mourning.

Certainly, influenced by apocalyptic disasters, Jung was born in 1875, a little more than a decade after the end of the US Civil War; he lived through WWI, WWII, and the 1918 Pandemic so it is not a surprise that he would have been affected by and interested in spiritualism. Jung's fascination with the dead seems to have been shaped by family history and early childhood experiences within a Christian context: he came from a long line of ministers on both sides of his family. He was probably affected by his mother's stories about her own childhood memories of standing behind her preacher father while he was writing sermons;

her charge was to shoo away the ghost of his first wife so that he could concentrate, unperturbed, by unwanted visitations. Jung suffered early childhood trauma with his mother's multiple reproductive losses and psychiatric hospitalizations; with witnessing bodies being pulled out of the Rhine River proximate to the family parsonage; and by possible sexual abuse by an older person. With a vivid imagination and powerful dreams, this lonely and isolated boy struggled to make sense of life, death and the possibility of realms beyond ordinary consciousness.

Like Mary Todd Lincoln and Sir Arthur Conan Doyle, who both had suffered tragic premature deaths of family members and who were avidly involved in seances and spiritualism, Jung, too, had been impacted by tragic losses and he coped via intellectual defenses by exploring questions about interactions with the dead as evident in his early research in medical school on "so-called occult phenomena" through observations of his cousin Helena Prieswerk, a medium. He concluded that Cousin Helly's spirits were actually split off subpersonalities of her own psyche and this revelation helped to launch Jung's ideas about complex theory that were further substantiated by his use of the Word Association Experiment at the Burgholzli. While involved in an intense relationship with Freud and his "psychoanalytic period," Jung leaned toward psychological understandings of invisible forces, but it seems that metaphysics was a central domain of curiosity and meaning throughout his lifetime. Notable evidence for Jung's belief in ghosts is apparent in reports of a time during 1916 when his children were convinced of a spectral presence frightening them and otherworldly figures rang the doorbell at 228 Seestasse (1965, p. 190). These incidents prompted Jung's rapid-fire writing of "The Seven Sermons to the Dead" along with creation of his first mandala, *Systema Munditotius*. He created both an imagistic organizing model and a written description for a system of containment connecting multiple aspects of what would be an overall psychological theory but also a metaphysical means for connection with the Infinite (Carter, 2023). We might see these organizing structures as in some ways similar to what Fra Angelico created in his painting and what we will see in another system for understanding invisible but powerful forces from the point of view of Norse mythology to be presented shortly.

Ancestral spirits live on through us as, I believe, they are depicted in Jung's final *Red Book* image; it is understandably, in this context, incomplete and in keeping with the infinite flow of life with individual faces clearly articulated but part of the sea of humanity that stretches from the beginning of time and on into the future. With the ebb and flow of the tides, we begin—emerging from the sea as source and Great Mother—and return to Her through rivers and streams to rejoin all who have walked this earth before our conception was imagined. Jung describes this flow of life toward death in visionary form as follows:

> I see densely pressed multitudes of men, old men, women, and children. Between them I see horses, oxen and smaller animals, a cloud of insects swarms around the multitude, a forest swims near, innumerable faded flowers, an utterly dead summer…. they are all flowing past in an enormous stream. (2009, p. 264)

We, too, will inevitably join this "enormous stream" with tears of lament, an essential aspect of continuity that flows from the love of others and love of life itself. Sonu Shamdasani and James Hillman had a series of conversations following the 2009 *Red Book* publication as Hillman was consciously facing his own death in 2011. Their dialogues were recorded and put into print as a book, *The Lament of the Dead* (2013). As I understand their views, we are always embedded in history and, therefore, always surrounded by the dead. Similarly, from a Complex Adaptive Systems view of emergence, life is self-perpetuating and self-replicating and has become ever-more complex over time. Humanity has evolved from those who have gone before and there is a natural unfolding of generations that cannot be denied; the dead are always among us. As our lives come to end, we inevitably create space for our children, their children, and their children's children. Continuity persists beyond our own physical mortality.

Etymological Intertwining: *Carry, Bear, Suffer, Burden*

As we walk through the transitions of this life and into what is to follow, we *carry*, *bear* and *suffer* various *burdens*. Each of these words imply images of physical weightiness and instinctual movement from one place to the next. They also share similar etymologies and meanings: To bear from Old English *beran* means "to carry, bring; bring forth, give birth to, produce; to endure without resistance; to support, hold up, sustain; to wear"[8]; while *to suffer* from Latin *sufferre* means "to bear, undergo,

---

[8] https://www.etymonline.com/word/bear

endure, carry or put under; from *sub* 'up, under' + *ferre* 'to carry, bear,' from PIE root *bher* or 'to carry,' also 'to bear children'" [9] Each of these interrelated words imply endurance, difficulty, work, pain but also signify birth and new life. We shoulder responsibility with hope that our efforts will be fertile and bear fruit.

An illustration of the god Odin with his two ravens Huginn and Muninn, from and 18th century manuscript, 1760 [10]

Ravens Perched on Each Shoulder

When reflecting on ideas having to do with shouldering and balancing grief, mourning and loss with joy and pleasure, stories about the Norse

---

[9] https://www.etymonline.com/word/suffer
[10] https://commons.wikimedia.org/wiki/File:NKS_1867_4to,_94r,_Odin.jpg

Allfather Odin's two ravens have flitted through my mind. Huginn and Muninn take off each morning as the sun rises and after surveying the world with keen vision, they return in the evening to perch again on their master's shoulders and whisper news from across the landscape into his welcoming ears. We might think of Odin as a somewhat vulnerable god who has only one eye (among other liabilities), so that his perspective is limited leaving him dependent on these winged helpers, along with others in his retinue. Further, this wind god of sky and war relies on the wisdom of Mimir whose decapitated talking head lies at the bottom of a well where the Norns (similar to the Greek fates) also reside underneath the tree Yggdrasil that functions as a world axis. Two wolves are part of the surrounding daily scene, and it has been found that wolves and ravens, in fact, often collaborate in the natural world. Ravens have curved beaks that cannot penetrate the skin of land animals so that they often follow the wolves who help in tearing apart animal carrion. In turn, wolves have learned over the millennia to follow the clear-eyed ravens whose overview perspectives allow them to locate dead and dying food sources that earthbound creatures (including early human hunters) cannot (Wheelwright, 2013). As a result of these natural interdependent activities, both ravens and wolves are associated with uroboric notions of life feeding on itself. This intricately intertwined mythological system, informed by our progenitors lived and generationally transmitted experiential knowledge, also includes a squirrel that runs up and down Yggdrasil from the realm of the Norns and Mimir underground to the tops of the tree carrying information. Communications, both horizontal across the world and vertical from above and below, were imbued with mystical wisdom conveyed from other worldly sources along with the drinking of mead. (Think here of resonances with the crucifix as another kind of world tree and with mystical communion rituals). Over time, Norse stories, myths, beliefs and shamanic practices became interwoven creating a culture and lifestyle to make sense of complex and otherwise inexplicable events such as mass illnesses and natural disasters (similar to myths about the Greek Titans). We find in these elaborate tales, a remarkable vision of an interdependent, highly networked system that is threatened throughout the sagas by the upcoming war Ragnarök that will eventually destroy Odin and his realm. However, hope persists that life will begin again following the demise of the community, as described in surviving texts.

Listening, Moving, and Gratitude

This system from an ancient time mirrors our own with the contribution of each member as a needed active component adding to the balance of the whole (whether that be an individual body or a national corpus) and with threats of ultimate destruction, not unlike our current situation with discussions of escalating wars and nuclear armaments. We need collaborating helpers to work together for survival of each individual and collective communities as a totality. As I struggle to move forward with the weighty issues of our time and with lessons learned from necessary

Oluf Olufsen Bagge, Yggdrasil, The Mundane Tree 1847

suffering and burdens myself, I continue to imagine the intelligent black ravens who have the capacity to fly in the wide skies above and who have the amazing ability to see and remember the world as it is—in perspective. I sometimes feel the windy movement of wings across my face and welcome their evening return to my very limited human shoulders, strengthened by burdens of life-lived; then listen to the balanced wisdom they have gleaned at the end of the day and settle into gratitude for the life granted me and whatever time remains.

Addendum: Reflections of Process

Of note to readers: The need for systems of orientation and organization around a central axis reaches far back into human history as evident in Norse mythology, in the traditions of Roman Catholicism, in Jung's *Systema Munditotius* and in the Three-tiered Systems Model (see below and Carter 2023 for further explication). When confronted with overwhelming loss and devastation, especially by invisible, incomprehensible forces, there is a human inclination to move from chaos to order by seeking organizing and orienting structures and models that offer grounding when anxiety spins emotions into the air, separating us from a sense of secure base. Jungian amplification, at its best, emerges from the co-created analytic relationship of mutual influence. The image, association or story comes into being through contributions arising from the two partners playing together in a "free and open space" with collaborative back-and-forth that includes turn-taking and switching pauses. As Jung has clearly said, the way into both the complex as well as active imagination is through emotion; cognitive understanding comes later. True transformation, whether in the context of analysis or religious ritual, requires embodied, active, visceral engagement and, of fundamental importance, accurate pattern match. Seeing through to archetypal underpinnings is a skill that takes time and experience to cultivate. Specific, emotionally imbued amplification offers companionship and a sense of belonging and inclusion in a larger cosmos. We influence and are influenced at multiple levels, most often without conscious awareness. Without intending to do so at the outset of writing this paper, I have been led by psyche into the *vitality* of these resonant systems.

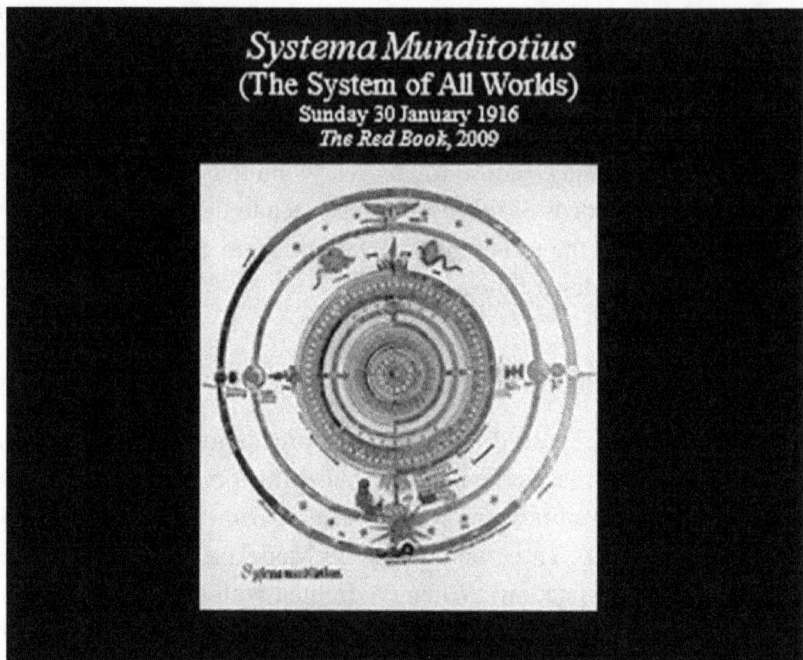

Systema Munditotius
(The System of All Worlds)
Sunday 30 January 1916
The Red Book, 2009

Three-Tiered Systems Model: Interaction Patterns of Mutual Influence Sol and Luna (macrocosmic, collective); Jacoby (clinical, transference/countertransference); Trevarthen (microcosmic, dyadic/intersubjective)

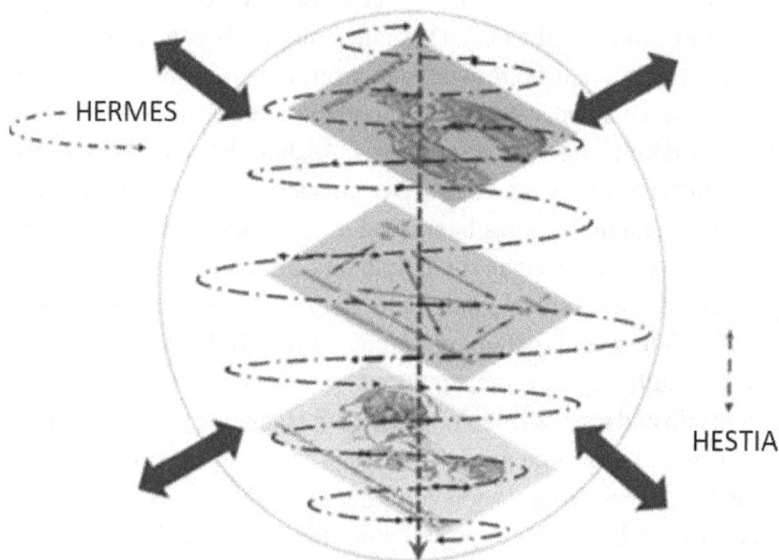

HERMES

HESTIA

Three-Tiered Systems Model:Interaction Patterns of Mutual Influence
Created by L. Carter. Graphics by B. William Brennan (2022)

Linda Carter, MSN, CS, IAAP, (USA) is a Clinical Nurse Specialist and a Jungian analyst practicing in Carpinteria, California and has been a psychotherapist for more than 40 years. A graduate of Georgetown, Yale, and the C.G. Jung Institute-Boston, Linda was the Journal of Analytical Psychology's Book Review Editor, US Editor-in-Chief and Film & Culture Editor. Founder and Chair of the Art and Psyche Working Group, she initiated and edited the service outreach project "Art in a Time of World Crisis: Interconnection and Companionship" that recently won a Gradiva Award from the National Association for the Advancement of Psychoanalysis (NAAP). Art and Psyche won a Gradiva previously for the art exhibition affiliated with the Illuminated Imagination Conference in 2019. Her paper "Amazing Grace" was a short listed nominee for a 2022 Gradiva. Linda has published widely and taught internationally, especially in China. Email: lcarter20@earthlink.net

References

Becker, Ernest. (1997). *The Denial of Death.* Free Press.

Bristow, Nancy. (2017). *American Pandemic: The Lost Worlds of the 1918 Influenza Epidemic.* Oxford University Press.

Carter, L. (2008). "Reflections on Bidirectional Influence in the Matisse/Picasso Relationship and in Clinical Practice from a Complex Adaptive Systems Perspective (CAS)," *Quadrant,* 38(1).

Carter, L. (2023). "Going the Full Circle: Pattern Resonance from Microcosmic Interactions to Macrocosmic Amplifications," *Jung's Red Book for Our Time*, ed. Murray Stein. Chiron Publications.

Christianity Stack Exchange. (2022). "Is there a written tradition that would explain why John the Evangelist is often depicted in art as effeminate?" https://christianity.stackexchange.com/questions/90549/is-there-a-written-tradition-that-would-explain-why-john-the-evangelist-is-often (Accessed February 25, 2023)

Cools, G. (2021). *Performing Mourning Laments in Contemporary Art. Amsterdam.* Valiz.

Danforth, L. (1982). *The Death Rituals of Ancient Greece.* Princeton University Press.

Delistraty, C. (2019). "Fra Angelico's Divine Emotion." *The Paris Review.* https://www.theparisreview.org/blog/2019/08/19/fra-angelicos-divine-emotion/ (Accessed February 25, 2023)

Ferenczi, Sándor. (1933/1955). "Confusion of tongues between adults and the child." *Final Contributions to the Problems and Methods of Psychoanalysis* (p. 156-67). Hogarth Press. (Original work published 1932 in German).

Freud, A. (1936/1992). *The Ego and the Mechanisms of Defense.* Routledge.

Hazan, Y. (1999). "From Ferenczi to Kohut: From Confusion of Tongues to Self-Object." *American Journal of Psychoanalysis*, 59(4): 333-343.

Hirsch, M. (1996). "2 Forms of identification with the Aggressor--according to Ferenczi and Anna Freud," Prax Kinderpsychol Kinderpsychiatr, 45 (6), 198-205. (In German) https://pubmed.ncbi.nlm.nih.gov/8966185/ (Accessed May 30, 2023)

Hillman, J. and Shamdasani, S. (2013). *Lament of the Dead: Psychology After Jung's Red Book*. Norton and Company.

Hood, W. (1995). *Fra Angelico: San Marco, Florence*. George Braziller.

Jung. C.G. (1965). *Memories, Dreams Reflections*. Vintage Books.

Jung, C.G. (2009). *The Red Book: Liber Novus, A Reader's Edition*, (Ed., S. Shamdasani). W. W. Norton & Company.

Klein, C. (February 12, 2020). "How America Struggled to Bury the Dead During the 1918 Flu Pandemic." History: A&E Television Networks, LLC. https://www.history.com/news/spanish-flu-pandemic-dead (Accessed March 20, 2021)

Kommel, A. (2019). "Seances in the Red Room: How Spiritualism Comforted the Nation During and After the Civil War." Washington, DC: The White House Historical Association.

McNamer, S. (2010). *Affective Meditation and the Invention of Medieval Compassion*. University of Pennsylvania Press.

Menarini, (2021). "Menarini Pills of Art: Crucifixion with Saints by Fra Angelico." *Menarini Blog*. Florence, Italy: Menarini Group. https://www.menariniblog.com/menarini-pills-of-art-crucifixion-with-saints-by-fra-angelico (Accessed February 25, 2023)

Mormando, F. (1995). "The Painted Visions of Fra Angelico." *America: The Jesuit Review.* December 19, 2005 Issue.

Oliver, M. (2007). "Heavy," *Thirst*. Beacon Press.

Seremetakis, C. N. (1991). *The Last Word: Women, Death and Divination in Inner Mani*. Chicago University Press.

Wheelwright, B. C. (2013). "A Storytelling of Ravens," *Jung Journal: Culture and Psyche*, 7 (1).

Psychological Types and the Individuation of Unique Personality

James Johnston

Murray is the most welcoming and gregarious Jungian analyst I know. He is tirelessly interested and willing to consider new ideas and insights from all sources. With his clear and present love of Jung's psychology and his lifelong quest to thoroughly understand the phenomenon of individuation, he has provided leadership and guidance for many.

Murray was exceptionally helpful in introducing me to other analysts who could be interested in a deeper understanding of Jung's type model for individuation. My project—to develop an instrument and training to thoroughly explore the value of Jung's types for individuation—was catapulted forward when I met Murray Stein in Zurich. As our friendship has matured over the years, my admiration for his commitment to Analytical Psychology has matured with it.

Psychological types are modes of consciousness and are useful for understanding the dynamics of individuation—the gradual unfolding and unification of unique personality. Not exclusively ego orientations, these modes of conscious awareness saturate the whole psyche. They influence the attributes of soul, shadow, ego, and persona. Jung provided a map of the psyche in his 1925 Seminars. It can serve as a useful context for the consideration of psychological types and their role in individuation.

The Living Architecture of the Psyche

The diagram Jung used in 1925 depicts key relationships in the human psyche.

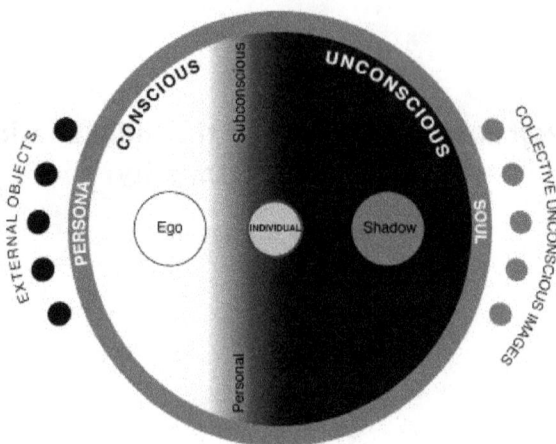

Jung's diagram was simple. The *ego* is the center of the consciousness side and includes two "objects" of ego awareness—the outer objects of the world *out there* and the mythopoetic world of archetypal images *in there*. The inner world of the archetypal images are objects for consciousness in the same way that our perceptions of the outside world are objects—they exist independent of the consciousness that perceives them. Perceptions of the outer or inner objects are always perceptions of the representations of those objects, rather than the things in themselves (*ding an sich*).

These two "objects" constitute an important division for each of Jung's eight psychological types—each is oriented either to the outer objects (extraversion) or to the inner objects (introversion). The orientations are so different in character that we could consider them a *great divide* in consciousness, a divide that is gradually bridged, by degrees, with the advancement of individuation. The *persona* that intervenes between ego and outer objects is a mode of relationship with others in the world. Its typological orientation is an extension of the ego's.

The *personal subconscious* in Jung's diagram, shown just behind the ego, is the storehouse of memories and accumulating complexes. It forms over time as the archetypes of the collective unconscious meet the experience of consciousness. The personal subconscious is relatively unconscious, yet its memories and complexes can be enlisted or autonomously activated to engage with or interrupt ego consciousness.

The *individual* is positioned at the center of the psyche, joined there by the archetypal Self to form the "central government" of the psyche. The Self pervades the center and circumference of the whole psyche and shares the same center as the individual personality.

In a lecture delivered at the 1952 Eranos conference on "reality planes," Erich Neumann illustrated the Self as the nucleus of the personality. In the same lecture he introduced the now frequently used term: ego/Self axis. But ego consciousness was not the main theme of his lecture. Rather, he was intent on uncovering other forms of knowing.

> The fact that we associate knowledge exclusively with the system of ego-consciousness is the result of our obsession with the ego-complex, with which we habitually identify our total personality. This identification was historically significant and necessary for our development, but it is nevertheless false and responsible for a narrowing of our horizon and of our "knowing." (1989, p.7)

For both Jung and Neumann, the Self is centered in the nucleus of the personality; they form an axis of alignment that shares a common center. The gradual development and unfolding of the central personality is the purpose of individuation.

> The meaning and purpose of the [individuation] process is the realization, in all aspects, of the personality originally hidden away in the embryonic germ-plasm; the production and unfolding of the original, potential wholeness.
> (CW, 7, para.186)

The ego has its complementary opposite in the unconscious: the *shadow*. In terms of psychological types, the shadow is the harbinger of those type dispositions incongruent with the salient ego identity. With individuation, the shadow's dispositions become increasingly available as the whole personality increasingly becomes more unified.

Just as the ego has its compatible intermediary in the persona, the shadow has a cohort in the *soul* (anima/animus). The soul carries the same type dispositions as the shadow. The persona and soul are typological complements, just as the ego and shadow are complementary. Jung's essay in Volume 17 on "The Development of Personality" amplifies the importance of the individuating personality.

> "To the extent that a man is untrue to the law of his being and does not rise to personality, he has failed to realize his life's meaning." (CW 17, para.314)
>
> "Just as the great personality acts upon society to liberate, to redeem, to transform, and to heal, so the birth of personality in oneself has a therapeutic effect. It is as if a river that had run to waste in sluggish side-streams and marshes suddenly found its way back to its proper bed, or as if a stone lying on a germinating seed were lifted away so that the shoot could begin its natural growth. (CW 17, para.317)
>
> "But in the end, the hero, the leader, the saviour, is one who discovers a new way to greater certainty. Everything could be left undisturbed did not the new way demand to be discovered, and did it not visit humanity with all the plagues of Egypt until it finally is discovered. The undiscovered vein within us is a living part of the psyche; classical Chinese philosophy names this interior way 'Tao,' and likens it to a flow of water that moves irresistibly towards its goal. To rest in Tao means fulfillment, wholeness, one's destination reached, one's mission done; the beginning, end, and perfect realization of the meaning of existence innate in all things. Personality is Tao (CW 17, para.323).

Jung refers in his 1925 diagram to ego and shadow as a "subjective personality" and an "objective personality" respectively, but neither of these sub-personalities characterize the person who permeates the whole psyche. The person has an ego and a shadow, but the person is not his or her ego or shadow. The aim of individuation is to unite the subjective and objective personalities in one individual.

The distinction between personality and the ego structure is an important one, both for depth psychology and for common parlance. Jung's type model has been frequently used as a system of assembling categories of ego/persona structures as "personality types." Even the English paperback edition of *Psychological Types* uses the term "personality types" in referring to Jung's model. To conflate ego and personality is to banalize the exalted position of personality in Jung's psychology and to obfuscate the central purpose of individuation.

Ego and Personality

With our tightly constrained modes of ego consciousness, we are not privy to the origins or real nature of consciousness, only our *experience* of it. We are endowed with the self-reflective capacity to *notice* our conscious awareness. From noticing that awareness, we are capable of assembling paradigms of understanding—conceptual *hypotheses* about consciousness, as Neumann did in his 1952 lecture: "I am offering here tentative interpretations, neither facts nor proofs, more questions than answers" (p. 3). Or as Jung did in his essay on the development of personality:

> Yes, this thing we call personality is a great and mysterious problem. Everything that can be said about it is curiously unsatisfactory and inadequate, and there is always a danger of the discussion losing itself in pomposity and empty chatter . . . I should like to regard all I say here only as a tentative attempt to approach the problem of personality without making any claim to solve it. (CW 17, para. 312)

The following comments about ego and personality are offered in the same spirit of open inquiry.

We are not the only conscious beings on the planet. There is a myriad of other sentient life forms in this world; many possess modes of awareness that are well outside human consciousness. Some modes we share in common; some of our extraverted orientations to consciousness are notable elsewhere. The orientation to communal relationships, sensual perceptions, decisive actions, the pursuit of possibilities, are all in evidence among other species.

But the introverted orientations, and their awareness of the "eternal images" generated by what Jung called the "archetypal collective unconscious," enable ideas that have generated religious epiphanies, scientific breakthroughs, philosophical insights, literary masterpieces,

231

and artistic expressions that advance the human experience beyond other organic forms of life.

We could consider ego consciousness as a limited spectrum of conscious awareness. As Kant noted, it is constrained by restrictive parameters of perception and assessment. Ego consciousness includes the perception and assessment of the two central objects of ego consciousness. Both the extraverted and introverted modes of consciousness are attributes of ego consciousness.

But there is yet another field of awareness apparently not included in our ego consciousness. We also have an *awareness* of that ego awareness. We humans alone appear to have a meta-awareness—to be self-reflective and aware of being conscious. The central "I" who we are apart from ego consciousness, as observers of ego consciousness, the "I" of the individual who knows that the "I" who experienced life at age eight is also the same "I" experiencing life at age eighty.

The endowment of the "I," or who we call a person, or using Jung's term "personality," elevates the human experience to an arena of consciousness that is different *in kind* from other forms of ego consciousness. Personality is a mystery. It seems an endowment from above rather than an evolutionary feature. Personality has no antecedent cause in the evolutionary climb to higher and more complex forms of consciousness. Personality is not an innovative organic response to an environmental condition. There was no causal reason for it; it was not induced by the need for an environmental adaptation. Personality separates the human experience from the experience of all other forms of life in this world. Personality seems to be an endowment destined for more august purposes than merely material survival.

In *Memories, Dreams, and Reflections* (1989), Jung's comments about his personality #1 and #2 could illustrate the difference between the ego identity and personality. He noticed two personalities within himself as a young boy. He said one of these ". . . went to school and was less intelligent, attentive, hard-working, decent, and clean than many other boys. The other was grown up—old, in fact—skeptical, mistrustful, remote from the world of men, but close to nature, the earth, the sun, the moon, the weather, all living creatures, and above all close to the night, to dreams and to whatever 'God' worked directly in him. As soon as I was alone I could pass over into this state. At such times I knew I was worthy of myself . . . I therefore sought the peace and solitude of this 'other,' second personality."

In that reflection we are privy to a new center of conscious awareness: the objective awareness of his ego/persona identity as a young boy, and also the awareness of the "I" of his endowed personality.

Jung continued, ". . . it was as though a breath of the great world of stars and endless space had touched me, or as if a spirit had invisibly entered the room—the spirit of one who had long been dead and yet was perpetually present in timelessness until far into the future. Denouements of this sort were wreathed with the halo of the numen."

We might say that the ego identity is *what* we are in the world and the personality is *who* we are in the universe. Our position, our status, our gender, our background, our nationality, our body size, our age all conditions the ego identity, but not personality. Personality experiences life through a field of awareness that transcends the ego structure.

In the Bhagavad Gita, Arjuna found that elevated perspective with the help of his charioteer, the divine Krishna. At the threshold of a great battle, Arjuna was full of anxiety. He was to meet those he knew well in battle, and he quivered with the misgivings of his ego identity: "In the dark night of my soul I feel desolation. In my self-pity I see not the way of righteousness."

In an extensive and enlightening dialogue with Krishna, one that is easily grouped with the most beautiful scriptures ever written, Krishna reminds him who he truly is, and the way of the cosmos that he lives in: "Energy, forgiveness, fortitude, purity, a good will, freedom from pride— these are the treasures of the man who is born for heaven." By the end of their long dialogue, Arjuna found his way to his more transcendent self: "By thy grace I remember my Light, and now gone is my delusion."

Thomas Merton, the Trappist monk, writer, theologian, mystic, social activist, and scholar of comparative religion, meditated regularly for the purpose of moving from his ego identity to the more transcendent consciousness of personality, his "higher self."

Personality awareness seems also to include an awareness of the presence of other personalities. Remote conferencing has illuminated the difference between ego consciousness and personality awareness. In a remote video call, we see and hear people, just as they would be in a room with us, but we do not qualitatively sense their presence. When we are with other people in a room, we have a qualitative sense that we are with the living breathing individuals—a sense that is not present through a digital channel. Anyone who has been alone with someone moving through the dying process is aware of that moment when the dying person takes the last gasp. Prior to death, there were two in the room. Instantly at the end of mortal life, the attending person experiences the stark reality of being alone.

There may also be a spirit consciousness for personality that transcends ego consciousness—a knowing of that presence, in the same way there is a knowing about the presence of other personalities. Jung famously noted that he does not "believe" in God; he "knows." The Latin verse above the entry to his home in Kusnacht speaks to his own awareness: "Called or uncalled, God is present."

The Compass of Ego Consciousness

Psychological type dispositions are fundamental modes of ego consciousness. Those orientations to consciousness are also found in the persona, the personal unconscious, the shadow, and the soul. But they are *not* dispositions of personality.

Jung used a simple compass diagram to depict his model of psychological types. The types, he would be the first to acknowledge, do not encompass all of the elements of consciousness, but they do account for significant elements that substantially influence the personal biography and the oppositions in the unconscious.

The compass consists of four "functions," two receptive functions oriented to perceiving: intuition (N) and (S); and two rational functions oriented to assessing: thinking (T) and feeling (F). Upon these four functions, his entire model of psychological types is built. Jung's compass was his indispensable aid: "I would not for anything dispense with this compass on my psychological voyages of discovery" (CW 6, para.959).

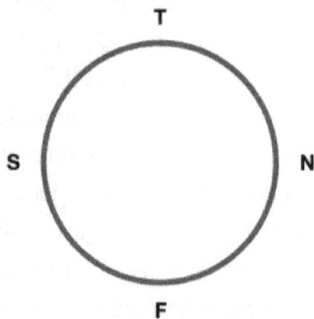

In only four paragraphs in Volume 6 of the Collected Works (666-669), Jung delineated how these functions might align with one another. Those alignments were brilliantly articulated in a 1977 article, "Typology Revisited: A new Perspective." The observations in that article are the *only* conclusions that can be explicitly drawn from Jung's four key paragraphs. The authors noted that a receptive function (sensation or intuition) as the lead function could align with either thinking or feeling. A rational function (thinking or feeling) as lead could align with either of the receptive functions (sensation or intuition).

They depicted the resulting combinations as "umwelts." Thinking with intuition would form the Ethereal Umwelt; feeling with intuition would form the Oceanic. Each umwelt had characteristic attributes of those combinations. Ethereal for example would be more philosophical and Oceanic would be more oriented to holistic values.

Thinking aligned with sensation would form the Structural Umwelt; Feeling aligned with sensation would form the Experial Umwelt. The Structural Umwelt is oriented to creating tangible order; the Experial Umwelt is oriented to relationships and experiencing sensual life in the moment.

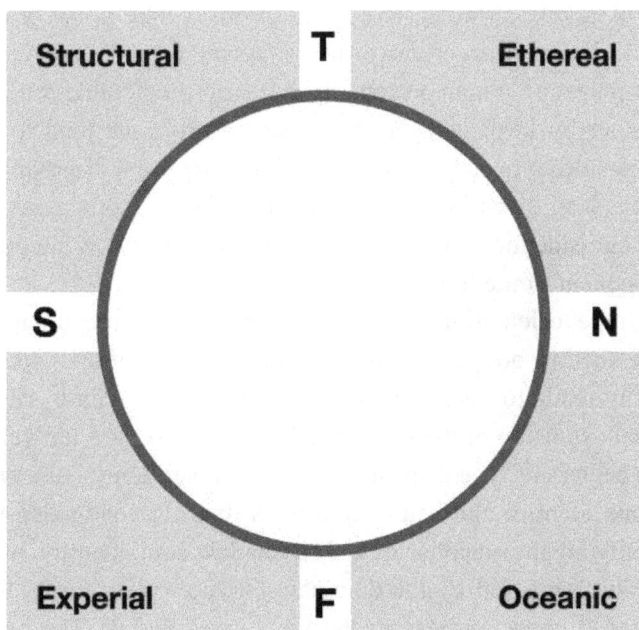

Using the umwelts to generalize the types in collaboration renders our work in this article easier. Each of the four umwelts is characterized by a rational function, thinking or feeling, and additionally characterized by a receptive function. The resulting attributes of the Oceanic and Ethereal Umwelts, for example, would implicitly include combinations of introverted feeling (Oceanic) or introverted thinking (Ethereal), each joined by intuition. The Experial and Structural Umwelts would include extraverted feeling (Experial) or extraverted thinking (Structural) each joined by sensation.

In that way, we can simplify our discussion of the role of the four introverted and four extraverted types as they are actively engaged collaboratively in the processes of individuation. Rather than consider all the types and their collaborative alignments separately, we will consider them as these simple vignettes of four umwelts.

The Process of Individuation

At last, with the architecture of the psyche, the review of ego and personality, and the compass of consciousness in hand, we can turn to the theme of psychological types and their relationship to individuation.

For other animals, the journey to wholeness is swifter and more direct; it is largely an instinctive proposition. Unlike geese or sheep or squirrels, living more according to an instinctual response to environment, the development of human personality is far less predictable or congruent.

Whether by birth or by culture, early in life, we tend to develop certain one-sided type dispositions. For simplicity, we will assume that the dispositions lean toward one of the umwelts. The persona gains strength from that one-sidedness, adopting the same umwelt, and is integrated as a vital component of the individual's ego identity.

The type orientations in the unconscious assume compensatory roles. The shadow adopts an opposing umwelt orientation—one that the ego identity tends to disown as incongruent or unwelcome. The soul, a typological extension of the shadow, adopts the shadow's umwelt.

Two centers of type dispositions vie for sovereignty—the one-sided ego/persona identity and a less conscious, but also one-sided shadow/soul identity in the unconscious. The shadow/soul identity will insist on not being repressed by the dominant ego/persona identity, for it too brings needed consciousness to the whole personality. The opposition

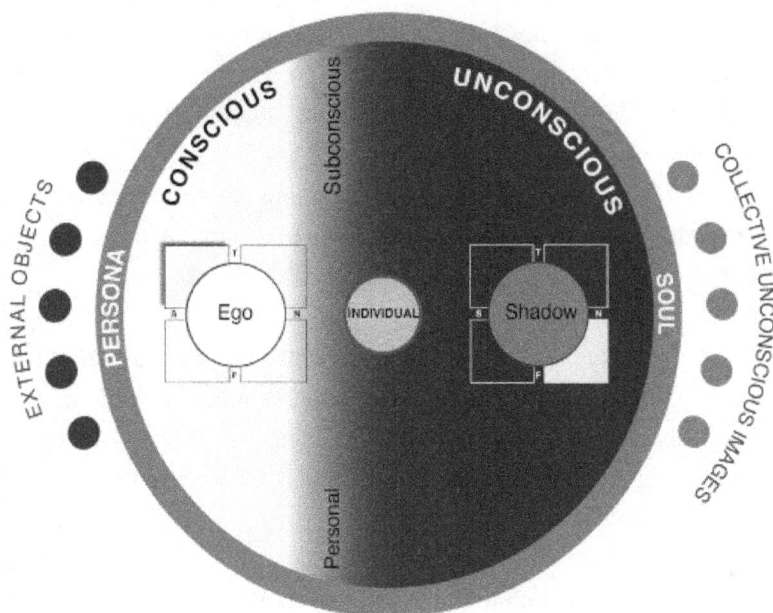

engendered by the lead ego type versus the lead shadow type forms what Jung called the "knock-down battle" in life. For the analyst, the task is to work with the ego's and shadow's auxiliary types, where the oppositions are not as conflictive.

For the whole personality with its broader awareness to emerge more fully, the conflicting factions need to be unified. In the first half of life, the ego/persona identity with its one-sidedness may have become quite stable, but for the central personality to become whole, the less conscious shadow and soul need to become increasingly conscious. The persona must fade, for it is an obstacle to individuation. As the one-sided ego identity diminishes, the perspective of the individual broadens and figuratively sees life from both sides—ego consciousness and the less conscious shadow and soul.

> If you can succeed in breaking down that dividing wall made by the personal unconscious, the shadow can be united with the ego and the individual becomes a mediator between two worlds. He can now see himself from the "other side" as well as from "this side." (Jung, 2012, p.142)

But the ego/persona identity may not accept that transition without a struggle. The ego may vie for dominion, for the shadow and soul dispositions may seem foreign, and the ego identity has become well established and defensible. Should the ego gain supremacy and completely suppress the promptings of shadow and soul, the less conscious types rise up to disrupt and disassemble the one-sided and pretentious ego identity. The individual will suffer neurosis, for he is investing his life's energy in egoistic *individualism* rather than the intended *individuation*.

> "But individualism is not and never has been a natural development; it is nothing but an unnatural usurpation, a freakish, impertinent pose that proves its hollowness by crumpling up before the least obstacle." (CW 17, para. 292)

With individuation, the greater personality gains an increasingly comprehensive connection to others, and to creating value in the world.

> ". . . there arises a consciousness which is no longer imprisoned in the petty, oversensitive, personal world of the ego, but participates freely in the wider world of objective interests. This widened consciousness is no longer that touchy, egotistical bundle of personal wishes, fears, hopes, ambitions which always has to be compensated or corrected by unconscious counter-tendencies; instead it is a function of relationship to the world of objects, bringing the individual into absolute, binding and indissoluble communion with the world at large. The complications arising at this stage are no longer egoistic wish-conflicts, but difficulties that concern others as much as oneself." (CW 7 para. 275)

The aim of individuation is the full growth and development of the whole personality, guided by the archetypal Self. The unifying personality must emerge with cooperative connections to ego, shadow, and soul.

The two initially opposing identities of ego and shadow gain unity through the gradually ascending penumbra of the personality/Self "central government."

CONSCIOUS Subconscious UNCONSCIOUS COLLECTIVE UNCONSCIOUS IMAGES EXTERNAL OBJECTS PERSONA SOUL Ego INDIVIDUAL Shadow Personal

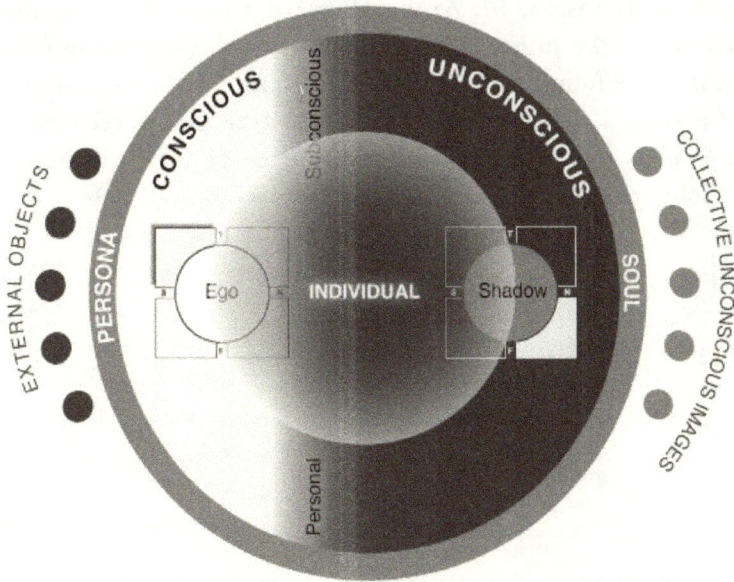

The value of Jung's astonishing insights about psychological types and their potentially disruptive nature from the unconscious is in our ability to become more self-aware, to recognize the leanings of ego identity, to understand the sources of disruptions from the unconscious, to understand that *what* we are in the world in terms of ego and persona pales in comparison to *who* we are becoming as persons with a potentially immortal destiny.

The Self guides the greater development of the whole personality. The Self is our connection to the infinite. If we invest our life energies in defending and promoting an ego identity, we have missed the real import of our lives.

> The decisive question for man is: Is he related to something infinite or not? That is the telling question of his life. Only if we know that the thing which truly matters is the infinite can we avoid fixing our interest upon futilities, and upon all kinds of goals which are not of real importance . . . In the final analysis, we count for something only because of the essential we embody, and if we do not embody that, life is wasted. (Jung, 1989, p. 325)

James G. Johnston, M. Arch., Harvard University, B.A. DePauw University, is the author of *Jung's Indispensable Compass* and *The Call Within*. He is founder of Gifts Compass and Life Atlas and architect of the Gifts Compass Inventory (GCI), the online self-assessment that depicts nuanced dispositions for each of Jung's original eight psychological types. He is also a lecturer at CGJI Zurich.

References

Humphrey, Siegler, & Smoke. (1977). "Typology Revisited: A New Perspective." *Psychological Perspectives.* Vol. 8, No. 2, pp. 206-219.

Jung, C.G. (1989). *Memories, Dreams, Reflections.* Vintage Books.

Jung, C.G. (2012). *Introduction to Jungian Psychology, Notes of the Seminar on Analytical Psychology* (given in 1925).

Neumann, E. (1989). *The Essays of Erich Neumann, Vol 3, The Place of Creation.* Princeton University Press.

Who is a Friend?:
Friendship in the Process of Individuation

Henry Abramovitch

When I think of Murray, the first word I think of is "mensch." In German, mensch means a person; but in Yiddish, it means something more profound, a truly decent human being. A person may be wise, rich, or beautiful, but if they are not a mensch, they are really "nothing" at all. For me, Murray embodies the idea in his fairness, his humanity, and mid-western decency.

In his short masterpiece *Men Under Construction,* Murray Stein (2020) discusses the archetypal dynamics of male friendship and mourns the scarcity of real friendship between men in contemporary life. Remarkably, Murray is the first depth psychologist to write about friendship and explore its unconscious and developmental aspects. Following his pioneering essay, I want to reflect upon the role of a true friend in the process of individuation, drawing on inspiring quotes. I will also briefly discuss the role of friendship in the therapeutic setting. But first, I want to discuss my friendship with Murray.

My Friendship with Murray

My friendship with Murray is a little like a fairy tale. We were good colleagues who met regularly as part of the International Jungian Community at congresses or committees. At one point, he asked me to contribute the entry on "Erich Neumann" (2006) for the Encyclopedia he was co-editing which deepened our dialogue. Mutual respect increased.

For many years, I wanted to bring Murray to Israel and finally he agreed to come in April 2015. He said he did not want to give a lecture or a workshop: "Let's just have a conversation in front of an audience" he proposed. I arranged an encounter at Jerusalem's prime culture and hospitality center, *Mishkenot Sha'ananim*, facing the walls of the old city where Saul Bellow, Simone de Beauvoir, and the Dalai Lama had lectured.

At one point, he was asked about Jung's antisemitism and Murray replied painfully, "It was like learning that someone very close to you had done a bad thing." The next day, I took him to the unique Masada complex overlooking the Dead Sea. When we were together on top of Masada, we discovered we had both been born in Canada and both attended Yale University. I mentioned that when I was an undergraduate, I had been very involved with an ensemble, acting, directing, even writing plays.

Suddenly, Murray whirled around toward me and said in a Biblical Voice: "You are the Man!" He explained that he wanted to write play about the historic meeting between Rabbi Leo Baeck and Carl Jung and was looking for a partner familiar with the Jewish tradition. A partner who would know what a Rabbi might say. I was indeed the man Murray had been seeking. I immediately said yes. There, on top of Masada.

As we began, I taught Murray the Hebrew word, "dugri," meaning "straight talk." We agreed that we would each say honestly what we felt about the evolving script, for the sake of the Work. Mostly, we worked on Skype, at crucial points both our wives made key suggestions that helped bring the play together. When we had a working script, the actors in Murray's ensemble, also made significant suggestions, saying, "I don't think Jung/Baeck would say that!" leading to key revisions. It is amazing to consider that the entire production team, authors, director, actors, musician, even the film director, are all Jungian analysts. "The Analyst and the Rabbi" was performed in France and Switzerland, and later revived with an American cast in Helena, Montana, made into a film available on Youtube (see References).

For me, the fairy tale continued. Chiron Publications, the press that Murray himself had founded, published a book version of the play in 2019. Each participant in the project added a personal chapter of reflection to the final script. In the spirit of our collaboration, Murray and I decided to put our Afterword in the form of a dialogue between us. Each night we would email each other back and forth. This conversation, now in front of print audience, was itself a most moving experience. I only knew how moving when, I read Murray's final entry:

> It has been a pleasure to work with you on this play, Henry. I don't have a biological brother, but now I have the feeling that must come with such a fraternal relationship. You have written a perceptive book on this topic, *Brothers and Sisters: Myth and Reality*, your Fay Lectures in 2014. Writing this play with you has brought a fantasy of brotherhood into the realm of reality for me. (Stein & Abramovitch, 2019, p. 75)

Ever since, Murray has been a brother and a friend.

Murray Stein on Male Friendship

Prior to Murray, only a single theorist—Harry Stack Sullivan—discussed the psychological importance of friends. Sullivan (1953) wrote about the need for a "chum" or a close friend for children and young adolescents. A chum teaches about the reciprocity of relationships and fosters sensitivity to the needs of another person. The child learns what to do to contribute to the happiness and sense of self-worth of his or her chum. Most significantly, a chum provides validation of self-worth. Growing up, like Jung, as a lonely replacement child, on an isolated farm in upper New York State, one can feel how much Sullivan was speaking how a chum redeemed him from a life of isolation and self-doubt. Sullivan writes however as if the importance of friendship is limited to a single developmental period. Yet, contemporary research, has shown how friendship play is crucial throughout the life cycle, and if anything, becomes more and more important as we age. It is associated with overall well-being, a better quality of life at all ages, as well as improved physical and mental health (Holt-Lunstad, Smith, & Layton, 2010). Having a friend is the best anti-depressant; not having friends is as damaging to one's health as being obese. The friendless die before their time. Living without close friends is damaging to the psyche at any age.

As noted above, Murray mourns the scarcity of real friendship between men in contemporary life. Friendship in America is indeed in a crisis. The May 2021 American Perspectives Survey finds that Americans report having fewer close friendships than they once did and rely on friends less often for emotional support. Americans today have fewer best friends and rely less on them for personal support. Most American men have only limited, situational friends or activity-based friendships—people they see only in specific contexts such as work, gym or the park. Significant numbers of American males have no friends at all, or only "online buddies" they have never actually met. Only a tiny fraction of men can talk openly about personal issues; even less about intimate concerns.

Stein (2020) picks up from Sullivan in asserting that "for most men in our present postmodern times, a close friendship with another man is but a memory from adolescence when one had a buddy with whom one shared innermost thoughts…" (p. 9). Male friendships, he argued, come to a halt "upon serious engagement with a female partner" (p. 9).

He then analyzes the stages of friendship between men. The first type of friend, he claims, is an "in-the-mother friendship" characterized by psychic fusion and unconscious identity and reflects a lack of psychologically differentiation from the mother complex. Such relationships are largely unconscious "intuitively, often in a quasi-magical way" express an unconscious longing for paradise. "Words are not needed to express feelings because they are communicated via unconscious channels" (p.101). The image is of two identical heads on one body who mirror each other, uniting against others. As a result, such men are usually silent, undeveloped, unformed, and infantile.

A more advanced type of friendship is based on overt, conscious masculine identity, in which physical prowess, competitiveness and aggressiveness are highly valued. Such bonding may begin with a fight as occurred between Gilgamesh and Enkidu, who start as rivals but go onto be fast friends. The psychic dynamic of such male friends is of a shadow brother. The relationship is based on an ego-shadow axis and therefore always with some measure of inequality. "Something in us knows that when the shadow friend dies, something in us also dies. Our lives are irrefrangibly joined to one another" (p. 103). Indeed, this is Gilgamesh's reaction to the death of Enkidu. Yet his mad grief sends him on this first individuation journey in recorded history.

Once a man has decisively differentiated his ego from the mother complex and integrated elements of shadow, then a "maturity friendship" may emerge. But, here too, shadowy emotions of hierarchy and envy predominate. The adult man's preference for hierarchical relationships derives from Oedipal anxieties of castration and then also sibling rivalry. "…sibling rivalry runs through the bible like a Wagnerian leitmotif" based on the idea that one is special (or gifted) in a way that the other is not. The rival feels deeply deprived and so retaliates (Abramovitch, 2014). Such friendship may have closeness, but they also have inherent instability.

Finally, Murray points toward true friendship when the anima facilitates deep connectedness and bonding, through the ability to speak of tender feelings, and with sincerity. He ends this discussion of friendship by quoting Emerson, that great student of friendship: "The essence of friendship is entireness, a total magnanimity and trust" (Emerson, 2016, pp.179-180). It is only an entire person who can offer this or accept it. And this is the reason for its rarity among us (Stein, 2020, p.110). This type of friendship, I call "true friendship" and in rest of the chapter I want to explore its essence.

Kinship vs. Friendship

Anthropologists emphasise a fundamental distinction between kinship and friendship. Kinship refers to obligatory social bonds within the family network. Friendship refers to relationships with others that are freely chosen. There are ritual friendships, like blood brotherhood that are kinship-like; and there are cases when a sister, is not just a sister, but also a friend. In Israel, there are high expectations from friendship, as expressed in the oft heard Hebrew phrase which translated means, "friends (are) like family." Just as you choose your friends, so too, you can unchoose them and definitively end the relationship. Even if you are not speaking with your father, he remains nevertheless your father. An estranged friend is a stranger.

Semantics of Friendship

Friendship exists along a broad spectrum of varying degrees of closeness and commitment. Cultures differ dramatically in their words for these different kinds of friends. English is particularly deficient in the vocabulary of friendship. The English word "friend" covers a vast semantic range from best friend to a recent, casual acquaintance. It is supremely ambiguous concerning the nature of the relationship, and the depth of mutual responsibility. The Russian language has a rich vocabulary for the type and depth of friendship that has no equivalents in the English language. I dramatically encountered it when I was giving group supervision many years ago to a group of talented "routers," a word Murray coined for those on the *route* to becoming Jungian analysts in countries without training programs. At that time, I was doing group supervision in Moscow with a translator (Abramovitch, 2015).

Friendship and Individuation

Jung had little to say about friendship, but many people spoke about him as a friend, like a wonderful, older brother. I believe that having friends is an essential part of the individuation process. The paradox is that while individuation is individual, it is not something you can do by yourself.

At one point, the translator translates what the therapist has said in Russian to the group, saying, "The patient said to me, 'I feel like you are my friend.'" Somehow, I am wary. Curious. Uneasy. I know that the Russian language has many nuanced words for different kinds of friendship. Using my intuition, I ask, "What was the actual Russian word, the patient used?" and I am told *drug*. I am unfamiliar with this term but come to understand that the only possible English translation for *drug* is friend, but friend is certainly not an adequate translation for *drug*. *Drug* and friend occupy entirely different emotional and interpersonal spaces. In Russian, *drug*, indicates someone extremely close and implies an intense, demanding, enduring relationship that is both exhilarating and exhausting. *Drug* is a deep friend who can ease the pain of life and is more of a soul brother or soulful sister. In Soviet times, your *drug* was the one person who could be chosen freely. For only children, they took the place of missing brothers and sisters and to whom they had a total commitment. Polish, too, has six terms for degrees and genders of friendship with the most important, *przyjaciel*, indicating a strong loyalty and attachment bordering on love. Understanding that Russians and Poles have specific words for relationship with more depth, devotion and duration than is implied by the English word, friend, cannot be without consequences for analysis. When I listen to those cases involving a positive transference to the therapist, I sense there is a culture-specific *drug*-like or *przyjaciel*-like relationship that primes patients to open their souls to their therapists. In this sense, there is a cultural concept or cultural complex that connects to the therapeutic situation that does not exist in the English-speaking world.

"A friend is someone who knows all about you and still loves you," writes Elbert Hubbard. This motto reveals how true friendship has a therapeutic quality. When a friend knows all about you, there is no reason to hide or present a persona barrier. Most people tend to hide parts of themselves to be liked or accepted. But true friendship dissolves that persona anxiety entirely. In a metaphoric sense, true friend functions like the Self, seeing all of us, accepting all of us.

The security that a true friend provides is illustrated in Epicurus' phrase: "It is not so much our friends' help that helps us as it is, as the confidence of their help." This emotional security that true friends provide is expressed poignantly in this phase: "It's the friends you can call up at 4 a.m. that matter." — Marlene Dietrich. In Israel, I have had that 4 a.m. experience of friendship. It was the middle of the night and I urgently needed to borrow a car. With trepidation, I called upon a friend. I was worried he might say that he never loans his car, that he would have to check with his insurance, that he would need the car back at 7 a.m. that he would agree but leave me terrified about what would happen if it received a scratch or a dent. Instead, when he heard my predicament, he said, "I will be outside in two minutes" and without a word, gave me the keys with a smile. He said good luck and bring it back when you can. This experience taught me a lot about what it means to be a friend.

True Friendship has a timeless quality. It is timeless both in the moment of an actual meeting, but also when, after a long break, true friends just effortlessly pick up where they left off. Friendship is, therefore, a never-ending conversation. Two other crucial aspects of the true friend are accompaniment and absence of hierarchy. Albert Camus gives a poetic expression of these qualities in his famous phrase: "Don't walk behind me; I may not lead. Don't walk in front of me; I may not follow. Just walk beside me and be my friend." Camus highlights how much friendship is a shared journey without walking ahead or behind but walking side by side in the long journey toward becoming ourselves. Pythagoras of Samos provides perhaps the best summary of the role of friends in the individuation: "Friends are as companions on a journey, who ought to aid each other to persevere in the road to a happier life."

True Friends are not "yes men." They do not tell us what we want to hear, but rather speak with refreshing directness. True Friends give clear, focused, critical feedback that does not trigger a defensive ego rection. They tell us what we need to hear, but what no one else will tell us. Oscar Wilde put it succinctly: "A friend stabs you in the front."

Love Your Friend as Yourself

One of the Bible's best-known phases is *Love your neighbor as yourself* (Leviticus 18:19). Surprisingly, the standard English translation, *neighbor* does not reflect the Hebrew original, which is *re'acha, literally 'your re'a'*. The Biblical term *re'a* does not mean "neighbor," *but* "friend" as is clear in numerous biblical passages, Exodus 2:13, II Samuel 13:2, Proverbs 17:17. The same root is used in one of the Blessing at a Jewish Wedding, when bride and groom are encouraged not only to share love, but also friendship. In the Bible, as in modern Hebrew, there is an entirely different word for neighbor, *shachen.* A "shachen" is a "friendship" based on geography. Why this historic mistranslation occurred remains a mystery. Moreover, this famous passage is usually understood as a stand-alone motto. But a close reading of the text reveals that, in fact, it is not a motto, but rather a conclusion. Here is the text in my translation:

> *Do not hate your brother in your heart*
> *Rebuke, yes, rebuke your fellow, so that you will not sin because*
> *of him.*
> *Do not to take revenge, Do not hold onto your anger…*
> *But love your friend as yourself. I am the Lord. (Lev. 19:17-8,*
> *my translation).*

The usual interpretation of the passage is a "negative" formulation of a golden rule: "Do not do unto others what you would not have them do unto you." While this formulation is a powerful statement of mutual empathy, it cannot be the original intension of the passage from Leviticus. The language of the prelude to the golden rule, "your brother" and "your fellow" clearly indicate that connections is far more powerful than mere neighbors. Instead, Leviticus presents us with a tense situation of a hurtful, hateful grievance between friends.

Scripture warns sharply against the natural tendency to nurture this wound and let it grow into an undermining grievance. It is this situation that the Text sees as extremely dangerous. A person may act out his shadowy complexes in a destructive, impulsive way and bring sin upon himself through revenge, such as humiliating a friend in public, which Jewish tradition considered a form of "bloodshed" since shaming brings blood to the face. Scripture remarkably urges a direct, quasi-therapeutic approach. It calls upon the injured person to speak directly to one's friend about the hurtful behavior, to rebuke him. Such openhearted sharing will clear the air and allow one to love one's friend, as yourself.

Eros & Philia

How does eros-based love differ from love among friends? Seneca, the Roman philosopher and stateman identified a key distinction between love and friendship asserting: "Friendship always benefits; love sometimes injures." In the original Latin, Seneca is contrasting *eros* with *philia.* Relations based on eros may have an intense, magnetic quality of profound togetherness. But inevitably, there will be tensions, clashes, misunderstanding and worse. In contrast, philia, love of friends, does not. Deep friendship has an exciting serenity. I ask my friend of over four decades, "When are we going to have our fight?" He smiles back. We both know it is never going to happen. Seneca asserts that true friendship embodies a longstanding attachment that no fear, nor self-interest, can ever sever. This bond is expressed in famous conversation between Piglet and Winnie the Pooh: "'We'll be Friends Forever, won't we, Pooh?' asked Piglet. 'Even longer,' said Winnie."

Frenemies

Frenemies is a word coined by the American columnist, Walter Winchell, in 1953, to refer to someone who pretends to be a friend but turns out to be enemy. In the archetype of the friend, one pole is the trusted, devoted friend but in its shadow is the frenemy, the false friend who betrays, like Judas. Recent research (Bishop et.al. in press) has revealed that frenemies are much more common than previously thought. This is also true in the history of psychoanalysis.

Freud's emotional life was dominated by such a fundamental frenemy dynamic. Freud, in his correspondence, confessed that it was based on his relationship with his nephew John, with whom he grew up during the first three years of his life and who was one year older. Freud wrote:

> Until the end of my third year we had been inseparable; we had loved each other and fought each other, and . . . this childhood relationship . . . had a determining influence on all my subsequent relations with contemporaries. Since that time my nephew John has had many re-incarnations. . . . All my friends have in a certain sense been reincarnations of the first figure. . . . My emotional life has always insisted that I should have an intimate friend and a hated enemy. I have always been able to provide myself afresh with both, and it has not infrequently happened that the ideal situation of childhood has been so completely reproduced that friend and enemy have come together in a single individual. (Freud, 1960, p. 423)

Freud's frenemy complex, seeing comrades as intimate friends or/and hated enemies, no doubt played itself out in his relationship with Jung, as with so many others. His split love-hate friend transference played itself out not only with friends and disciples, but, most likely, also within his consulting room. This idea led me to consider how friend dynamics plays itself out in the transference-countertransference matrix.

Friend Transference and Countertransference: Case Example

A new patient enters my consulting room crying out, "I don't need an analyst, I need a friend." The inequality of therapeutic situation does not allow for true friendship to develop between analyst and patient. But I have had patients who needed a friend and for a phase of the course of treatment, I allowed them in symbolic sense to experience me as their friend. We might call this a "friend transference." In contrast, I also have patients who I feel that had we not met through analysis, we most certainly could have been friends. We might call this a positive friend countertransference. The analysis continues helpfully until one day he enters and says, "I don't have the energy to talk. You're my friend, tell me something about yourself. Even better, let's go out for a beer." I don't know what to say, so I say nothing. I suddenly realize why, indeed, this man has no friends. Usually, he is self-absorbed. But when he is depleted, he needs a friend. When I do not respond to his offer, he says sullenly, "I thought you were my friend."

Shadowy thoughts start intruding into my mind. Because I am not his "friend," he will start slandering me, telling lies about me. In his mind, I am now the Judas who has betrayed him. In syntonic countertransference/ projective identification, I experience him as betraying me.

I know he is alone, abandoned, vulnerable, friendless. How can I say to him that we were never meant to be friends, without hurting him and destroying his illusion that we are friends. How can I explain that I deliberately allowed him to experience me as a friend for the sake of his healing journey. I am cautious. But I do want him to reflect to reflect on our relationship. Drawing on Hebrew tradition of asking questions, I say, "Who is a friend?" He is an intellectual and relishes intellectual puzzles. To my amazement, he quotes Hubbard, almost word for word, "A friend is someone who knows all about you and still loves you." Then, to my own amazement, I say, "Yes! I am your friend." The analysis proceeds.

Ending as Friends

I also believe that a good ending to an analysis can transform the relationship between analyst and analysand to something closer to friendship. Elsewhere (Abramovitch, 2021), I used the final scene of the classic movie Casablanca as an amplification of this transformation. The ending of Casablanca is perhaps the most famous parting scene in cinematic history. I want to reframe this romantic scene where Rick, played by Humphrey Bogart, is the analyst and Ilsa, played by Ingrid Bergman, is his patient. Bergman, responds as if in the role of the patient. Rick tells Ilsa that instead of going off together, she must leave with her husband, "You're getting on that plane." Ilsa, startled, asks: "But what about us?" Patients often wonder what the therapist's true feelings towards them are. Do they really care, or even love them? Bogart, as analyst, replies: "We'll always have Paris." To "always have Paris," means to be able to permanently hold onto the intimate experience between analyst and patient within the temenos, the therapeutic container. Rick the analyst, is pointing to all the good enough, even loving work that was done together in analysis. Regardless of the current and painful separation, our "Paris" can never be taken away. Rick's final phrase to Ilsa: "Here's looking at you, kid," embodies a profound sense of seeing and being seen, which is the essence of all good therapeutic work. It cannot be coincidence that Rick's iconic, last line of the film is, "I think this is the beginning of a

253

beautiful friendship." The exploration of clinical aspects of friendship dynamics is worthy of further investigation.

Finally, I want to assert that true friendship has a transcendent quality. This sentiment was expressed poignantly by Goethe:

> To know someone here or there with whom you can feel there is understanding in spite of distances or thoughts expressed, that can make life a garden.
>
> Here, the polymath from Weimar, highlights how true friendship, even just knowing that there is a friend out there, has a transformative ability of returning us to a state of grace, to a state before the fall, when life was truly a garden.

Henry Abramovitch (Israel) is founding president and senior training analyst at the Israel Institute of Jungian Psychology in Honor of Erich Neumann, Professor Emeritus at Tel Aviv University Medical School and Past President of Israel Anthropological Association. He has served on Ethics and Programme Committees of the International Association for Analytical Psychology (IAAP) and is active in Israel Interfaith Encounter Association. He teaches and supervises Routers in the IAAP Developing Groups in Eastern Europe and Kazakhstan. He is author of *The First Father* (2010*); Brothers and Sisters: Myth and Reality* (2014); *Why Odysseus Came Home as a Stranger and Other Puzzling Moments in the Life of…Great Individuals* (2020), and with Murray Stein, the play, *The Analyst and the Rabbi* (2019). For the past year, he has led a Reflection Group for Ukrainian Analysts on Zoom. His special joys are poetry, dream groups and the holy city of Jerusalem. Email: henry.abramovitch@gmail.com

References

Abramovitch, Henry. (2006). "Erich Neumann." *The Edinburgh International Encyclopedia of Psychoanalysis*. Edinburgh University Press. (Ed. RM Skelton).

Abramovitch, Henry. (2014). *Brothers and Sisters: Myth and Reality. Fay lecture series in analytical psychology*. Texas A & M University Press.

Abramovitch, Henry. (2015). "Pioneers or Colonialism?" *Between Innovation and Tradition: Jungian analysts working in different cultural settings* (Eds. C. Crowther and J. Weiner). Spring Books. pp. 51-69. Reprinted by Routledge 2022 as *Jungian Analysts working in Different Cultures.*

Abramovitch, Henry. (2021). "When is it time to stop? When good enough becomes bad enough." Journal of Analytical Psychology 66(4): 907-925.

Bishop Mills, Carol, Yu, Panfeng & Mongeau, Paul (in press). "Frenemies: Acting like friends but feeling like enemies."

Emerson, R. W. (2016). *Essays*. Diamond Books.

Freud, S. (1960). *The Letters of Sigmund Freud*. (Ed. Ernest L. Freud). Basic Books.

Holt-Lunstad, J., Smith, T.B., and Layton, J.B. (2010). "Social Relationships and Mortality Risk: A meta-analytic review." PlosMedicine 7(7): e1000316. Published: July 27, 2010. https://doi.org/10.1371/journal.pmed.1000316

Sullivan, H. S. (1953). *The Interpersonal Theory of Psychiatry*. Norton.

Stein, M. (2020). *Men Under Construction: Challenges and Prospects*. Chiron Publications.

Stein, M. & Abramovitch, H. (2019). *The Analyst and the Rabbi: A Play.* Chiron Publications. Performance available at https://www.youtube.com/watch?v=JsAMVbRYaGA.

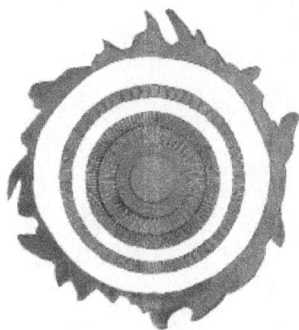

CROSSING BORDERS

The Transformative Plumbed Serpent of the Americas: Quetzalcoatl

Nancy Swift Furlotti, PhD

Murray is a special human being, so full of life and creativity. As Erich Neumann has described in his books on the nature of creativity, Murray is one of the "Great Individuals" who is in touch with the creative essence of the unitary reality, that transpersonal realm that creates new light. It has been and continues to be a privilege to know him.

This chapter is in honor of Murray Stein's 80th birthday. I first *"discovered"* Murray's brilliance years ago before I began my formal Jungian training. He would periodically come to Los Angeles/Santa Monica to speak, not at the L.A. Institute, but always impressive large conferences focused on some important and timely topics, like feminism, where Murray stood his own among the likes of Betty Friedan. I have had the pleasure of working with Murray on many occasions, from the challenging days of the *Red Book* to many seminars, online and in person, most recently at the Zurich Lecture Series where we—now two older analysts—could relax, laugh and talk about the joys and tribulations of lives thoroughly lived.

At its inception Murray invited me to be a member of the Mercurius Prize Committee to observe and celebrate through film the wonderful serpent Mercurius and its ever-transformative nature. This is where we have fun, watching films and having lively discussions of whether Mercurial energies are present or not. Murray is a special human being, so full of life and creativity. As Erich Neumann has described in his books on the nature of creativity, Murray is definitely one of the "Great Individuals" who is in touch with the creative essence of the unitary reality, that transpersonal realm that creates new light. It has been and continues to be a privilege to know him.

Quetzalcoatl, The Plumbed Serpent

In light of our involvement with Mercurius—as in the Prize Committee—where we look for that transformative serpent stalking the shadows of characters and film makers, and relate to it ourselves, I have chosen to talk about Quetzalcoatl, the plumed serpent in Central American mythology. His myths reflect the Mercurius energy that is so important for individuation psychology as a different manifestation of Mercurius, the bird-snake god that inherently carries the opposites. While I mostly speak about Maya mythology, an earlier time period and further south, this mythology from Central Mexico is equally interesting, especially this central god figure, the beautiful-plumed serpent and his shadow brother, Tezcatlipoca. The interplay between these two gods is a further union of opposites of earth and air, or spirit and matter, creation and destruction, consciousness and the unconscious. Quetzalcoatl was considered a savior god in Central Mexican mythology, the white god of light, who struggled constantly with his evil black brother. The Nahua believed that Quetzalcoatl would one day return as the savior god.

The black god, Tezcatlipoca, was seen as a primordial god, a part of preconscious nature, similar in regard to Dionysus' relationship to Apollo in Greek mythology. Tezcatlipoca was called the god of the smoking mirror since he wore a mirror on his missing foot. The mirror that emerges from the unconscious brings with it our shadow and encourages us to look at it to see our wholeness. Quetzalcoatl was caught in this mirror as his shadow was reflected back to him in his regression to lustful, incestuous passions, as described in the first myth we will discuss. He could not tolerate this in himself and instead shamefully disappeared across the waters (Bierhorst, 1998). This represents another manifestation of the archetype of Mercurius at work, always at work, pushing us to become more conscious. The myth points to the importance of symbolic sacrifice, which in contrast was played out as real sacrifice in the myth.

As an archetypal figure, the snake is a cold-blooded saurian that live in the dark recesses of caves or under rocks. It can be poisonous or harmless, but it evokes a reaction of fear in humans as well as in most other animals. Metaphorically, they can be seen as feminine or masculine, and as frequent visitors to dreams they represent a new primordial element emerging from the unconscious that the dreamer needs to take very seriously. Jung (1984) refers to a patient who always got sick after dreaming of a snake. He says, "So whenever life means business, when things are getting serious, you are likely to find a saurian on the way. Or when vital contents are to appear from the unconscious, vital thoughts or impulses, you will dream of such animals" (p. 645). Snakes and worms are part of the same archetypal energy pattern. They come from the body or the psychological earth, the preconscious realm, and have to do with the sympathetic nervous system. In other words, their archetypal energy represents movement out of the primordial aspect of the psyche. Although, potentially dangerous and frightening, snakes also carry the germs of human development and potential transformation. Symbolically, they are connected to rebirth. They shed their skins yearly in transformation into a new self.

Quetzalcoatl's name derives from two words: *quetzal*, a rare bird with brilliant green feathers, and *coatl*, which means serpent. The combination means the plumbed serpent. Coatl is a combination of the words *atl*, or water, and *co*, or serpent. Coatl also means *twin brother*. Quetzalcoatl can also be translated, *Precious Brother*, alluding to the earthly self and the spiritual self. Quetzalcoatl's aspect of himself as his fleshy twin is called Xolotl, that takes the form of a dog. He is also the personification of Venus, the morning star, *Lord of the Dawn*, and as the evening star, Xolotl, *Lord of the Land of the Dead*.
According to Ester Harding,

> The serpent represents several standpoints: as the demon of earth, darkness and evil, as the representative of the light, spirit and wisdom, as the ouroboros of cyclic life and the symbol of renewal as well as the ghosts of the dead, and as the uniter of opposites and the means of communication with the divine. (2001)

Birds, on the other hand and one half of Quetzalcoatl, represent air, spirit, wind, breath, creative inspiration, ideas, fantasy, imagination, and the realm of the psyche. The bird is a hunch which has to come down to earth or into consciousness to be understood. The plumed serpent is an archetype that represents a combination of the ultra-violet and infrared spectrum for light and energy—opposites. If they are too far apart, then both extremes are acted out in different ways.

Quetzalcoatl is a banished figure waiting to return. Quetzalcoatl reflects through his myth and struggle the essence of what Jung describes in *Symbols of Transformation* and what Erich Neumann elucidates in *The Origins and History of Consciousness*. His is the struggle to successfully accomplish the *Night Sea Journey* rather than succumbing to mortal instincts, complexes and shadow, and falling incestuously back into the arms of the Great Mother, the unconscious. Quetzalcoatl succeeds and emerges as the united duality of dark and light, mortal and spirit which is represented by the morning star, Venus. Through his struggle, he canalizes the sexual, incestuous instinct into a higher form of spiritual love.

Two Important Myths

The myth and religion of Quetzalcoatl first arose in Mesoamerica during the Teotihuacan Civilization, 150 B.C. to 650 A.D. Teotihuacan was the "City of the Gods" where the current Fifth Sun was created, and also the birthplace of the Nahua culture. It is located 30 miles north of Mexico City and still standing are the Pyramids of the Sun and Moon, in the center of which lies the Temple of Quetzalcoatl.

There are two important myths related to Quetzalcoatl: the first is the creation myth and the second is his journey into the underworld. In the Nahua (including Aztec, Mixtec, Zapotec, Tlaxcala, Puebla and Oaxaca) religion, the supreme dual creator was Ometeotl, both masculine and feminine in the one, that were omnipresent and omnipotent. It existed in the *Place of Duality*, at the navel of the universe, the highest point in heaven. It created the world through the abstract forces of the four directions, represented as their sons, which were created one after the other as four successive suns, worlds or ages and lasted different lengths of time. The eras make up a quincunx, the four directions with the fifth as the source of movement in the center. The birth and death of eras made the Nahuas very much aware of the finiteness of life as if life were just a transitory stage we pass through to get to death. The human body and life have little value, much like a corn stalk that grows and is cut down. A nahuatl poem reflects this belief:

It is not true, it is not true that we come on this earth to live.
We come only to sleep, only to dream. Our body is a flower.
As grass becomes green in the springtime, so our hearts will
open and give forth buds, and then they will wither. (M. Leon-
Portillo. p. 72)

In the creation myth, the four sons of Ometeotl represent the four
quadrants of space, the four directions, each represented by a color
which is connected to a god. East was represented by Red Tezcatlipoca,
north by Black Tezcatlipoca, west by White Tezcatlipoca, also known as
Quetzalcoatl, and south by Blue Tezcatlipoca, whom the Aztecs called
Huitzilopochtli, the god of the sun and war. Black Tezcatlipoca, called just
Tezcatlipoca, was the god of darkness and evil, and White Tezcatlipoca,
known as Quetzalcoatl, was the god of goodness and light. These two
reflect the opposite and conflicting dualities of the supreme creator god.
They were in constant opposition from the beginning of creation, each
striving to become the sun and rule the world.

The earth and sky were dark, in need of light. The council of gods
chose Black Tezcatlipoca to become the god of the First Sun of the
world inhabited by giants, an *era of earthbound matter*. Quetzalcoatl or
White Tezcatlipoca struck him with a club, knocking him into the water.
There he changed into a jaguar and devoured the giants. Quetzalcoatl
became the god of the Second Sun in the *era of air*, enduring until Black
Tezcatlipoca struck him down with his jaguar paw. A great wind arose that
destroyed the world. Thaloc, the god of rain and water, was chosen as the
god of the Third Sun, in the *era of fiery rain*. That world was destroyed by
Quetzalcoatl through a rain of fire. Tlaloc's wife Chalchiuhlicue, or *She of
the Jade Skirts, goddess of running water*, was the goddess of the Fourth
Sun in the *era of water* and was destroyed when Tezcatlipoca caused it to
rain so long that the earth flooded. This flood caused the watery sky to fall
down upon the earth. With this dangerous result, it now became necessary
for the two opposing rivals, Tezcatlipoca and Quetzalcoatl, to lift the sky
off the earth so they could continue with the creation of the next sun. The
four gods cycled through the elements, matter, air, fire, and water but still
could not make a sustainable world. So, all the gods gathered in council
to try again and decide who among them would be sacrificed and changed
into the Fifth Sun, in *the era of movement* at the center of the wheel.

It is told that when yet (all) was in darkness, when yet no sun had shown and no dawn had broken—it is said—the gods gathered themselves together and took council among themselves there at Teotihuacan. They spoke; they said among themselves; come hither, O gods! Who will carry the burden? Who will take it upon himself to be the sun, to bring the dawn? (Sahagún's transcription of the myth of the creation of the Fifth Sun from the Florentine Codex. vol. 3)

One god from the group of council volunteered, Tecuciztecatl. Another god, Nanauatzin, stood and listened to the discussion, then the gods called upon him to be the second one and he agreed. He said, "It is well, O gods; you have been good to me" (Sahagún, Vol. 3). Both gods now did penance and fasted for four days. During this time the fire was laid, and it burned in the hearth that was called *teotaxcalli*. Tecuciztecatl who was rich and powerful, offered quetzal feathers, pellets of gold, copal, thorns made of coral and precious stones. His incense was of a very good quality. Nanauatzin, on the other hand, was poor and scabby with sores, offered branches of green water reeds, pellets of hay, and maguey thorns dyed with his own blood. For his incense, he used the scabs from his own sores.

On the fifth night the gods gathered in front of a divine hearth where the large fire had been burning for four days. One of the two chosen gods had to cast himself into the fire as the supreme sacrifice and emerge purified to light the world. The gods directed Tecuciztecatl to enter the fire, and he attempted to jump in four times, but the heat was too great, and he was afraid and held back. Then they asked Nanauatzin, and unafraid, he quickly hurled himself into the flames. "Thereupon, he burned; his body crackled and sizzled" (Sahagún, Vol. 3). Hearing the crackling and roasting, Tecuciztecatl then found his courage and threw himself into the fire. After this an eagle and then a jaguar followed them into the flames, the eagle becoming blackened and the jaguar dotted with black spots, both splashed with black ash from the fire. The two animals represented spirit and matter. The jaguar was Texcatlipoca's animal counterpart.

The gods sat and waited for the dawn for a long time before they saw a reddening in all directions around them as the light broke. The gods fell to their knees to watch the god who had become the sun, Nanauatzin, begin to rise and it was red, swaying side to side with a blinding brilliance that could not be looked upon. Then Tecuciztecatl, the moon, rose from the east where the sun had burst forth. Both sun and moon, too, were on the same path and had the same brightness. The gods were not happy about this. This could not be! Suddenly, one of the gods came running out with a rabbit and threw it into the face of Tecuciztecatl, the moon. It darkened his face, killing off some of its brilliance. But the sun still did not move, and the still air began to kill the gods, while one named Xolotl, the dog-headed god who was Quetzalcoatl's fleshy twin, escaped to hide first in the maize stalks, then in the maguey, and then threw himself into the water turning into a salamander. Here he was finally killed with the other gods. Still the sun did not move until the wind from Quetzalcoatl, as the god of wind, Ehecatl, began to blow with all its might and made the sun move on its course. Thus, the Fifth Sun of Movement was created through purification and sacrifice in fire and water and was ruled by Quetzalcoatl. To keep it constantly moving on its course, a specified period of time within the Fifth Era was allotted to each of the gods of the four directions, as the wheel of time turned.

This myth addresses the basic conflict of opposites, the polarities of earth and sky, light and dark, fire and water and their reconciliation through penance and sacrifice as that which begins creation, giving energy and movement to life. The gods had to sacrifice themselves for life to begin. The movement from the center of the wheel is the libido, or the flow of energy from one's nature out into life. This creation myth reflects not only how the Fifth world was created but it also reflects the transformative process within individuals in need of healthy development and creative change. Sacrifice is always required to set this in motion. We frequently see individuals who are stuck in the realm of the gods, so to speak, in spirit above the uncomfortable grounded matter of being, unwilling to burn in the flames of emotion and heated passion in order to purify and transform the elements/complexes to allow energy to flow into a middle ground between earth and spirit, and into balanced, conscious relationships with self and others.

This situation of the split is represented in this myth by the image of the plumed serpent, which is Quetzalcoatl before his transformation. He was all unconscious spirit, and his shadow was all unconscious matter. As von Franz says in *The Psychological Meaning of Redemption Motifs in Fairytales*:

"The Alchemists speak either of the dragon or the hermaphrodite monster, something monstrous and unnatural and not positive. It has to be cut in pieces, destroyed, or redeemed because it represents a union of the opposites on a too-unconscious level." (p.78)

The Aztecs on a cultural level remained on the side of matter trying to bring in spirit for their redemption and connection to the gods/ancestors, and in their attempt, concretized the process as seen in their human sacrificial rituals, much like the gods sacrificing themselves in the fire to commence the Fifth World. In the second myth, Quetzalcoatl journeys into the underworld, demonstrating a symbolic sacrifice as opposed to the earlier concrete sacrifice.

There is a myth of Quetzalcoatl as the ruler/priest of the Toltec city of Tula, but we will now focus on the Hermetic myth of his death and journey into the underworld. As the ruler of the City of the Gods established after the creation of the Fifth Sun, Quetzalcoatl was wise, good and chaste. His old rival and antithesis shadow, Tezcatlipoca, who is also called *Smoking Mirror* for the mirror he wears in place of his amputated foot, a motif similar to the foot injuries characteristic of chthonic gods. (Through their struggle with the Great Mother the gods, her sons, lose a foot but gain *second sight*, or eyes into the creative unconscious, much like the Greek god, Hephaestus). Tezcatlipoca appears in disguise, along with two demons, to plot Quetzalcoatl's downfall. He brings Quetzalcoatl a mirror and Quetzalcoatl sees his earthly form for the first time but is frightened by what he sees. Tezcatlipoca then temps him with a drink of pulque, an alcoholic beverage. After refusing, he finally agrees to taste it and likes it. After five drinks he becomes quite drunk and calls for his sister, Xochiquetzal, the goddess of love, beauty, and pleasure, his sisterly anima. She, too, drank five drinks of pulque, and then they slept together. The incest—falling into the unconscious realm of the Great Mother via the anima is much like Eve and the serpent in the Garden of Eden, seducing Adam away from his perfect, chaste world to one that required knowledge. Jung, in *Symbols of Transformation* says, "In so far as the mother represents the unconscious, the incest tendency, particularly when it appears as the amorous desire of the mother or of the anima, is really only the desire of the unconscious to be taken notice of" (p. 299).

Quetzalcoatl committed the ultimate sin: incest. With shame and regret, he had to go away as punishment, and therefore ordered a stone box adorned with turquoise to be made in which he lay for four days. He then went to the shore of the Divine Sea where he put on his feathers and mask, built a great fire and cast himself into the flames. (or in another version, he cast off in a canoe made of snakes, fled to Yucatan, took on the name Kukulcan and Gucumatz and was imported into the Maya pantheon). All the rare birds gathered to watch his ashes rise (or his ashes turned into birds). He then went into the underworld to *Miclan, the Land of the Dead*. Eight days later, after a difficult journey and many challenges through the nine levels of the underworld, his heart rose like a flaming star, Venus, the Lord of the Dawn. He was accompanied by his double, Xolotl, who took the shape of a dog, a soul guide to the dead. From Mictlantecutli, Lord of the Dead, he managed to acquire what he was after, the bones of a man and woman, and sprinkled them with his own blood. This redeemed them so that they could populate the earth and the Fifth World. He spent four more days making arrows and on the eighth day he made his ascent.

Quetzalcoatl's journey through the underworld for eight days is very much like the journey described in the *Tibetan Book of the Dead* and the Maya *Popol Vuh*'s myth of The Hero Twin's journey into the underworld where they were killed and resurrected. Quetzalcoatl's trials are seen in the pictures of the *Codex Borgia*.

He begins his journey of transformation by suffering death to his mortal body by being burned in the Land of the Red and Black, east and north. His heart is then transformed into Venus which journey's west and south to the Region of Sin where he recognizes sin. He then goes south to the Place of Thorns, of cutting, dismembering and decapitating, where sin is cut away. Black Tezcatlipoca (Quetzalcoatl's other half) emerges from the head of the goddess of voluptuousness, (perhaps Coatlicue) where two huge flints have been placed, while Red Quetzalcoatl emerges from a flint in her heart. Aspects emerge from the head and heart.

From here he passes through the Masculine House of the Black Serpent and the Feminine House of the Red Serpent in the west, the place of re-birth, where there is the bundle of ashes of the dead man and woman who were redeemed to populate the earth, and the ashes of his father who when resuscitated becomes the Evening Star. In these two houses, Quetzalcoatl acts as the transcendent function that integrates the masculine with the feminine resulting in the creation of mortals and of a god, from the union of head and heart, reflecting the creation of spirit and matter.

It is not over yet as he then disappears into Cipactli, the earth dragon. From there the two Quetzalcoatls, black and red representing earthbound matter and fiery rain, north and east, emerge carrying sacrificial knives and enter the Region of the Dead, the lowest level in hell. The heart of this darkness is pictured as a great vessel, a "well of the water of precious stone," which is the blood of sacrifice. This well may correspond to the Self, the source of life from which all else flows, and it is equated with blood which would explain the Aztecs obsession with this precious life substance. Tlaloc, the god of water, pours the blood over Red Quetzalcoatl, the one who was born out of the heart, indicating that he is destined to die, while the Black, who was born out of the head, will live.

The sacrificing of the *red* may have to do with the taming of the instincts or passions and feelings in favor of the *black* which may represent the expression of literal earthbound darkness and evil expressed through rational purpose. Red Quetzalcoatl is sacrificed, his heart being torn out, by his fleshy twin, Xolotl, the dog god, while his opposite, Tezcatlipoca (Black Quetzalcoatl) drinks the blood that spurts from the wound. The body of Red Quetzalcoatl is then thrown down to disappear into Cipactli, the earth. (The Aztecs would throw the sacrificed bodies down the temple stairs giving the body or the material shell as an offering back to the earth, the Great Mother, while the heart, or spirit, is raised up to the sun.)

Now Black Quetzalcoatl immolates himself in fire-water, the eastern domain of Red Quetzalcoatl, as a re-enactment of Nanauatzin, the original god who threw himself into the fire to help create the Fifth World, and is himself re-born in the east. Xolotl (also Quetzalcoatl) is born out of an eagle vessel filled with a yellow liquid and surrounded by a sea of fire and emerges empowered with lightening in his hand. The mortal body and the instincts have now been canalized into a potent spiritual nature. The eagle represents spirit, wisdom, and clear vision. The move from the red, to the yellow, (from affect to solar consciousness) is part of an alchemical process, culminating with the symbol of lightening or illumination from above.

Quetzalcoatl now moves to Cinalco, a cave which is the opening to the west and the Land of the Origin of Corn. From there, he passes through the House of Stone Knives and the Realm of Fire Flowers, the region of destruction, where stars, representing the force to keep one unconscious, are torn apart by a bat, jaguar, eagle, and the aquatic monster. He then becomes the multicolored quetzal bird; the serpent half has been transformed. The knives of discrimination show a greater consciousness towards the unconscious.

Quetzalcoatl is then re-united with his sister who, after her self-sacrifice is transformed into the young moon. She is shown in the center of the images in the *Codex Borgia* with a large-rayed disc on her belly with the hieroglyph of the human heart in the center. The feminine has been transformed from unconscious lust and sexual instinct to love as *eros:* love with feeling and relationship. From the disc rises a tree with flowers on the ends of the branches, and on top is perched Quetzalcoatl as a hummingbird, which is a symbol of rebirth. The hummingbird hibernates in the winter like the bear. It is a symbol of the seasonal decent into the underworld and rebirth or renewal. It also represents the god Huitzilopochtli or Blue Tezcatlipoca, the god of war, sun, human sacrifice, called hummingbird of the west. Quetzalcoatl now ascends into the eastern sky, becoming the Morning star, Lord of the Dawn, the dwelling place of sacrificed warriors who have gone to the House of the Sun, while Xototl is the evening star, the dark aspect of Venus.

Venus repeats his ritual journey, rising in the western sky as the Evening Star and dying in the eastern sky as the Morning Star as it meets the sun, whose fire extinguishes its light, just as the fire of consciousness defeats the waters of the unconscious. The myth represents the integration of the masculine with the feminine as seen in Venus, and the moon, represented by Quetzalcoatl and his sister who appear in the sky. To quote Erich Neumann (1991) in *The Great Mother*:

> The progress to the male consciousness and the autonomy of the spirit-principle require the "ritual slaying" of the Great Mother and the heavenly father's support of the son principle that has grown independent of the Earth Mother. Wherever the night sea voyage in pursuit of the sun is undertaken, by the gods or the human soul, it signifies this development toward the relative independence of an ego endowed with such attributes as free will...It achieves its highest form in the myth of Quetzalcoatl... He is not a hero who transforms the outside world, but one who transforms himself by atonement. He is the dying and resurrected god, but he is also the hero king and the culture

bringer, the earthly and divine representative of the principle of light and humanity. (pp. 203-4)

As the morning star, Quetzalcoatl is the bringer of knowledge and spirit, the ascending power of the masculine, or the son, the masculine as it relates to and subdues the devouring aspect of the feminine. He transforms the Terrible Mother, the devouring aspect of the unconscious, into a more conscious feminine connected to *eros,* her feeling, compassionate side. As the evening star, he is the old king who must die in order to fertilize the world with his sacrifice. The old life and attitudes and way of being must die to bring forth the birth of the new. When the negative shadow energy, the influence of the unconscious Terrible Mother prevails, the individual can behave like an Aztec sun god demanding to be fed blood. Quetzalcoatl's struggle with Tezcatlipoca represents what was a needed transformation for the culture at the time, to find a balance between the light and dark, and because it is archetypal it also remains human's struggle with the same negative shadow. When the dark half is disowned and rejected, falling back into the unconscious, it can become a monster of regression and destruction. The reverse is also true in denying the light half of the shadow—the spiritual or light aspect of the personality. Here, one falls into a defense of lofty spiritualization and disconnection from the ground of matter.

Human sacrifices were not advocated when Quetzalcoatl was priest, but with his banishment the religion of his dark counterpart, Tezcatlipoca/Huitzilopochtli, regressed and sacrifice became prevalent. The darker influence of the consuming Great Mother took hold once again, while the banished Quetzalcoatl became the hoped-for-savior who would sail back across the waters after his long exile to reclaim his position of prominence. Sacrifice would again become symbolic, resulting in an internal self-transformation rather than the literal taking of life. When the Spaniards arrived in their large, strange sailing vessels on the coast of Mexico, it is thought the joy of Quetzalcoatl's return was in the air. Unfortunately, this was not the case. A much more virulent intruder had arrived that would put an end to life as it was known. Quetzalcoatl did not have the opportunity to bring the message of an inner symbolic transformation to his people. Life became brutal and remains so in many ways. Even today, Mexico suffers terribly from the drug dealers and their violence and disregard for human life, the kidnappings, the serial killing of women, the general danger and violence that persists in that country. It shares the dark, senseless disregard for life. That life is the flower that will be plucked, that blood will be fed to the gods through literal sacrifices, in order that the balance between the conscious and unconscious, spirit and matter will not prevail. We see the hope and possibility in the mythic stories that offer the guidance to establish cultures and values to live by. They point to the development of consciousness in a culture. Most are archetypally similar, some succeed, and others do not. The invasion by the Spanish truncated whatever future possibilities may have emerged and left Quetzalcoatl in exile.

A Clinical Example

I worked with a woman who suffered from a split similar to what we have just seen in the Quetzalcoatl myth. The images from her dreams and fantasies were those of birds and snakes, including the plumbed serpent. She tended to live very much in the realm of archetypal images and lofty fantasies. As an artist and a therapist who grew up in Germany, she brought in drawing after drawing, stories, poems and discussions of her images, yet all with a disembodied quality. The down to earth, feeling world, her conscious connection to her instincts, was missing. Her disowned nature showed up in a dream of a wild, frenzied snake whipping back and forth in a glass aquarium while she stood transfixed in front of it like a terrified child. Her mother, who stood behind in the shadows, came forward to irritate the snake further by dropping a folded piece of paper into the water. As the paper unfolded, the snake went crazy.

In drawing this scene, she drew a burned tree trunk, representing her dead grandfather next to the aquarium. This is an interesting image because the tree can be a feminine image, which it has been for her as the container for her growing child-self, but it can also be phallic and masculine. The fire of the Terrible Great Mother, acted out by her own mother and grandmother, burned down the tree through violent and fiery affect rages from their animus. Her grandfather was the only caring figure in her life, but he died when she was eight. Her father was imprisoned shortly before her birth. She does not have enough of the father/masculine to temper the negative feminine. Her mother never wanted her and was too narcissistic to pay any attention to her. Very much like the witch in the fairytale *Snow White*, her mother had to be the most beautiful. My patient became the young, admiring suitor who night after night listened while her mother masturbated, simulating her own youthful sexuality in response to the wrong object— the mother. At 13, she was molested by her uncle. Brutalized by the masculine and drawn to/repulsed by the mother, by way of escaping, she became a prostitute and embarked on a life of faceless sex, where she used men. During this period, she was brutally raped and beaten by a gang of men and almost died. After this horrific event, she managed to recognize how out of control her life was and sought help.

In her dream, the glass aquarium is not a safe container for this kind of energy; it needs to be brought into the analytical container. The glass represents a too rigid defense against intense and violent affects, which could shatter if not contained properly. It also represents a cold distance between her and the violent forces within herself, the result of a life of trauma; she sees it but cannot touch it. It is actually a dream representing the stage of whitening in alchemy, when we gain a perspective on what exists within us, but it is not yet embodied in our conscious sense of self. She is terrified, afraid the rage-full, primitive instinct symbolized by the wild snake will destroy her and those around her. It would be like the destruction of the world through a rain of fire or flood. The dark and light are polarized in this immense struggle. Her affect rages and hisses out through her animus/shadow; it is important to encourage some of that snake energy to burn itself out in a benign way, through stories, movement, her expressions of creativity, even at me. Certainly, the impulses toward self-sacrifice and sacrificing others are there, yet rather than unconscious destructive sacrifice, she needs to hold on to her ego and consciously make a sacrifice, as Quetzalcoatl did after his shameful incest with his sister. What needs to be sacrificed now is the strong affect—the serpent in the flames—and the airy, lofty defense—the bird, when she cuts herself off from the world and her feelings, both regressions to the unconscious. As Quetzalcoatl, she needs to burn and then descend into the underworld and be dismembered and put back together, emerging re-born with a new more conscious relationship to her feelings and affects and a stronger more stable ego. The flighty bird and the secretive snake when united bring spirit and instinct together so that one can live out one's true nature, where instincts are mediated by consciousness and love is expressed as *eros* through relationship to oneself and to others. This same process of learning and transformation was a very significant piece of Jung's (2009) own inner journey as laid out in *The Red Book*, in his dialogues with his spirit soul, the bird, and his earthly soul, the serpent.

This Mercurial transformation, seen both in the myth of Quetzalcoatl and in our own lives, is the essential archetypal energy of individuation that leads us to healing the split in our soul which prevents us from living our lives to their full capacity.

Nancy Swift Furlotti, Ph.D. is a Jungian Analyst living in Aspen, Colorado. She is a past president of the C.G. Jung Institute of Los Angeles, where she trained, a founding member and past president of the Philemon Foundation and is on the Mercurius Film Prize Committee. She is a member of the C.G. Jung Institute of Colorado and the Interregional Association of Jungian Analysts. She is on the boards of Pacifica Graduate Institute in Santa Barbara and the Smithsonian National Asian Museum. Dr. Swift Furlotti lectures internationally on Jungian topics such as dreams, mythology, trauma, the feminine, and the environment. Her company, Recollections, LLC, publishes early analysts' unpublished material, such as the manuscripts of Erich Neumann. She has two forthcoming books, *The Splendor of the Maya: A Journey Into the Shadows at the Dawn of Creation*, and *Eternal Echoes: Erich Neumann's Timeless Relevance to Consciousness, Creativity, and Evil.*

References

Bierhorst, J. (Trans.) (1998). *History and Mythology of the Aztecs: The chimalpopoca codex.* The University of Arizona Press.

De Sahagún, B. (1950). *The General History of the Things of New Spain; The Florentine Codex.* (12 Volumes). (Trans in English: A.J.O Anderson & Charles Dibble). Original date, 1577. School of American Research.

Diaz, G. & Rogers, A. Eds. (1993). *The Codex Borgia.* Dover Publications, Inc.

Edinger, E. (1994). *Transformation of Libido: A Seminar on Jung's Symbols of Transformation.* Los Angeles C.G. Jung Institute Bookstore and Library.

Harding, E. (2001). *Women's Mysteries.* Shambhala Publications.

Harding, E. (1973). *Psychic Energy: Its Source and Goal.* Pantheon.

Jung, C.G. (1990). *Symbols of Transformation.* Princeton University Press.

Jung, C.G. (1984). Seminar on dream analysis. Princeton University Press.

Leon-Portillo, M. (1990). *Aztec Thought and Culture: A Study of the Ancient Nahuatl.* University of Oklahoma Press.

Neumann, E. (1991). *The Great Mother.* Trans. Ralph Manheim. Princeton University Press.

Neumann, E. (1970). *The Origins and History of Consciousness.* (trans. R. F. C. Hull). Princeton University Press.

Von Franz, M.L. (1982). *The Psychological Meaning of Redemption Motifs in Fairytales.* Inner City Books.

Individuation and Pre-Hispanic Mythology: A Tribute to Murray Stein

Patricia Michan

Murray Stein is not only a special friend, a valued teacher, colleague, supervisor, and mentor, but also played a key role in sowing the seed of Jungian training in Mexico. For me, it has been a privilege and an honor to have been mentored in my work and relationship to the life of the Centro Mexicano C.G. Jung by Murray, by his generous heart, by his open-handed sharing of his knowledge, gifts, and discipline, and by his unwavering support.

I am privileged to participate in this Festschrift for Murray Stein. Sometimes we are honored to be mentored in our work by a gifted generous-hearted individual, a figure who supports a bridging through successive stages of development toward individuation whether pertaining to the professional, institutional or personal. Murray was just such a figure in my professional relationship to the life of the Centro Mexicano C.G. Jung.

When I was invited to contribute a dedicatory essay to the Festschrift to honor Murray, I was immediately drawn to writing about the figure of the psychopomp in pre-Hispanic mythology in order to honor the myriad inexpressively generous ways in which Murray functioned as a bridge to the realization of the Centro. He functioned as advisor, mentor, supervisor of students, faculty member, and member of the Academic, Admissions, and Evaluation Committee of the Training Program in Jungian-Oriented

Psychotherapy, culminating, over time, in the building of a deeply valued friendship.

It is precisely the central concept of the process of individuation in Jung's psychology that is the overall topic of this Festschrift for Murray. Jung states that individuation is "the process by which a person becomes a psychological 'in-dividual,' that is, a separate, indivisible unity or 'whole'" (CW 9.i, para. 490).

Paradoxically, individuation processes are, however, in truth, rarely if ever completed. The mercurial figure of the psychopomp is the psychic structural and functional *sine qua non* which supports psychic processes including the individuation process. The Mercurial structure and function of the psychopomp in the pre-Hispanic creation myth of Ometeotl, the supreme God/Goddess, unfolds in successive permutations of differentiation culminating in the personification of Quetzalcoatl, a psychopompic figure necessary to linking conscious and unconscious. Each of these permutations expresses through the capacity to cross from the accessing of source level resources to a further state of realization/ differentiation.

In order to illustrate the structure and function of the Mercurial energies in the pre-Hispanic creation myth, it serves to further map the relationship between the psychopomp and the mercurial function.

The arc of Jung's thought casts the complex figure of Mercurius as an expression of a guiding orienting agency personifying the territory of psychic energy that sponsors movement including crossing boundaries, linking, sponsoring psychic process, and playing the role of the mediating psychopomp. Mercurius is then an expression of the in-between as the primary territory of linking energy that can then allow the opposite poles to come into relationship.

Mythologically, Mercurius (he/she) presents as a messenger of the gods between Heaven and Earth, a guide to travelers, an interpreter and boundary crosser, a Spirit Guide. This is the all-important territory of the psychopomp who bridges between worlds. Most elaborated mythologies express this bridging function through particular figures including Mercurius, Hermes, Toth, and their partial counterparts such as Cerberus, the hound of Hades in Greek mythology; Anubis, the jackal-headed god of death in Egyptian mythology; or Xolotl, Quetzalcoatl's dark twin. It also includes such specific references as glue in alchemy which can manifest creatively or destructively, for example, in stuckness or in secure fertile connection. All these dualities/duplicities point to the rich territory of paradox.

Because of the "double nature of Mercurius," (CW 9.ii, para. 234) he/she also represents a pervasive twoness, (carrying the opposites including masculine and feminine), ambiguity, and potentiality. The possibility of process always carries both potential and risk. This bivalence is expressed by the paradoxical qualities of the alchemical figure of Mercurius, which are "inherent in all things in a latent state" (CW 14, par. 318). The soul per se, the in-between, is and is not of both extremes. Here lies the structural and functional sponsorship which allows opposite poles (like any opposing pairs, including the broad arc of the immaterial and the material) to support them in coming into relationship.

Jung emphasizes the unsurety of outcome, of whether process may be creative or destructive. He says, "Though Mercurius has a bright side concerning whose spirituality alchemy leaves us no doubt, he also has a dark side, and its roots go deep" (CW 14, para. 19). Further, he says, "Mercurius is not only split into a masculine and a feminine half but is the poisonous dragon and at the same time the heavenly lapis" (CW 14, para. 235). The positive realization of Mercurial potentiality rests on the relationship between ego consciousness and conscientiousness and the rich wealth of the non-ego.[1]

In *Aion*, Jung states that "the heart of Mercurius," … lies in the North Pole, and contains the "…true fire within" (CW 9.ii, para. 206). The true fire within is itself bivalent. It corresponds to the "*stella maris*" which "stands for the fiery center in us from which creative or destructive influences come" (CW 9.ii, para. 212). The position of the heart of Mercurius (i.e., true north) expresses its importance as a guiding orienting agency. Mercurial bivalence is endemic to psychic material

---

[1] Although the dance between the ego and the non-ego is complex and highly orchestrated, I include the entire arc of expression which comes dominantly from the source level whether through images, dreams, visions, synchronicities, constellations, as well as through defenses, symptoms, and projections. By non-ego, I refer to what we might think of as the source level provisions, sponsorships, and agencies, whether expressed closer to instinct or archetype. I engage with the non-ego as the agency Jung refers to in 9ii as "immortal" (par. 348-349) as the agency outside the conscious ego which prompts, directs, and stirs us. I choose to use the terms ego and non-ego in order to further a "working" differentiation between those agencies coming from nearer the pole of the unconscious and those coming from nearer the pole of the conscious ego.

and essential to psychic movement. Understanding this pervasive truth provides a primary tool in clinical practice.

The core aspect that allows the function of Mercurius and its magnetic heart of ambiguity to bridge between true opposites is that they are both the same and different. This is the alchemical *concidentia oppositorum* which is itself a paradox. Mercurius is the paradox par excellence. He/She is the arcane substance, which is identical to the scintilla, the little soul-spark, the "spark of stellar essence" (CW 14, para. 42). The figure of Mercurius is the most fully explicated treatment of the psychopomp in the Jungian cannon.

The mapping of the structure and function of the psychopomp, in its myriad forms, is in clear evidence in the tripartite pre-Hispanic creation myth of Ometeotl, the four creator gods, and the Five Aeons,[2] albeit in unique and culture-specific permutations. The presence of psychopompic energies occurs in most, if not all, myth systems.

In *Alchemical Studies,* Jung in beautiful detail summarizes the structural and functional aspects of Mercurius. "Mercurius' duality is also expressed in *Aion* thusly: He/She is *'undoubtedly akin to the godhead;* ... [and is] ... *found in sewers* '" (CW 13, par. 269).

The arc of Jung's thought thus casts the complex figure of Mercurius as an exemplar of structural wholeness and dynamic sponsorship of wholeness. Mercurial energy supports process. It supports coming apart. It supports equilibration. It supports linking.

Within the Jungian cannon, the structures and functions which support process, in particular linking, are then ubiquitously expressed through the personification of Mercurius. The mercurial function of linking, of bridging, of having the capacity to cross boundaries is the role of the psychopomp. The psychopomp, however, does in fact express through a myriad of other personifications and processes. As Jung says, it is a "psychic factor that mediates unconscious contents to consciousness,... [and is] often personified in the image of a wise old man or woman, and sometimes as a helpful animal" (Sharp, 1991). It may also include other

---

[2] It is important to note that the Aztec concept of Age is equivalent to that of aeon in Western thought, which refers to a 2000-year period, like the Age or Aeon of Pisces. Embedded in the idea of a 2000-year period, is the dual aspect of being in time and out of time. Psychically speaking, each cosmogonic era, each sun parallels a psychic era whose archetypal personification is not only progressively amplified symbolically, but also brings with it changes in the individual's attitude, a new consciousness, and a different relationship with the objective psyche

agencies of linking or, conversely, of stuckness, like the aforementioned image of the alchemical glue. The psychopomp is then an expression of the unconscious potentiality for bridging between the ego and the collective unconscious.

The word psychopomp comes from the Greek *psukhopompos,* derived from *psukhē,* meaning soul and *pompos,* meaning conductor. Mythologically, the psychopomp is the archetypal personification of the energy of the conductor of souls which provides a "guide along the road of our soul's travels" (Shalit & Furlotti, 2013). Further, it supports psychic process in general, both connection and disconnection. In Greek mythology, psychopompic energy is expressed by the figure of Hermes, the messenger of the gods who, with winged sandals, a winged helmet, and carrying the caduceus (itself bivalent) descends from Olympus to deliver messages from the gods. Hermes rules roads, boundaries, and commerce. He is the figure par excellence which has the ability to cross the threshold between worlds: the divine realm, the human world, and the underworld. The figure of the psychopomp, then, has the capacity to cross that all-important "critical line of demarcation"(CW 9.ii, para. 44) between conscious and unconscious, between the ego and the contents of the unconscious.

Pre-Hispanic myths and cultures are imbued with the presence of intercessory figures that personify the psychopompic function, including the smith, the shaman, the priest, the healer, the *nahual*/shapeshifter, and the sorcerer, among others.

The mercurial function, so critically important to analytic process, is also commonly in active evidence in teaching and mentoring relationships. This was powerfully true of Murray at the Centro. The psychopompic function, of course, is not free from challenges, tests, and even endangerments. This was in evidence in the development of the training at the Centro and is as well a more generally expressed reality in both psychic process and myth.

The larger schema of the pre-Hispanic myth of Ometeotl and the generation of the Five Ages or Aeons is a clear stage-specific expression of multiple processes of coming apart and re-linking, i.e., of the Mercurial psychopompic function. These expressions of Mercurius in both myth and psyche have the nature of a "ligament." In alchemy, Mercurius is the "ligament" of the soul, uniting spirit and body. Mercurius's "dual nature enables him to play the role of mediator; he is bodily and spiritual and is himself the union of these two principles" (CW 14, para. 635). These multiple aspects are also laid bare in Quetzalcoatl's descent to the underworld.

For the purpose of this Festschrift, I have chosen to illustrate the arc of expression from pre-differentiated original unity through further differentiation of the four creator gods and the successive stages of the five cosmogonic ages. This arc of expression reverberates to the deeply familiar Jungian notion of the axiom of Maria Prophetissa: "One becomes two, two becomes three, and out of the third comes the one as the fourth." In the pre-Hispanic myth, Ometeotl, the one, gives way to the two, Ometecutli and Omecihuatl. The two then join together to create a third: four creator gods. My primary focus is on the culminating psychopompic figure of the pre-Hispanic creator god Quetzalcoatl. He is a quintessence, and as such expresses a form closer to realization. Interestingly, in the myth of Ometeotl, Quetzalcoatl is both the second iteration of the four ages, as well as the fifth uniting figure.

The movement between the fourth and the fifth as in the myth of Ometeotl expresses in realized form the deeply important quintessence. Jung says, "the One born of the Four is the Quinta Essentia" (CW 14, para. 439).

The energies supporting the psychic realities expressed by each of the transformations, culminating in the figure of Quetzalcoatl, resonate powerfully with Jung's articulation of the figure of Mercurius. In the myth, each of the successive forms is implicitly an expression of the paradox of multiplicity and unity. The opposites in the narrative of each successive age are both destructive and creative.

Jung's aforementioned summation of the structural and functional aspects of Mercurius in *Alchemical Studies,* applies likewise to the mythological figure of Quetzalcoatl who is a duality, but is also named a unity in spite of his innumerable inner contradictions. He is both material and spiritual. He is the process by which the lower and material is transformed into the higher and spiritual, and vice versa. He is a redeeming psychopomp and an evasive trickster. He is a primary sponsor then of process and the potential for process. This process of bringing spirit into matter and mattering (realizing) spirit is the alchemical circular distillation. "The alchemists were fond of picturing their opus as a circulatory process, as a circular distillation or as the uroboros, the snake biting its own tail" (CW 9.ii, para. 418). This expresses the energies of both separation and conjoining. The circular process supports ongoing rounds of differentiation in any never complete individuation process. Quetzalcoatl, like Mercurius, sponsors the entire arc of any round of movement from unconsciousness to consciousness.

In this pre-Hispanic creation myth, we see the structural and functional provisions that support process. The first permutation of this arc of sponsorship is expressed by the figure of Ometeotl. Ometeotl personifies the original uroboric state of pre-conscious/unconscious undifferentiated unity and wholeness prior to the separation of opposites. He/She paradoxically expresses both implicit multiplicity as well as unity, and, hence, the potential for process. In other words, the life force inherently holds the as yet unrealized bivalent potentiality to differentiate.

Ometeotl, like an aspect of Mercurius, is a paradoxical unconscious original unity that carries the capacity to come apart and back together. He/She is a unity and is named as such, despite his/her given structural paradoxical capacity to divide.

The concept of a given and pervasive paradoxical twoness within original unity is present in the pre-Hispanic cosmovision just as in psychic process. The paradox of multiplicity and unity is key both to understanding Jungian thought and psychic functioning. This paradox supports the realization of the opposites, as well as their re-integration. As Jung says in *Mysterium,* "the opposites are the ineradicable and indispensable precondition of all psychic process" (CW 14, para. 206). In other words, without the structural and functional support of paradoxical nature, there would be no structural or dynamic support for process. Jung describes in *Mysterium Coniunctionis* how paradoxes cluster in a deeply intense way around the mysterious transformative arcane substance. The arcane substance contains the opposites in undifferentiated form, as *prima materia* or *lapis exilis*, the stone of little worth, at the beginning of any round of process. It shifts to an amalgamated form (albeit generally to a relative degree) as the *lapis philosophorum* at the end of any round of transformation.

Of course this is relative and ongoing. We see successive iterations which support the possibility of increasing degrees of lived/realized conscious wholeness. The figure of Ometeotl exemplifies this mysterious paradoxical territory from which the psychic medicine is made. As introduced above, the figure of Ometeotl, through an initial stage of discrimination/separation produces the emergence of Ometecutli, the masculine pole, and Omecihuatl, the feminine pole. The coming into being of this couple mythologically expresses an early manifestation of the potential for process. It expresses, as well, an early stage of consciousness.

Jung's statement, "There is no consciousness without discrimination of opposites" (CW 9i, para. 178) expresses the necessity and potential for differentiation out of the pre-conscious uroboric state. The achievement of the state of the two is essential to self-reflection, as well as to relatedness to self or other. This movement from the one to the two is an initial manifestation of the psychopompic energies. As such, it is both a condition for and the expression of process. In analytic process, this movement from the one to the two results in an energic pair, variously expressed by an ambivalent attraction, negative or positive, ego dystonic and/or ego syntonic. As Jung says, "The factors which come together in the *coniunctio* are conceived as opposites, either confronting one another in enmity or attracting one another in love" (CW 14, par. 1).

Following the creation of this first pair of opposites, Ometecutli and Omecihuatl then come together in a lesser *coniunctio*. This leads, in turn, to the creation of a quaternion in the form of the four sons, the creator gods: Tezcatlipoca, Quetzalcoatl, Huitzilopochtli, and Tlaloc.

The four sons represent differentiated bivalent complementary opposing poles of the multi-layered aspects of multiplicity inherent in Ometeotl in his/her pre-differentiated form. The narrative of these four creator gods expresses a succession of creations and destructions through five cosmogonic Ages that culminate in the Fifth Age ruled by Quetzalcoatl. This Fifth Age describes a more conscious differentiation and progression, representing the creation of humankind and the present world. As in both myth and psychic process, multiple expressions of both separative and integrative processes end with some degree of incompletion or failure. In the creation myth, before the fifth era was achieved, there had been four prior partially successful/partially failed attempts to create human beings.

The arc of development in the myth begins in the First Age with a world of giants and culminates in the Fifth Age with the creation of human beings. The First of these five ages, that which was inhabited by giants, is ruled by Tezcatlipoca, the God of the Night Sky and Darkness. The destructive element came in the form of an eclipse.

The Second Age, ruled by Quetzalcoatl, God of the Wind, was inhabited by unbaked clay beings. It was destroyed by a hurricane. The Third Age, ruled by Huitzilopochtli, the God of Fire, was inhabited by baked clay beings. Note the forward movement from unbaked to baked clay beings, a further step toward the realization of humankind. This era was destroyed by a rain of fire coming from a volcanic eruption. The Fourth Age is ruled by Tlaloc, the God of Rain, and was inhabited by beings made with the ashes of the ancestors of the preceding Ages. It was destroyed by a catastrophic flood. Note the introduction of the element of water so dominant in human life. In the myth, each age is expressive of successively gained ground in the movement toward the creation of human beings.

Each one of the first four ages, then, is ruled by the element that both created it and, paradoxically, brought about its destruction. These four ages are characterized by a quality of the one-after-the-other, manifesting inherent structural support for function/process, a further step toward wholeness.

This is reflective of the pre-Hispanic belief that processes of instability, whether experienced objectively or subjectively, were not only inherent in the world and in our existence in it, but if worked through also allowed for the possibility of the emergence of a new order.

This pre-Hispanic belief in the usefulness and endangerment inherent in processes of instability is reflected in Jung's formulation regarding the potential for negative as well as positive outcomes in what he refers to as the right path. As he wrote, "the right way to wholeness is made up, unfortunately, of fateful detours and wrong turnings. It is a longissima via, not straight but snakelike, a path that unites the opposites in the manner of the guiding caduceus . . . It is on this *longissima via* that we meet with those experiences which are said to be 'inaccessible'" (CW 12, para. 6). Such "fateful detours and wrong turnings," i.e., all those distortions and pathologies that attend upon symptom, complex, and defense hold within them important and useful resources (bones) which are indeed part of "the right way to wholeness"

After the destruction of the Fourth Age, the Fifth Age maps a more conscious differentiation and progression. The Fifth Age is again ruled by Quetzalcoatl. This is the Age in which humankind was created. During the Fifth Age, when the experiment finally succeeded, its inhabitants were made with the bones of the ancestors combined with the divine blood of

Quetzalcoatl. This culminating era is characterized by the fulfillment of the capacity for movement.

Psyche characteristically has just such a potential for process. Individuation processes, similar to the unfolding of this creation myth, map a highly differentiated series of processes moving from initial pre-differentiated states and content through extensive patterns of differentiation and, ideally, to re-memberment/reintegration. Typically, when this occurs, there is movement toward successive rounds of differentiation.

Having created the sun (consciousness) and the moon (the unconscious) and provided them with movement, the gods then realized the need and possibility for a creative third, i.e., new inhabitants for the Earth. At this point, the circle of Gods commissioned Quetzalcoatl, God of Wind, primary sponsor of movement, to make the all-important descent to the Underworld, the Mictlán, ruled by Mitlantecutli, the Lord of the Underworld. Quetzalcoatl is a primary personification of these energies which map the agencies of process that are paradoxically a unity, a duality, and are, at the same time, characterized by innumerable inner contradictions.

This provision is expressive of the structure and function of mercurial psychopompic figures. Thus, psychically speaking, we can see that out of the foregoing of the old way in the congress of the Gods, an agency which sponsors wholeness comes to the fore. This parallels the stage in which individuals can take a reconciling position between the content and agencies of the ego and the non-ego. There is then a provision for the emergence of a third creative possibility. Only an ambiguous and paradoxical symbolic third is capable of reconciling psychic opposites.

Quetzalcoatl's task in his journey to the underworld was to retrieve the roots of humankind from Mictlán, that is, the bones of the ancestors from the initial iterations of the four Ages. These are known as the "precious bones" by the Aztecs. These "precious bones" brought forward successively through the reiterations of the Aeons are, indeed, "the gold seeds" in the residues of the past Ages. The Fifth Age, as well as correspondent psychic stages, expresses the culmination and integration of the full dynamic of the creation of a conscious human being. Quetzalcoatl is a key factor in making process possible and thus serves as a culminating unifying figure.

According to Aztec mythology, everyone who dies goes to Mictlán, the Underworld. The journey to the underworld is comprised of nine levels or thresholds in which the souls have to face different challenges before gaining admission to their destination: Mictlán. Quetzalcoatl went through this lengthy process and, once he reached the underworld, Mitlantecutli, the Lord of the Underworld was initially unwilling to let go of the bones of the ancestors. In their interaction, Mitlantecutli functions as another all-important trickster figure, and a worthy counterpart/opponent of Quetzalcoatl. Mitlatecuntli placed conditions upon Quetzalcoatl much as psyche supports and challenges through the processes Jung speaks of as the deeply important "fateful detours and wrong turnings" (CW 12, par. 6). Mitlantecutli required that Quetzalcoatl circumambulate the Underworld four times. Further, he said he would give Quetzalcoatl the "precious bones" only if Quetzalcoatl played Mitlantecutli's sacred instrument: his conch shell. Quetzalcoatl immediately realized that Mitlantecutli was tricking him as the instrument lacked the necessary hole through which to blow. Quetzalcoatl had the wisdom to value and summon his humble allies, the worms, bees, and bumblebees to assist him. The worms drilled the hard shell of the conch and the bees and bumblebees entered through the hole and helped Quetzalcoatl produce and amplify the sacred ritual sound. Mitlantecutli's trick had failed, and he had no option but to yield and allow Quetzalcoatl to take the "precious bones." However, Mitlantecutli, unhappy with this state of affairs, told Quetzalcoatl that he could take the bones, so long as he would bring them back again. Quetzalcoatl was not willing to bring the bones back. This time, Quetzalcoatl played the trickster. He asked his theriomorphic and darker twin brother Xolotl to inform Mitlantecutli that he himself [Quetzalcoatl] would come back to return the bones. Thus, Quetzalcoatl enlisted body-instinct-self to commit the necessary crime. Having enlisted Xolotl to make this false promise, Quetzalcoatl was able to start his ascent.

Metaphorically speaking, when we think of the true as opposed to the false, we tend to think of the good as opposed to the not good. But that does not make room for the fact that the non-ego can be so purposively deeply dark, risky, and negative in service of individuation. In other words, there is a way in which the communications of the non-ego psyche, like the figure of Hermes or the trickster, Mercurius, can be very ruthless, even "the lowest" (CW 13, para. 267) of the low, despite the positive or creative potentials that lie in this path. Quetzalcoatl then took the male and female bones, put them in a bundle, and again in a step-by-step process, carried them back up to the world of consciousness. However, Mitlantecutli upon realizing that Quetzalcoatl was ascending with the bones, tricked him a third time by instructing the energies at his service to open up a hole in order to trip and trap Quetzalcoatl. Quetzalcoatl, upon falling into the hole, dropped the bones which scattered and broke into pieces. The male and female fragments became mixed up. Note the correspondence to the *intermedia res* and the *mixtum*. Quetzalcoatl injured himself badly in the fall, and quails appeared out of nowhere and started pecking and gnawing at him. In his fear, he fainted. He later recovered his senses and, overwhelmed, began to cry. He realized the bones were broken. He was suffering the pecks of the quails. In his despair, he asked Xolotl, his twin brother, "What shall we do?" The all-important framing of the question itself led Quetzalcoatl to a response from ego consciousness. Quetzalcoatl proceeded to answer himself, "Be that as it may, although the bones got ruined, they'll be good enough!"

The challenges that Quetzalcoatl faced on his journey both to and from the underworld are correspondent to psychic risks and dangers encountered in any encompassing depth process, perhaps particularly in the engagement with the unconscious. We must not take the powers of the unconscious lightly.

Quetzalcoatl's fall brings to mind Jung's (1989) reflection in *Memories, Dreams, Reflections* regarding the challenges in any process of inner transformation/individuation:

"But when one follows the path of individuation, when one lives one's own life, one must take mistakes into the bargain; life would not be complete without them. There is no guarantee not for a single moment that we will not fall into error or stumble into deadly peril. We may think there is a sure road. But that would be the road of death. Then nothing happens any longer at any rate, not the right things. Anyone who takes the sure road is as good as dead"(p. 297).

Xolotl, who knows the shadows of the underworld like the palm of his hand, and whose eyes are accustomed to such darkness, was cunning and fast. He proceeded to help Quetzalcoatl collect all of the fragments of the bones with great discriminated attention to detail, care, and patience. He then made a bundle of them, and thus brought the bones back together. Xolotl partnered Quetzalcoatl in this round of the journey. The ubiquitous role of the two-in-one nature of the psychopomp is here evidenced as

Quetzalcoatl and Xolotl working together as differentiated counterparts. This leads, in both the myth and, correspondently, in the psychic realm, to a possibility of recombining in a more encompassing whole.

Upon returning to the realm of the gods, Quetzalcoatl proceeded to ask the earth goddess Cihuacoatl, "Serpent Woman," to grind the bones into meal (to a greater degree of differentiation), on her sacred grinding stone. Once the bones were ground into a fine meal, Quetzalcoatl pierced his phallus, thus releasing precious drops of divine blood. He sprinkled the ground bones of the ancestors with this life-giving force thus transforming them into a dough. The expression between the conjunction of female and male is clear here. The ground bones provide the flesh (the substance) for the new humankind; the blood, the enspiriting energy. The new humankind was thus differentiated into masculine and feminine, into "the two" upon which process is conditional. Jung states, "In Dorn's philosophical explanation of this in 'Physica Trismegisti,' he says: 'In the beginning God created *one* world (*unus mundus*). This he divided into two—heaven and earth. Beneath this spiritual and corporeal binarius lieth hid a third thing, which is the bond of holy matrimony...'" (CW 14, para. 659).

Similarly Jung states, "Mercurius ... is not just the medium of conjunction but also that which is to be united, since he is the essence or 'seminal matter' of both man and woman. *Mercurius masculinus* and *Mercurius foemineus* are united in and through *Mercurius menstrualis*, which is the 'aqua'" (para. 659).

Jung's mapping here clearly evidences the structure and function of the Mercurial psychopompic personification. "The division into two was necessary in order to bring the 'one' world out of the state of potentiality into reality. Reality consists of a multiplicity of things. But one is not a number; the first number is two, and with it, multiplicity and reality begin" (para. 659). The dough with which to make the new humans is made out of the ground bones (the concrete material) and the sacred blood of Quetzalcoatl (already a *mixtum*). With this dough Quetzalcoatl molded the new humans as a potter shapes his clay, thus creating new life. Like with the figure of Mercurius, the energies personified by Quetzalcoatl sponsor processes of coming apart and back together.

The recovery of the bones of the ancestors in particular is resonant to processes of reintegrating core psychic energies of the layers of our past. In depth psychic process, we strive to claim the "bones" of the past, not just the personal past, but also the ancestral, generational, historical past. Jung eloquently references how residues of the entire history of humankind live within the individual psyche. Part of the work of individuation is to engage the energies of the underworld (the unconscious) in order to retrieve the all-important bones (core seeds) of the past and future. That said, this process includes the separating out and forgoing of elements both foreign to and contaminating of individual psyche.

Quetzalcoatl carries the ego closer to the mercurial, bringing these essential riches from the unconscious to consciousness despite the challenges and obstacles. This is accomplished in both the myth and in psyche through step-by-step, careful, dedicated processes of discrimination. In the process, a higher level of responsibility and consciousness may be achieved.

Quetzalcoatl does accomplish the creative putting back together and reconfiguring of the ancestral bones so that masculine and feminine—in a new creative differentiated form—come into being as humans capable of participating in the creation of something new. Quetzalcoatl's conscious quest for the recovery of the ancestral bones was accomplished by both his conscious and unconscious suffering of the descent to the underworld and by his interactions with the core energies of the earlier iterations of the four ages. As it pertains to parallel psychic process, this expresses the recovery of aspects of historical collective constructs in psyche.

The motif of Quetzalcoatl as a personification of the energies sponsoring process maps the core functioning of the psychopomp in general. Psychopomp figures bear and sponsor process. They are the paradoxical two in one. As Jung makes clear in *Mysterium*, the opposites express through an endless number of forms. This ubiquity points to a vast potentiality. Primary amongst these forms, for example, is the masculine/feminine.

In the creation Myth of Omeoteotl, the figures of Quetzalcoatl and Xolotl express the opposites of light and dark, conscious and unconscious, although both are masculine. The differentiated contents of the two figures reveal that they are both the same and different. The sameness supports a bridging, a linking; the difference sponsors creative elaboration. Although there are no guarantees as to the outcome of this process, as a rule it involves both loss and gain.

Quetzalcoatl's act of self-sacrifice does not destroy him. It is an at least partly conscious self-sacrifice. It also brings the more conscious

288

aspect into conjunction with the deeper source level and its generative quality, the fiery spark of origin that gives forth the precious engendering aspect of the sacred.

Quetzalcoatl is a seminal figure in the cultural foundation of the entire pre-Hispanic civilization. He is the giver, renewer, and preserver of life. His blood is paradoxically both blood and no ordinary blood. This itself is another pair of opposites and thus supports the making real of the potential. In the figure of Quetzalcoatl, the generative provision brings the opposites, spirit and matter, into closer proximity and potential movement toward linking and integration. Quetzalcoatl, as a bivalent figure, is connected to the concrete *materia* as well as to the illimitable immaterial and is, as such, an expression of the psychopomp par excellence. He is thus richly endowed with the ability to sponsor process. He functions fluidly. He has the capacity to move from one pole of a pair of opposites to the other, as well as to the all-important in-between (the alchemical *intermedia res*).

The myriad processes of coming apart and ultimately back together in a new form, when it is creative, expresses processes of coming into being. It is, as Dorn implies, a back-and-forth process. It is the *via longissima*. This may, ideally and to varying degrees, result in the stabilization of the self, of the stone of the philosophers (individuation). In order for the process to unfold creatively, there needs to be a strong relationship between ego and self (non-ego). Although the interplay between these opposing/differentiated energies is in evidence in the narrative of the Five Ages, the oppositional nature of the relationship between Mitlantecutli and Quetzalcoatl is more dramatic than in the initial iterations of the Five Ages.

The bivalent mercurial trickster energy, as personified by Mitlantecutli, resides in the unconscious, in the underworld. As such, it is both distant from consciousness and, most likely, ego dystonic at certain points. Quetzalcoatl, on the other hand, as the myth's primary psychopomp figure, is both closer to consciousness and characterized by a connection, albeit less conscious, to the resources of the unconscious. Bear in mind, as Jung says in volume 8, there is consciousness in the unconscious.

Quetzalcoatl's energies thus carry the potential for linking consciousness and conscientious ego function with the purposiveness of the unconscious. There is, however, an all-important difference. The role of the psychopompic energy here expressed by the underworld figure of Mitlantecutli provides the crucially important obstacles and also stimulates the heroic efforts of Quetzalcoatl which ultimately play a primary function in the retrieval of contents from the underworld/the unconscious.

In the myth, the interplay between the opposites of conscious and unconscious, Quetzalcoatl and the Lord of the Underworld, requires the descent of Quetzalcoatl. He thus achieves a greater relationship with the darker trickster energy of Mitlantecutli, the Lord of the Underworld. As the narrative unfolds, we see Mitlantecutli, in defensive conservative fashion, attempting to foil the efforts of Quetzalcoatl.

In psychic process, the non-ego provision may express through a dominant conservative, even defensive, energy. This is correspondent to the pole of Mercurius named as the lowest of the low, although it has a conservative protective function as well. Quetzalcoatl makes three passes at negotiating with Mitlantecutli. In the first, Mitlantecutli demands a four-fold circumambulation of the underworld. This implies the necessity of the finding or making of a center (so clear in alchemy), as well as through the circumambulation of psychic contents in the analytic process. It also corresponds to Quetzalcoatl's function as a potter. Note that pre-Hispanic potters built by hand rather than by using a potter's wheel. Nonetheless, the critical point here is that circumambulation implies the creation of a space with a center and yet with the imposed limitations necessary to realization.

In the second trick, Mitlantecutli requires that Quetzalcoatl play his musical instrument, a conch shell. The conch shell, however, as we saw above, has no hole. Hence it is impossible to play. This confronts Quetzalcoatl with the necessary heroic act of doing the impossible. As in psychic process, this meeting such obstacles hinges on the respect for and reliance on the critical role of humble helpers. In the third trick, Mitlantecutli with the aid of his helpers designs the means of the fall and entrapment of Quetzalcoatl. This trick again has a double nature and can either constructively contain or hopelessly entrap. These three challenging acts of Mitlantecutli's trickery map the crucial steps of: 1) creating a "mandalic space" with a center; 2) meeting the impossible creatively and with the aid of humble helpers; and 3) accessing the resources embedded in both falling/failing and containment. Quetzalcoatl's journey to the Underworld and back provides a rich amplificatory resource that mirrors, sometimes in an encompassing arc, sometimes in bits and pieces, the *via longissima* of the path of individuation within the individual psyche.

In each of the five mythical aeons or ages the relation of the opposites expresses this dominant dynamic. Things come apart. Things come back together ideally at a higher degree of conscious wholeness. Ultimately, the new human beings (realized in the fifth aeon/age) are achieved through processes of both fragmentation and differentiation, on one hand, and through *mixtum* and integration, on the other.

The breaking of the bones is essential to the processes which support shifting from a pre-differentiated unconscious unity to the achievement of a new differentiated consciousness. In processes of differentiating and recombining, there is indeed an accessing of the resources necessary to psychic realization. This taking apart and bringing back together lays bare the difference between the paradoxical pre-existent/non-existent god (archetypal potentiality) and the manifest god. The pre-existent/non-existent god cannot pass from potentiality into existence without being 'mixed' with the limited manifest human contents. The exchange between the material and immaterial (the circular distillation of the alchemists) is in full evidence in both mythology and, here in particular, in the myth of Ometeotl and the Five Suns. It pertains as well to psychic process. The realization of the godhead in lived terms depends upon it. Psychopompic energies, characterized by a *coincidentia oppositorum* in their core natures, are both necessary to and, in fact, sponsor and/or underlie all psychic processes, creative or destructive.

The dynamic supported by the twofold reach of the psychopomp opens a potential path toward a creative recombining, toward a greater wholeness, although not without its dangers. Clearly, the provisions which support these processes are the province of psychopompic structures and dynamics. The myth of Ometeotl and the five aeons/ages expresses the universal provision in the structures and dynamics of psychopompic energies. It is also endemic to pre-Hispanic mythology and the myth of Ometeotl, in particular. The particularities of the realization of the training at the Centro bore the marks of parallel processes of coming apart and back together.

291

Conclusion

At least since the 1980s, there had long been a deep interest in Jungian thought in Mexico. In 1991, in conversation between me and Thomas Kirsch, glimmers of hope and inspiration regarding a bridging training in Jungian-oriented psychotherapy in Mexico began to blossom. I later met Murray in 1992. He proceeded to join our conversations involving the structuring and development of a Training Program in Jungian-Oriented Psychotherapy in Mexico. Murray became a seminal figure in giving public seminars at the Centro (from 1993 to 1995). Later, from 1996 to 2010, he taught and supervised the four different generations of students at the Centro. He was key to bridging the gap from deeply desired but previously unrealized training in Jungian-oriented psychotherapy. He, Thomas, and I joined together in these seminal stages. Soon after, Beverley Zabriskie joined the three of us in the formation of the Academic, Admissions, and Evaluation Committees. Ultimately, many other analysts from around the world participated. The first generation of trainees in Jungian-Oriented Psychotherapy began in 1996. One of the goals was to provide a pathway for those students interested in applying for individual membership with full IAAP certification.

From the beginning and throughout, Murray carried the archetypal function of bridging, bringing himself, lending his experience and expertise to both the development of the Program and to teaching and supervising the students at the Mexican C.G. Jung Center. He bridged the opposites between the dearth and desire for serious Jungian training in Mexico to reach its fruition. He brought a wealth to our shared endeavor. The development of the Center, as is the case in most serious endeavors, was attended by extreme difficulty, frustration, and cost. It was indeed characterized at times by the "lowest of the low," as well as the "highest of the high." Murray was central to the fulfilment of our mission and to the navigation of this rocky and long journey. It was a journey of almost twenty years of challenges, stumbling blocks, and steppingstones. At times, it seemed overwhelming, impossible. It was indeed a *longissima via*, a path replete with labyrinthine twists and turns.

With this Festschrift, I honor Murray for providing in the most wonderful way his function as the carrier of the most positive aspect of the psychopomp. Hats off to Murray!

Patricia Michan is a Jungian psychoanalyst certified by the International Association of Analytical Psychology (IAAP) in 1995. She has a private practice in Mexico City, first as a psychotherapist (as of 1982) and later as a Jungian psychoanalyst (since 1995). She has lectured in Mexico, Latin America, United States, and Europe. Her many achievements include serving as founder and directress of the Centro Mexicano C.G. Jung, assistant editor for the JAP's Editorial Board, member of the International Association of Analytical Psychology (IAAP) and the Inter-Regional Society of Jungian Analysts (IRSJA). Her published works include "Reiterative Disintegration: Historical and Cultural Patterns and the Contemporary Mexican Psyche," a chapter in *Confronting Collective Trauma: Jungian Approaches to Treatment and Healing*, edited by Grazina Gudaite and Murray Stein; "Analysis and Individuation in the Mexican Psyche: Culture and Context," published in the *Journal of Jungian Theory and Practice; Analysis and Individuation in Latin Cultures and Contexts: The Mexican Psyche;* and *Dismemberment and Reintegration: Aztec Themes.* She is currently working on an extensive research and study on the relationship between analytical psychology, pre-Hispanic mythology and clinical practice.

References

Jung, C.G. (1967). The spirit Mercurius (R. F. C. Hull, Trans.). In H. Read et al. (Eds.), *The Collected Works of C.G. Jung: Vol. 13. Alchemical Studies* (pp. 191-250). Princeton University Press. (Original work published 1948) https://doi.org/10.1515/9781400850990.191

Jung, C.G. (1968). Introduction to the religious and psychological problems of alchemy (R. F. C. Hull, Trans.). In H. Read et al. (Eds.), *The Collected Works of C.G. Jung: Vol. 12. Psychology and Alchemy* (2nd ed., pp. 1-37). Princeton University Press. (Original work published 1943) https://doi.org/10.1515/9781400850877.1

Jung, C.G. (1968). *The Collected Works of C.G. Jung: Vol. 9 pt. 2. Aion: Researches Into the Phenomenology of the Self* (R. F. C. Hull, Trans.) (H. Read et al., Eds.). Princeton University Press. (Original work published 1951) https://doi.org/10.1515/9781400851058

Jung, C.G. (1969). Archetypes of the collective unconscious (R. F. C. Hull, Trans.). In H. Read et al. (Eds.), *The Collected Works of C.G. Jung: Vol. 9 pt. 1. Archetypes and the Collective Unconscious* (2nd ed., pp. 3-41). Princeton University Press. (Original work published 1954) https://doi.org/10.1515/9781400850969.3

Jung, C.G. (1970). *The Collected Works of C.G. Jung: Vol. 14. Mysterium Coniunctionis* (R. F. C. Hull, Trans.) (H. Read et al., Eds.). Princeton University Press. (Original work published 1955-56) https://doi.org/10.1515/9781400850853

Jung, C.G. (1989). *Memories, Dreams, Reflections*. Vintage Books.

Shalit, E. & Furlotti, N.S. (2013). *The Dream and its Amplification*. Fisher King Press.

Sharp, D. (1991). *Jung Lexicon: A Primer of Terms & Concepts*. Inner City Books.

The Self and the Heart, Individuation Psychology and Chinese Culture

Heyong Shen

Murray Stein and Tom Kirsch, along with many Jungian analysts, started the development of Analytical Psychology in China, continuing the task left by C.G. Jung and Richard Wilhelm.

Self and Individuation are the heart of Jungian analysis and analytical psychology. In 1921 Jung published *Psychological Types*, created the systematic framework for his system, and gave the subtitle of the book *The Psychology of Individuation*. For Jung, and in the context of the work then, Self and individuation contain a wholeness of fulfilling the nature of humans. But how? Where is the way?

As Jung (2009) described in *The Red Book*, "there is a knowledge of the heart that gives deeper insight" (p. 233). In his later years, Jung tried to bring a new method which he called the "intuitive method," like the inspiration from the dialogue with Mountain Lake, thinking with the heart could yield measurable results and at the same time give us an insight into the psychic nature of synchronicity and a method of grasping the total situation.

Murray Stein has published a series of books focused on Self and Individuation including: *Practicing Wholeness: Analytical Psychology and Jungian Thought* (1996), *Transformation: Emergence of the Self* (2004), *Principle of Individuation: Toward the Development of Human Consciousness* (2006); *Minding The Self* (2014), *Soul: Treatment*

295

and recovery (2015), and *The Collected Writings of Murray Stein: Individuation* (2020). In the Chinese context, Self and Individuation carry very special images and meanings, especially in the I Ching, the Book of Changes, or the Book for Transformation (转化). For example, the Chinese characters for Self(自性), the heart (心), and individuation (自性化), contain and convey inspirational connotations. When Jung went into the spirit of the depth seeking the knowledge of the heart, and imagining the "intuitive method," he embodied the meaning of Chinese culture and the wisdom of I Ching. As Jung said: "I therefore turned my attention first of all to the intuitive technique for *grasping the total situation* which is so characteristic of China, namely the *I Ching* or *Book of Changes*" (CW 8, para. 863).

As we know, Jung capitalized the "S" of self, giving it a special meaning for analytical psychology. In the Chinese context, there is a similar expression, putting "Da" (大, which means great or real) before "self," almost like capitalizing the self. The image of the character Da (大) combines the character for One (一) into self or man (人). According to the Chinese classic dictionary, the One means nature for everything: From the very beginning to the beginning, the Dao stands in oneness, creates the heaven and the earth, and turns into all things. The character for man （人, human）, has the basic meaning: the most precious nature of heaven and earth. So the image for Da, conveys the meaning for "Da Ren" （大人）, generally translated as a great man, or a real human.

I Ching, the Book of Changes, described "Da Ren" as follows: "The great man has the virtue vast as heaven and earth and the wisdom brilliant as the sun and the moon. He works in the good order as alteration of seasons and reveals good fortune and disaster in his divination miraculous as ghosts and spirits do"(2008, p.15). It is precisely the image and situation of Self and individuation in the Chinese context; it conveys the meaning of transformation and the Tao. In my imagination, C.G. Jung would like such an expression. Jung learned I Ching very well and even learned Chinese characters. He once described them as "readable archetypes" (1973, p. 584-585). One of the characteristics of Chinese characters and I Ching hexagrams is that they simultaneously reflect the meaning of Self and individualization, as we described above, while also containing the method for how to attain to Self and individuation.

In his first lecture at the Eranos East and West Round Table Conference in 1933, *A Study of the Process of Individuation*; Jung used his knowledge and wisdom of I Ching, to analyze the symbols of a client's Soul-Flower, for the understanding of the individuation process, and the significance of transformation. Therefore, the theme of Self and individuation includes how to experience self-nature and how to obtain and fulfill the individuation process. In fact, the sustained search for how to embody the connotation and meaning of Self and individuation was also the continuous effort of C.G. Jung, as well as post-Jungian analysts, such as Stein.

Confucianist, Taoist, and Zen Buddhist teachings and practice in Chinese culture echo and respond to the wisdom of I Ching, the Tao. For such understanding, the culture contains a way of life, a kind of life wisdom, which is also the embodiment of Self and individuation. For example, the influential book: *Secret of the Golden Flower* translated by Richard Wilhelm with commentary by Jung, is subtitled *A Book of Chinese Life*. This book brought me to Jungian analysis and allowed me to get to know Murray Stein and Tom Kirsch.

In 1993, I was alone in the forest of Southern Illinois (USA) and conducted several months of self-analysis. I worked on the dream diary that I have recorded since 1982 and reflected on the psychology I have studied for over 10 years. The forest is a container of self-nature, and there I encountered new dreams, experienced "fasting of the Heart" described by Chuang Tzu, and planted the seed for Psychology of the Heart. *The Secret of the Golden Flower: A Book of Chinese Life* was beside me all the way; it was as if I was accompanied by Richard Wilhelm and C.G. Jung. According to van Franz, the tree (from the writings of Chuang Tzu) contains the symbol of Self, and getting through the forest carries the symbolic meaning of the individuation process.

During that period, I contacted Murray Stein and Tom Kirsch. Shortly afterward in 1994, Tom Kirsch, Murray Stein, Jean Kirsch, and Jan Stein visited China on behalf of the IAAP, and started the official development of Analytical Psychology in China. In the report to the IAAP by Murray Stein, he introduced the translation and discussion about the Self and individuation. "We wanted to be sure that a distinction was drawn between the concepts of ego and self as Jung used these terms, and Dr. Shen and his colleagues struggled visibly with this point. At this moment we could have chosen to be archetypalist/deconstructionist Jungians, classical Jungians, or developmentalist Jungians, and a debate sputtered in our own brainpans about how subtle to become with our new friends. We took the easy way out, probably a grave mistake for which future generations will have to pay, and said that the Self is like the Tao, it cannot be grasped directly. If you think you know what it is and can define it, you don't have it. It is both inside and outside. It is everywhere, it is nowhere, etc. The analogy to Tao seemed at the moment to get Jung's intent across the cultural barrier better than other concepts and terms of a more technical psychological nature could have done." (1995, vol 15). Then, Murray said: "I wrote to Dr. Shen some weeks later and asked him to reconstruct that bit of dialogue if he could remember it." He replied: "In the Chinese language, there is one word for both the English words 'I' and 'me' (wo;我)…three Chinese words can be used as English 'self.' 1) zi wo (自我): myself; 2) zi ji (自己): me; and 3) zi shen (自身): my body. So, the first one (zi wo) is closer and can be used as 'self,' and actually, we used this word for every Western psychologist who uses 'self' and 'ego' in his theories, including Jung." But in my experience, I prefer to use a fourth one, zi xing (自性), to translate Jung's Self. Zi Xing originally is a special term of Buddhism and mainly means a) the heart of fa (法 i.e. TAO) and b) the first truth, the cause of everything. But in my theory about the Psychology of the Heart, zi xing is better than zi wo, zi ji, and zi shen for Jung's theory. Since xing (性) is 'heart' and 'life' together, it means the original psychological truth which we carried from the very beginning and the psychological meaning of our life (1995, vol 15). I engraved a chapter for Stein, which highlights the imagery of the stone; and fifty yarrow stalks for divination taken from King Wen's platform for practicing the I Ching.

The Way of Individuation in Chinese Culture

In fact, my understanding of the Self then and for the translation was inspired by the Sixth Patriarch Huineng and the teaching of Zen Buddhism. C.G. Jung wrote of the origin of this branch of Buddhism in his foreword to Suzuki's book *Introduction to Zen Buddhism*: "The origin of Zen, as Oriental authors themselves admit, is to be found in Buddha's Flower Sermon. On this occasion he held up a flower to a gathering of disciples without uttering a word. Only (Maha) Kasyapa understood him." (CW 11, para. 877). At that moment, when Maha Kasyapa smiled faintly, Gautama Buddha said, "I possess the true Dharma eye, the marvelous heart-mind of Nirvana, the true form of the formless, the subtle dharma gate that does not rest on words or letters but is a special transmission outside the scriptures. This I entrust to Mahākāśyapa (Maha Kasyapa)" (2005, p. 9). We can imagine at this moment the images of "seed," "sprouting"; the "core," the Self and the "heart" are all present. At the level of archetypal symbolism, this flower corresponds to the secret of the golden flower, and to the "heart/soul flower" in analytical psychology.

The original name for Chinese Zen Buddhism is "Heart Sect" (Xin-zhong; 心宗). It's fundamental teaching is "from the heart to heart" and seeks to achieve an "enlightening of the heart nature." The Sixth Patriarch Huineng expressed the nature of the self in such way:

How unexpected? The self-nature is originally pure in itself.
How unexpected! The self-nature is originally neither produced nor destroyed.
How unexpected! The self-nature is originally complete in itself.
How unexpected! The self-nature is originally without movement.
How unexpected! The self-nature can produce the ten thousand dharmas
(2007, p. 16-18)

The fifth Patriarch Hongren responded to Huineng at that moment: "Studying the Dharma without recognizing the original heart is of no benefit. If one recognizes one's own original heart and sees one's original self-nature, then one is called a great hero, a teacher of gods and humans, a Buddha." Therefore, in the basic teaching of Zen, contains the meaning of Self, and the way of individuation and spiritual transformation.

The development of Chinese Zen is influenced by Taoism, especially the concept of Tao in the Chinese context. In the earlier period of Jung's Psychology of Individuation, for instance in the Psychological Types, Jung paid particular attention to Tao, especially to Lao-Tzu, getting great inspiration from it.

C.G. Jung's first speech given at the Eranos East and West Round Table was titled "A Study of the Process of Individuation" (1933). He started with the 21st chapter of Lao-tzu's Tao Te Ching:

Tao's working of things is vague and obscure.
Obscure! Oh vague!
In it are images.
Vague! Oh obscure!
In it are things.
Profound! Oh dark indeed!
In it is seed.
Its seed is very truth.
In it is trustworthiness.
From the earliest Beginning until today
Its name is not lacking
By which to fathom the Beginning of all things.
How do I know it is the Beginning of all things?
Through *it!*

Before Jung gave his talk, he said in this way: "The European comes seeking the perfumed air of the Orient…" That is the reason I have set a certain motto as the foundation of my talk. My motto is to be found in Chapter 20 of the Tao Te Ching. There Lao-tzu wrote:

Give up your learning; then you will be free of anxiety!
Between 'yes' and 'yea,' what is the difference?
Between good and evil, what is the difference?
However, what all revere cannot with impunity be set aside.
O Solitude! Have I not yet attained to your heart?

After that introduction, Jung began his formal talk on "A Study of the Process of Individuation." As described in the Chinese description of "Da" and "Da Ren," Lao Tsu used Da for the name of Tao. In chapter 25 of *Tao Te Ching*, Lao Tsu said: "Therefore, the Dao (the Meaning and the Way) is great: Heaven is great, the Earth is great, and Man is also great. In the universe there are four 'greats,' and Man is one of the four" (1994, p. 50-51). If I were to try to put this in the language of Analytical Psychology, then I would want to say that the Dao is great because, like the Self, it is a container of everything. Indeed, a Chinese proverb says: "The capacity of containing makes greatness." But of course, Lao Tzu has added the thought that only through greatness may things transform. This has profound implications for our understanding of individuation, including the individuation that sometimes will not happen because the patient cannot embrace his or her capacity to take their place among the "Greats" in life.

In Chapter 4: "Way of the Human World," in addition to teaching about the fasting of the heart principle and emptiness of the heart, Chuang-tzu described a practical method of "intuiting heart" to attain heartfelt influence. Jung understood this approach and incorporated it into analytical psychology: "If you have insight, says Chuang-tzu, 'you use your inner eye, your inner ear, to pierce to the heart of things, and have no need of intellectual knowledge.' This is obviously an allusion to the absolute knowledge of the unconscious, and to the presence in the microcosm of macrocosmic events." In this same chapter, Chuang-tzu introduces the story of a gigantic old oak tree, which appeared in the dream of a wandering carpenter, and which led, in the dream, to a wonderful conversation between the tree and the carpenter. Marie-Louise von Franz used this story in her essay on "The Process of Individuation." She wrote: "This is a process in which one must repeatedly seek out and find something that is not yet known to anyone. The guiding hints or impulses come, not from the ego, but from the totality of the psyche: the Self" (1988, p. 164).

In Jung's mind, Tao is not only the expression of Chinese Taoist philosophy but also the crystallization of the entire Chinese culture, including Zen and Confucianism. The classics of Confucianism, such as *the Analects, Mencius, the Great Leaning*, and *the Doctrine of the Mean* also contain connotations and images of self-nature and individuation, as well as enlightenment, reflected in Jung's analytical psychology.

The Tao of Confucius can be expressed by the way of loyalty（忠; the upper part is a symbol of the Mean, and the lower is the symbol of the heart）and forgiveness（恕; the upper part is a symbol of the same, and the lower is the symbol of the heart）as *The Analects* of Confucius recorded. Richard Wilhelm translated "loyalty" as "loyalty to oneself" (Treue gegen sich selbst) and translated "forgiveness" as "kindness to others" (Gutigkeit gegen andre); which already contains the inspiration of Jung's analytical psychology. In Wilhelm's view, the "Zhong"(忠) of Confucianism—contains one kind of depth spirit or transcendental function. According to Wilhelm, by just using this "Zhong"（中）and the "heart" (心) you can realize your own human nature, go into the depth and transcendental realm, and understand the meaning of destiny.

After Confucius, Meng Zhi (Mencius, 372-289 BC) became the leading figure of Confucianism. One of his most important essays is called "To Fully Develop the Kindness of the Heart." He begins with: "To fully develop the kindness of the heart is to understand human nature. To understand human nature is to understand the mandate of Heaven. And to preserve one's kind heart and one's nature is to serve Heaven" (1999, p. 291). Then, Meng Zhi went on further and said: "Benevolence, righteousness, decorum and wisdom are deeply rooted in the heart. That is the nature of Junzi (a person of noble character, quite close to Self and individuation in Chinese culture context)." (p. 299). Benevolence (Ren), righteousness (Yi), decorum (Li) and wisdom (Zhi) are the four pillars of Confucianism, and they can also be seen as the embodied expression of the primary energies of the I Ching: Yuan, Heng, Li, Zhen[1] (CW 9i, para. 640).

These four pillars have supported the cultural education of the Chinese, including the way of Self and individuation, and they are all deeply rooted in the heart, which can be said to be the core and seed of Confucianism, the I Ching and our cultural teachings.

The text of *The Great Learning* starts with: "The object of a higher education is to bring out the intelligent moral power of our nature; to make a new and better society (literally people); and to enable us to abide in the highest excellence" (1992, p. 2-3). The book presents a realm that is possible for the human heart and soul to achieve. But how does one achieve that? How does one get to this living in "highest excellence?" This is reminiscent of the earlier discussion of the symbols for Self and individuation in which the way and the method is embedded? *The Great Learning* teaches what can be called the heart method, and gives a simple and firm answer: (to have) "the right, and most sincere, heart" (1992, p. 4-5).

In *The Doctrine of the Mean*, the use of and application of this "heart method" is also described, as can be seen in the first sentence of the first chapter of this work: "Human nature is endowed by Heaven." The right way of behavior is to follow one's nature and all nature should be cultivated in the right way of behavior. As mentioned previously, this book goes on to explain the concepts of Zhong (中) and He (和; harmony). In this book, although speaking of the individual and his or

---

[1] For Yuan, Heng, Li, Zhen, Jung described them as: *Yuan*, generative power; *Heng*, all-pervading power; *Li*, beneficent power; and *Zhen*, unchangeable, determinative power

her living with a basis in *Zhong* and expressing things using the concept of *He*, the text interestingly writes that when Zhong and He are achieved, "the world...runs smoothly" (2006, p. 4-5) the Self and the heart, and the individuation process in it.

As Confucianism developed further during the Song dynasty of China (960—1279), we have the work of Zhou Dunyi (1017-1073), considered the founder of Neo-Confucianism, who left us a famous essay the *Taiji Tushuo* (*Explanations of the Diagram of the Supreme Ultimate*). In this essay, Zhou Dunyi referred to a diagram and explained the image and meaning of Taiji (supreme polarity) and Wuji (limitless potential), expounded on the concepts of yin/yang and the theory of wu xing (which describes five elements and phases). Through this writing, Zhou Dunyi illustrates the law of changes in the universe and also how these occur in the heart & Soul. He describes "human" as the heart of heaven and earth and describes the nature of the human being as "Ren" (仁, "benevolence" or, as translated by Richard Wilhelm, "menschlichkeit" and "wohlwollen" - humanity and goodwill). C.G. Jung appreciated Zhou Dunyi's theory very much. Later, Dora Kalff, used Zhou Dunyi's *Diagram of the Supreme Ultimate* in forming her methodology and foundation for Sandplay therapy.

Individuation and Enlightenment: East and West

The theme of the 8th International Conference for Analytical Psychology and Chinese Culture was: "Enlightenment and Individuation: East and West." Murray gave the keynote address: *Psychological Individuation and Spiritual Enlightenment: Similarities and Differences*. Murray started his presentation with these words: "The attainment of enlightenment as understood traditionally in the East and the process of individuation as understood by analytical psychology in the West share a common goal: the transformation of consciousness" (2018).

Liu Dajun, Chinese I Ching scholar, gave the presentation with the title: *Obtaining Enlightenment from the I Ching: Entering a Spiritual or Numinous Realm*. According to Professor Liu Dajun's view, the *Book of Changes* is an ancient Chinese classic by which human affairs can be ascertained on the basis of the Dao (the Meaning and the Way) of Heaven. Focusing on the unity of Heaven, Earth, and Human, not only does the I Ching reveal the waxing and waning of the *yin* and *yang* energies in the natural world, but it also fuses and articulates human nature and destiny, contains the meaning of Self and individuation of Analytical Psychology, and in which spiritual cultivations and enlightenment are conceived—a kind of wisdom which deserves to be explored and valued.

Joe Cambray, Tom Kelly, Jeorge Hogenson, Martin Schmidt, John Merchant, Wu Yi (Confucian scholar), Yan Zexian (philosopher of science), Hu Fuchen (Taoist scholar), Chen Bing (Buddhist scholar), Shi Jiqun (Buddhist priest), Ren Farong (Taoist leader) also presented their insights and wisdom around the theme: Enlightenment and Individuation: East and West. I gave the presentation: *Enlightenment and Individuation, Psychology of the Heart and Jungian Analysis*. In Chinese culture, "enlightenment" means the encounter between the Self and the heart, a kind of understanding of the heart nature, and the integration of the self and the heart. "Psychology" in Chinese also includes "learning the truth from the heart." Chinese culture advocates "enlightenment," a state that can only be reached by the heart; it is also like Buddha is the heart, and the heart is Buddha; Self is the heart, and the right heart is enlightenment. The effort of the Psychology of the Heart is also an echo of Jung's quest for the knowledge of the heart and intuiting heart method; practicing wholeness.

For Wilhelm, Confucian benevolence is humanity, the principle of human beings, just like the Delphic motto that originated from Western psychology: Know yourself and fulfill your talents. Therefore, Wilhelm deduced the "benevolence" of Confucianism as "human nature" (menschlichkeit), "good deeds" (wohlwollen), and "perfection" (vollkommenheit). Thus, Confucian "benevolence" naturally entered Jung's analytical psychology system, whether it is its Psychological Types or its concept of Self and the individuation process. The development trend contained in human nature is integrity and wholeness.

In Richard Wilhelm's view, the maintenance and development of the Chinese Confucian tradition can make the world a great harmony. Wilhelm had been in China for 25 years. He had gradually devoted himself to Chinese culture and integrated Chinese culture into himself. Because of Richard Wilhelm, China's Confucius and Confucianism, as well as China's Taoism and Buddhism, especially I Ching, all have had far-reaching psychological significance for the west. Among them, it is not only the dissemination of knowledge, but also the passion and devotion to Life. The endowment of fate and the experience of the self and individuation have achieved a perfect combination in him.

The life of Confucius is also a life of integrity and practicing the wholeness, his individuation process, that was expressed in six stages by him:

At fifteen I set my heart upon learning.
At thirty, I had planted my feet firm upon the ground.
At forty, I no longer suffered from perplexities.
At fifty, I knew what were the biddings of Heaven.
At sixty, I heard them with docile ear.

At seventy, I could follow the dictates of my own heart; for what I desired no longer overstepped the boundaries of right (1999, p. 10-11).

Such a description of six stages, in fact, is the expression of the archetypal imagery of the Qian hexagram of the I Ching:

Nine at the beginning: Hidden dragon. Do not act.
Nine in the second place: Dragon appearing in the field. It furthers one to see the great man.
Nine in the third place: All day long the superior man is creatively active. At nightfall his mind is still beset with cares. Danger. No blame.
Nine in the fourth place mean: Wavering flight over the depths. No blame.
Nine in the fifth place: Flying dragon in the heavens. It furthers one to see the great man.
Nine at the top: Arrogant dragon will have cause to repent."
As the great symbol of Qian Hexagram presented: The movement of heaven is full of power. Thus, the superior man makes himself strong and untiring.

Superior man, Junzi (君子) or Da Ren in Chinese, is another kind of expression of Self and individuation. As we discussed earlier relating to Self and individuation in I Ching: "The great man (Da Ren) has the virtue vast as heaven and earth and the wisdom brilliant as the sun and the moon. He works in the good order as alteration of seasons and reveals good fortune and disaster in his divination miraculous as ghosts and spirits do"

(2008, p.15). These descriptions and images also contain the methods and the way of individuation. For instance, "the virtue vast as heaven and earth" manifested in the first and second hexagram of I Ching: Qiang and Kun. The "wisdom brilliant as the sun and the moon," it is also the image and significance of Kan (29) and Li (30) hexagrams. For understanding of that, as Stein said: "In fact, it was these similarities between individuation as he experienced it in himself in his *Red Book* period and with his patients thereafter, and what he discovered in the Chinese alchemical text, *The Secret of the Golden Flower* sent to him in translation by his friend Richard Wilhelm, that he concluded that there is an archetypal basis for the individuation process, i.e., that it is a human universal." What Jung expressed in the Red Book also left us with inspiration: "But how can I attain the knowledge of the heart? You can attain this knowledge only by living your life to the full" (2009, p. 233). This is what he expressed when he reflected on the spirit of depth. The previous paragraph is: "One would like to learn this language, but who can teach and learn it? Scholarliness alone is not enough; there is a knowledge of the heart that gives deeper insight" (2009, p. 233). What is contained in it is the key to individuation and transformation. We have the Red Book and Black Books of C.G. Jung today, and learned that, in his exploration of the spirit of depth, along with the way for the individuation process, he pursued the knowledge of the heart and the method of grasping the total situation, intuitive heart method…all related to I Ching and Chinese culture.

Conclusion

In a letter that Jung wrote to Richard Wilhelm on May 25, 1929, Jung said: "Fate seems to have apportioned to us the role of two piers which support the bridge between East and West" (1973, p. 66). Jung especially mentioned that in his memorial speech for Wilhelm: "I may perhaps speak of Wilhelm and his work, thinking with grateful respect of this mind which created a bridge between East and West" (CW 15, para. 74).

Murray Stein and Tom Kirsch, along with many Jungian analysts, started the development of Analytical Psychology in China, continuing the task left by C.G. Jung and Richard Wilhelm. As Jung says: "We must continue Wilhelm's work of translation in a wider sense if we wish to show ourselves worthy pupils of the master. The central concept of Chinese philosophy is *tao*, which Wilhelm translated as 'meaning.' Just as Wilhelm gave the spiritual treasure of the East a European meaning, so we should translate this meaning into life. To do this—that is, to realize *tao*—would be the true task of the pupil" (CW 15, para. 89).

As we know, one of the last dreams Jung left to us, just a few days before his death in 1961, was recorded by Hannah (1976) in her *The Work and Life of Jung*: "He saw a big, round block of stone in a high bare place and on it was inscribed: 'This shall be a sign unto you of wholeness and oneness'" (p. 347). I heard from David Rosen that the last piece of stone engraved by C.G. Jung included four Chinese characters: Tian-Ren-He-Yi（天人合一, Heaven-Man-Unity-One）.

Tian-Ren-He-Yi, Heaven-Man-Unity-One, is the embodiment of Self and the heart, the witness of the individuation process. Stein (2018) considers three stages of mature (or, as I call it, "late stage") individuation as described by Jung in *Mysterium Coniunctionis*, his last major work: "I can briefly summarize these stages as follows: a) attainment of mental discipline and self-knowledge, b) embodiment of insights, and c) *unus mundus* awareness." Murray Stein elaborated them in his presentation: *Psychological Individuation and Spiritual Enlightenment*. For the third stage of the process of self-naturalization, Jung's development of the alchemical fusion (*coniunctio*) as Gerhard Dorn, Jung writes: "The thought Dorn expresses by the third stage of conjunction is universal: It is the relation or identity of the personal with the suprapersonal atman, and of the individual *tao* with the universal *tao*." (para. 762). In this sentence Jung again references Chinese Daoism. He goes on to relate this to the individuation process. Here we arrive at the third and highest degree of conjunction, "the union of the whole man with the *unus mundus*... a union with the world – not the world of multiplicity as we see it but with a potential world, the eternal Ground of all empirical being, just as the self is the ground and origin of the individual personality past, present and future." Then, Murray said, individuation becomes enlightenment.

According to Stein, "Individuation is a lifelong journey toward a destination shared by Jungian psychology and Eastern spiritual traditions. In the practice of individuation, West joins East in a common enterprise of transformation" (As. 29). Then, the addition of the West to the East is also the blending of the heart and soul.

I am very honored to join the *Individuation Psychology: Essays in Honor of Murray Stein*, with this "Self and the heart, individuation psychology and Chinese culture," as a tribute to Murray Stein.

Heyong Shen, Ph.D., is the author of *Psychology of the Heart* (Fay Lecture), *C.G. Jung and Chinese Culture*, and *The Heart of Chinese Culture Psychology*, as well as numerous articles on the interface between analytical psychology and Chinese culture. Dr. Heyong Shen is a professor of psychology (City University of Macao), Jungian analyst (member of the International Association for Analytical Psychology), Sandplay therapist (member of the International Society of Sandplay Therapy), founding president of China Society for Analytical Psychology (CSAP) and China Society for Sandplay Therapy (CSST), speaker at the Eranos East and West Round Table Conferences (1997, 2007, 2019, and 2022), main organizer of the International Conference of Analytical Psychology and Chinese Culture (1998-2020), chief editor of Chinese translation of *Collected Works of C.G. Jung*; and founding member of the Garden of the Heart & Soul project. Email: shenheyong@hotmail.com

References

Campbell, J. (1964). *Papers from the Eranos Yearbooks*: foreword. Vol. 5. Pantheon Books.

Dumoulin, H. (2005). *Zen Buddhism: A History (India & China)*. (J.W. Heisig, Paul F. Knitter, Trans). World Wisdom, Inc.

Hannah, B. (1976). *Jung, His Life and Work: A Biographical Memoir*. Putnam.

I Ching. (2008). *The Zhou Book of Changes*. Hunan People's Publishing House.

Jung, C.G. (1966). Richard Wilhelm: In memoriam (R. F. C. Hull, Trans.). In H. Read et al. (Eds.), *The Collected Works of C.G. Jung: Vol. 15. Spirit in Man, Art, and Literature* (pp. 53-62). Princeton University Press. (Original work published 1957) https://doi.org/10.1515/9781400850884.53

Jung, C.G. (1969a). A study in the process of individuation (R. F. C. Hull, Trans.). In H. Read et al. (Eds.), *The Collected Works of C.G. Jung: Vol. 9 pt. 1. Archetypes and the Collective Unconscious* (2nd ed., pp. 290-354). Princeton University Press. (Original work published 1950) https://doi.org/10.1515/9781400850969.290

Jung, C.G. (1969b). Concerning mandala symbolism (R. F. C. Hull, Trans.). In H. Read et al. (Eds.), *The Collected Works of C.G. Jung: Vol. 9 pt. 1. Archetypes and the Collective Unconscious* (2nd ed., pp. 355-384). Princeton University Press. (Original work published 1950) https://doi.org/10.1515/9781400850969.355

Jung, C.G. (1969c). Synchronicity: An acausal connecting principle (R. F. C. Hull, Trans.). In H. Read et al. (Eds.), *The Collected Works of C.G. Jung: Vol. 8. Structure and Dynamics of the Psyche* (2nd ed., pp. 417-519). Princeton University Press. (Original work published 1952) https://doi.org/10.1515/9781400850952.417

Jung, C.G. (1969d). Foreword to Suzuki's "Introduction to Zen Buddhism" (R. F. C. Hull, Trans.). In H. Read et al. (Eds.), *The Collected Works of C.G. Jung: Vol. 11. Psychology and Religion* (2nd ed., pp. 538-

557). Princeton University Press. (Original work published 1939) https://doi.org/10.1515/9781400850983.527

Jung, C.G. (1970). *The Collected Works of C.G. Jung: Vol. 14. Mysterium Coniunctionis* (R. F. C. Hull, Trans.) (H. Read et al., Eds.). Princeton University Press. (Original work published 1955-56) https://doi.org/10.1515/9781400850853

Jung, C.G. (1973). *Letters.* (G. Adler & Jaffe, A, Eds.) Bollingen Series, Princeton University Press.

Jung, C.G. (1988). *Man and His Symbols.* Anchor Press.

Jung, C.G. (2009). *The Red Book.* Ed. Sonu Shamdasani. W.W. Norton & Company.

Kuan, V.C. (2007). (trans.) The Dharmic Treasure Altar-Sutra of the Sixth Patriarch (The Altar Sutra). Neo-Carefree Garden Buddhist Canon Translation Institute.

Lao Zi. (1994). *Tao Te Ching* (A. Waley, Trans.). Hunan Publication.

Legge, J. (trans). (1992). *Four Books: The Great Learning.* Hunan Publication.

Meng Zhi. (1999). *Gaozhi (Part A).* Changsha: Hunan People's Publishing House.

Stein, M. (1995). Report on an IAAP Visit to China. IAAP Newsletter. Vol 15.

Stein, M. (2018). "Psychological Individuation and Spiritual Enlightenment: Similarities and Differences." Keynote address to the 8th International Conference for Analytical Psychology and Chinese Culture, Xian, China.

Zisi. (2006). *The Doctrine of the Mean.* Sinolingua.

"Let it happen": *Wei Wu-Wei* for Individuation

Ann Chia-Yi Li

Dr Murray Stein's presence along my study path has inspired me in many ways. I studied at ISAP Zurich, and once in a reading seminar on Jung's Alchemy and Psychology, Murray tried to depict the numinous experience, using the example of one's encounter with God, an archetypal image of Self. He was too moved even to speak, and a tremendous supportive silence immediately filled the lecture room. He has significantly impacted me in those few seconds, making me comprehend that psychology is not knowledge but life itself.

Prelude

"Let it happen." Murray said gently. This short sentence puzzled me for years until I came out from the other end of that project, which was fraught with dilemmatic difficulties.

It was a fresh morning in early autumn. I visited Dr Murray Stein, as usual, in that small café in Zurich's old town. The café was cozy, and the delicious smell of freshly made coffee constantly wafted from the bar. But I was uneasy. Hearing that the project was somewhat distorted, Murray said gently, "Let it happen."

This open endedness of our discussion settled the nature of the process. I could not understand why I should "let it happen" instead of "dealing with it." I left the café feeling that I was heard and yet not heard. Nevertheless, an indescribable certainty sprouted in me despite being deeply puzzled. On the tram home, I couldn't stop thinking, "Let it happen. But who *lets it happen* and what happens when and where?"

The Role of the Ego

That unendurable suspension naturally reminded me of the crucifixion. It is so true that the background of a transformation process is a state of suffering. I immediately experienced the difference between reading the crucifixion as a metaphor and living it as part of everyday life. The suspension and inflexibility due to the crucifixion make me feel trapped in complicated situations like a tangled knot. I desired to cut it open, but I was advised to give enough space to let situations develop to untie the knot.

Describing the nature of the psyche, Jung (1954/1969b) argues, that theoretically, no conscious content can be claimed to be absolute consciousness. He therefore comes to this paradoxical conclusion: "There is no conscious content which is not in some other respect unconscious. Maybe, too, there is no unconscious psychism which is not at the same time conscious" (p. 188). Because this is the grey zone where we live, it is not surprising that the initial state of wholeness is depicted as a watery abyss. In addition, our shadows, complexes, projections, and transference naturally aggravate this condition, turning this abyss into infinite chaos.

From this *massa confusa*, people strive for order beginning with differentiation. Be it the other from within or the other from without, only when an object and a subject are both present can the dialogue be possible. Whether it be the water and fire, the King and Queen, the *Sol* and *Luna*, or one's conscious and unconscious, Jung refers to the integration of the conflicting opposites as the *individuation process*.

Despite this arcane description, the profound mystery of individuation is empirical and occurs in our everyday life. In this short essay, I limit my discussion to the presence of ego on finding the inner light to anchor oneself in this impenetrable darkness and on its ways of navigating in the life jungle of modern man. Psychologically speaking, the ego surfs on the waves of constant psychic disturbance. How might the conscious ego be challenged by controversial problems? What risks will the conscious ego undergo when attempting to integrate diametrically opposed opposites?

On one hand, as Jung (1951/1968) observes, "the progressive development and differentiation of consciousness leads to an ever more menacing awareness of the conflict and involves nothing less than a crucifixion of the ego, its agonizing suspension between irreconcilable opposites" (p. 44). This is not an unusual situation in current life. Particularly when confronting the insoluble conflicts between ethical obligations and eros, people claim that the more they recognize, the more they feel stuck, to the extent that they are incapable of thinking but are simply functional in life. On the other hand, in indicating another subtle danger that involves one when operating the *opus* in the unknown realm of the psyche, Jung cites the oldest Chinese alchemist, Wei Po-yang:

> Ghostly things will make their appearance, at which he will marvel even in his sleep. He is then led to rejoice, thinking that he is assured of longevity. But all of a sudden he is seized by an untimely death. (c. 42 C.E./1932, as cited in Jung, 1951/1968, p. 364)

On this point, Jung warns about inflation due to one's identification with archetypal unconscious content. As soon as the ego is assimilated by the unconscious material or overwhelmed by its archaic numinosity, one is not oneself anymore. It appears that, either torn apart and disintegrated or devoured and dissolved, the ego is surrounded by perpetual danger and risks extinguishing itself in descending to the depths of life.

Nevertheless, Jung (1937/1968) also comprehends that "the chaos is a *massa confusa* that gives birth to the stone" (p. 325). In other words, this unknown world beyond our consciousness is dark and void on the surface but buries within itself the light of Nature. Psychologically speaking, it turns out that the ego is obliged to venture on this journey. Regarding this type of perilous condition, Jung (1954/1967) provided a tale from a Persian alchemical text involving "a tree that grows on the tops of the mountains, [and] a young man born in Egypt, a prince from Andalusia, who desires the torment of the seekers." Referring to this prince's attack on the seekers, the teller of the tale states,

> He has slain their leaders. ...The sages are powerless to oppose him. I can see no weapon against him save resignation, no charger but knowledge, no buckler but understanding. If the seeker finds himself before him with these three weapons, and slays him, he [the prince] will come to Life again after his

death, will lose all power against him, and will give the seeker the highest power, so that he will arrive at his desired goal. (Berthelot, 1924, as cited in Jung, 1954/1967, p. 320)

Jung argues that the tree and the prince are synonymous with the *lapis*, the philosopher's stone, and psychologically the Self. However, in presenting this tale, Jung especially wants to address its chthonic side: the prince "desires the torment of the seekers." Indeed, the *lapis* is a treasure that is hard to obtain. Moreover, it is a living thing and challenges its seekers. How, then, can the sages master the relationship with the hostile stone?

Apply this tale metaphorically to the situation I discussed with Murray, the weapon, the charger, and the buckler (shield) seem to resonate with my desire to forcefully deal with the dilemmatic difficulties and cut the tangled knot open, whereas the three suggested accoutrements— resignation, knowledge, and understanding—remind me of the act of taming the dragon. This approach—making progress by way of holding and containing—naturally calls my attention to the Daoist *wei wu-wei* (為無為) approach, the practice of doing by not doing. In the teaching of the Daoist alchemical treatise *The Secret of the Golden Flower* (Wilhelm, 1929/1962), this practice is the contemplation (*fan-chao,* 反照) to which the Daoist Master Lü-tsu refers. The text adds, "When Confucius says: 'Perceiving brings one to the goal'; or when the Buddha calls it: 'The vision of the heart'; or Lao-tse says: 'Inner vision,' it is all the same" (p. 34).

These contemplation practices are discussed later in this essay, but at this point, the *wei wu-wei* (為無為) approach recalls Jung's (1954/1969a) assertion about the process of confronting one's unconscious. In terms of relating to and integrating the autonomous unconsciousness, especially the numinous contents sent forth by the archetypes, he emphasises that those psychic contents "cannot be integrated simply by rational means, but require a dialectical procedure" (p. 40). In Jung's analytical work with his clients, he observed this kind of inner dialogue taking place of their own accord with their dreams or drawings or visions. Jung associates this internal dialogue with "the *meditatio*: 'an inner colloquy with one's good angel'" (p. 40), as the alchemists defined it.

The Role of the Self

One might question why a modern person would be encouraged to seek help from the inner Self when attempting to untie the dilemmatic difficulties? My image of *untying a knot* is an action of rearranging the posture of the strings. As one can see, when strings are formed in a knot, they are fixed in a definite posture. The tighter the knot is, the more rigid is the posture of the strings. To all appearances, a knot is constructed at the expense of the strings' inflexibility.

In the same way, one-sided consciousness is intended by the individual to adapt to the external environment, especially in one's first half of life. However, no matter how convincing a person's one-sided conscious attitudes might be, their rigidity will unavoidably block the natural flow of the psyche, leaving one stuck in a specific situation in a particular position. In other words, the more one singles out certain conscious attitudes toward life, the more one represses the right of unconsciousness to existence. It is not difficult to imagine that, sooner or later, one's unconscious will stand up to express itself.

Jung (1929/1969) observes, "People often fail to see that consciously willed one-sidedness is one of the most important causes of an undesirable complex, and that, conversely, certain complexes cause a one-sided differentiation of doubtful value" (p. 122). I suspect that this psychic entanglement is where the difficult dilemmas in our lives are born. Naturally, this situation reminds me of the *nigredo*. Jung once borrowed the words from the alchemist Michael Maier, describing this confusion stage of nondifferentiated conscious and unconscious as a "'black blacker than black' (*nigrum nigrius nigro*)" (1617, as cited in Jung, 1937/1968, p. 327).

From the perspective of Jungian psychology, the ego is only the centre of consciousness, whereas the Self shares the paradoxical character of archetypes. Self contains beginning and end; it nurtures and devours; it is the subject of the whole being as well as the ideal entity of the individual. Moreover, being the center of the psychic matrix, the Self exerts its influence on the ego with dynamic enantiodromia and compensation; if the ego can receive and transmit the messages sent forth by the Self without losing its presence, autonomous self-regulation results.

This collaboration between ego and Self draws attention once more to the dynamics of *wei wu-wei*; in other words, the partnership result from the resignation, knowledge, and understanding of the ego.

For example, helped with the reflection on the dream about shooting down the hero Siegfried, Jung (1961/1963) comprehends that this heroic idealism and identity in his conscious attitude are no longer suitable and must be "abandoned" (p. 181). He eventually understands that "there are higher things than the ego's will, and to these one must bow" (p. 181). A similar opinion can be found in the Daoist teaching in the *Golden Flower* (Wilhelm, 1929/1962). Daoist sage Lü-tsu says, "If today people sit and meditate only one or two hours, looking only at their own egos, and call this reflection, how can anything come of it?" (p. 34) The sage claims that with contemplation, the "self-conscious heart" must be reversed and directed to "where the formative spirit is not yet manifest" (p. 34).

The importance of introspective observation of the dynamics of the inner world is reinforced by one's inborn relationship with the Self. On the structure and dynamics of the Self, Jung (1951/1968) argues that the Self is the life force and subtle essence of one's being underlying ego-consciousness. On this point, he refers to the Brihadāranyaka Upanishad:

> "He who dwells in all beings, yet is apart from all beings, whom no beings know, whose body is all beings, who controls all beings from within, he is your Self, the inner controller, the immortal." (as cited in Jung, 1951/1968, p. 223)

Correspondingly, Master Lü-tsu understands it as the primal spirit, "the place whence heaven and earth derive their being" and, hence, "beyond the polar differences" (Wilhelm, 1929/1962, p. 24).

From Jung and Master Lü-tsu, we understand that the Self is not only paired with the ego as its opposite. Paradoxically, being one's entity, the Self contains the pairs of opposites within itself. Daoists practice synchronizing themselves with Dao, which gives birth to eternity by generating constant changes through the interaction of the paired *Yin* and *Yang* energies. Similarly, we can understand that conscious and unconscious tendencies will be equally appreciated when the Self shepherds them. The tension and the relation between this pair of opposites will eventually form the transcendent function, which "makes the transition from one attitude to another organically possible, without loss of the unconscious" (Jung, 1958/1969, p. 73). Naturally, this organic transition from one attitude to another leaves no space for the rigidity of one-sidedness. In this ideal condition, life blooms, unfolding in a circumambulatory way instead of creating knots one after another.

Wei Wu-Wei as a Format of the Ego-Self Axis

In *The Secret of the Golden Flower*, Master Lü-tsu[1] reveals, "The most important things in the great Tao are the words: action through non-action" (Wilhelm, 1929/1962, p. 53), or in Chinese, *wei wu-wei*. As for this specific Daoist presence of *wu-wei*, it has been variously translated as an "effortless action" (Slingerland, 2000, p.298) and an "actionless action" (Roberts & Ertubey, 2022, p.133). Similarly, Jung (1921/1971) understands that "*wu-wei* means 'not-doing'" but specifies that it does not mean "doing nothing" (p.217). Harold Coward (1996) depicts *wu-wei* as a "spontaneous action centred not in the ego but in the self" (p.489). Regarding this perspective, I argue that action through nonaction manifests the phenomenon of the ego-Self axis and hence a practical operation of individuation in everyday life.

Regarding the term *wu-wei* from the Daoist teaching of Lao-tzu (ca. 400 B.C.E./1891) the word *wei* (為) may be approached from three perspectives. First, literally, the word *wei* is a verb meaning "to action" and refers to a particular way of dealing with situations; the word *wu* (無) relates mainly to the determiner *no* or the adverb *not*. Together, these two words, *wu* and *wei*, form the opposition of *wei* and consequently indicate *wu-wei*, nonaction. Second, in the context of Lao-tzu's *Tao Te Ching*, *action* implies the operation of the human mind. To some extent, it includes situations in which the ego dominates one-sidedly, hence "to action" also suggests artificial doings operated by the ensnared ego. Lao-tzu therefore encourages people to be *wu-wei*: to let go of ego domination and judgement but be with the flow of Nature as it is. In other words, to rest oneself in Dao could be understood as the moment when one tries and takes action to manifest this *wu-wei* dynamic in one's life, and therefore, it is to *wei wu-wei*. Third, when the word *wei* is a noun, it can signify the universe's eternal motion, which is Dao. The goal of one's self-cultivation is therefore to be present in the great Oneness, to centre in the Self, and to live one's life in a way that is like the motion of Dao, which is action through nonaction.

---

[1] Lü Dongbin is generally regarded as the author of The Secret of the Golden Flower.

This kind of *wei wu-wei* life dynamics resonates with Jung's experience and understanding. In 1928, Jung received a copy of the German translation of *The Secret of the Golden Flower* from the sinologist Richard Wilhelm (1929/1962). Recalling that significant moment, Jung (1961/1963) says that he "devoured" the manuscript. He explains, "The text gave me an undreamt-of confirmation of my ideas about the mandala and the circumambulation of the centre" (p. 223). In the background of this historical encounter, Jung was creating *The Black Books* (2020) and *The Red Book* (2009), during the years 1913-1932. In these works, Jung explored the unknown world which he encountered by honestly writing down whatever came through him. He also took pains to turn his emotions into drawings.

It cannot be overlooked that in 1916, Jung formulated his experiences of this creative writing process as active imagination and derived an understanding of the transcendent function. This conjoint process of the conscious and unconscious resonates with Jung's (1946/1966) reading in *Rosarium Philosophorum* that one should "employ venerable Nature, because from her and through her and in her is our art born" (as cited in Jung, 1946/1966, p. 212). From the viewpoint of this alchemical treatise, the *opus* is the work of Nature; correspondingly, the individuation process driven by the Self is a journey surfing the current of one's inner necessity. Jung (1934/1954) associates this "inner vein of life" with Dao, which is "a flow of water that moves irresistibly towards its goal" (p. 186). From my point of view, the natural blooming of life operated and driven by the Self resonates with the motion of what I have explained as *wu-wei*. In the *wu-wei* phenomenon, no ego-centric artificial construction is conducted, yet everything manifests itself in its own way; therefore, Jung's holding onto this natural flow of unconscious and mediating the manifestation of the inner images exemplifies *wei wu-wei*.

Recalling Jung's (1921/1971) reminder that *wu-wei* does not mean "doing nothing" (p. 217), the greatest challenge for people might be the task of *wei*—the ego's action of holding the *wu-wei* process and putting this metaphysical dynamic into practice. One might question how to set sail in this grey zone where conscious and unconscious converge and how to rest in Dao where ego and Self are both present. In other words, we are challenged to reunite with the numinous Self and manifest self-realization in practical everyday life. In *The Secret of the Golden Flower*, Master Lü-tsu elucidates this situation and states, "Nothing is possible without contemplation (*fan-chao*, refection)" (Wilhelm, 1929/1962, p. 34). Furthermore, Master Lü-tsu reminds us that the goal of contemplation is reversing our self-conscious hearts towards "the form which existed before the laying down of heaven and earth" (p. 34) and rather than observing only our own egos. To be more precise, when reversing the self-conscious heart, we not only look at our own egos but also extend our attention to the Oneness where life is not yet born.

In this context, the Chinese word *fan* (反) refers to a reverse motion. Eventually, it draws the latent meanings of *return* and *reunion*. The word *chao* (照) indicates the act of mirroring and reflection. Combining these terms, *fan-chao* depicts the action of the ego reversing its attention inwards, and paradoxically, because of its presence, the ego may mirror the existence of the Self and reflects the light of Nature. This Daoist form of contemplation indicates an essential nature—the witness—in Lao-tzu's teaching of *wei wu-wei*.

The ego's action, *fan-chao*, brings forth the actuality of the Self. Sharing the Daoist viewpoint, Jung (1937/1968) maintains that the latent paired opposites in the unconscious must "be activated by the intervention of the conscious mind," and if not, they will "merely remain dormant" (p. 334). In his discussion on realizing the Self, Leslie Stein (2021) asserts a similar opinion: "In the absence of a numinous experience, we cannot grasp the Nature or extent of totality, yet we must attempt to make sense of it" (p. 212). It is as if the ego becomes the reference point for one's existence in the world. This view resonates with Jung's (1954/1969d) claim that the Self "is the subject and the object of the process" (p. 280). He likens the Self to a lamp and the ego to the one who perceives it and asserts, "Its light is invisible if it is not perceived; it might just as well not exist" (p. 280). To this extent, the ego and the Self depend on each other and form a paradoxical subject–object relationship.

A similar formula can be observed in Erich Neumann's (1952/1989) model of the ego-Self axis (pp. 56–61). If the ego can assert itself in relation to the totality of life—the Self—then the ego would be capable of navigating this numinous realm, like surfing the waves in the ocean. The surfer observes the waves, feels the push of the waves, tunes into this eternal changing motion, stays patient, remains present, and awaits the right timing to act. I would argue that this way to relate to the Self embodies the suggested accoutrements—resignation, knowledge, and understanding—which the sages need to "slay" the prince from Andalusia.

However, it must be noted that even if successfully standing on the surfboard, the surfer would fall back into the ocean in no time when losing contact with the hidden force in motion. This is by no means an easy task! Yet it might be the way people conduct their lives. In confronting the numinous power of archetype, "the ego enters into the picture only so far as it can offer resistance, defend itself, and in the event of defeat still affirm its existence" (Jung, 1955–56/1970, p. 546). The ego lets itself be guided by archetypal patterns but only with active and engaging gestures. This process of coming to know the counterposition in the unconscious is what Jung (1955–56/1970) called the *transcendent function* (pp. 199–200).

Master Lü-tsu reinforces the importance of *fan-chao* with reference to Confucius's instruction on self-cultivation: "Perceiving brings one to the goal" (Wilhelm, 1929/1962, p. 34). This sentence is a translation of the Chinese term *zhi-zhi* (致知), which is an amplification of the *wei wu-wei* ego–Self relationship in Confucian terms. *Zhi-zhi* is a core belief conveyed in the Confucian classic *The Great Learning*, or *Daxue*. The first four sentences in this book help illuminate its meaning: "What the Great Learning teaches,/ is to illustrate illustrious virtue;/ to renovate the people;/ and to rest in the highest excellence" (Legge, 1893, p. 356).

Before exploring the meaning of the phrase "to illustrate illustrious virtue (明明德)" (Legge, 1893, p. 356) it is necessary to consider Confucius's deep belief that one's illustrious virtue is inherent. *Ming-de* (明德), the original Chinese phrase for "illustrious virtue," contains the latent meaning of a brightness contributed by both the sun and moon; in this very obscure way, illustrious virtue entails an eternal natural light as a goal; however, life ensnares people easily in their needs and sensational desires. Naturally, people end up losing contact with their innate illustrious virtue. The task of perceiving therefore includes not only recognizing one's inner light but also facing oneself honestly. Daoist Master Lü-tsu portrays this course of events as a procedure "to melt out completely the slag of darkness" (Wilhelm, 1929/1962, p. 26); psychologically, this means the process of recognising one's own shadows and projections. In terms of the Western alchemical stage *putrefaction*, this is "the decomposition of the old matter that prepares for the birth of the new, the death that must precede rebirth" (Willard, 2015, p. 273).

With the word *illustrate* (明), people are reminded of the obligation to illuminate and demonstrate the inherent illustrious virtue, the natural light within; therefore, "perceiving" becomes a necessity. One's ego-conscious helps one recognize the right direction for self-cultivation and, simultaneously, to distinguish the snares and lures during the practice.

The Process

Thus far, this essay has established the importance of the ego's action and the ambivalent essence of the archetypal Self, both nourishing and devouring; however, the process of integrating the irreconcilable opposites itself must not be forgotten. At this point, it is helpful to add that the meaning of Confucian self-cultivation of *zhi-zhi* (致知) is carried out and completed by its twin-like core instruction in *The Great Learning*— the instruction of *zhi-zhi* (知止) (Legge, 1893, p.356). This phrase shares the exact spelling as the term *zhi-zhi* (致知), meaning "perceiving brings one to the goal" (Wilhelm, 1929/1962, p. 34), but as the Chinese characters indicate, it is pronounced differently. Literally, the first word *zhi* (知) means "to know"; the second word *zhi* (止) means "to stop." In this context, the term hints at two layers of meaning. First, it reminds people to make sure to know where their thoughts end and where their conjecture starts; namely, it advises one to distinguish clearly between one's thoughts and conjecture to avoid falling victim to one's unconscious. Second, it reminds people to bear in mind their supreme goal of self-cultivation. *Zhi-zhi* (知止) implies that despite all the complications and confusion during the long process, one should hold to the direction and give absolute priority to the goal: the redemption of and reconnection with one's illustrious virtue. Be it the Great One or Dao or the Self, this is the ultimate place where one shall rest.

According to the teaching of *The Great Learning*, only when one's innate natural light is perceived and operating in worldly everyday life can one "renovate the people" (Legge, 1893, p. 356). More precisely, this teaching means that those who can re-establish a connection with their inner virtue are obliged to guide others to pursue the journey of self-cultivation, hence renovating the people. Consequently, the renovation starts from the personal level, arrives at the collective level, and enables people to "rest in the highest excellence" (p. 356), the ultimate goodness; thus, "perceiving brings one to the goal" (Wilhelm, 1929/1962, p. 34).

This instruction indicates that Confucian scholars believe personality maturation helps individuals relate instead of being individualistic. That resonates with Jung's understanding of individuation.

Additionally, on the inner process of contemplation, *fan-chao*, Master Lü-tsu includes the Buddhist practice as a reference. This Buddhist instruction, "the vision of the heart" (Wilhelm, 1929/1962, p. 34), refers to the practice of "fixating contemplation," or *zhi gwan* (止 觀). Literally, the word *zhi* (止) means "to stop," and *gwan* (觀) indicates the action of observation; therefore, during the practice, "when the flight of the thoughts keeps extending further, one should stop and begin contemplating. Let one contemplate and then start fixating again" (p. 36). This process echoes the Confucian instruction *zhi-zhi* (知止). Step by step, with this self-awareness, one pursues a circumambulating way to revive the inner light. The practice of fixating contemplation also resonates with an alchemical distillation process. In Master Lü-tsu's words, "This is the washing of the heart and the purification of the thoughts; this is the bath" (p. 59); however, he also warns, "To kill the heart does not mean to let it dry and wither away, but it means that it has become undivided and gathered into one" (p. 42).

The oneness to which Master Lü-tsu refers is a mode of transcendental nondual presence derived from the tension and cooperation of the ego and the Self. In Jung's (1954/1969c) "Psychological Commentary on '*The Tibetan Book of The Great Liberation*,'" he delves into the differences between Western and Eastern thought. He perceives this nonduality in Eastern practice and comments, "Such an ego-less mental condition can only be unconscious to us, for the simple reason that there would be nobody to witness it" (p. 484); however, regarding the ego-less state of mind, I would argue that instead of extinguishing itself, actually the ego is fully present, though invisible. In terms of the Eastern practice of contemplation, *ego-less* depicts more of a purified ego whose subjectivity is free from the limitation and domination of bodily sensations. This ego is as pure and transparent as a piece of glass; therefore, with this ego's witness, "one hears only that there is no sound" and "sees only that no shape is there" (Wilhelm, 1929/1962, p. 44).

This ego-less state of mind demonstrates the ego's reunion with the source of life, hence sharing its essential objectivation. In this state of mind, the ego makes itself the best messenger of the Self. Namely, the ego is subjective and can distinguish differences, yet the ego is also objective and capable of perceiving the duality as it is without involving personal judgement and preference. This ability enables one's inner dialogue and encourages one to rest in Dao and follow the natural flow of life directed by the Self. In the same manner, the co-presence of the ego and Self contributes the flexibility for navigating life's complications and limitations. As Jung (1954/1969d) says,

> without the objectivation of the Self the ego would remain caught in hopeless subjectivity and would only gyrate round itself. But if you can see and understand your suffering without being subjectively involved, then, because of your altered standpoint, you also understand "how not to suffer," for you have reached a place beyond all involvements. (p. 281)

Postlude

"Let it happen!"

Only after I had borne the process could I understand that "letting it happen" implies keeping the dialectical procedure alive and listening carefully to this dialogue located either inwardly, between my conscious and unconscious, or outwardly, between myself and the surrounding environment.

I should have remembered one of the first dreams that came to me in my initial month of studying in Zurich:

> I arrived in a vast cave. With the dim light, I recognised hundreds of rocks surrounding me. But soon, from a distance, I noticed many different Chinese words engraved on each piece of rock. Then, when I attempted to figure out all those small writings at a distance, one of the Chinese words was suddenly enlarged and zoomed in towards me. I recognised it clearly; it is this word---在 (be).

To be and to be in it; this kind of purified ego-less state of mind is desired. It is authentic to its role in actualizing the occurrence of *wu-wei*. This might be a way to depict the essence of letting it happen: one is fully present to what is happening but not passively waiting and doing nothing; hence this process generates movement instead of collapse. I recall that chilly afternoon in the early spring; the tangled dilemmatic project was not resolved as wished but happened as it did. The flow of life remains, and I move on again.

Ann Chia-Yi Li is a supervising analyst at the International School of Analytical Psychology and has a practice in Zurich. Her interest lies in the relationship between Daoist practice, alchemy, and analytical psychology. Her chapter, "The Receptive and the Creative: Jung's Red Book for Our Time In the Light of Daoist Alchemy," was published in 2018 in *Jung's Red Book for Our Time: Searching for soul under postmodern conditions, Vol. II*, edited by Murray Stein and Thomas Arzt; and the chapter, "The 'Secret' of the Golden Flower: The Individuation Process by Way of Daoist Practice," was published in 2022 in *Eastern Practices and Individuation: Essays by Jungian Analysts*, edited by Leslie Stein.

References

Coward, H. (1996). Taoism and Jung: Synchronicity and the self. *Philosophy East and West, 46*(4), 477–495. https://doi.org/10.2307/1399493

Jung, C.G. (1954). The development of personality (R. F. C. Hull, Trans.). In H. Read et al. (Eds.), *The Collected Works of C.G. Jung: Vol. 17. Development of Personality* (pp. 165–186). Princeton University Press. (Original work published 1934)

Jung, C.G. (1963). *Memories, Dreams, Reflections* (Rev. ed.; A. Jaffé, Ed.; R. Winston & C. Winston, Trans.). Vintage Books. (Original work published 1961)

Jung, C.G. (1966). The psychology of the transference (R. F. C. Hull, Trans.). In H. Read et al. (Eds.), *The Collected Works of C.G. Jung: Vol. 16. Practice of Psychotherapy* (2nd ed., pp. 163–323). Princeton University Press. (Original work published 1946)

Jung, C.G. (1967). The philosophical tree (R. F. C. Hull, Trans.). In H. Read et al. (Eds.), *The Collected Works of C.G. Jung: Vol. 13. Alchemical Studies* (pp. 251–349). Princeton University Press. (Original work published 1954)

Jung, C.G. (1968). *The Collected Works of C.G. Jung: Vol. 9ii. Aion: Researches into the Phenomenology of the Self* (R. F. C. Hull, Trans.) (H. Read et al., Eds.). Princeton University Press. (Original work published 1951)

Jung, C.G. (1968). Religious ideas in alchemy (R. F. C. Hull, Trans.). In H. Read et al. (Eds.), *The Collected Works of C.G. Jung: Vol. 12. Psychology and Alchemy* (2nd ed., pp. 225–472). Princeton University Press. (Original work published 1937)

Jung, C.G. (1969a). Archetypes of the collective unconscious (R. F. C. Hull, Trans.). In H. Read et al. (Eds.), *The Collected Works of C.G. Jung: Vol. 9i. Archetypes and the Collective Unconscious* (2nd ed., pp. 3–41). Princeton University Press. (Original work published 1954)

Jung, C.G. (1969b). On the nature of the psyche (R. F. C. Hull, Trans.). In H. Read et al. (Eds.), *The Collected Works of C.G. Jung: Vol. 8. Structure and Dynamics of the Psyche* (2nd ed., pp. 159–234). Princeton University Press. (Original work published 1954)

Jung, C.G. (1969c). Psychological commentary on "The Tibetan Book of the Great Liberation." In H. Read et al. (Eds.), *The Collected Works of C.G. Jung: Vol. 11. Psychology and Religion* (2nd ed., pp. 475–508). Princeton University Press. (Original work published 1954)

Jung, C.G. (1969). The significance of constitution and heredity in psychology (R. F. C. Hull, Trans.). In H. Read et al. (Eds.), *The Collected Works of C.G. Jung: Vol. 8. Structure and Dynamics of the Psyche* (2nd ed., pp. 107–113). Princeton University Press. (Original work published 1929)

Jung, C.G. (1969). The transcendent function (R. F. C. Hull, Trans.). In H. Read et al. (Eds.), *The Collected Works of C.G. Jung: Vol. 8. Structure and Dynamics of the Psyche* (2nd ed., pp. 67–91). Princeton University Press. (Original work published 1958)

Jung, C.G. (1969d). Transformation symbolism in the Mass (R. F. C. Hull, Trans.). In H. Read et al. (Eds.), *The Collected Works of C.G. Jung: Vol. 11. Psychology and Religion* (2nd ed., pp. 201–296). Princeton University Press. (Original work published 1954)

Jung, C.G. (1970). *The Collected Works of C.G. Jung: Vol. 14. Mysterium Coniunctionis* (R. F. C. Hull, Trans.) (H. Read et al., Eds.). Princeton University Press. (Original work published 1955–56)

Jung, C.G. (1971). *The Collected Works of C.G. Jung: Vol. 6. Psychological Types* (R. F. C. Hull, Trans.) (H. Read et al., Eds.). Princeton University Press. (Original work published 1921)

Jung, C.G. (2009). *The Red Book: Liber Novus* (S. Shamdasani, Ed.) (S. Shamdasani, M. Kyburz, & J. Peck, Trans.). W. W. Norton and Company.

Jung, C.G. (2020). *The Black Books, 1913–1932: Notebooks of Transformation* (Vols. 1–7) (S. Shamdasani, Ed.; M. Liebscher, J. Peck, & S. Shamdasani, Trans.). W. W. Norton and Company.

Lao-tzu. (1891). *Tao Te Ching* (J. Legge, Trans.). Sacred Books of the East, Vol 39 (Original work published ca. 400 B.C.E.)

Legge, J. (1893). *The Chinese Classics: Vol. 1. Confucian Analects, the Great Learning, and the Doctrine of the Mean*. Oxford University Press.

Neumann, E. (1989). The psyche and the reality planes: A meta-psychological essay (H. Nagel, I. Roberts, & W. Goodheart). In W. McGuire (Ed.), *The Essays of Erich Neumann: Vol. 3: The Place of Creation* (pp. 3–62). Princeton University Press. (Original work published 1952)

Roberts, W., & Ertubey, C. (2022). Flow the wu-wei way: A thematic analysis of charity runners' experience of wu-wei in enhancing wellbeing and flourishing. *International Journal of Well-Being, 12*(4), 132–154. http://dx.doi.org/10.5502/ijw.v12i4.2129

Slingerland, E. (2000). Effortless action: The Chinese spiritual ideal of wu-wei. *Journal of the American Academy of Religion, 68*(2), 293–327. https://doi.org/10.1093/jaarel/68.2.293

Stein, L. (2021). *The Self in Jungian Psychology*. Chiron Publications.

Wilhelm, R. (Trans.). (1962). *The Secret of the Golden Flower* (C. F. Baynes, German to English translation). Harvest. (Original work published 1929)

Willard, T. (2015). Beya and Gabricus: Erotic imagery in German alchemy. *Mediaevistik, 28*, 269–281. https://doi.org/10.3726/83024_269

Approaching Zen Buddhism via Individuation Psychology

Mari Yoshikawa

It was not long after the founding of ISAP that I studied in 2009. There, I could feel the passion for the internationalization of analytical psychology that was shared among the analysts, lecturers, staff, and students. Dr. Stein was at the center of it all, standing there so quietly, so calmly, like a hermit, who seemed to be enjoying his new life in the mountains.

In *Where East Meets West* (2017), Dr. Murray Stein notes that there are many roads to what Jung calls "individuation." One of them is spiritual cultivation like that of Zen Buddhism in the East. He defines individuation clearly as "serious efforts to become more conscious through encounter with unconscious contents and process" (p. 264) while passionately insisting that it is a general human project and not limited to a few specific cultural enclaves. The hypothesis that individuation is aimed at a certain experience and development that exists across cultures would be agreed upon by many Jungian analysts. However, when the structure of the mind differs across cultures, the process may also differ from culture to culture.

Dr. Murray Stein presented his paper in memory of Dr. Kawai Hayao, the Father of Jungian psychology in Japan. As a lifelong student of the psychological differences between the West and of his own culture, Kawai's research into Buddhism was featured in the 1995 Fay Lectures, *Buddhism and Jung* (Kawai, 1995a). In it, Kawai describes conscious and unconscious transformation in his analytic practice in relation to Buddhism, which is deeply rooted in the land of Japan, through his own experience of 30 years of clinical practice as a Jungian analyst in Japan. In his lectures, Kawai recalled his childhood, in which he perceived Buddhism as something close to death. Kawai continued: "I am still afraid of death at my age, and I have never experienced any kind of enlightenment. However, my attitude toward the issue of death, which I will spend the rest of my life thinking about, has not changed" (Kawai, 1995b, p. 29). This was Hayao Kawai's fundamental attitude toward death and religion. This fundamental stance was carried through in the many books he published on death and religion during his lifetime.

In the Fay Lectures, he reports on his study of the dream series of Myoe, a high priest of the Kozan-ji Temple. There, he introduces the Kegon-sutra, the scripture of the Buddhist sect to which Myoe belongs, with reference to the writings of Toshihiko Izutsu. (Izutsu, 1989) I would like to summarize his introduction of the Kegon-sutra here.

In contrast to the ordinary world of reality, the world from which the boundaries that distinguish things from each other are removed is called the Dharmic World of Principle. This is the "nothingness" of Zen and the "absolute emptiness" of Kegon: Garland Sutra. In Buddhism, the "discriminating mind" refers to the daily awareness that distinguishes each thing and tries to see the differences between them. By emptying the discriminating mind, one becomes "nothingness" or "emptiness" of existence.

Kawai further quotes Izutsu to explain the characteristics of Kegon. In Hua-yen philosophy, Izutsu (1989) says: "The Principal permeates phenomena without the slightest hindrance and is thus none other than the phenomena themselves. Therefore, every single thing in our world of experience is the exact embodiment of 'Principal.'" Kawai states: "Once a person acknowledges their emptiness before or beneath such discrimination, one can see the world entirely nondiscriminatory" (Kawai, 1995a, p.100). However, here again, Kawai states in Japanese version of this book, "I would like to make it clear that I have never had an experience that can be called 'empty' consciousness" (Kawai, 1995b, p.151).

Kawai's description of the World of Hua-yen, called "the Dharmic World of Principle" here seems to be in line with Jung's description of the "psychoid" realm. Murray Stein, in his book *Jung's Map of the Soul*, introduces the concept of "psychoid" realm in an easy-to-understand manner,

On Jung's map, the psyche is a region that is located in the space between pure matter and pure spirit, between the human body and the transcendent mind, between the human body and the transcendent mind, between instinct and archetype. He shows it as stretched between two ends of a spectrum that has openings at either end permitting an entrance of information into the psyche. At the ends of the psyche are the psychoid areas that produce quasi-psychic effect like psychosomatic symptoms and parapsychological happenings. As information passes through the psychoid area, it becomes psychized and transformed into psyche. In the psyche, matter and spirit meet. (Stein, 1998)

As is well known, Jung had knowledge of classical Eastern philosophies and religions such as the Chinese I Ching, Chinese alchemy, and Taoism through Richard Wilhelm and of Zen Buddhism through D. T. Suzuki.

Jung (1939) wrote, "The idea of synchronicity and of a self-subsistent meaning, which forms the basis of classical Chinese thinking and of the naïve views of the Middle Ages" (para. 944). Jung clarifies here that the concepts of synchronicity and meaning as the Way in Taoism have their origin in classical Eastern philosophy. Further, he grounds the principle of synchronicity by arguing that "Nor has the determinism of a scientific epoch been able to extinguish altogether the persuasive power of the synchronicity principle" (para. 944). In fact, Jung himself was interested in ancient Eastern philosophies, and this knowledge was one of the sources of his consideration of the psychoid realm and synchronicity.

Satori and Individuation in the East

In *Where East Meets West*, Stein informed us of Harry Murray's question to Jung: What does the individuated person look like? Jung replied in 1956 that the individuated human being is just ordinary and therefore almost invisible. Jung's reply continues and shows a Zen Buddhism teaching as example: "First mountains are mountains and the sea is the sea. Then mountains are no more mountains, the sea is no more sea and in the end the mountains will be the mountains and the sea will be the sea" (Adler, 1975). The source of the above teaching might be D. T. Suzuki's lecture, "The Role of Nature in Zen Buddhism." at the Eranos Conference in 1953. In the lecture, D. T. Suzuki presented a Zen master's remarks: "When I began to study Zen, mountains were mountains; When I thought I understood Zen, mountains were not mountains; but when I came to full knowledge of Zen, mountains were again mountains" (Suzuki, 1953).

Returning to his reply, Jung says that nobody can have a vision and not be changed by it. First, he has no vision, and he is the man A; then he is himself plus a vision, the man B; and then it might be that the vision may influence his life, if he is not quite dull, and this is the man C (Adler, 1975). This explanation of Jung's views seems to me not about Zen, but rather about Jung's method, the individuation process through active imagination. According to Jung, visions greatly influence the individuated person psychologically, but from the outside the person remains a very ordinary and invisible, or unremarkable person. On the other hand, D.T. Suzuki explained this monk's remarks as follows: "When the mountains are seen as not standing against me, when they are dissolved into oneness of things, they are not mountains, they cease to exist as objects of Nature. When they are seen as standing against me as separate from me, as something unfriendly to me, they are not mountains either" (Suzuki, 1953). Here Suzuki made it clear that both mystical fusion and objectification are far from the state of enlightenment. Suzuki continued: "The mountains are really mountains when they are assimilated into my being and I am absorbed in them." Suzuki wrote that in the stage of completion of Zen wisdom, the stage of enlightenment, the ego is not fused with the mountain; they are independent of one other, the mountain being assimilated into the psyche and the psyche being absorbed into the mountain while facing each other.

It seemed to me that many of the participants in the Eranos Conference at that time had been puzzled. At the 42nd Eranos Conference in 1973, after Jung's death, Toshihiko Izutsu attempted to explain the quoted words of a Chinese Zen master. (Izutsu, 1973). The summary is as follows: The first stage of satori is the everyday human experience of the world. There the seeing subject is clearly distinguished as a separate entity from the seen thing, the object thing, the mountain. The second stage corresponds to the mental state of subject-object undifferentiation. The ego-consciousness has disappeared, and the subject is immersed in meditation on its object, feeling a deep empathy for the object. The subject feels as if it has "become a mountain" itself. It is considered an absolute undifferentiated awareness of "something" that illuminates the entire world. In the third stage, the undifferentiated "something" divides into subject and object in the midst of this primordial unity. Although it is divided, its unity remains intact. When I, the viewer, and the object, the mountain, arise from the "something," there is a connection between us. At this point, the mountain is established as the "absolute mountain." It is just a mountain, although it has a complicated nature within. In other words, it is both a "mountain" in the spiritual world and a mountain in the ordinary real world. In light of the above explanation, in this third stage of satori, the inner world and the ordinary real world are two sides of the same coin from the perspective of the "something" that illuminates the world as a whole, and furthermore, the division between the objects of the real world is fundamentally connected and indivisible.

Jung's Reflections on Zen Buddhism

The Preface to *An Introduction to Zen Buddhism* (1939) is a valuable document that shows Jung's understanding of Zen Buddhism. In the Preface, Jung states that "Zen itself is the most important fruit to have sprung from the tree whose roots are the collections of the Pali Canon: the intellectual world of Buddhism" (1939, para. 877).

In Zen satori, Jung wrote, "When one reads the Zen texts attentively, one cannot escape the impression that, however bizarre, satori is a natural occurrence, something so very simple, even, that one fails to see the wood for the trees, and in attempting to explain it invariably says the very thing that throws others into the greatest confusion" (para. 884).

Jung thought that the author of *Deutsche Theologie* "tells us a good deal about the 'content of enlightenment.' The occurrence of satori is interpreted and formulated as a break-through, by a consciousness limited to the ego-form, into the non-ego-like self. This view is in accord not only with the essence of Zen, but also with the mysticism of Meister Eckhart" (para. 887). Further, Jung clarified: "In this sense, therefore, it is not a question of 'actual fact' but of psychic reality, i.e., the psychic process known as satori. Every psychic process is an image and an 'imagining,' otherwise no consciousness could exist, and the occurrence would lack phenomenality. Imagination itself is a psychic process, for which reason it is completely irrelevant whether the enlightenment be called 'real' or 'imaginary'" (para. 889).

According to Jung, in the West the emphasis has been on consciousness, and such 'changes in consciousness itself' have not been focused on except in the realm of mysticism. In the East, on the other hand, the focus has been on the changes in consciousness that occur through practice. Jung recognized the Eastern practice to transform the Psyche, as "it was yoga and in China Buddhism which supplied the driving force for these attempts to wrench oneself free from bondage to a state of consciousness that was felt to be incomplete" (para. 892).

Jung calls the Satori in the East 'an experience of totality' and continues "that consciousness is always only a part of the psyche and therefore never capable of psychic wholeness: for that the indefinite extension of the unconscious is needed" (para. 906). Then he noticed: "The attainment of wholeness requires one to stake one's whole being. Nothing less will do; there can be no easier conditions, no substitutes, no compromises" (para. 906). He concluded that "Zen shows how much 'becoming whole' means to the East" (para. 907, p.7203) and that "Zen demands intelligence and will power, as do all greater things that want to become realities" (para. 907).

The Paths to Enlightenment and the Messages of Two Japanese Zen Masters

In this section, I will examine the process leading to the enlightenment of two Japanese Zen masters and the works in which they attempted to convey the Buddhist mind to the people after their enlightenment. I expect this examination from the perspective of Jung's individuation could deepen our understanding of Zen Buddhism.

The first is Muso Soseki from the late Muromachi period. During the Muromachi and Kamakura periods, he seems to have attracted the faith of those in power at the time and provided spiritual support to them based on Buddhist teachings. He received the title of National Master and, under the support of the Shogunate, created gardens in many temples, which are still maintained at present. The other was Hakuinn Ekaku of the Edo period. At that time, Zen temples had gained socioeconomic stability through the Shogunate's system of obtaining Danka (parishioners), but the development of teaching and learning the Buddhist theory had stagnated. Hakuin actively practiced and trained disciples, gave easy-to-understand lectures to the public, published Zen paintings and writings and came to be called the reformer of the Rinzai school of Zen Buddhism.

Muso Soseki (1275-1351)

Muso lived in a time of warfare in the Japanese middle Age. His family lost their land because of war and became refugees in a rural area, where his mother passed away when he was four years old. He was keen to learn about Buddhism already from childhood. At first, he studied in a Kegon school and at age of 18 received the Buddhist ecclesiastical vows at Todai-ji Temple, the greatest temple of esoteric Buddhism in Japan. By the age of 19, he became disappointed with esoteric Buddhism when he witnessed a Buddhist lecturer die upset by the prospect of death. He started a 100 days esoteric meditation to overcome the fear of the border between death and life. On the 97th day of the retreat, he had a dream.

> *A strange old man guided him into a deserted Zen temple, where he met two famous Chinese monks, first Sozan, and then Sekito, both of them fathers of Chen Buddhism in China. Then the eldest master of the temple invited him to his private room where they exchanged greetings. The Master gave him a portrait of Bodhidharma.* (Muso, 1342)

After this dream, he decided to turn to Zen Buddhism and change his name into Muso Soseki, which is a combination of So- from Sozan and -seki from Sekito.

Muso Soseki's experience of Satori at age of 31

One day in early summer, he meditated under a tree until midnight. When he went back to the bedroom, he tried to lean against the wall which he assumed he was standing beside in the dark only to tumble down since there was no wall. He could not help laughing, and suddenly enlightenment occurred. He wrote a poem about this:

For many years, I had dug in the earth to search for blue heaven.
It had been misdirected, piling worldly desires on desires.
One dark night, a piece of tile spun off
to hit the bone in the empty air with a crash. (Muso, 1342)

In Japanese Zen Buddhism, monks did various kinds of arts— calligraphy, writing poems, painting. Muso loved deeply designing landscape gardens.

There are those who regard mountains, rivers, grass, trees, tiles, and stones to be their own Original Nature. Their love for gardens may resemble worldly affection, but they employ that affection in their aspiration for the Way, using as part of their practice the changing scenery of the grasses and trees throughout the four seasons. One who can do this is truly an exemplar of how a follower of the Way should consider a garden. (Muso, 2015)

Why did Muso make gardens? He wrote a poem:

The person of benevolence loves quiet mountain
the person of wisdom enjoys clear water
Please don't be wondering
why a fool enjoys design landscape garden.
I expect, it makes my mind clear and sharp.

The ancient masters tell us, 'The mountains, rivers, the great earth, and everything that exists are all oneself.' If you have made this truth your own, then no activities are outside of cultivation. You put on your clothes and eat your meals in cultivation; you walk, stand, sit, and lie down in cultivation; you see, hear, perceive, and know in cultivation; you experience joy, anger, affection, and pleasure in cultivation. Those who can do this are said to 'perform worldly activities in the midst of practice.'" (2015)

This is the practice of nonpractice, the striving of non-striving.

In the first phase of Muso's garden design, he showed preference for rocks. He caught an inspiration from the rock to make the garden as a part of landscape. At Eihō-ji Temple in Gifu prefecture, he found a big rock and made a pond in front of the Rock.

336

Eihō-ji Temple

In Kamakura-Era, 1330, Muso was invited by the governor of the area to open Erin-ji Temple in the Yamanashi prefecture. In the year 1332, He designed the garden of the temple. He started to arrange small rocks around the pond and build an island in the pond. He shaped these rocks in the form of a mountain and hills around it and a waterfall flowing into it.

Erin-ji Temple

He was invited to restore Saihō-ji Temple in 1339. He designed gardens with two layers surrounded by beautiful landscape. On the upper layer, he arranged rocks on the slope to look like fish swimming against the stream. On the lower layer, he made a path around the pond, which was accented with rocks to resemble a tortoise, a crane, and a waterfall as well as planting bushes and flowers in natural ways.

The upper garden of Saihō-ji Temple

The lower garden of Saihō-ji Temple

Tenryu-ji Temple was built by General Ashikaga Takauji at the suggestion of Muso as a National Zen Master to mourn the soul of Emperor Godaigo. Ashikaga Takauji had rebelled against the Emperor and driven him to Yoshino, where Emperor Godaigo died in 1339. The ceremony for the completion of Tenryu-ji Temple and the memorial service for the late emperor was held in 1345, the seventh anniversary of his death. The temple was named Tenryu-ji Temple after the dream of Takauji's younger brother, in which a golden dragon rose from the river located in the south of the temple. The temple has a large pond named Sogen-ike, on the opposite bank of which rocks are arranged to resemble a fish trying to swim upward against a waterfall to become a dragon.

Sogen-ike pond in Tenryu-ji Temple

Hakuin Ekaku in Edo Period

According to his biography, Hakuin was born in 1865 to a family that ran an inn and transportation business in a town at the foot of Mt. Fuji on the Tōkaidō road. At that time, some 80 years after the Edo shogunate was established, the Tōkaidō road was frequently traveled, and the family business was probably thriving.

When he was 8 or 9 years old, his mother took him to hear a lecture by a high-ranking priest of the Nichiren sect of Buddhism, in which the priest described hell lively in detail. He was so afraid of the story that he grieved day and night, anguishing and not enjoying himself. At the age of 13, he saw a Joruri play about a high priest of the Nichiren sect who smiled and did not panic even when a burnt iron pot was put on his head. Finally, he received permission from his parents to attain ordination at Shōin-ji Temple, a Zen Buddhist monastery at age of 14. After that, Hakuin traveled to visit various Zen temples to continue his Zen practice. When Hakuin returned to Shōin-ji Temple at the age of 23, he encountered the great eruption of Mt. Fuji in 1707. It is said that during the eruption, he continued his zazen meditation, saying, "If I open my eyes to see the truth, I will gain the protection of the sages and escape the disaster."

The following year, Hakuin embarked on another journey, this time to Eigan-ji Temple in Echigo, where he listened to a lecture by a monk and practiced Zen meditation. One night and just at dawn, he heard the sound of temple bells in the distance. It was a small sound, but to him it seemed as if a large bell had been struck. At that moment, he was suddenly enlightened and gained great confidence, saying, "In the past 300 years, no one has been so brilliantly enlightened as I have been." With this conceit, 24-year-old Hakuin went to Shinshu to see Shoju-Rojin, only to have Shoju-Rojin abuse him, calling him a useless dead Zen monk. After continuing his rigorous training, he was finally accepted by Shoju-Rojin and continued his journey further. Soon after, Hakuin began to suffer from a headache, cold feet and legs, ringing in his ears, fear of bright places, and depression, probably due to his excessive training. This was the so-called "Zen sickness." Someone told the disturbed Hakuin that a Hakuyū hermit in the mountains of Shirakawa in Kyoto would be able to teach him a cure. According to Hakuin's writing, *Yasenkanwa*, he visited Hakuyuu in Shirakawa and learned the method of introspection, namely Naikan. Naikan is a regimen of contemplating the circulation of qi and blood in the body and gathering qi in the lower abdomen to activate it. In his 33rd year, Hakuin became the abbot of the dilapidated Shoin-ji Temple. At this temple, Hakuin practiced Zen meditation and the Naikan, and many of his disciples began to gather there.

In the fall of his 42nd year, while reading the Lotus Sutra, Hakuin heard crickets chirping in his garden and suddenly had a profound enlightenment. In Hakuin's Chronological records, he describes his experience of enlightenment: "I have suddenly realized the profound truth of the Lotus, and my previous experience of enlightenment was a mistake. I now understand for the first time what Shoju-Rojin told me when I was young." (Enji, 1820) Then the significance of the sutras preached by the Buddha came into view. Regarding the content of this great enlightenment, his biography records, "Bodhicitta is nothing but the practice of the four vows of the bodhisattva." The four vows of

341

bodhisattva summarize the vows of the seeker of enlightenment in four paragraphs as follows.

To save all living beings without limit;
To put an end to all passions and delusions however numerous;
To study and learn all methods and means without end
To become perfect in the supreme Buddha-law.

Hakuin understood that through study and practice in the way, vexations would be cut off and the Way of Buddha would be fulfilled. It can be said that Hakuin placed the utmost importance on the practice of saving people based on study of Buddhism theory.

Katsuhiro Yoshizawa (1945-), who studied with Hakuin, has published a catalogue of 1050 of Hakuin's Zen paintings. (Yoshizawa, 2009) The majority of Hakuin's Zen paintings were given as gifts, depicting the teachings of Zen Buddhism in a form that could be easily conveyed to the recipient of the painting, based on his or her personality and ability to understand, and considering the circumstances of the time. That over a thousand Zen paintings have survived is astonishing. In this section, we will discuss three of Hakuin's Zen paintings and elucidate the Zen Buddhist teachings contained in them.

Fuji Daimyo Gyoretsu by Hakuin

On the First Zen painting, "Fuji Daimyo Gyoretsu (means Procession)" painted at the request of the monk Sosan of Jiseiji Temple (Nakatsu City, Oita Prefecture), depicts a procession of lords passing at the foot of the sacred mountain Mt. Fuji.

In the "Compliment" (Chinese poem on the left of the painting), it is written, "I have been asked to paint Daruma for a long time, and here I have depicted the true essence of Daruma." In this painting, Daruma is nowhere to be seen, but rather Mt. Fuji standing majestically and a procession of feudal lords and common people pass by without paying attention to it. Fuji in the upper half of the painting represents Daruma, or the truth of Buddhism, and the procession of lords in the lower half of the painting are a representation of the secular world. In the lower right part of the painting, a teahouse is depicted, and we notice a traveling monk sitting on the porch, looking out at Mt. Fuji. In order to further understand Hakuin's intent in this Zen painting, it is necessary to look at the old Chinese characters used to represent "Fuji." In the Edo period, Fuji was sometimes written using the Chinese character for "fuji," which means "not two" or "only one." Hakuin's intention in this Zen painting is that Daruma, or the Dharma of Truth, is represented not only by the mountain Fuji, but by the painting as a whole, in which the two poles of the world, the sacred and the profane, are inextricably linked.

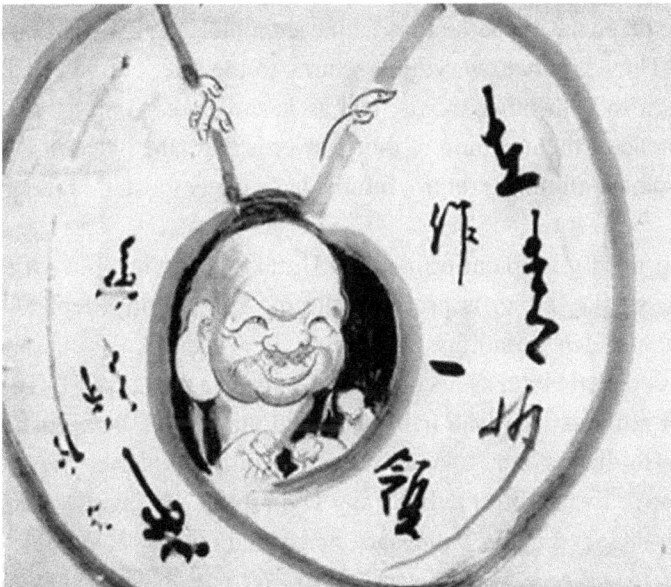

Hotei by Hakuin

The second Zen painting depicts Hotei with three children playing around his chest. Hotei is holding up a sheet of paper, twisted around. The paper reads, "When I stayed in Qingzhou, I made a hemp robe, which weighed 4200 grams." Since the hemp robe is supposed to be very light, the description that it weighed 4200 grams is a paradox. The trick of this Zen painting is that the paradox is twisted around and the statement "weighed 4200 grams" is written on the back of the paper. Regarding the meaning of this Zen painting, Yoshizawa reasoned, "The twists and turns may express the Zen world of the two sides of the same coin, where there is no front or back, where there is no distinction, where the two sides are the same, where existence is nothingness, where right is wrong and where vexation is Bodhi." (Yoshizawa, 2012) Yoshizawa cites as evidence for this the statement in the second volume of Hakuin's *Oradegama*: "If you say 'existence,' there is no existence; if you say 'nothingness,' there is no nothingness." In the West, it is known as the "Möbius strip," where twisting a piece of paper creates a loop that connects the front and back of the paper. What is being presented here is a Zen teaching that turns the polarization of consciousness on its head. It is a teaching that can be found in the many Koans of Zen. The sentence in this painting, "When I made a hemp robe in Qingzhou, it weighed 4,200 grams," was taken from the Blue Cliff Record, a Chinese Zen Buddhist text. These words were the response of the famous Chinese monk Zhao Zhou when he was asked, "They say that everything returns to the one, but where does the one return to?" In other words, just as in the *Orategama,* "existence is not existence," the meaning of this answer is that "the place to which the One, to which all things return, returns have never existed in the physical world."

The third Zen painting depicts Hotei as blowing out Ofuku like cigarette smoke. Hotei is probably the most frequently depicted figure in Hakuin's Zen paintings. According to Yoshizawa's interpretation, Hakuin depicted Hotei as his double. (Yoshizawa, 2012, p. 51) The figure of Hotei reminds us of the half-naked old man in the last illustration in Ten Ox Herding Pictures. Hotei was a legendary Buddhist monk who is said to have lived from the late Tang Dynasty to the Five Dynasties. He was characterized by the large sack he carried on his back. Although his appearance was eccentric, he was said to have had an honest heart and the mysterious power to make people feel content.

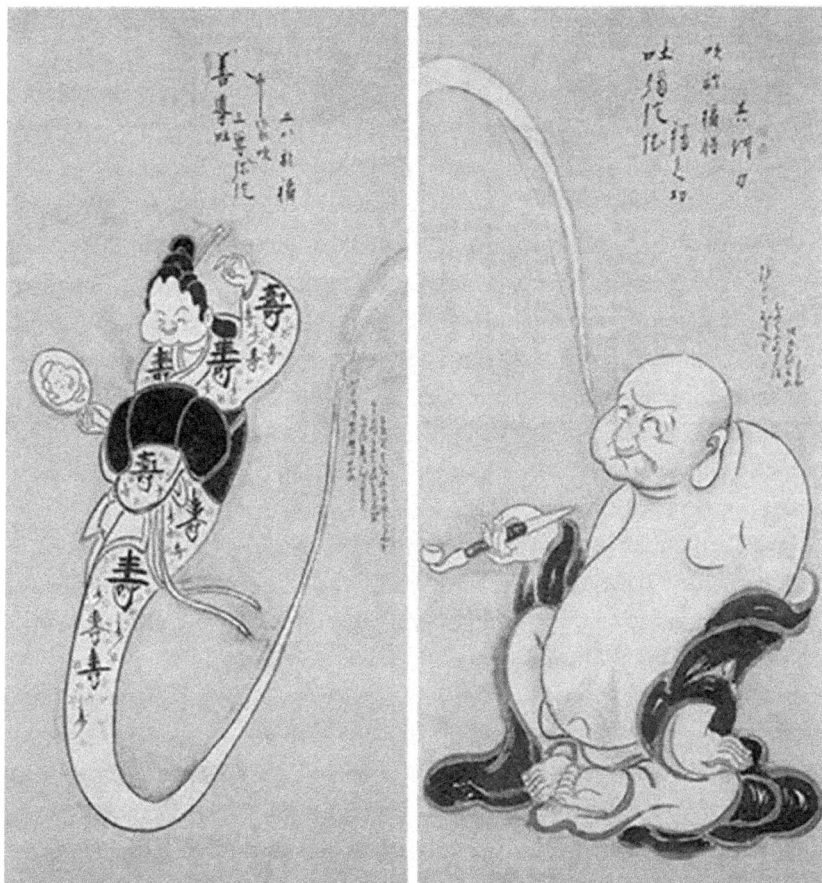

Hotei blows out Ofuku by Hakuin

When Hotei passed away, he left the verse, "O Maitreya Bodhisattva! The real Maitreya Bodhisattva. He has taken on a thousand billion forms in different incarnations, and has appeared to all people in all ages, but they do not know it." (Shi, 1004) A complimentary inscription to this painting reads. "Zendo Daishi blows out Amida, but Hotei blows out 16-year-old Ofuku. The reason Zendo Daishi blows out Amitabha is because of the merit of Nembutsu (repeating the name of the Buddha). What power is it that blows out Ofuku?" This sentence is followed by Hotei's humorous words, "I blow smoke as hard as I can, but it is difficult to blow out Ofuku." Now what message does this Zen painting contain? Yoshizawa (2012) reasoned, "Hakuin is incarnated as Hotei, blowing out Ofuku and wishing people to be happy." Indeed, the name Ofuku means blessing. Here, I would like to examine the meaning of this Zen painting in more detail.

Ofuku is a woman with a so-called "Okame" face. About Okame, Atsutane Hirata, a scholar of Japanese classical culture in the late Edo period (1603-1868), wrote: "Around the end of the Ashikaga period, there was a shrine maiden named Kame-jyo who worshipped the goddess Ama-no-Uzume[1], who was charming and sincere at heart. When the most evil person saw her face, his evil heart vanished. So, people made a mask in the shape of her face, named it Otafuku, and spread it. This is the origin of Okame-mask." (Hirata, 1829) The way she wears her obi tied in front of her and the way her hair is styled indicate that she is a "Jyoro," or a prostitute. Hakuin often depicted Ofuku in his Zen paintings. In one of his paintings, "Otafuku Jyoro-zu," Hakuin wrote the words, "Ofuku has a low nose but high cheekbones, and she is a nice girl. then Ofuku replied, It does not matter, I am an incarnation of Kannon, the Bosatsu of Mercy." Hakuin also depicted Ofuku drawing flour and Ofuku skewering dumplings. In the Edo period (1603-1867), inns on the main road were frequented by "Meshimori Onna" (means female food server) who, along with serving meals, also provided sexual services at the request of their customers. They were girls who were sold to the inns to support the livelihood of their poor families. Her kimono has a plum blossom pattern written on it. The pattern is the symbol of Kitano Tenman-gu Shrine, which enshrines Sugawara Michizane as the god of heaven. It is suggested there that there is some kind of connection between Ofuku and Michizane.

During the Heian period, Michizane excelled at writing and was highly valued by the Emperor of Japan, but he died of a broken heart in a place where he had been relegated because of false accusations. He was enshrined at Kitano Tenman-gu Shrine to appease his grudge. In the Muromachi period (1336-1573), there is a legend of Michizane's visit to Tang Dynasty China. According to the legend, Michizane appeared in the dream of a Zen monk and traveled to China to study Zen and returned with a vestment as a token of Satori in just one night. By wearing a kimono with a plum blossom pattern symbolizing Michizane, it is suggested that Ofuku also possessed the qualities of Michizane. This might be pureness of heart despite one's unfortunate circumstances.

---

[1] Ama-no-Uzume: A Goddess in Japanese Mythology, who is known for her attractive and sensual dancing in front of the cave where Amaterasu Oh-Mikami withdrew because of her anger at her naughty brother, Susano.

In this Zen painting, Ofuku is happily looking into a mirror. At the moment we see the face of Ofuku reflected in this mirror, we are drawn into the same line of sight as Ofuku peering into the mirror. Before we know it, we have become the the Ofuku whom Hakuin blew out.

From the perspective of Jung's analytical psychology, this Zen painting is composed of the pairing of the old man, Hotei, and the young, 16-year-old Ofuku; of Hotei as a man and Ofuku as a woman; of Hotei as a saint and Ofuku as a secular public prostitute. There, the three opposites, old and young, male and female, and sacred and secular, are connected into one. However, it is not the pattern of the two opposites of the King of the Sun and the Queen of the Moon in the illustration of "The Philosopher's Rose Garden" confronting and deeply meeting, but rather the relationship of one blowing out the other. The breath that Hotei blows takes the form of Ofuku. From this, we can understand that Ofuku is the embodiment of Hotei's "chi," or spirit.

Here we are reminded that Hotei was originally the embodiment of Maitreya. From the above verse left by Hotei, we can understand that each of us is a manifestation of Maitreya Bodhisattva. And when we look at this Zen painting, especially when we look into the mirror held by Ofuku, we realize that each of us is the embodiment of Hotei's spirit, or Maitreya Bodhisattva.

It can be deduced that the picture of Hotei blowing Ofuku was a device to induce the viewer to realize that he or she was Ofuku, as Maitreya Bodhisattva. This realization is deeply related to the content of Hakuin's enlightenment. It can be said that Hakuin was thus trying to convey his experience of enlightenment to as many people as possible through his Zen paintings.

Conclusion

The two Zen monks mentioned here aspired to become monks in their childhood and adolescence. They traveled around the world, contemplating and answering the questions of their masters, and practiced Zen meditation in search of enlightenment. For them, enlightenment was the experience of transforming their ego-centered way of being, or the experience of learning the meaning of the Buddha's teachings. In Buddhism, the two directions required of seekers are "Jugubodai Gegeshujo" (self-training and seeking Nirvana every day while looking up and converting others to the religion while looking down).

The National Zen master, Muso, reported a process of mental conditioning through the process of designing a garden based on a sense of oneness with nature. In his gardens, the image of a fish going up against a waterfall is expressed. This is an expression of the never-ending Jugubodai: self-training and seeking Nirvana every day while looking up.

Hakuin, on the other hand, through his Zen paintings, shows that the sacred and the profane are two sides of the same existence. By depicting a woman, his double, he tried to convey the teachings of Buddhism, which preaches love for people in society and the practice of saving people. It is none other than Gegeshujo: converting others to the religion while looking down.

In the Zen paintings in which Hakuin demonstrated enlightenment to people, a scene was shown in which Hotei blows his female double, Ofuku, or as Jungian psychology might call it, anima.

Now I would like to try to understand the message in this Zen painting according to Jung's theory of individuation. In this painting, Maitreya could be positioned as Self in Jungian psychology. Maitreya is taking the form of a Hotei, who blows out Ofuku as each one of us. From the side of Self, to blow out Ofuku, i.e., each one of us, means that the Self emerges in a certain form. This is nothing but self-realization, or individuation. What is interesting about this scene is that it depicts this individualization from the Self's side.

When the same individualization is depicted from the ego's side in the West, the first step is for the subject of consciousness to encounter and unify with its opposite. The illustration of "Rosarium Philosophorum" is an example of this. The ego and its opposite are depicted as equal beings, the king of the sun and the queen of the moon. The union of the two occurs on a cosmic scale, bringing about a new birth after death. The process suggests how firmly constructed the ego as the subject of consciousness is in the West, and how difficult it is for it to change.

In contrast, enlightenment in Japanese Zen Buddhism may involve recognizing that one is an entity blown out by Self, as if it were smoke. However, Hakuin's Zen paintings tell us that the blown-out blessing is a manifestation of Self and can be a person of charm, purity of heart, good health, and happiness to those around him or her.

Mari Yoshikawa, Ph.D., is originally from Osaka, Japan and educated at Kyoto University (Ph.D.). She is Professor of Gakushuin University in Tokyo, and is engaged in training certified clinical psychologists in Japan. In 2008, she studied at ISAP in Zurich, and received a diploma of AJAJ (Association of Jungian Analysts, Japan) in 2016. She manages Yamanashi Hakoniwa Institute (www.yamanashi-hakoniwa.com) for her practices with imagery. She collaborated in many Japanese books on psychological assessment, personality psychology and psychotherapy. Her English writings include *The Shadow of Modernization in Japan as Seen in Natsume Soseki's Ten Night's Dreams*, and *Confronting Cultural Trauma-Jungian Approaches to Understanding and Healing* (Edited by Granzina Gudaite and Murray Stein, 211-226, Spring Journal Books 2014), "A Japanese Perspective of the Meaning of the Serpent in the Red Book" *(Jung's Red Book for Our Time Vol. 3,* Edited by Murray Stein, and Thomas Arzt, 217-232, Chiron Publications, 2019).

References

Adler, G. (Ed.) (1975) *C.G. Jung letters,* Vol. 2. Princeton University Press.

Enji/Yoshizawa, K.(Ed.) (1820/2016) *Takizawakaiso Jinkidokumyo Zenshi Nennpu Ingyokaku, /Shinpen Hakuin Zenshi Nennpu.* Zen Bunka Kenkyusyo.

Hirata, A. (1829). *Miyabinokamigodenki.* https://doi.org/10.20730/100227127

Izutsu, T. (1973/2008). The Interior and Exterior in Zen Buddhism, *The Structure of Oriental Philosophy: Collected Papers of the Eranos Conference* Vol. I, Keio University Press.

Izutsu, T. (1989). Cosmos to Anticosmos, *Cosmos and Anticosmos.* Iwanami Syoten.

Jung, C.G. (1939/1958,1969). Foreword to Suzuki's *"Introduction to Zen Buddhism," The Collected Works of C.G. Jung.* Princeton University Press.

Kawai, H. (1998a). *Buddhism and the Art of Psychotherapy.* Texas A&M University Press.

Kawai, H. (1998b). *Jungian Psychology and Buddhisum*, Tokyo:Iwanami Syoten (In Japanese) Muso, S., Otaka, S.(ed.) (1342/2015) *Dialogues in a Dream: The Life and Teaching of Muso Soseki.* Trans. by Thomas Kirchner. Wisdom Publications.

Shi, D. (1004/1993). *The Jingle Record of the Transmission of the Lamp/ Keitoku Dento Roku* (In Japanese). Zen Bunka Kenkyusyo

Stein, M. (1998). *Jung's Map of the Soul.* Chicago: Open Court.

Stein, M. (2017). "Where East Meets West: In the House of Individuation." *Outside Inside and All Around.* Chiron Publications.

Suzuki, D.T. (1953/2014). The role of Nature in Zen Buddhism. *Selected Works of D.T. Suzuki.* Vol. I. University of California Press.

Yoshizawa K. (2009). *Hakuin Zenga Bokuseki.* Nigen-Sha.

Yoshizawa, K. (2012). *Hakuin Zenga wo Yomu.* Wedge.

Individuation Theory and Practice: The Promising Emergence of a Nonbinary Transcendent "Third" Between Temporal Depth Psychology and Non-Temporal Dzogchen Psychology

Jim Manganiello

Murray's writing is often soaked in the hermetic secret sauce needed to transform letters, words and paragraphs into music for the inner ear. He is a judicious student of Jung's work and a capable keeper of the flame. Murray's original work has given rise to an individuation psychology that extends and deepens existing writing. His words carry the melodic harmony needed to convey the psychological meaning that is far beyond the reach of the intellect. Murray's work helped bring Jung's individuation sheet music notations into song.

This essay explores the basis for a nonbinary "third" position between depth psychology and Dzogchen psychology, one that resolves the duality between depth psychology's view of individuation as gradual stages in time and Dzogchen psychology's view of individuation as immediate and beyond time. The trans-binary view recognizes temporality and non-temporality as interdependent elements of different dimensions of mind. It also recognizes psychology and spirituality as interdependent. A collaboration between individuation psychology and Dzogchen psychology holds great promise. They each partake in a notion of individuation that the other is missing. Jung explained his life as a story about his becoming conscious of elements in his mind that were outside his awareness. Dzogchen contemplative scientists made a Copernican-like discovery about the mind's innermost essence, known as the Nature of Mind. The Nature of Mind is beyond ordinary awareness. Although Mind's innermost Nature is unconscious, it's the essence of who we truly are—beyond time. Dzogchen's contemplative science's methods offer us valid and reliable access to the unconscious numinous elements Jung identified as the spiritual and mystical constituents of individuation. Depth psychology methods offer access to the unconscious psychological forces at play in the temporal mind that Dzogchen psychology too often misses. With knowledge of how to access both temporal and nontemporal consciousness, collaborators can consider opportunities for reconsidering individuation theory and practice accordingly.

I first read Murray Stein's work in his 1983 book, *In Midlife: A Jungian Perspective.* The book was like a long-awaited desert rain, and has remained a beacon for me. It is as if one dark night I saw it flash on the horizon and I approached with a vision in mind, a vision born of sacred heat. Our meaningful conversations led to a collaboration exploring the opportunities for a transcendent bridge between individuation theory and Dzogchen psychology. We wrote an essay in a book edited by Les Stein: *Eastern Practices and Individuation: Essays by Jungian Analysts* (M. Stein, J Manganiello, 2022, pp. 291-326).

My conviction is, there is a transcendent "Third" emerging. And it could hold great promise. Murray Stein's body of work on individuation psychology is a solid foundation for us to understand and steward temporal individuation. It gives us the opportunity to consider that the notion of individuation is incomplete unless we recognize and understand its nontemporal elements. Dzogchen psychology is about the non-temporal dimension of Mind. The Mind's innermost timeless nature is the Unus Mundus, known in Dzogchen as the Nature of Mind.

What needs to be worked out is individuation psychology's own "individuation"; to understand that "who we truly are" in time, is different than "who we truly are" beyond time. Different, yet interdependent. No individuation can be complete unless we realize them both as integrated experiential knowledge and wisdom.

This essay is a tribute to Murray Stein and his work that I will now gratefully stand on to extend our consideration of individuation.

Individuation Psychology and Dzogchen Psychology are Interdependent

Individuation psychology and Dzogchen psychology need capable bridging if they are to transcend the dilemma of conflict as opposites. At first glance, the two appear to be diametrically opposed and separate individuation paths. One, a progressive path in time, the other, an immediate path beyond time. An interdependent view of temporal and non-temporal individuation points us towards a far-reaching revision of individuation psychology and depth psychology. For starters, psychology and spirituality are not two separate things. They are interdependent parts of the mind. The intellect separates them by mistaking its ideas about reality for reality itself. The thinking-conceptual mind is a remarkable resource for many things. Developing a psychology to understand the non-temporal, spiritual elements of mind is not among them. Conceptual views and theories can be like quicksand. Once stuck in them it's hard to realize we are stuck, let alone to break free.

The intellect draws a blank when it tries to fathom the spiritual, timeless dimension of mind. The Western "agnostic reflex" loses the connection between thinking and being. When it comes to recognizing the sacred, timeless part of the mind, the intellect is like a birdwatcher looking for birds with binoculars that still have the lens caps on. All the intellect can possibly see are its projections. Such a birdwatcher returns home with mistaken views. Feeling that he spent the day observing a vast array of birdies "out there."

Murray noted something essential for becoming who we truly are. In his words: "The demanding requirement for individuation is to return to one's nature, to one's true being" (Stein, 2006, p.11).

I agree. I am a depth psychologist with decades of experience studying and teaching psychology, doing therapy, and training and supervising therapists. I have also been a Dzogchen practitioner for nearly as long under the direction of accomplished "grandfather" teachers. And I have done many years of inner work in therapy and analysis, most with Jungian analysts.

I have learned one thing that is unshakably certain: The work we must do to return to our nature, to our true being is— "in time" *and* "beyond time" because they are in fact interdependent. Neither alone will do. Believing otherwise is a risky misconception. Separated and alone both will run out of road and get lost. Let us consider what is needed for an interdependent trans-binary vision for individuation.

The Sine Qua Non for Emergence of a Trans-Binary Position

The essential condition for the emergence of an interdependent nonbinary vision for individuation is that each of the binary positions must understand the other experientially. Depth psychology and Dzogchen psychology must walk in one another's shoes. In our context, temporal individuation must understand immediate individuation beyond time. Non-temporal individuation must understand temporal in time. Only then will the seams of interdependence between them be unveiled and understood. Only then can the interdependence of "in time" individuation and "beyond time" individuation be well considered and realized.

Any East-West duality can be resolved if the lights within the mind are turned up. Jung's admonitions about westerners turning to the East and Eastern practices were well-taken cautions, not prohibitions. And Dzogchen psychology's hesitations about psychology stem from its lack of familiarity with depth psychology. Dzogchen misses the importance of temporal individuation and the unconscious psychological forces at play in the dimension of mind in time.

I think of Jung as part contemplative scientist. His core vision arose from the direct experience of his own mind. Not just from his intellect. Jung was awake at 3 in the morning talking to Philemon, taking dictations from Basilides, and painting mandalas while others were sleeping. In some ways, conditioned views aside, Jung was more Eastern in his sensibilities than Western. He focused on the numinous, not ego adaptation or curing maladies. We tend to regard time and timelessness as distinct opposites. But they are not.

Theoretical Physics Illustrates a Reconciling Path

Let us consider work being done in theoretical physics to develop a "Third" position capable of reconciling the differences between classical physics with quantum mechanics. Scientists holding tight to a classical view of physics initially felt that quantum mechanics wasn't valid physics. Because it seemed counterintuitive to their absolute, causal views about physical reality. Einstein maintained well known reservations about quantum reality, e.g., entanglement as "spooky science at a distance." But his own experiments showed that quantum mechanics could account for the behavior of light and matter on the smallest of scales. He intuited early that chaos and upheaval in physics were necessary if physics was to move beyond binary conflict and integrate quantum science.

Individuation psychology will have to undergo its own chaos and disruption, if is to recognize and overcome its biases. Including the preconception that psychology, the temporal part of the mind, and spirituality, the non-temporal part of the mind, are two separate things. A refreshed and revisioned depth psychology can realize that the differences between psychology "in time" and spirituality "beyond time" are more accurately understood as interdependent, not separate, elements of mind.

Keys for the Emergence of a Trans-Binary Position

The heated opposition between classic and quantum physicists as to whether physical reality is fundamentally causal and determined, or acausal and random, created opportunities for recognizing them as interdependent. A nonbinary position evolved resting on a twofold premise: 1) Reality is not what it appears to be and 2) The principles governing large-scale bodies are not the same as those governing small-scale bodies. The ongoing work to unify Quantum Mechanics and Special Relativity would not be possible unless all collaborators understood what they were working to unify. In well informed collaboration, a reconciling "third" position has emerged, one that integrates both general relativity and quantum mechanics in new frontier research on black holes (Almheiri. et al, 2020; Musser, 2020).

This is also true for the proposed work on unifying the temporal and nontemporal dimensions of mind, and for integrated individuation in both. Our opportunities to realize the interdependence between temporal individuation (individuation psychology) and nontemporal individuation (Dzogchen psychology), are similar. 1) Individuation is not what it appears to be from a temporal or nontemporal point of view alone; and 2) The principles governing the temporal and-non-temporal elements of the mind, and individuation, are not the same.

Individuation psychology needs to understand and integrate what is known about the timeless dimension of mind, including consciousness beyond time, and the nontemporal immediate individuation that arises naturally from it. Nontemporal, i.e. Dzogchen psychology, needs to understand and integrate what is known about the temporal elements of mind, including consciousness in time, and the temporal individuation that can gradually arise in it.

A Meta Psychology-Spirituality

Individuation in time and individuation beyond time need to be worked out as a meta psychology-spirituality. The alchemical individuation opus is both gradual and temporal and immediate and nontemporal. Time and Timelessness can lean into each other with mutual recognition and understanding. Timelessness is the unmanifest source of time, and time is the manifestation of timelessness. We need a new trans-binary transcendent position that integrates both psychology and spirituality as interdependent parts of the mind. Again, we may need to ring the bells of chaos more than a few times to work out a vision of mind that enables the emergence of such a vision. The issue of interdependence between psychology and spirituality is also the issue of interdependence between "in time" and "beyond time" individuation. In temporal individuation, we encounter unconscious forces, both conditioned and teleological, at play in the progressive process of realizing "who we truly are." In non-temporal individuation, realization is immediate. In an instant, we encounter and recognize non-dual pure Being as our ultimate "nonidentity." Now let us turn to Dzogchen.

About Dzogchen

Dzogchen came to the West from Tibet. The indigenous Tibetan spiritual tradition is known as Yungdrung Bon, or just Bon. Bon gave Tibetan Buddhism its unique form and character. Both Tibetan traditions share common features, though they have different lineages and histories. The Tibetan Bon and Buddhist traditions both share similar gradual progressive paths, each comprised of nine stages or vehicles, aimed at spiritual realization. Dzogchen is the ninth and final stage in both traditions, but it can stand alone—as an immediate path. The Bon and Buddhist Dzogchen teachings have been intermingled for so long, they are indistinguishable. Now known as Bon-Buddhist Dzogchen. Or just Dzogchen.

While Dzogchen is the highest stage of spiritual development in the Tibetan Bon and Buddhist gradual path traditions—Dzogchen can stand free of both. As an independent direct nontemporal immediate path dependent on nothing other than itself. Dzogchen can exist separate from Bon and Buddhism, as well as from the Tibetan cultural tradition. Anyone can practice Dzogchen, no religious, spiritual, or cultural affiliation is required or needed. There are no Dzogchen organizational doctrines. The task is to learn how to be conscious and undistracted. We simply must learn how to enter the timeless dimension of mind.

The Natural State: Rigpa

Tibetan contemplative scientists discovered Dzogchen, using "experiential" methods; they directly and systematically observed their own mind. Dzogchen arose out of these experiments. It is predicated on "Rigpa," the mind's Natural State. Rigpa is the direct experience of mind's primordial Nature, it's nondual, timeless awareness—as who and what we truly are. We find Rigpa and the mind's Natural State in the only place it could possibly be—in the nondual now. More about Rigpa and the nontemporal now up ahead.

I want to make a simple note on dual vs. non-dual. If we look out at the sunset, that is dual. There's the sunset and there is us. Dualistic awareness has a subject and an object. Someone is aware of something else. Non-dual awareness is just awareness, on its own. It's timeless awareness now, free, on its own. No object, no subject. We're so accustomed to awareness being dual and temporal that we fail to experience timeless awareness, as awareness free from ego as a centering and determining point.

Namkhai Norbu Rinpoche, (1938-2018), a celebrated Tibetan Buddhist Dzogchen master, scholar and author explains:

> In Dzogchen, there is no object to be known. Instead, it's about experiencing the state beyond the mind, the state of contemplation.... our real nature is also called the state of *rigpa* or the primordial state (or Natural State). It consists of the discovery of true knowledge. The essential point is to be truly in this state and experience it. (Namkhai Norbu Rinpoche, 2011, *Guruyoga, Arcidosso,* IT, p.15)

Rigpa is the immediate experience of timeless awareness, known in Dzogchen as "contemplation." When in contemplation, in the Natural State, we are who we truly are, beyond the temporal mind.

Renowned Yungdrung Bon Dzogchen master, Yongdzin (teacher of teachers) Lopon Tenzin Namdak Rinpoche, (1926-), explains further:

> Rigpa, the Natural State, is neither the calm state nor the movement of thoughts, but a state of immediate awareness which transcends all thought and working of the mind. It is like a mirror reflecting what is set before it, without judgment or thought. (Bonpo Dzogchen Teachings, Freehold, NJ., 1992, p.8)

The Natural State is very easy to find, but only after we find it. Until we experience Rigpa directly, it is not so easy. Keep in mind the effortful sequence of learning a foreign language, how to ride a bike, skate on ice, dance, or play a musical instrument. First, we must meet the Natural State. Then we practice familiarizing ourselves with it, again and again. So, we become confident and certain about what it is. Then we strengthen and stabilize our connection to the Natural State so we can bring it into the circumstances of daily life. And so, we learn how to manage the transitions in between temporality and non-temporality. Ultimately our Dzogchen practice posture becomes whatever position we find ourselves in.

The conflict and unnecessary separation between the temporal (psychological) and non-temporal (spiritual) dimensions of mind can be resolved, in an interdependent vision of individuation that includes them both. The reconciliation includes the direct experience that time, and timelessness are not two separate things. They are interdependent. Time flows from timelessness and returns to timelessness.

In this context, our first obligation as individuation psychologists is to learn how to directly experience Rigpa and the Nature of Mind, as our non-temporal identity, known as nonidentity. Keith Dowman is a longtime Dzogchen practitioner and an esteemed translator of Tibetan Dzogchen texts. Keith is an astute commentator on the Dzogchen View and its implication for understanding timeless individuation as who we truly are, in our innermost essence. Discussing the Dzogchen View, he explains that:

Dzogchen is being here and now. It's not about what we want to be, but what we already are, what we have been from beginningless time, changeless time. That is what Dzogchen insists upon, and what it asserts from beginning to end. There is nothing much more to Dzogchen than identity with the nature of mind…than the knowledge of, or the memory of, who we are (2020, p. 56). Let us move on to look at Dzogchen as a contemplative science discovery.

Copernican-Like Contemplative Science Discovery

We can view Dzogchen as a Copernican-like contemplative science discovery, rather than as an "Eastern spiritual path." Dzogchen contemplative science discovered the mind's innermost essence—its timeless Nature. The West learned about Dzogchen not that long ago, but it is not well understood. Dzogchen hasn't transplanted well in the West, for several reasons. A significant one is because Dzogchen arrived in a form best suited to another time and place. A "radical" western form of Dzogchen addresses some of these problems by liberating Dzogchen from Tibetan cultural and traditional formalisms. But it also lacks temporal individuation perspective and suffers accordingly.

The Dzogchen and individuation psychology collaboration needs to come alive with visionary enthusiasm. Each has what the other is missing and needs to fulfill individuation's full promise. Together, they have an opportunity to recognize the possibilities for complete individuation. And to advance those possibilities as well as their own.

The Dzogchen Discovery

The breakthrough discovery: The human mind has an innermost Nature that escapes our ordinary awareness. The detection and recognition of the mind's essential nature is not cognizable by the intellect. Thought and concepts, along with Western scientific methods, will drive right by it and miss and then conclude that it doesn't exist. An important next step in depth psychology's individuation is to understand and use phenomenological methods to make reliable and valid inquiry into the mind, including inquiry into the interdependence between mind's temporal and nontemporal dimensions. Third-person empirical study of the mind misses the mark. For Western psychology to use the experimental scientific method to investigate the mind is another variation on the materialistic nightmare. Western science can no more understand the mind than a pigeon can understand a tax audit.

Dzogchen contemplative scientists used first-person experiential methods to make their discovery about the mind's innermost timeless Nature. In the future, direct, firsthand experience of one's own mind must be understood as essential for becoming an individuation and depth psychologist and for working with others as one. Intellectual and conceptual knowledge and training are important but woefully insufficient. Experiential self-knowledge is necessary.

Underscoring important points: Dzogchen cannot be known intellectually. It must be experienced, as nondual timeless awareness, i.e., "Rigpa." By missing Rigpa and the timeless spiritual dimension of mind, depth psychology misses the critical elements of individuation beyond time. By missing the psychological dimension of mind, Dzogchen fails to recognize the temporal elements of individuation. They both suffer the consequences, as do the prospects for recognizing complete individuation. The two are interdependent and individuation psychologists need to learn how to experience timeless awareness, and so understand the nontemporal dimension of individuation and its interdependence with individuation in time. Dzogchen psychologists must learn how to experience the temporal dimension of individuation and temporal individuation's interdependence with becoming who we truly are beyond time.

Dzogchen as Potentially Transformative

Dzogchen contemplative science's discovery of the mind's essential nature as akin to Copernicus' groundbreaking discovery that the Sun, not the Earth, is the center of our solar system. His discovery changed our vision of our solar system, and ultimately the science and practice of astronomy as well. Dzogchen contemplative science research unveiled the Nature of Mind. We are only just beginning to learn and understand the details of this important discovery, one that could sit well with Jung's work as he imagined, experienced, and lived it. Dzogchen psychology positions timeless awareness at the center of the mind as an accessible direct experience, not as a concept or theory. Dzogchen is not a view of what is, it *is* what is. It's a "viewless" experience of pure Being. Dzogchen revelation is Gnosis experienced on its own, in the nontemporal state.

Copernicus' discovery was ignored, scoffed at, and misunderstood initially by astronomers and other scientists, as well as artists and church authorities. Yet in 100 years, his work changed the role of astronomy in society. Similarly, the discovery of Mind's innermost Nature can have transformative implications, especially if its timeless dimension becomes interdependent with the temporal dimension of individuation psychology. Dzogchen psychology also offers us an opportunity to understand what egocentrism is and what a sound, healthy mind looks like and how to cultivate and protect such a mind. Dzogchen gives us a unique experiential lens to recognize and consider what hinders temporal individuation. A lens that also sheds light on our social problems, including much of the hell that characterizes human life.

Avoiding Indifference and Costly Misunderstandings

Great ideas too often die from a lack of blood supply. They are often just ignored or misunderstood. One of Einstein's colleagues, Hermann Minkowski (1864-1909) worked out the math demonstrating the distinct possibility of a fourth dimension. But despite Einstein's later support, it was ignored for decades.

I was shocked when I discovered that most of what I learned about Freud's ideas were not Freud's ideas at all. I was taken aback when Freud explained how many science-oriented psychology professionals, including many of his followers, were missing something important about him and his work. Freud explained why:

> Everybody thinks...that I started by the scientific character of my work and that my principal scope lies in curing mental maladies. This is a terrible error that has prevailed for years and that I have been unable to set right. I am a scientist by necessity, and not by vocation. I am really by nature an artist... And of this there lies an irrefutable proof: which is that in all countries into which psychoanalysis has penetrated it has been better understood and applied by writers and artists than by doctors. My books, in fact, more resemble works of imagination than treatise on pathology. (Papini, 1969, pp 130-134)

Keeping Jung's Vision for Individuation in Mind

As individuation psychologists informed and inspired by Jung's work, we should be certain we understand his views and vision. There's no doubt that Jung's vision of individuation included a sacred, nontemporal component, one that is too often glossed over and undervalued by those of us more comfortable and more aligned with his intellectual work. But whether we understand or like it or not, Jung was unequivocal that the numinous is central to his individuation vision and work. He told us that "Individuation is a philosophical, spiritual and mystical experience" (Jung, 1989, p. 294).

We should regard Jung's words as inviolable. But not because Jung says so, as the One Who Knows, but because a view of individuation without the spiritual and mystical elements misses the mark. In our understanding of Jung's views on individuation we often overlook or downplay its spiritual and mystical features. Many of Jung's followers fail to recognize these elements as fundamental and indispensable.

So, we should remind ourselves occasionally about what Jung said about Jungians and Jungian Training Institutes. In his own words: "Thank God I'm Jung and not a Jungian" (Stein, 2006, p. 11). Jung was not enthusiastic about the creation of training institutes using his name. When asked about the training program idea, Jung replied: "To tell the truth, I can think of nothing less I would rather hear about" (Stein, Manganiello, 2022, p. 324). Jung seemed to know that all educational and training organizations tend to contract into normative proprieties that lose track of the essential points.

A Key Point Requires Recognition and Understanding

Like Freud, Jung emphasized that his work was not focused on treating problems and illnesses. Jung told us that the main concern was the numinous. We should believe him and appreciate its implications for what we call therapy, analysis, and individuation.

Let's turn to a von Franz quote regarding Jung's views, and her commentary on their meaning and implications.

> The main interest of my work," writes Jung, "is not concerned with the treatment of neurosis but rather with the approach to the numinous. But the fact is that the approach to the numinous

is the real therapy and *inasmuch as* (italics mine) you attain to the numinous experiences, you are released from the curse of pathology. Even the very disease takes on a numinous character." Von Franz continues: "This citation cites everything of essential importance about a Jungian analysis. If it is not possible to establish a relationship with the numinous, no cure is possible; the most one can hope for is an improvement in social adjustment. But then, what is left for the analyst to do? (von Franz, 1990, p. 177)

As for von Franz's question as to what's left for the therapist/analyst to do, the answer is clear in an experiential psychology that understands how to access the numinous timeless dimension of mind. There's no reason we must wait for patients to catch the occasional numinous big fish to carry into sessions. Not when, if we know how, we can help them experience the numinous, in synergistic concert with their gradual individuation work.

Noting Jung's critically important words in von Franz's reference above, "...*inasmuch* (italics mine) as you attain to the numinous...." (i.e., in so far as, to the extent or degree to which you attain, achieve, accomplish, realize). This is a key issue. Too often we imagine that the task of someone who has had a numinous experience is to just integrate the experience in sessions and out. That's surely the case, at some level, but more is needed. Because the numinous is where we find the timeless depth of who and what we are. Understanding this, the critical additional work is then to find, stabilize and strengthen our connection to the numinous, so we can "attain to the degree to which we need" to realize who we truly are. This is the precise Dzogchen agenda, and it resonates perfectly with Jung's vision and with Murray Stein's position that the return to one's true being is the absolute prerequisite for individuation.

Jung's Nondual Near-Death Experience

After his Near-Death Experience (NDE) in 1944, Jung was quite clear on the intellect's shortcomings and inability to grasp the spiritual and mystical elements of individuation. Like psychedelic mystical experiences, a NDE can move us quickly into timeless nondual consciousness. Lillian Frey was by Jung's side during the time. She reported to James Hillman's first wife Kate that Jung:

>...lives now in an 'in-between' state somehow, most often he lets himself drop off into awake nondirective states, leaving the ego and mind out. He says he experiences truth as light, that is not with the consciousness that he has preached all these years, but another kind of awareness on a very deep level. ... Jung says he does not trust consciousness in the usual sense anymore ... it means giving up a great deal to enter into this state where truth so to say lingers on a different level, that Jung has always known about it, but not until now really taking it on as a change in himself. (Russell, 2013, pp. 468-469)

In his NDE, Jung apparently discovered the profound difference between dualist and nondual awareness. *"He says he experiences truth as light, that is not with the consciousness that he has preached all these years, but another kind of awareness on a very deep level."* Both NDEs and entheogen-induced mystical experiences can absent the conceptual mind, as pure awareness comes to the forefront. But we cannot just keep almost dying or taking entheogens to keep that awareness refreshed. But with Dzogchen methods, we can indeed do just that, with ongoing revelation in Nature of Mind.

NDE's and entheogens, like LSD and psilocybin, can awaken us to the spiritual dimension of mind and nontemporal identity. While the lights are turned on in these experiences we can "leave ego and the mind out" and see "truth as light." But our conditioned personality grows back, in time. With knowledge of how to access both temporal and nontemporal consciousness, without losing either, we can explore the transitional "in-between" states. This is critically important work.

Because the revelation of who we are beyond time only remains revelation if it can refresh enough to be sustained during the in-between transitions to and from temporal and the nontemporal. Therein resides the great potential for integrated progressive "in time" and immediate "beyond time" individuation psychology and inner work.

Time and timeless are state dependent experiences. In the inexperienced mind, the transition into one excludes the other. To remain conscious of both, they need to be bridged in direct experience as interdependent, so we do not fall into liminality amnesia. Jung suffered the pain of transition when "coming down" from his NDE. As if his sacred, nondual vision was dying and his timeless identity along with it.

As Jung described in harrowing words:

> I was profoundly disappointed…. The painful process of defoliation (shedding ego as centering and determining point), had been in vain. Disappointed, I thought, "Now I must return to the 'box system' again." For it seemed to me as if behind the horizon of the cosmos a three-dimensional world had been artificially built up, in which each person sat by himself in a little box. And now I should have to convince myself all over again that this was important! Life and the whole world struck me as a prison, and it bothered me beyond measure that I should again be finding that quite in order. I had been so glad to shed it all. . . And now all that would be a thing of the past! (1989, pp. 292-293)

Kandinsky's Materialist Nightmare Offers Depth Psychology Perspective

For amplification, let's visit Wassily Kandinsky (1866-1944) and his visionary work which was well aligned and resonant with Jung's vision. Kandinsky was the father of abstract art and a savvy depth psychologist. His and Jung's work were simpatico. They both prized the numinous, self-knowledge, and inner life. Parallels have been drawn between Jung's first public exhibit of the Red Book at NY's Ruben Museum and Kandinsky's simultaneous retrospective at the Guggenheim (Sherwood, 2010).

Kandinsky gives us a clear look at the poisonous materialistic nightmare we live in, as well as its causes, consequences, and only antidote. The nightmare's cruel reality testifies to the interdependence between psychology and spirituality. Kandinsky lived art, psychology, and spirituality as an interdependent whole. He understood the suffering born from the fragility of the human mind caught in dark egocentrism and the greedy evil marriage between science and commerce.

Here we have Kandinsky's words that ring mightily true for individuation psychologists today:

The all-important spark of inner life today is at present only a spark. Our minds, which are even now only just awakening after years of materialism, are infected with the despair of unbelief, of lack of purpose and ideal. The nightmare of materialism, which has turned the life of the universe into an evil, useless game, is not yet past; it holds the awakening soul still in its grip. This feeble light is but a presentiment, and the soul, when it sees it, trembles in doubt whether the light is not a dream, and the gulf of darkness a reality. (1977, p. 1)

Kandinsky offers a numinous vision central to Jung's view of individuation and a healthy mind. Kandinsky's recognizes psychology and spirituality as inter-reliant. The mind with little or no "light" is a lost and troubled mind. If you are in a room 120 degrees, you are hot. Not because you are ill, but because it's 120 degrees. If you live in a materialistic nightmare where life is an evil game that leaves you in the dark with woe and weary, you are not ill. You are suffering and your individuation is burdened or stopped.

The "light" has been marginalized and undervalued for so long, we can barely see it. For Dzogchen everything is light. When the grime of discursive thinking, intellectual concepts, and materialistic vision give way to the mind's primordial awareness, we realize that it's the nightmare that is false. In the mind's innermost essence, the radiant, timeless light shines on.

The great artist composer Robert Schumann (1810-1856) defined the artist's role 150 years ago: "To send light into the darkness of men's hearts - such is the duty of the artist" (Dwight, 1856, Vol. 7-8, p. 12). As depth psychologists, we share that obligation because it is truly our job, and the heart and soul of the individuation psychologist's work.

More on this later. For now, let us explore more of the issues facing our search for the famous transcendent "third."

Temporal and Non-Temporal Alchemy

Understanding individuation beyond time unveils a startling truth: We are already in the final temporal individuation stage, the Rubedo. Now and always. Because, from a timeless perspective, now is all there is. The Dzogchen View is that the future is a projected concept, not a reality. On close inspection, the "future" never arrives because when it does, it is now. And the past always shows up as now, as well. Now is the only real thing going on, ever. From the Dzogchen perspective, the Rubedo is the non-temporal first and last step, because it is the only step. Whether we are conscious of it or not, i.e., in the experience of now, or not. For Dzogchen, though we can imagine a temporal path, it's a conceptual projection. The solid identity known as "I" or "me" who treads the imagined gradual path is fictive. For Dzogchen, no one exists to individuate through progressive stages.

Looking to theoretical physics again for parallel perspective, we see that light is both wave and particle, not one or the other, and individuation is both temporal and non-temporal. Dzogchen elegantly explains nontemporal individuation as the identification with the numinous dimension of mind. But we miss a great deal about individuation if we regard the Dzogchen view as sole and complete. While embodied in time, we cannot deny the importance of temporal individuation. Depth psychologists and Dzogchen psychologists have the same problem— in reverse. Both risk falling into the egocentric trap of assuming their position is the only correct one.

The Egocentrism Dilemma

The collaborative work that must be done is not easy. Because each position is inclined toward an egocentric stance. Where it strives to protect and advance itself to maintain position and power. Binary conflict is hard to resolve because each position feels it is more or less than the other. Each position can fear being marginalized and colonized by the other. If adversarial stances flare, then projections will trigger and dominate and alliance and cooperation then become difficult, if not impossible. The egocentric dilemma is a binary power dilemma: I/my side is either right or wrong. It wins or loses. The dilemma is inherent in egocentric psychology. Once egocentrism has momentum, it cannot be easily relativized and deliteralized. Even psychologically sophisticated minds get stuck in it. Consider Jung and Freud.

What is essential is cooperation and focus on experiment. The physicists are fortunate. Most often they can see the results. Light is both wave and particle. The "third" that emerges is the both. The experiment for us is on ourselves. We use the same precise contemplative experimental methods Dzogchen used, to systematically explore our minds through direct experience. Then we consider our findings in collaborative engagement.

Dzogchen Psychology on Egocentrism

Dzogchen contemplative science research shows "egocentrism" to be an affliction, one central to understanding the mind, and individuation, in both its temporal and nontemporal aspects. Egocentrism means something different and more in Dzogchen psychology than the word usually implies in Western psychology. In Dzogchen, egocentrism is the hallmark of an unsound mind, separated from its innermost nature. It is a mind infected by materialism, a mind that lacks the light of non-dual awareness. Dzogchen contemplative scientists discovered its source and its remedy. Remarkably, if collaboration works, we can experience that directly as well, a transformative possibility.

The root of egocentrism is our inherent tendency to mistakenly impute solid identity to ourselves from the flow of discursive thought in our stream of consciousness. To avoid doing this is the key to a healthy mind. Using Dzogchen methods, we can replicate this finding easily. For most people, mistaken identity is wrongly presumed to be solid and real, and chronically vulnerable. This vulnerable identity is based on a projected presumption of self and external reality. It is the fictive identity who becomes egocentric. This too can be easily confirmed.

This mistaken identity becomes the heap on which our conditioning gets layered. As young children, we do not have the mind power to make sense of our circumstances and the problems therein. This coalesces into a self-image that, although fictional, nevertheless feels real, and determines much of what we think, feel, and do. We all become identified with our conditioned self-image until we develop the consciousness needed to see through and stand free from it. Our identification with this "I" or "me" is dominant and dangerous. It permeates all aspects of our psychological life. We live in it as something true and undeniable. As do nation states. The egocentric dilemma is to consider this mistaken identity as literally real and then fall prey to the consequences: The chronic striving to protect, defend and advance relative identity as absolute and literal.

Temporal and nontemporal individuation working together hold great promise for remedying the egocentrism problem. Active imagination can relativize and deliteralize the egocentric dilemma in time, when it's illuminated by the light of the Nature of Mind, beyond time. This is an "in time" and "beyond time" remedy that arises from a nonbinary interdependent vision.

Self-Liberation as Antidote to Egocentrism

Dzogchen is known as the Path of Self-Liberation through seeing with naked, timeless awareness. The key to understanding this path is to correct the error that arises from not properly understanding our stream of consciousness, and avoid attributing fictive identity to ourselves and the fall into egocentrism. In Dzogchen, instead of liking, disliking, or following our thoughts into storyline and narrative, we just let our thoughts "self-liberate." Thoughts come and go. But we do not go with them. When we do, we are in time, in a Waking Dream of sorts. A waking dream that feels very real, but on close inspection—isn't. If we learn the appropriate Dzogchen method, then we can "train" to "see with naked awareness," and avoid distraction and possession by waking dream narratives and storylines. We just remain more in non-dual awareness—NOW.

In the mind's Natural State, we can discover that thought is a manifestation of the mind's timeless, essential Nature. Here's what we can experience and understand: If we like, dislike or follow our thoughts, we miss the innermost Nature of Mind from which thoughts arise. We unconsciously ascribe solid identity to ourselves from our discursive thought flow. We then move into this imputed false identity as if it was who we truly are, and so we suffer the consequences. If we follow thought into storyline and narrative, we are in time, typically blindfolded and not fully conscious. But if we develop the capacity to release our thoughts, then they self-liberate on their own. When thought liberates, what's left then is the timeless source of thought's arising. Thought manifests from the ground of indescribable non-temporal Being. The open and spacious Ground beyond description or characterization.

Dzogchen practice is known as contemplation. Many secondary practices support our entering contemplation as the Natural State, as Rigpa. One secondary practice is to relax, observe and directly experience your mind to answer the following three questions: When thoughts arise where do they come from? When thoughts abide where are they? When thoughts leave, where do they go?

His Holiness Lungtok Tenpai Nyima Rinpoche, the former Abbot of Menri, the Bon Monastery in Northern India, gave key instructions on working with this issue, as follows:

Do not follow thoughts about the past or the future. When the past comes to mind, it is NOW. Do not follow thoughts about the future, when the future arrives, it is NOW. Stay in *rigpa*, Aware Presence, NOW.[1]

Easy to say, but hard to do—at first. But as we practice our capacity becomes more stable and stronger. We then experience thoughts as energy. As energy that arises from the Nature of Mind itself, as thought, as immaterial form. The thoughts can be charged with the grime of time: conditioned memories, complexes, hopes, fears, trauma and so on. They appear to be about us, but only if we follow them do we get sucked into the role of protagonist in recurring dramas. If we do not follow them we can stay in the mind's Natural State, as now, not as an "I" or "me" making egocentric efforts, but as effortless pure timeless awareness. From pure awareness, unburdened by what's not now, thought becomes spontaneously original, arising on the wings of the creative imagination.

This is not a spiritual bypass, the kind so prevalent for westerners using eastern meditation—what I call mindless mindfulness training—which leaves the unconscious, complex ridden, conditioned mind out of the picture. Correctly understood and practiced, Dzogchen is moving into who we truly are beyond time, and this identity is interdependent with who we truly are in time. To assume that it negates our temporal identity is an egocentric error made by many Dzogchen followers and teachers, who are unfamiliar with the temporal mind, including its teleological imperatives.

At carefully chosen points, this method of experiential self-observation and then contemplative non-dual awareness can be creatively woven into individuation work. The benefits that come with this level of self-knowledge are clear: Impartial awareness gives rise to a consciousness better able to release from troublesome states of mind, not in defense, but as knowledge and wisdom. Awareness gives the mind a means to liberate itself from negative and conditioned states of mind, and

---

[1] His Holiness Lungtok Tenpai Nyima Rinpoche, the 33rd Menri Trizin, former Abbot of Yungdrung Bon Menri Monastery. Personal communication about Dzogchen practice.

so avoid identification with and possession by them. Temporal awareness then can learn to create and engage the "free position."

"In time" and "beyond time" individuation are interdependent and individuation must be reciprocal if it is to be complete. For Dzogchen to miss the temporal psychology and the progressive work needed to consciously individuate, is to also put itself at risk in the West. The forces at play in the unconscious temporal dimension of mind cannot be spiritually bypassed. Dzogchen in the West is less than it could be if it could address the forces at play in temporal psychological life. Any numinous tradition that claims to embody ultimate truth, but which will not face the ordinary truths about itself, will be rightly seen as lacking character and credibility.

Missing either temporal or non-temporal individuation is an error. Seeing both together as interdependent is a breakthrough view. Both need to be considered and understood alone and together if we are to recognize and realize the entire individuation picture. To say that "in time," alchemical individuation work leads to the Self as some literal personal attainment of wholeness is fuzzy, intellectual, and incomplete. The intellect is in time. The spiritual core of individuation is beyond time, it must be experienced. To say that because our essential innermost being, our Nature of Mind, is who we truly and the timeless source of all that is true, but also incomplete. Because the beyond time view must recognize and acknowledge the reality of embodied existence in time, for the mind and the soul.

Dr. Jim Manganiello is a clinical psychologist with 45 years of experience working, teaching and supervising in the depth psychology and depth therapy tradition. Jim has an associate professor academic rank. He has also worked for 30 years in the Dzogchen contemplative science tradition, studying and practicing under the direction of Dzogchen "grandfather" teachers. Jim has presented his work internationally on the sacred interface between depth psychology and spirituality. He is the author of books and articles in this vein. Including *Unshakable Certainty* and *Your Creative Imagination—UNLOCKED—Become Who You Truly Are* (with Abstract Expressionist Artist Frank Arnold). In 2022, Jim co-authored an essay with Murray Stein published in *Eastern Practices and Individuation*, on the prospects of a transcendent third between individuation theory and Dzogchen psychology. www.jimmanganiello.com

References

Almheiri, A., Hartman, T., Maldacena, J., Shaghoulian, E., & Tajdini, A. (2020). Replica wormholes and the entropy of Hawking radiation. *Journal of High Energy Physics,* 13. https://doi.org/10.48550/arXiv.1911.12333

Dowman, K. (2020a). *Dzogchen nonmeditation.* Dzogchen Now! Books.

Dowman, K. (2020b). *The Dzogchen View.* Dzogchen Now! Books.

Hoeller, S. (1982). *The Gnostic Jung and the Seven Sermons to the Dead.* Quest Books.

Jung, C.G. (1950/1971). A study in the process of individuation. In *CW* 9i. Princeton University Press.

Jung, C.G. (1955–6/1970). *Mysterium Coniunctionis.* In *CW* 14. Princeton University Press.

Jung, C.G. (1961). *Memories, Dreams, Reflections.* Vintage Books.

Manganiello, J. (2013). *Unshakable Certainty* (2nd ed.). http://bitly.ws/ocIF

Manganiello, J. (2021). Depth psychology and depth therapy — Reset and refreshed. In. B. Panter, Ed. *Psychological Studies of Art and Artists.* Vol. 3, pp. 105-122. AIMED Press.

Manganiello, J. & Arnold, F. (2016). *Your Creative Imagination Unlocked: Become Who You Truly Are.* Ashford Books.

Musser, G. (Ed.), "The black hole information paradox Comes to an end." *Quanta Magazine.* https://www.quantamagazine.org/the-most-famous-paradox-in-physics-nears-its-end-20201029/

Namdak, T. (2010). *Masters of the Zhang Zhung Nyengyud: Pith Instructions from the Experiential Transmission of Bonpo Dzogchen.* Heritage Publishers.

Norbu, N. (1989). *Dzogchen: The Self-perfected State.* The Penguin Group.

Norbu, N. (2006). *Dzogchen Teachings.* Snow Lion Publications.

Reynolds, J. (1989). *Self-liberation Through Seeing with Naked Awareness.* Station Hill Press.

Ribi, A. (2013). *The Search for Roots: C.G. Jung and the Tradition of Gnosis*. Gnosis Archive Books.

Russell, D. (2013). *The Life and Ideas of James Hillman*. Helios Press.

Stein, L. (2021) *The Self in Jungian Psychology: Theory and Clinical Practice*. Chiron Publications.

Stein, L. (Ed.) (2022). "On a possible bridge between individuation theory and Dzogchen psychology: Challenges, pitfalls, opportunities for a transcendent 'third': A dialogue between Murray Stein and Jim Manganiello." In *Eastern Practices and Individuation: Essays by Jungian Analysts*. Chiron Publications.

Stein, M. (2006). *The Principle of Individuation*. Chiron Publications.

Stein, M. (2020). Individuation. In *Collected Writings of Murray Stein* (Vol. 1). Chiron Publications.

Stein, M. (2021). Transformations. In *Collected Writings of Murray Stein* (Vol. 3). Chiron Publications.

Stein, M. (2022). *Four Pillars of Jungian Psychoanalysis*. Chiron Publications.

Vyner, H. (2019). *The Healthy Mind*. Routledge.

Biographies

Henry Abramovitch (Israel) is Founding President and senior training analyst at the Israel Institute of Jungian Psychology in Honor of Erich Neumann, Professor Emeritus at Tel Aviv University Medical School and Past President of Israel Anthropological Association. He has served on Ethics and Programme Committees of the International Association for Analytical Psychology (IAAP) and is active in Israel Interfaith Encounter Association. He teaches and supervises Routers in the IAAP Developing Groups in Eastern Europe and Kazakhstan. He is author of *The First Father* (2010); *Brothers and Sisters: Myth and reality* (2014); *Why Odysseus Came Home as a Stranger and Other Puzzling Moments in the Life of... Great Individuals* (2020), and with Murray Stein, the play, *The Analyst and the Rabbi* (2019). For the past year, he has led a Reflection Group for Ukrainian Analysts on Zoom. His special joys are poetry, dream groups and the holy city of Jerusalem. Email: henry.abramovitch@gmail.com.

John Beebe, a past president of the C.G. Jung Institute of San Francisco, is the author of Energies and Patterns in Psychological Type: The reservoir of consciousness and also of Integrity in Depth. He is co-author, with Virginia Apperson, of The Presence of the Feminine in Film, and co-editor, with Ernst Falzeder, of The Question of Psychological Types: The Correspondence of C.G. Jung and Hans Schmid-Guisan. He founded the quarterly publication that is now called *Jung Journal: Culture & Psyche* and was the first American co-editor of the Journal of Analytical Psychology. John has spearheaded a Jungian typological approach

375

to the analysis of film. In his over 200 publications, he has often used type and archetype to explore developments in the cultural and political unconscious. His eight-function, eight-archetype model, which Murray Stein was the first editor to encourage John to present to an audience of Jungian analysts and candidates, is now widely studied and applied.

Paul Bishop is William Jacks Chair of Modern Languages at the University of Glasgow, UK. After studying at Oxford and (for a year) at Harvard, Paul has lived and worked in Glasgow for nearly three decades. He is interested in all aspects of German culture and thought, in tracing the progression of ideas through time, and in uncovering links between German culture and the concepts of psychoanalysis, with particular emphasis on analytical psychology. Although he is currently researching the philosophy of Ludwig Klages, the publication of the *Red Book* (and subsequently *The Black Books*) means he keeps returning to Jung's remarkably rich and fertile thought. He is the author of *Reading Goethe at Midlife: Ancient wisdom, German classicism, and Jung* (2011/2020), and other studies on aspects of Jung's thought in an intellectual-historical perspective.

Steven Buser, MD trained in medicine at Duke University and served 12 years as a physician in the U.S. Air Force. He is a graduate of a two-year Clinical Training Program at the C.G. Jung Institute of Chicago and is the co-founder of the Asheville Jung Center. He is board certified in psychiatry as well as addiction medicine. He has worked for over 30 years as a psychiatrist with a focus on Jungian oriented psychotherapy. He currently works in the field of addiction and serves as Publisher at Chiron Publications.

Maria Grazia Calzà grew up among the olive trees along Lake Garda, Italy. After a diploma in Art Restoration in Venice, she continued her studies at the Albert-Ludwigs-University of Freiburg, Germany receiving a MA and later a PhD in Medieval History, Theology, and Psychology. She has written a book on the role of the body in the mysticism of the first Beguine, Marie d'Oignies, published various articles (*e.g.* "The Thinking Heart. The Individuation Process in Late Medieval Mystic Women," in: *Jung Journal. Culture & Psyche*, 10:3, 3-14, 2016) and lectured internationally. In 2017 she graduated from the *International School of*

Analytical Psychology (ISAP) in Zurich, Switzerland. Dr. Calzà works in Riva del Garda as a Philosophical Counselor and Jungian Psychoanalyst. She is a co-founder of the *Embodied Jung Conference* held in 2022 and currently completing a book, entitled *The Feminine Taste of God. The Individuation Process of Medieval Women Mystics.*

Joseph Cambray, Ph.D. is the Past-President-CEO of Pacifica Graduate Institute; he is Past-President of the International Association for Analytical Psychology and has served as the U.S. Editor for *The Journal of Analytical Psychology.* He was a faculty member at Harvard Medical School in the Department of Psychiatry at Massachusetts General Hospital, Center for Psychoanalytic Studies. Dr. Cambray is a Jungian analyst now living in the Santa Barbara area of California. His numerous publications include the book based on his Fay Lectures: *Synchronicity: Nature and psyche in an interconnected universe.* He has published numerous paper in a range of international journals as well as book chapters and has edited three collections of research in analytical psychology.

Linda Carter, MSN, CS, IAAP, (USA) is a Clinical Nurse Specialist and a Jungian analyst practicing in Carpinteria, California and has been a psychotherapist for more than 40 years. A graduate of Georgetown, Yale, and the C.G. Jung Institute-Boston, Linda was the Journal of Analytical Psychology's Book Review Editor, US Editor-in-Chief and Film & Culture Editor. Founder and Chair of the Art and Psyche Working Group. She initiated and edited the service outreach project "Art in a Time of World Crisis: Interconnection and Companionship" that recently won a Gradiva Award from the National Association for the Advancement of Psychoanalysis (NAAP). Art and Psyche won a Gradiva previously for the art exhibition affiliated with the Illuminated Imagination Conference in 2019. Her paper "Amazing Grace" was a short listed nominee for a 2022 Gradiva. Linda has published widely and taught internationally, especially in China. Email: lcarter20@earthlink.net

Professor Ann Casement, LP, is a London-based licensed Jungian psychoanalyst, a member of professional bodies including the National Association for the Advancement of Psychoanalysis (NYC), The British Psychoanalytical Council, The British Psychological Society, and founder member of the International Neuropsychoanalysis Society. She served on the International Association for Analytical Psychology's Executive Committee as well as its Ethics Committee, the latter two terms as its Chair. She is a Fellow of The Royal Society of Medicine and the Royal Anthropological Institute, has worked in various parts of the world including the USA, Europe, Russia, Latin America, Israel, South Africa, China and Japan. She served in the House of Lords on a Private Member's Bill for the statutory regulation of psychotherapists/psychoanalysts. She contributes to *The Economist* and professional journals around the world, has authored articles, reviews, book chapters, eight books, the last titled: *Integrating Shadow: Authentic Being in the World* (is in press).

Len Cruz, MD is the Editor-in-Chief of Chiron Publications and co-founder of the Asheville Jung Center. He holds graduate degrees in medicine and business. With more than 40 years in psychiatric practice, he currently focuses on the treatment of substance use disorders. He is the Chief Medical Officer of a 72-bed substance abuse hospital.

Nancy Swift Furlotti, Ph.D. is a Jungian Analyst living in Aspen, Colorado. She is a past president of the C.G. Jung Institute of Los Angeles, where she trained, a founding member and past president of the Philemon Foundation and is on the Mercurius Film Prize Committee. She is a member of the C.G. Jung Institute of Colorado and the Interregional Association of Jungian Analysts. She is on the board of Pacifica Graduate Institute in Santa Barbara and the Smithsonian National Asian Museum. Dr. Swift Furlotti lectures internationally on Jungian topics such as dreams, mythology, trauma, the feminine, and the environment. Her company, Recollections, LLC, publishes early analysts' unpublished material, such as the manuscripts of Erich Neumann. She has two forthcoming books, *The Splendor of the Maya: A Journey into the Shadows at the Dawn of Creation,* and *Eternal Echoes: Erich Neumann's Timeless Relevance to Consciousness, Creativity, and Evil.*

Magi Guindi is a Jungian analyst in private practice in Los Angeles, California trained at ISAP, Zurich. Her main interest lies in the discovery and understanding of the mysterious language of the deeper psyche, as expressed through dreams, images, metaphors, and symbols. She has lectured at ISAP, at the Jung Institute, and at the Centro Mexican C.G. Jung on a wide diversity of themes ranging from myths, dreams and the archetype of the coniunctio, through depression and creativity, to the individuation process, among other themes. She has lived in Mexico, Spain, France, Switzerland, and the United States. She speaks Spanish, French, Italian, and English.

James G. Johnston, M. Arch., Harvard University, B.A. DePaul University, is the author of *Jung's Indispensable Compass* and *The Call Within*. He is founder of Gifts Compass and Life Atlas and architect of the Gifts Compass Inventory (GCI), the online self-assessment that depicts nuanced dispositions for each of Jung's original eight psychological types. He is also a lecturer at CGJI Zurich.

Ann Chia-Yi Li is a supervising analyst at the International School of Analytical Psychology and has a practice in Zurich. Her interest lies in the relationship between Daoist practice, alchemy, and analytical psychology. Her chapter, "The Receptive and the Creative: Jung's *Red Book* for Our Time In the Light of Daoist Alchemy," was published in 2018 in *Jung's Red Book for Our Time: Searching for Soul under Postmodern Conditions, Vol. II*, edited by Murray Stein and Thomas Arzt; and the chapter, "The 'Secret' of the Golden Flower: The Individuation Process by Way of Daoist Practice," was published in 2022 in *Eastern Practices and Individuation: Essays by Jungian Analysts*, edited by Leslie Stein.

Roderick Main, PhD, works at the University of Essex, UK, where he is a professor in the Department of Psychosocial and Psychoanalytic Studies and Director of the Centre for Myth Studies. His books include *The Rupture of Time: Synchronicity and Jung's Critique of Modern Western Culture* (Brunner-Routledge, 2004), *Revelations of Chance: Synchronicity as Spiritual Experience* (SUNY, 2007), and most recently *Breaking the Spell of Disenchantment: Mystery, Meaning, and Metaphysics in the Work of C.G. Jung* (2022).

Dr. Jim Manganiello is a clinical psychologist with 45 years of experience working, teaching, and supervising in the depth psychology and depth therapy tradition. Jim has an associate professor academic rank. He has also worked for 30 years in the Dzogchen contemplative science tradition, studying and practicing under the direction of Dzogchen "grandfather" teachers. Jim has presented his work internationally on the sacred interface

between depth psychology and spirituality. He is the author of books and articles in this vein, including *Unshakable Certainty,* and *Your Creative Imagination—UNLOCKED—Become Who You Truly Are* (with Abstract Expressionist Artist Frank Arnold). In 2022, Jim co-authored an essay with Murray Stein published in *Eastern Practices and Individuation*, on the prospects of a transcendent third between individuation theory and Dzogchen psychology.
www.jimmanganiello.com

Robert Michael Mercurio completed his undergraduate studies in philosophy and then moved to Rome for graduate studies in theology at the Gregorian University. He later completed a master's degree in management with a thesis project on the application of Jung's typology to teaching methods adopted in language schools. He subsequently enrolled in the C.G. Jung-Institut in Küsnacht, where he took his diploma in Analytical Psychology. Previously a member of the Centro Italiano di Psicologia Analitica (CIPA), he is presently a member, training analyst, and President of the Associazione per la Ricerca in Psicologia Analitica (ARPA). His interests include the practice of active imagination, the interface between spirituality, psychology, myth, and fairy tale interpretation.

Patricia Michan is a Jungian psychoanalyst certifi ed by the International Association of Analytical Psychology (IAAP) in 1995. She has a private practice in Mexico City, first as a psychotherapist (as of 1982) and later as a Jungian psychoanalyst (since 1995). She has lectured in Mexico, Latin America, United States, and Europe. Her many achievements include serving as founder and directress of the Centro Mexicano C.G. Jung, assistant editor for the JAP's Editorial Board, member of the International Association of Analytical Psychology (IAAP) and the Inter-Regional Society of Jungian Analysts (IRSJA). Her published works include "Reiterative Disintegration: Historical and Cultural Patterns and the Contemporary Mexican Psyche," a chapter in *Confronting Collective Trauma: Jungian Approaches to Treatment and Healing*, edited by Grazina Gudaite and Murray Stein; "Analysis and Individuation in the Mexican Psyche: Culture and Context," published in the *Journal of Jungian Theory and Practice; Analysis and Individuation in Latin Cultures and Contexts: The Mexican Psyche;* and *Dismemberment and Reintegration: Aztec Themes.* She is currently working on an extensive research and study on the relationship between analytical psychology, pre-Hispanic mythology and clinical practice.

Heyong Shen, Ph.D., is the author of *Psychology of the Heart* (Fay Lecture), *C.G. Jung and Chinese Culture*, and *the Heart of Chinese Culture Psychology*, as well as numerous articles on the interface between analytical psychology and Chinese culture. Dr. Heyong Shen is a professor of psychology (City University of Macao), Jungian analyst (member of the International Association for Analytical Psychology), Sandplay therapist (member of the International Society of Sandplay Therapy), founding president of China Society for Analytical Psychology (CSAP) and China Society for Sandplay Therapy (CSST), speaker at the Eranos East and West Round Table Conferences (1997, 2007, 2019, and 2022), organizer of the International Conference of Analytical Psychology and Chinese Culture (1998-2020), chief editor of Chinese translation of Collected Works of C.G. Jung; and founding member of the Garden of the Heart & Soul project. Email: shenheyong@hotmail.com

Thomas Singer, MD, is psychiatrist and Jungian analyst who trained at Yale Medical School, Dartmouth Medical School, and the C.G. Jung Institute of San Francisco. He is the author of many books and articles that include a series of books on cultural complexes that have focused on Australia, Latin America, Europe, the United States and Far East Asian countries, in addition to another series of books featuring Ancient Greece, Modern Psyche. He serves on the board of ARAS (The Archives for Research in Archetypal Symbolism) and has edited *ARAS Connections* for many years.

Chiara Tozzi is a psychologist and psychotherapist. She is a Training Analyst and Supervisor of *Associazione Italiana di Psicologia Analitica* (AIPA) and of the International Association for Analytical Psychology (IAAP). She is also a writer, screenwriter, and screenwriting professor. She lectures internationally and is visiting professor to different IAAP Developing Groups. She is the author of a research on active imagination supported by the IAAP which will be published by Routledge. She is artistic director of the international *"Mercurius Prize for Films of particular Psychological Significance and Sensitivity to Human Rights,"* based in Zurich. She is former editor of *"Studi Junghiani,"* the Journal for AIPA. Email: chiarat652@gmail.com

Jan Wiener is a Training Analyst and Supervisor at the Society of Analytical Psychology in London. She recently completed a second term of office as Director of Training. She was Vice President of the IAAP from 2010-2013 and co-chair of the IAAP Education Committee. She has taught and supervised extensively in the UK and abroad, especially in Eastern Europe. She is author of many papers and four books, the most recent of which *Jungian Analysts working across Cultures: from Tradition to Innovation*, was edited with Catherine Crowther and published by Routledge in 2021.

Mari Yoshikawa, Ph.D., is originally from Osaka, Japan and educated at Kyoto University (Ph.D.). She is Professor of Gakushuin University in Tokyo, being engaged in training certified clinical psychologists in Japan. In 2008, she studied at ISAP in Zurich, and received a diploma of AJAJ (Association of Jungian Analysts, Japan) in 2016. She manages Yamanashi Hakoniwa Institute (www.yamanashi-hakoniwa.com/) for her practices with imagery. She collaborated in many Japanese books on psychological assessment, personality psychology and psychotherapy. Her English writings include *The Shadow of Modernization in Japan as Seen in Natsume Soseki's Ten Night's Dreams*, and *Confronting Cultural Trauma-Jungian Approaches to Understanding and Healing* (Edited by Granzina Gudaite and Murray Stein, 211-226, Spring Journal Books 2014), "A Japanese Perspective of the Meaning of the Serpent in the Red Book" (Jung's Red Book for Our Time Vol. 3, Edited by Murray Stein, and Thomas Arzt, 217-232, Chiron Publications, 2019).

* 9 7 8 1 6 8 5 0 3 1 8 3 1 *